INFINITY

Volume 1

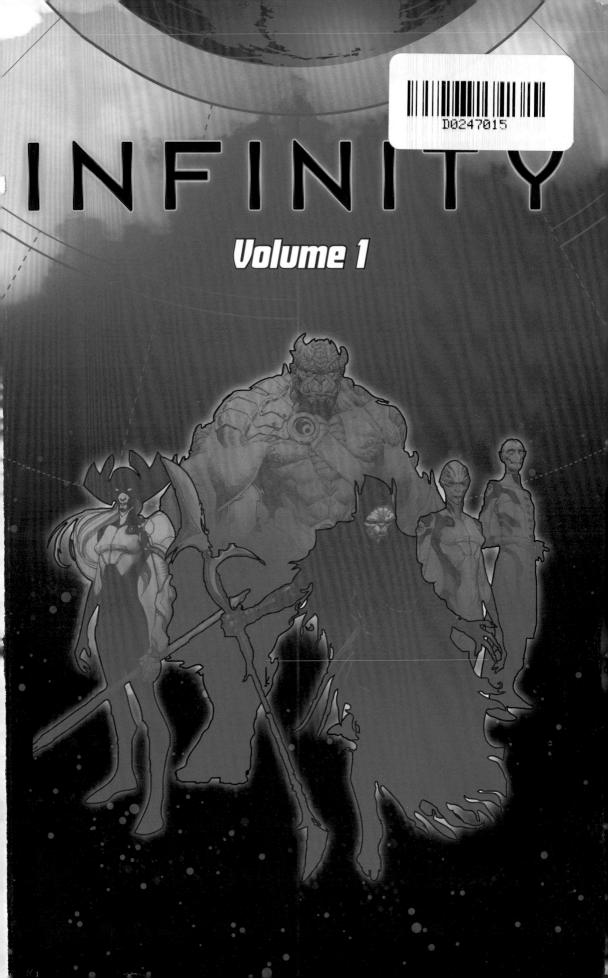

INFINITY

Volume 1

WRITER: JONATHAN HICKMAN

INFINITY
PENCILERS: JIM CHEUNG, JEROME OPEÑA
& DUSTIN WEAVER

INKERS: MARK MORALES, JOHN LIVESAY,
DAVID MEIKIS, JEROME OPEÑA
& DUSTIN WEAVER

LETTERS: VIRTUAL CALLIGRAPHY'S JOE CARAMAGNA
& CHRIS ELIOPOULOS

COLOURIST: JUSTIN PONSOR

COVER: ADAM KUBERT

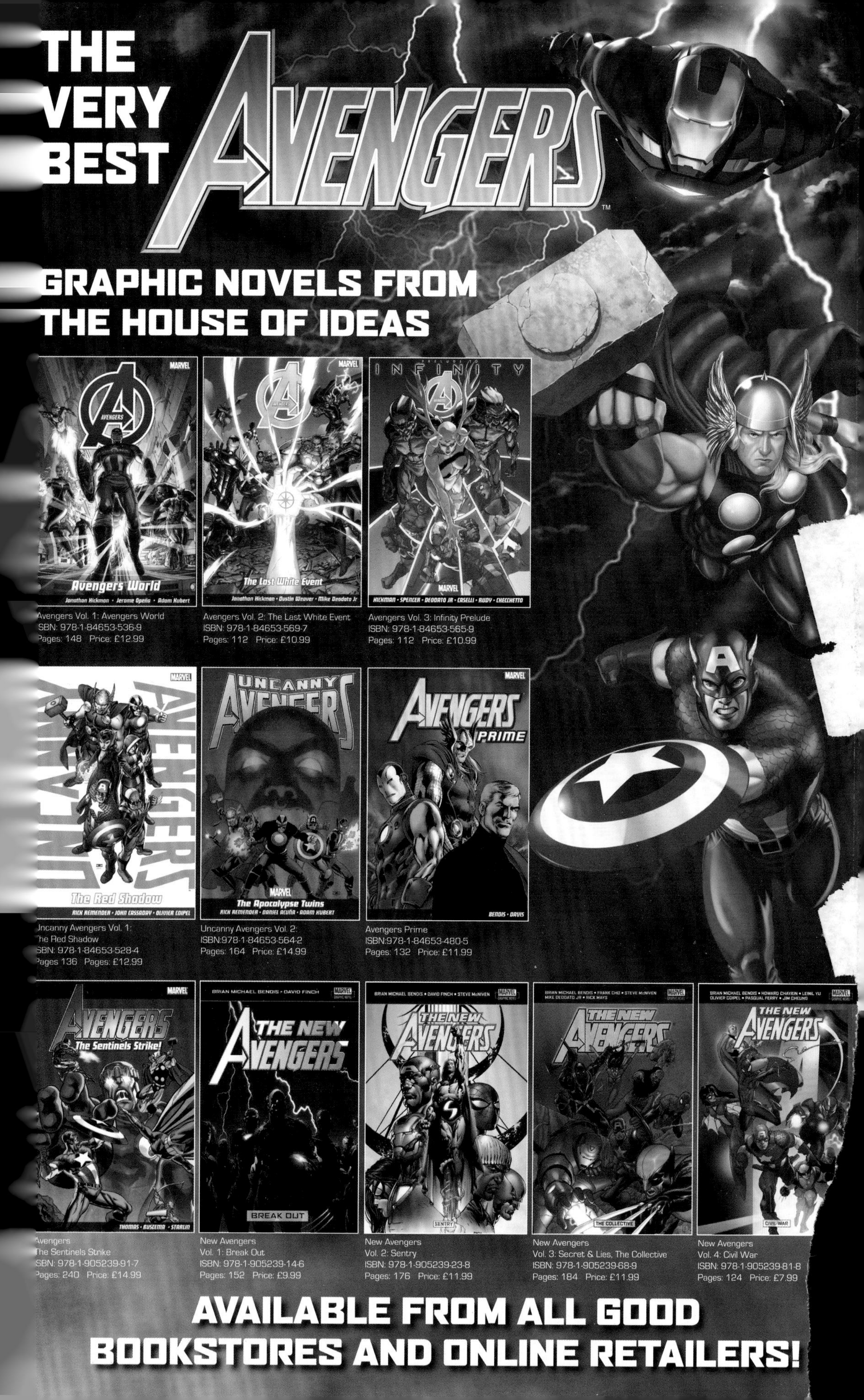
THE VERY BEST AVENGERS
GRAPHIC NOVELS FROM THE HOUSE OF IDEAS
Avengers World
Jonathan Hickman • Jerome Opeña • Adam Kubert
Avengers Vol. 1: Avengers World
SBN: 978-1-84653-536-9
ages: 148 Price: £12.99
The Last White Event
Jonathan Hickman • Dustin Weaver • Mike Deodato Jr
Avengers Vol. 2: The Last White Event
ISBN: 978-1-84653-569-7
Pages: 112 Price: £10.99
INFINITY
HICKMAN • SPENCER • DEODATO JR • CASELLI • RUDY • CHECCHETTO
Avengers Vol. 3: Infinity Prelude
ISBN: 978-1-84653-565-9
Pages: 112 Price: £10.99
The Red Shadow
RICK REMENDER • JOHN CASSADAY • OLIVIER COIPEL
Jncanny Avengers Vol. 1:
he Red Shadow
SBN: 978-1-84653-528-4
ages 136 Pages: £12.99
UNCANNY AVENGERS
The Apocalypse Twins
RICK REMENDER • DANIEL ACUÑA • ADAM KUBERT
Uncanny Avengers Vol. 2:
ISBN:978-1-84653-564-2
Pages: 164 Price: £14.99
AVENGERS PRIME
BENDIS • DAVIS
Avengers Prime
ISBN:978-1-84653-480-5
Pages: 132 Price: £11.99
AVENGERS The Sentinels Strike!
THOMAS • BUSCEMA • STARLIN
Avengers
he Sentinels Strike
SBN: 978-1-905239-91-7
ages: 240 Price: £14.99
BRIAN MICHAEL BENDIS • DAVID FINCH
THE NEW AVENGERS
BREAK OUT
New Avengers
Vol. 1: Break Out
ISBN: 978-1-905239-14-6
Pages: 152 Price: £9.99
BRIAN MICHAEL BENDIS • DAVID FINCH • STEVE McNIVEN
THE NEW AVENGERS
SENTRY
New Avengers
Vol. 2: Sentry
ISBN: 978-1-905239-23-8
Pages: 176 Price: £11.99
THE NEW AVENGERS
THE COLLECTIVE
New Avengers
Vol. 3: Secret & Lies, The Collective
ISBN: 978-1-905239-68-9
Pages: 184 Price: £11.99
THE NEW AVENGERS
CIVIL WAR
New Avengers
Vol. 4: Civil War
ISBN: 978-1-905239-81-8
Pages: 124 Price: £7.99
AVAILABLE FROM ALL GOOD BOOKSTORES AND ONLINE RETAILERS!

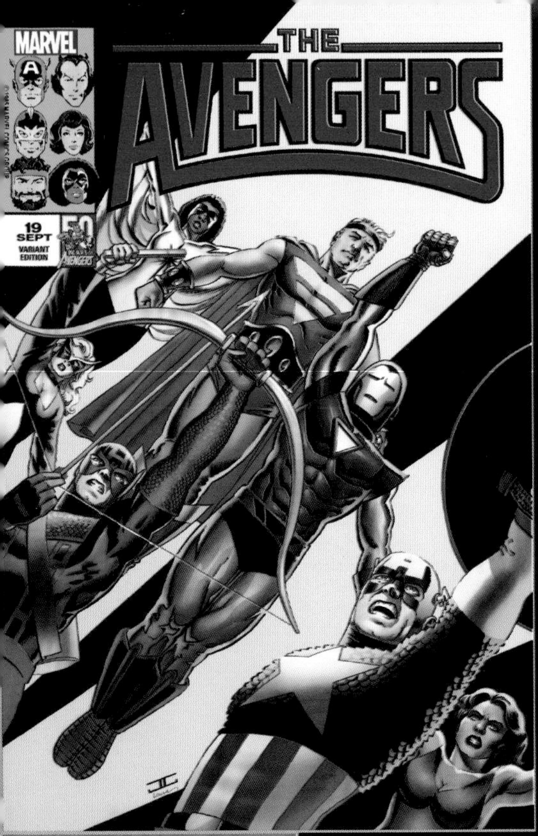
MARVEL
THE
AVENGERS
19
SEPT
VARIANT EDITION

Avengers #19 by John Cassaday

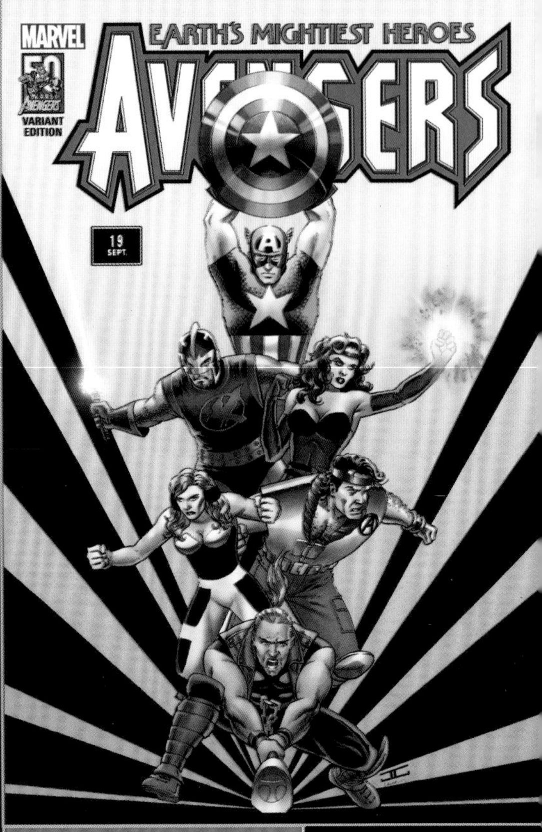
MARVEL
VARIANT EDITION
EARTH'S MIGHTIEST HEROES
AVENGERS
19
SEPT.

Avengers #19 by John Cassaday

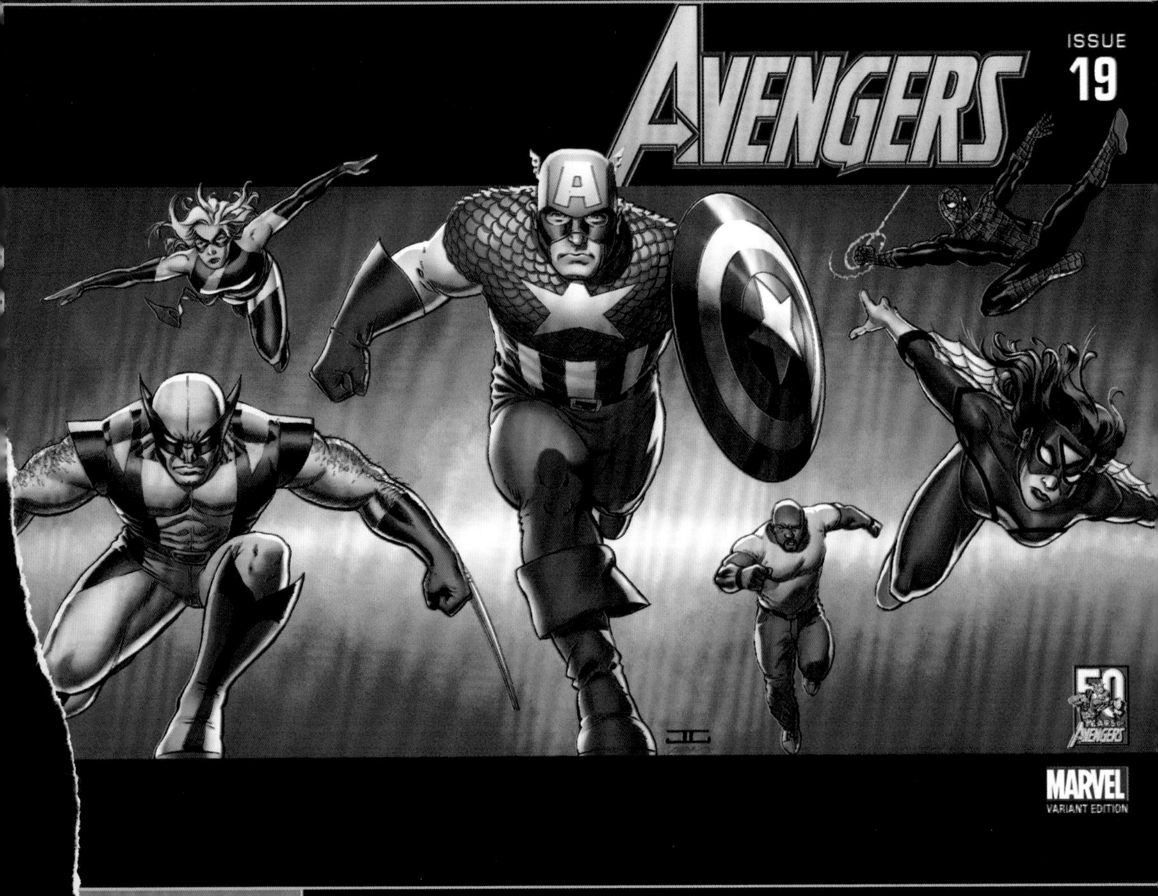
AVENGERS
ISSUE
19
MARVEL
VARIANT EDITION

ers #19 by John Cassaday

AVENGERS

PENCILERS: LEINIL FRANCIS YU

INKERS: GERRY ALANGUILAN
& LEINIL FRANCIS YU

LETTERS: VIRTUAL CALLIGRAPHY'S CORY PETIT

COLOURIST: SUNNY GHO

NEW AVENGERS

ART: MIKE DEODATO JR.

LETTERS: VIRTUAL CALLIGRAPHY'S JOE CARAMAGNA

COLOURIST: FRANK MARTIN

ASSISTANT EDITOR: JAKE THOMAS

EDITORS: TOM BREVOORT & LAUREN SANKOVITCH

CHIEF CREATIVE OFFICER: JOE QUESADA

PUBLISHER: ALAN FINE

EXECUTIVE PRODUCER: DAN BUCKLEY

Do you have any comments or queries about Infinity Vol. 1? Email us at graphicnovels@panini.co.uk
Find us on Facebook at Panini/Marvel Graphic Novels.

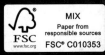

 First printing 2014. Thirteenth impression 2021. Published by Panini Publishing, a division of Panini UK Limited. Mike Riddell, Managing Director. Alan O'Keefe, Managing Editor. Mark Irvine, Production Manager. Marco M. Lupoi, Publishing Director Europe. Brady Webb, Reprint Editor. Angela Hart, Designer. Office of publication: Brockbourne House, 77 Mount Ephraim, Tunbridge Wells, Kent TN4 8BS. Printed in the United Kingdom by Zenith Media. ISBN: 978-1-84653-566-6

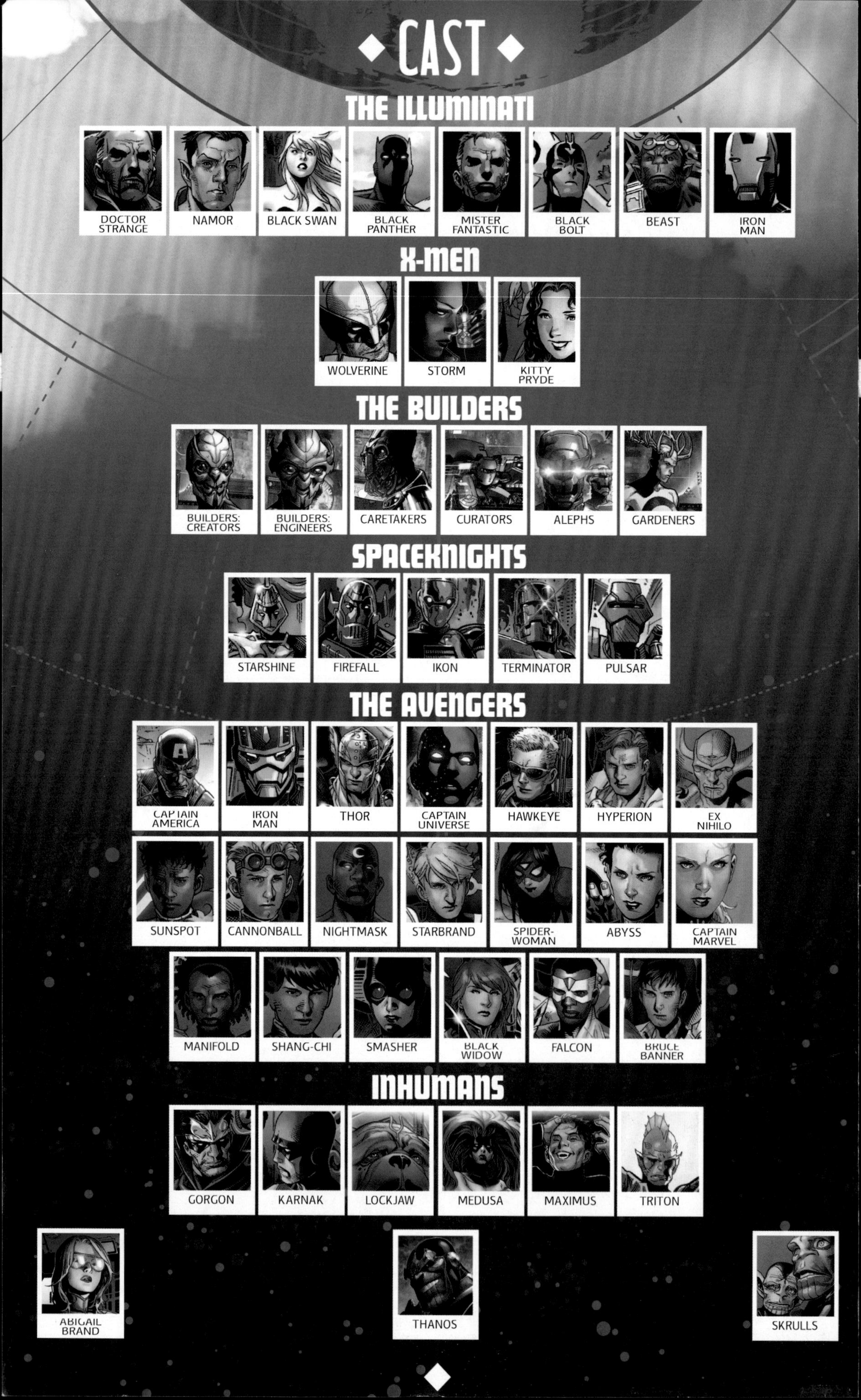
CAST
THE ILLUMINATI
DOCTOR STRANGE
NAMOR
BLACK SWAN
BLACK PANTHER
MISTER FANTASTIC
BLACK BOLT
BEAST
IRON MAN
X-MEN
WOLVERINE
STORM
KITTY PRYDE
THE BUILDERS
BUILDERS: CREATORS
BUILDERS: ENGINEERS
CARETAKERS
CURATORS
ALEPHS
GARDENERS
SPACEKNIGHTS
STARSHINE
FIREFALL
IKON
TERMINATOR
PULSAR
THE AVENGERS
CAPTAIN AMERICA
IRON MAN
THOR
CAPTAIN UNIVERSE
HAWKEYE
HYPERION
EX NIHILO
SUNSPOT
CANNONBALL
NIGHTMASK
STARBRAND
SPIDER-WOMAN
ABYSS
CAPTAIN MARVEL
MANIFOLD
SHANG-CHI
SMASHER
BLACK WIDOW
FALCON
BRUCE BANNER
INHUMANS
GORGON
KARNAK
LOCKJAW
MEDUSA
MAXIMUS
TRITON
ABIGAIL BRAND
THANOS
SKRULLS

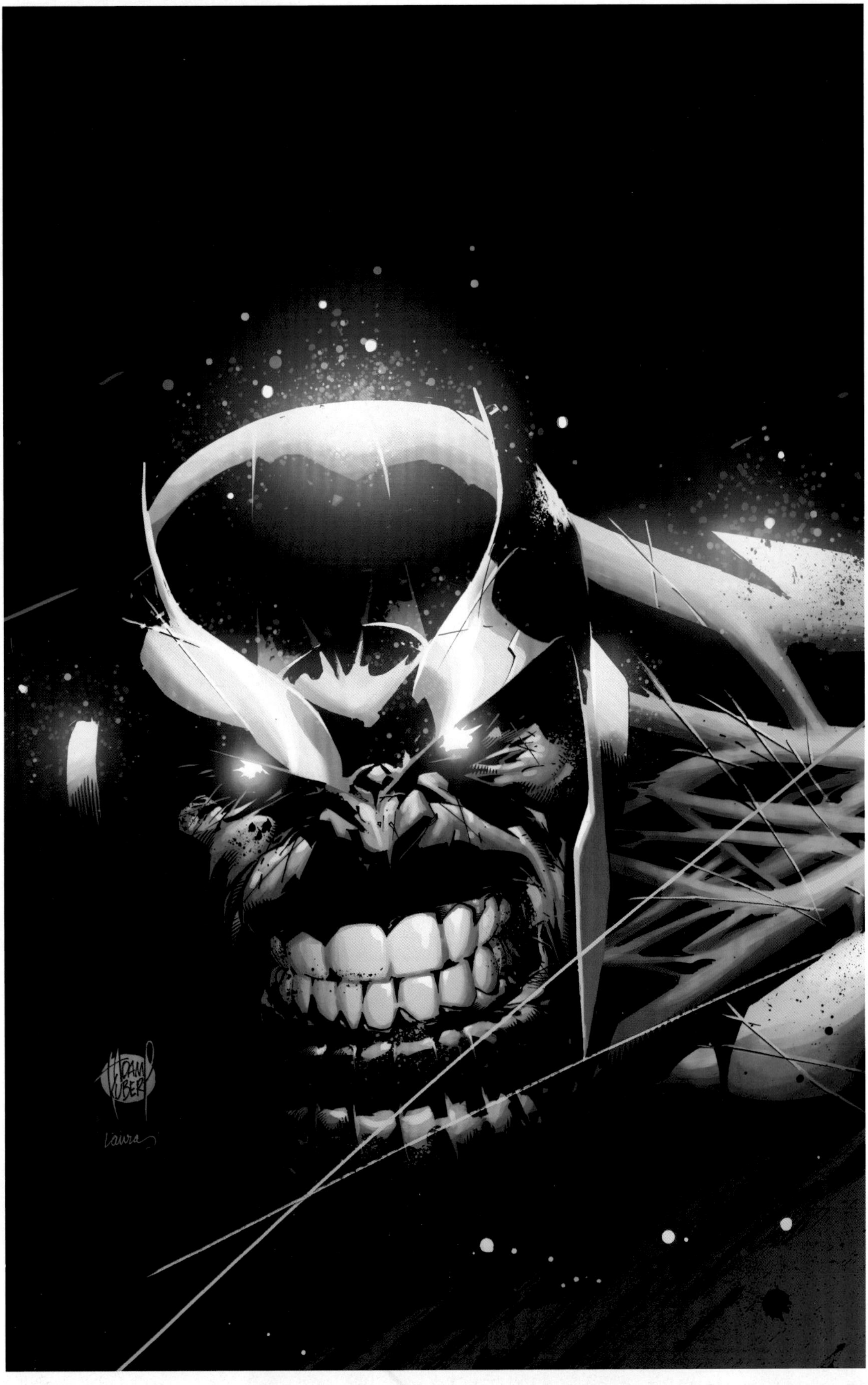

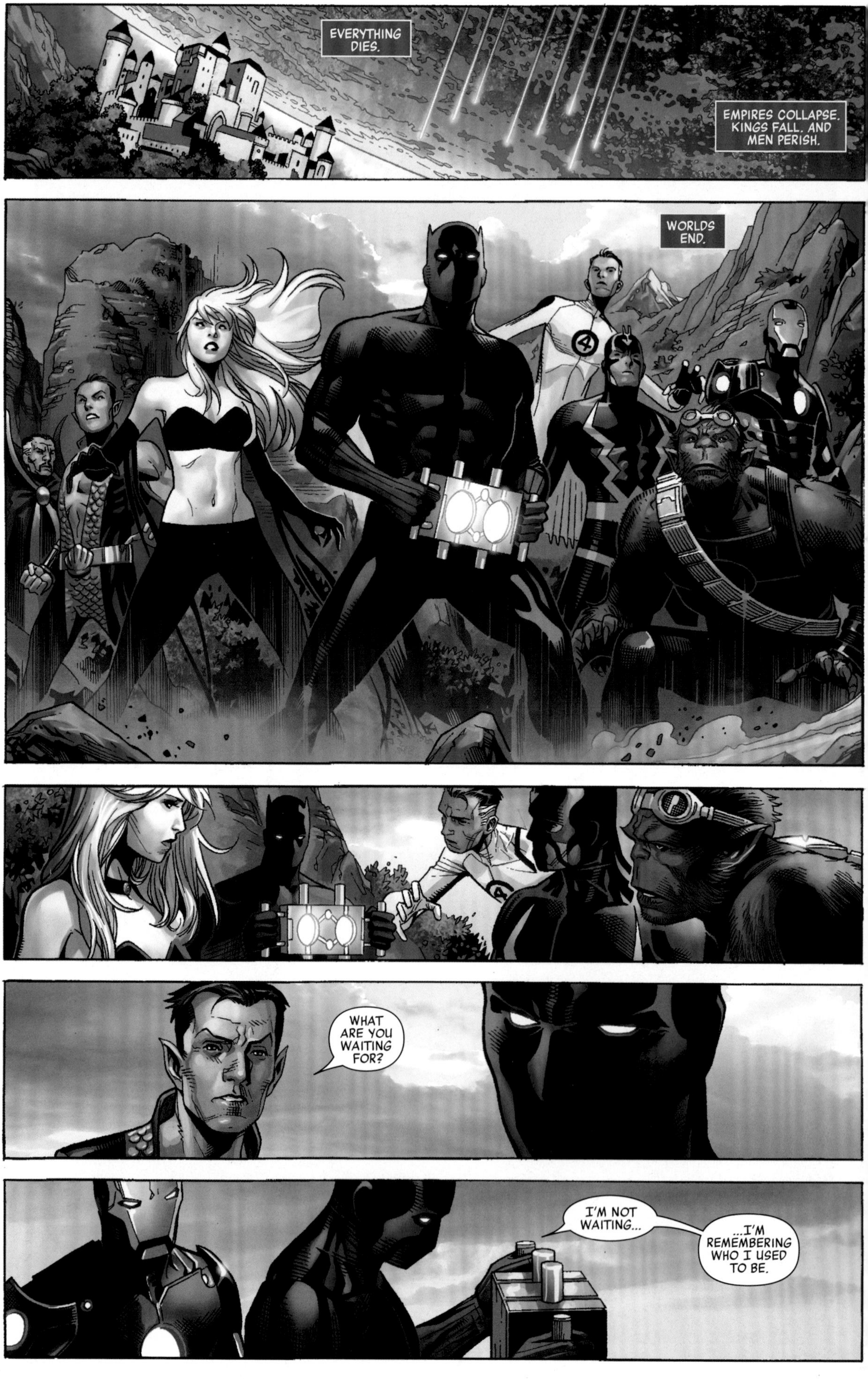
EVERYTHING DIES.
EMPIRES COLLAPSE. KINGS FALL. AND MEN PERISH.
WORLDS END.
WHAT ARE YOU WAITING FOR?
I'M NOT WAITING...
...I'M REMEMBERING WHO I USED TO BE.

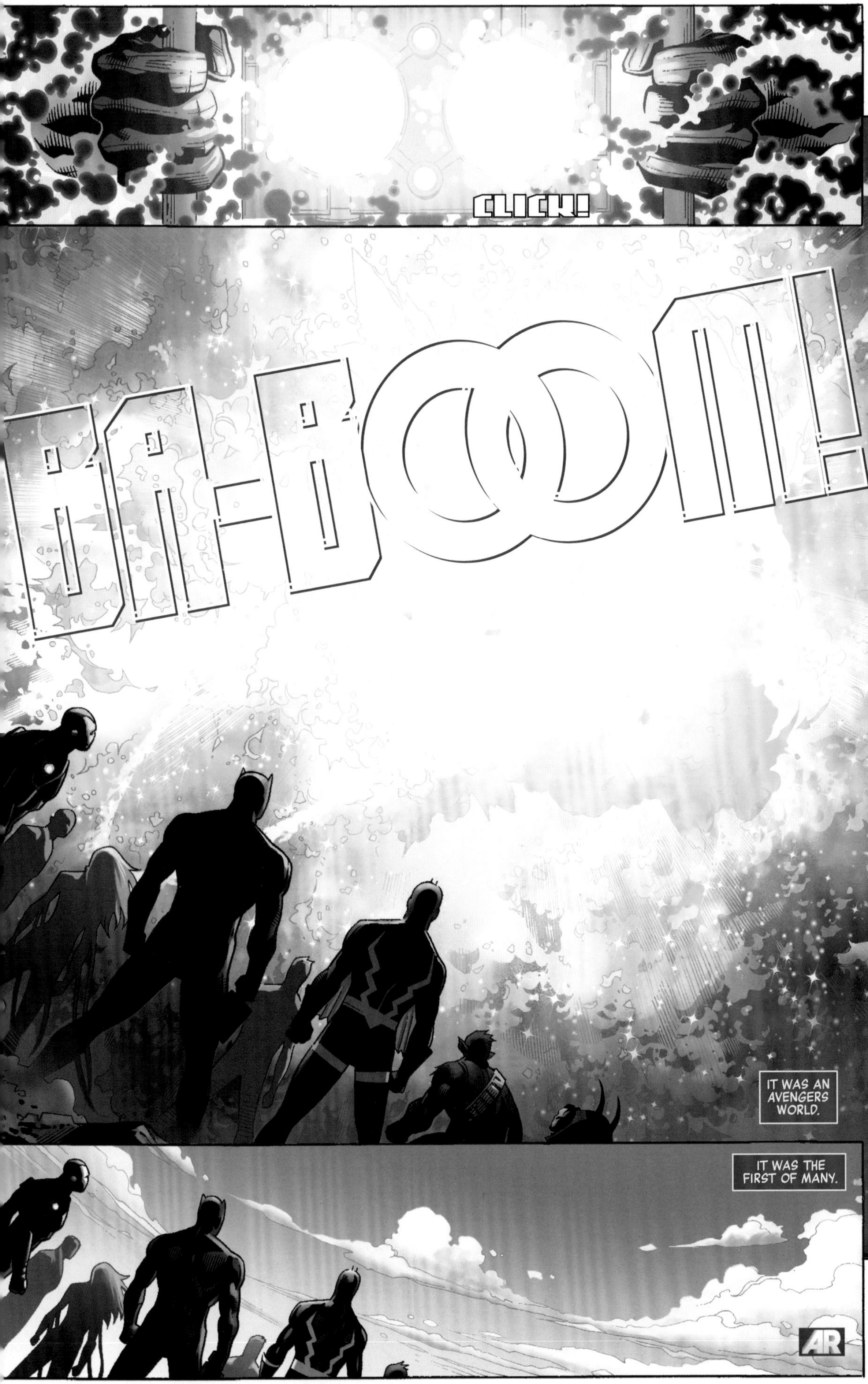
CLICK!
BA-BOOM!
IT WAS AN AVENGERS WORLD.
IT WAS THE FIRST OF MANY.

THE TRIBUTE

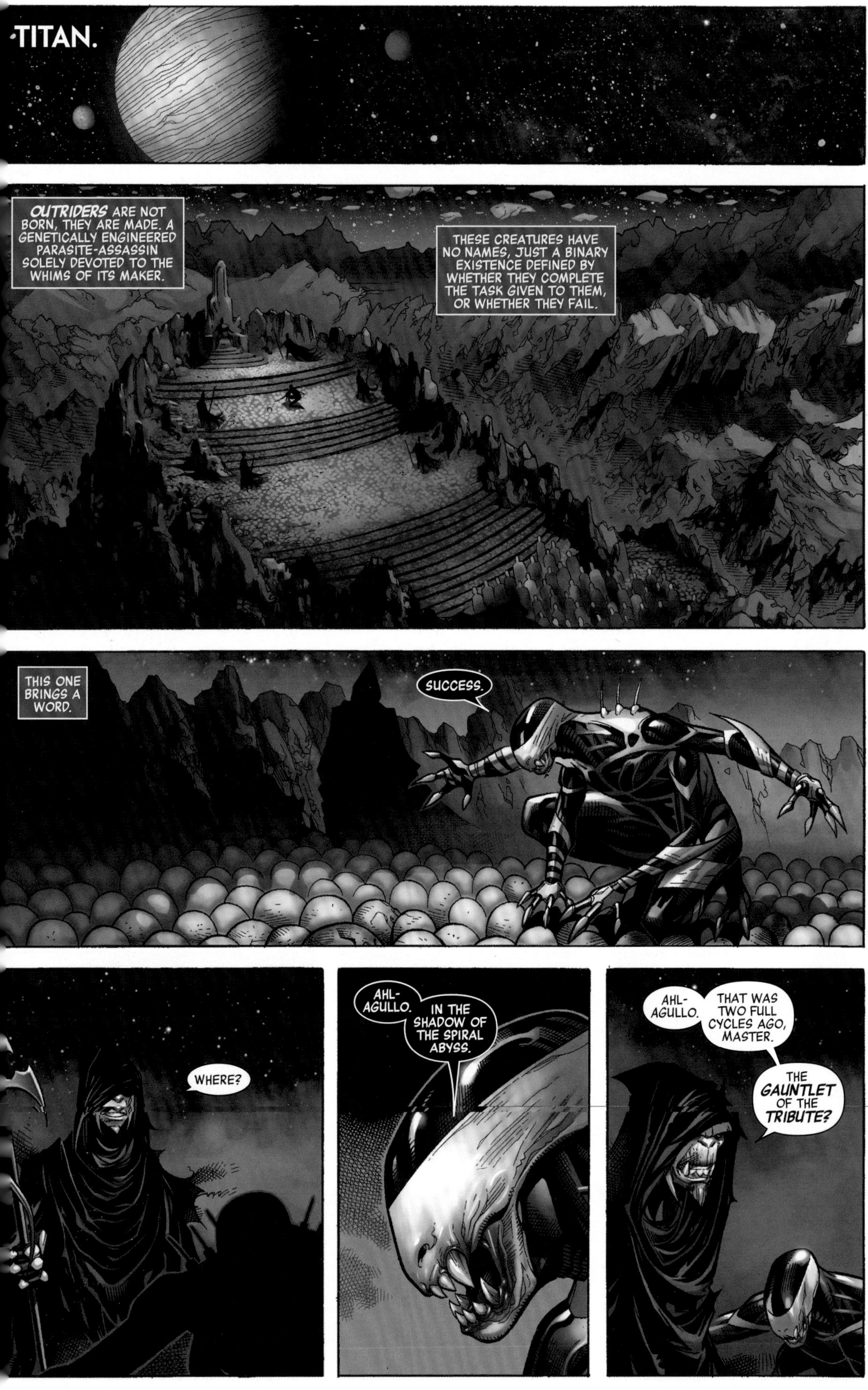
TITAN.
OUTRIDERS ARE NOT BORN, THEY ARE MADE. A GENETICALLY ENGINEERED PARASITE-ASSASSIN SOLELY DEVOTED TO THE WHIMS OF ITS MAKER.
THESE CREATURES HAVE NO NAMES, JUST A BINARY EXISTENCE DEFINED BY WHETHER THEY COMPLETE THE TASK GIVEN TO THEM, OR WHETHER THEY FAIL.
THIS ONE BRINGS A WORD.
SUCCESS.
WHERE?
AHL-AGULLO.
IN THE SHADOW OF THE SPIRAL ABYSS.
AHL-AGULLO.
THAT WAS TWO FULL CYCLES AGO, MASTER.
THE GAUNTLET OF THE TRIBUTE?

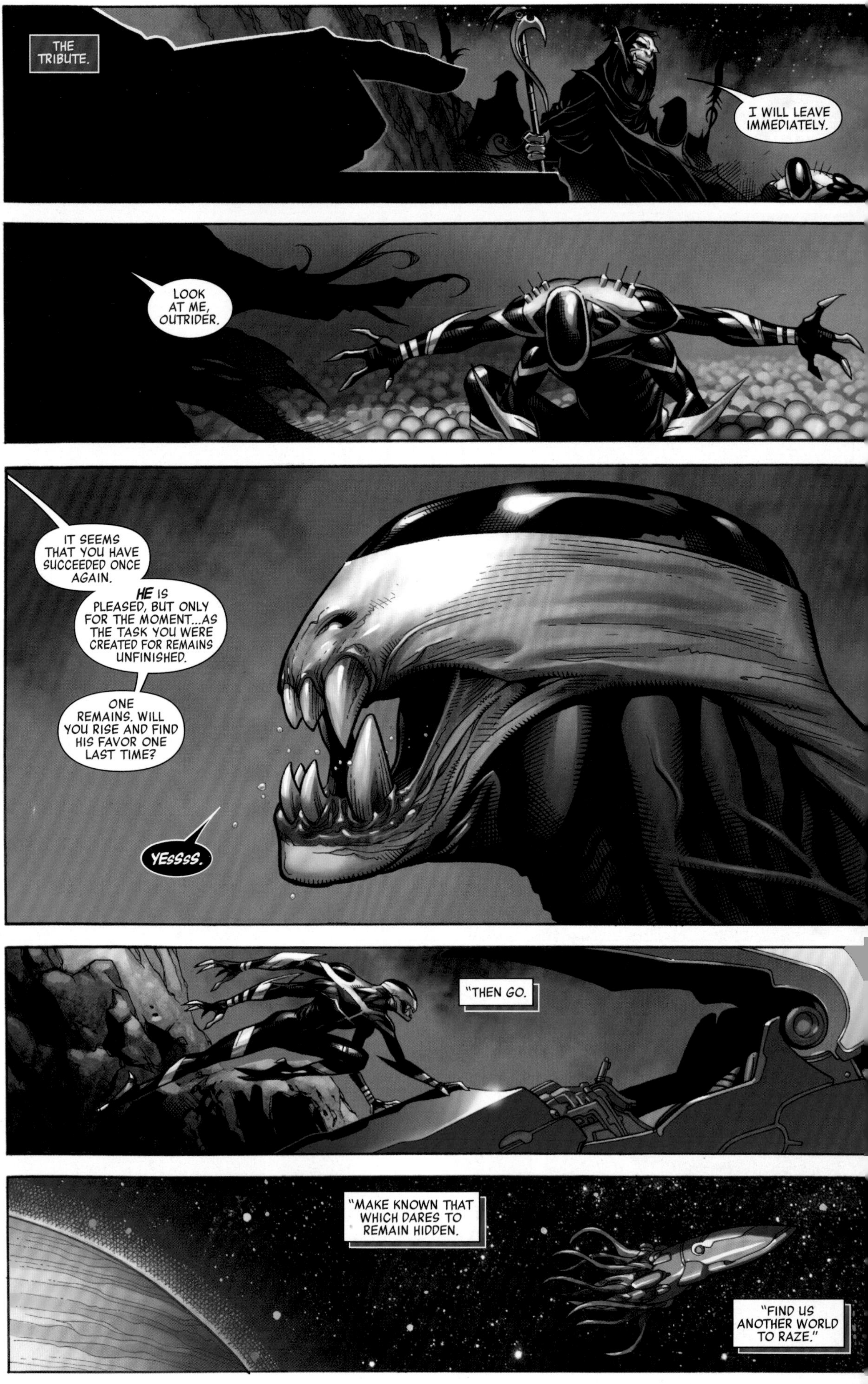
THE TRIBUTE.
I WILL LEAVE IMMEDIATELY.
LOOK AT ME, OUTRIDER.
IT SEEMS THAT YOU HAVE SUCCEEDED ONCE AGAIN.
HE IS PLEASED, BUT ONLY FOR THE MOMENT...AS THE TASK YOU WERE CREATED FOR REMAINS UNFINISHED.
ONE REMAINS. WILL YOU RISE AND FIND HIS FAVOR ONE LAST TIME?
YESSSS.
"THEN GO.
"MAKE KNOWN THAT WHICH DARES TO REMAIN HIDDEN.
"FIND US ANOTHER WORLD TO RAZE."

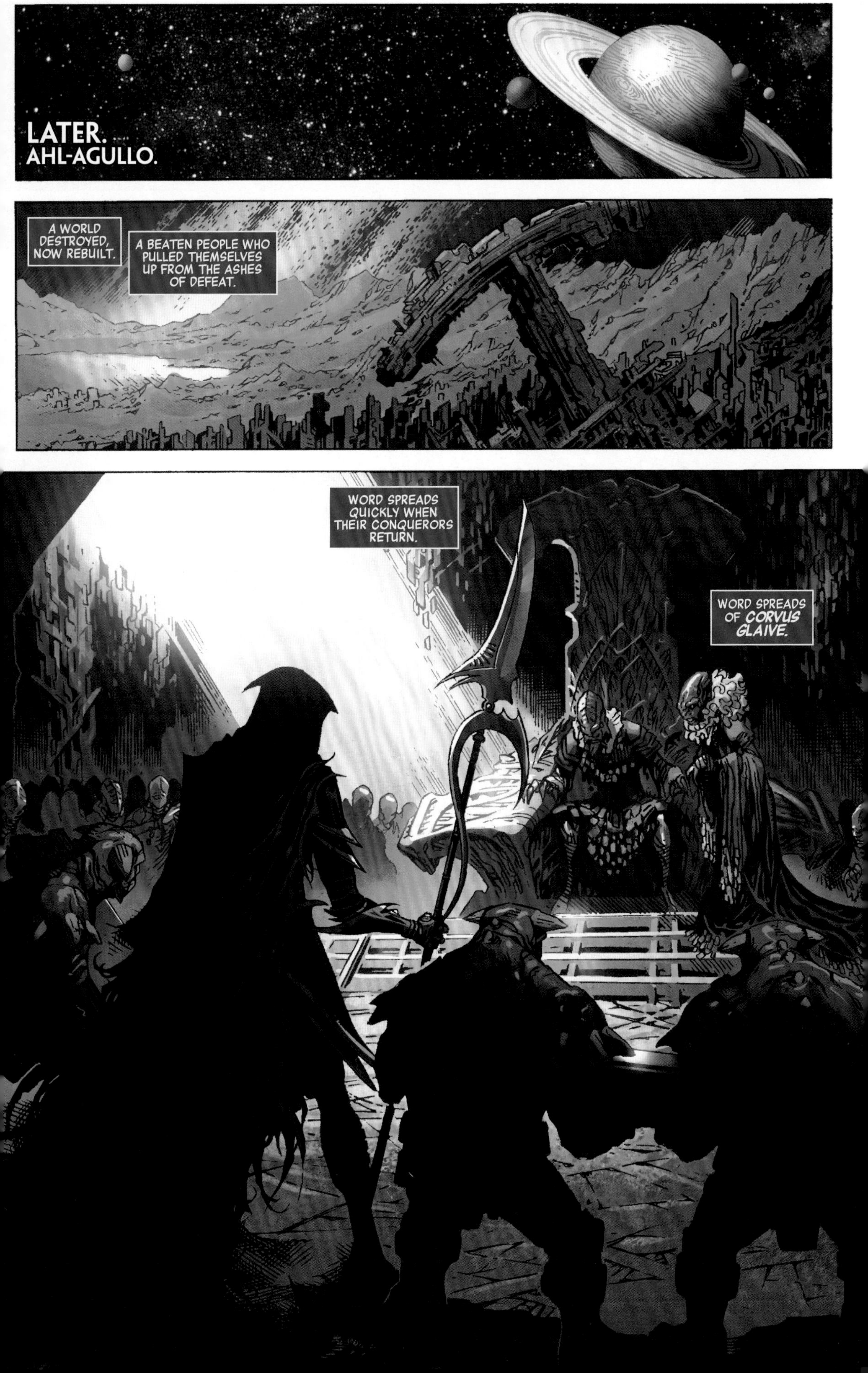
LATER.
AHL-AGULLO.
A WORLD DESTROYED, NOW REBUILT.
A BEATEN PEOPLE WHO PULLED THEMSELVES UP FROM THE ASHES OF DEFEAT.
WORD SPREADS QUICKLY WHEN THEIR CONQUERORS RETURN.
WORD SPREADS OF CORVUS GLAIVE.

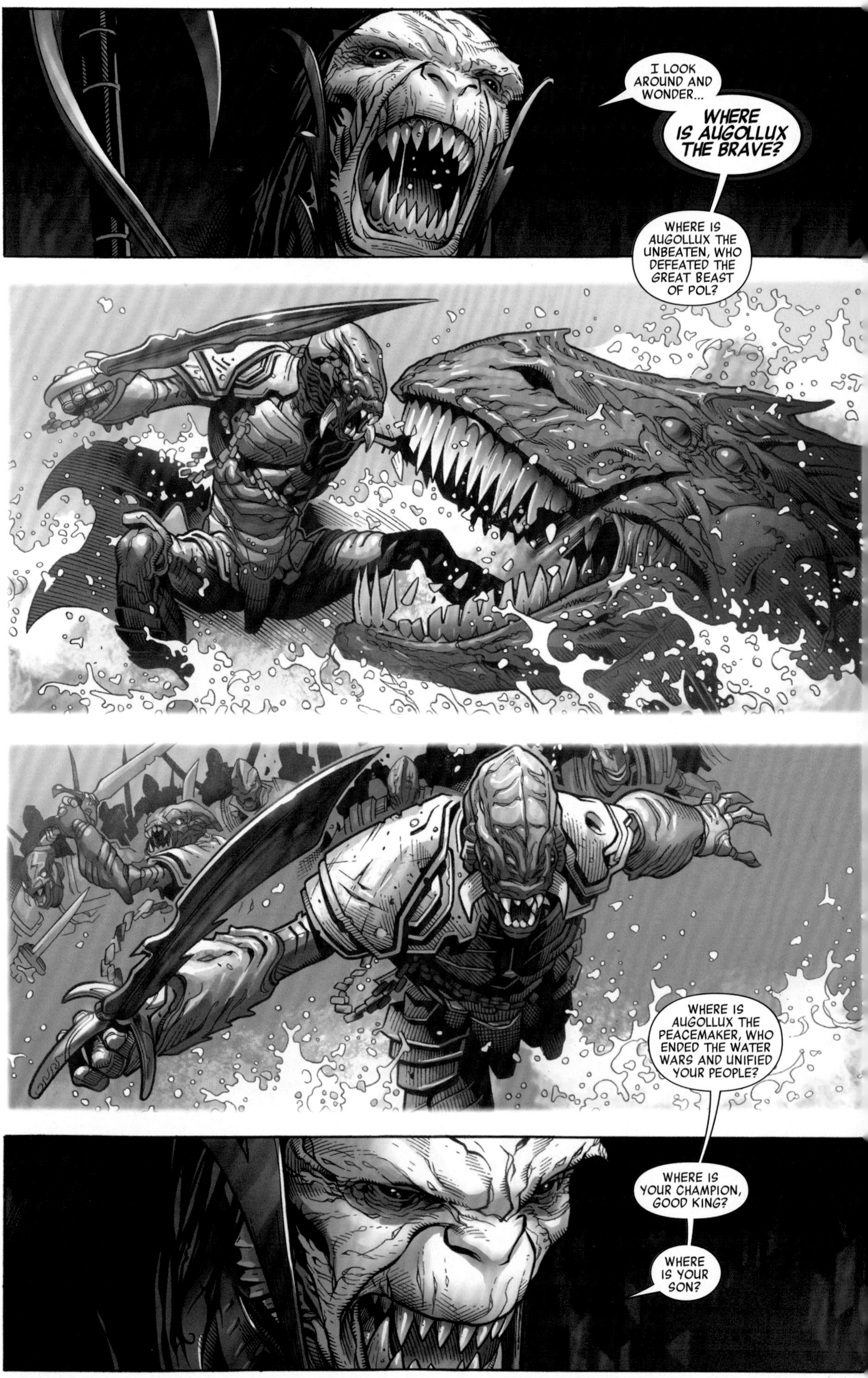
I LOOK AROUND AND WONDER...
WHERE IS AUGOLLUX THE BRAVE?
WHERE IS AUGOLLUX THE UNBEATEN, WHO DEFEATED THE GREAT BEAST OF POL?
WHERE IS AUGOLLUX THE PEACEMAKER, WHO ENDED THE WATER WARS AND UNIFIED YOUR PEOPLE?
WHERE IS YOUR CHAMPION, GOOD KING?
WHERE IS YOUR SON?

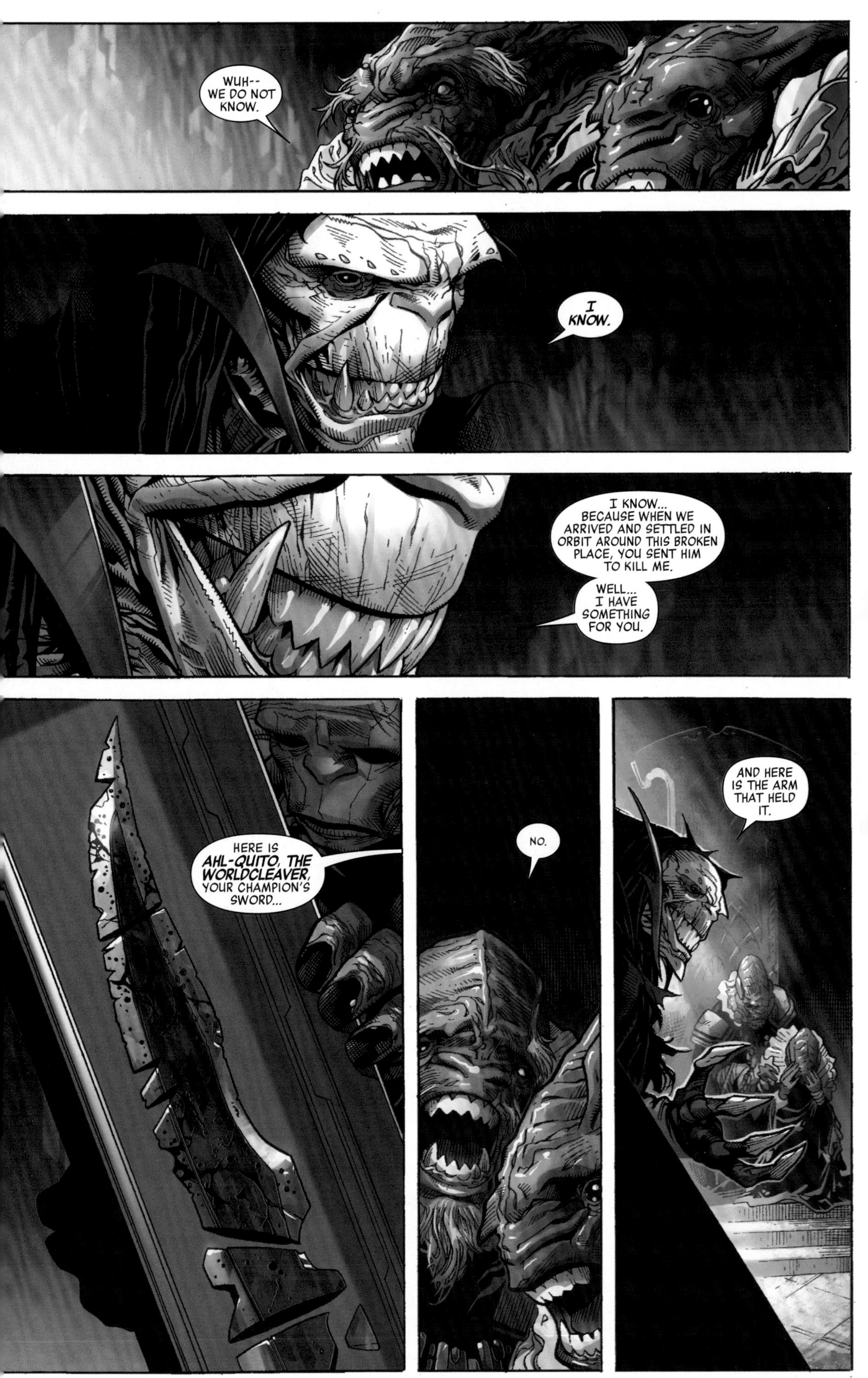
WUH-- WE DO NOT KNOW.
I KNOW.
I KNOW... BECAUSE WHEN WE ARRIVED AND SETTLED IN ORBIT AROUND THIS BROKEN PLACE, YOU SENT HIM TO KILL ME.
WELL... I HAVE SOMETHING FOR YOU.
HERE IS AHL-QUITO, THE WORLDCLEAVER, YOUR CHAMPION'S SWORD...
NO.
AND HERE IS THE ARM THAT HELD IT.

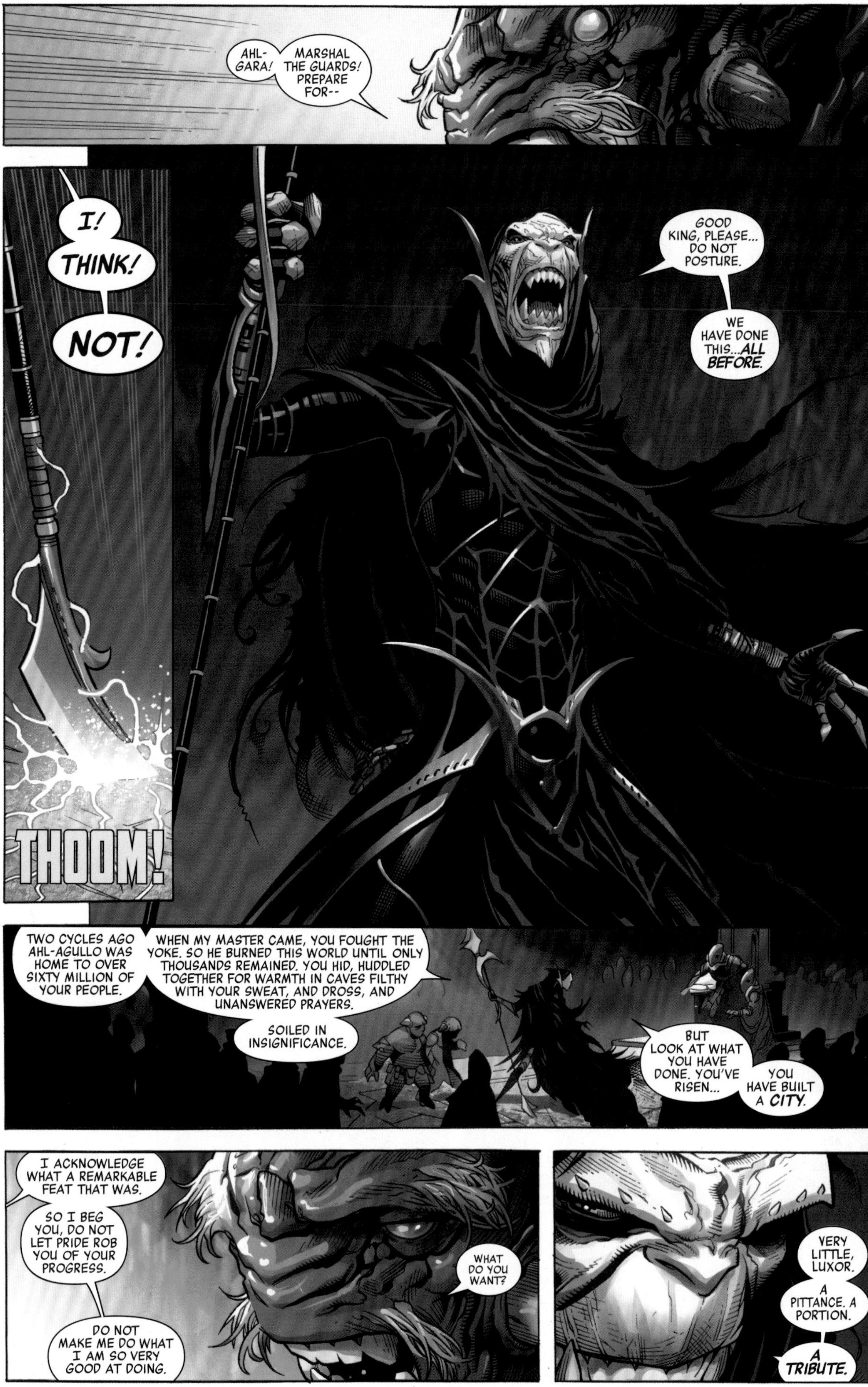

AHL-GARA!
MARSHAL THE GUARDS! PREPARE FOR--
I! THINK! NOT!
THOOM!
GOOD KING, PLEASE... DO NOT POSTURE.
WE HAVE DONE THIS...ALL BEFORE.
TWO CYCLES AGO AHL-AGULLO WAS HOME TO OVER SIXTY MILLION OF YOUR PEOPLE.
WHEN MY MASTER CAME, YOU FOUGHT THE YOKE. SO HE BURNED THIS WORLD UNTIL ONLY THOUSANDS REMAINED. YOU HID, HUDDLED TOGETHER FOR WARMTH IN CAVES FILTHY WITH YOUR SWEAT, AND DROSS, AND UNANSWERED PRAYERS.
SOILED IN INSIGNIFICANCE.
BUT LOOK AT WHAT YOU HAVE DONE. YOU'VE RISEN...
YOU HAVE BUILT A CITY.
I ACKNOWLEDGE WHAT A REMARKABLE FEAT THAT WAS.
SO I BEG YOU, DO NOT LET PRIDE ROB YOU OF YOUR PROGRESS.
DO NOT MAKE ME DO WHAT I AM SO VERY GOOD AT DOING.
WHAT DO YOU WANT?
VERY LITTLE, LUXOR.
A PITTANCE. A PORTION.
A TRIBUTE.

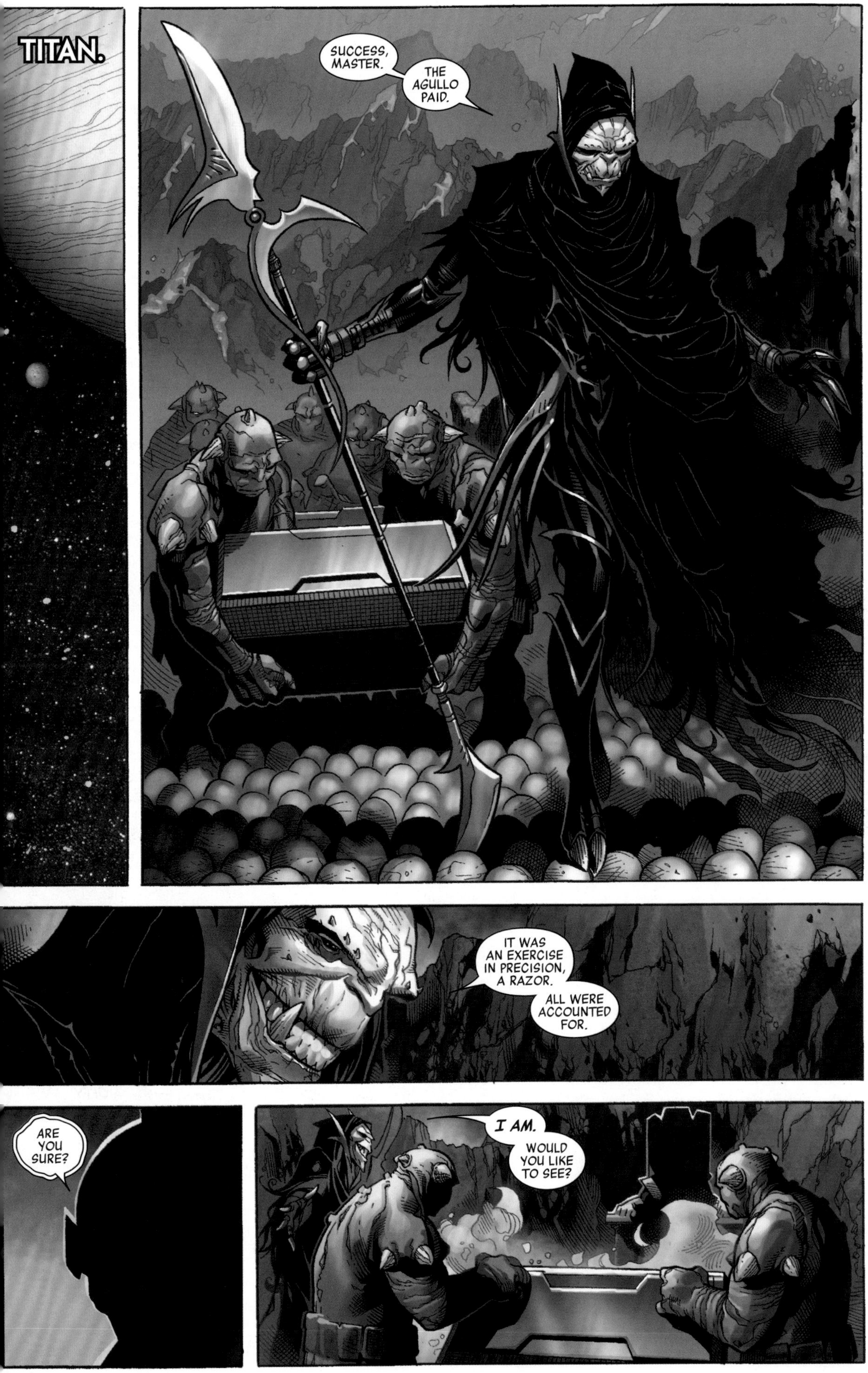
TITAN.
SUCCESS, MASTER.
THE AGULLO PAID.
IT WAS AN EXERCISE IN PRECISION, A RAZOR.
ALL WERE ACCOUNTED FOR.
ARE YOU SURE?
I AM.
WOULD YOU LIKE TO SEE?

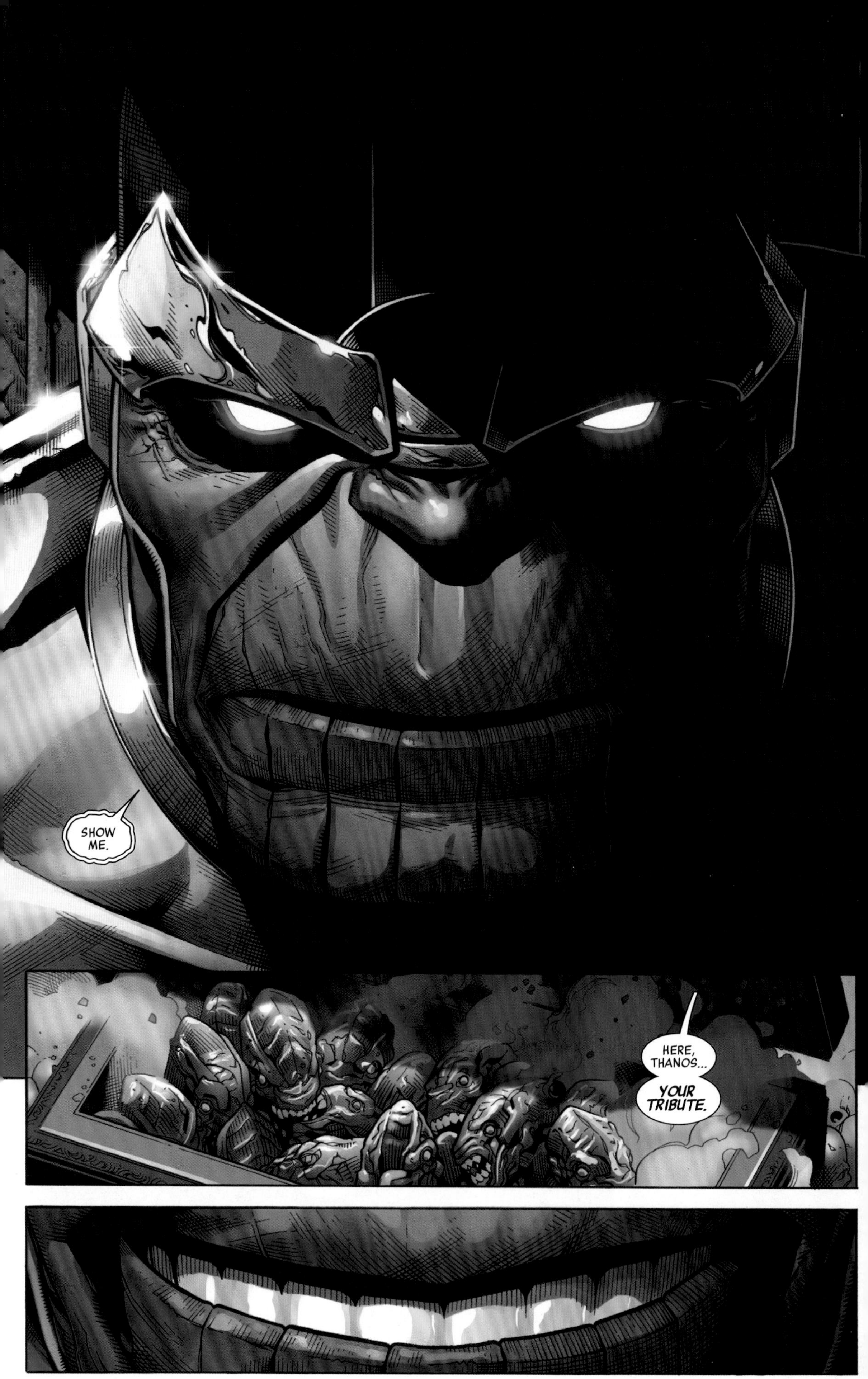
SHOW ME.
HERE, THANOS...
YOUR TRIBUTE.

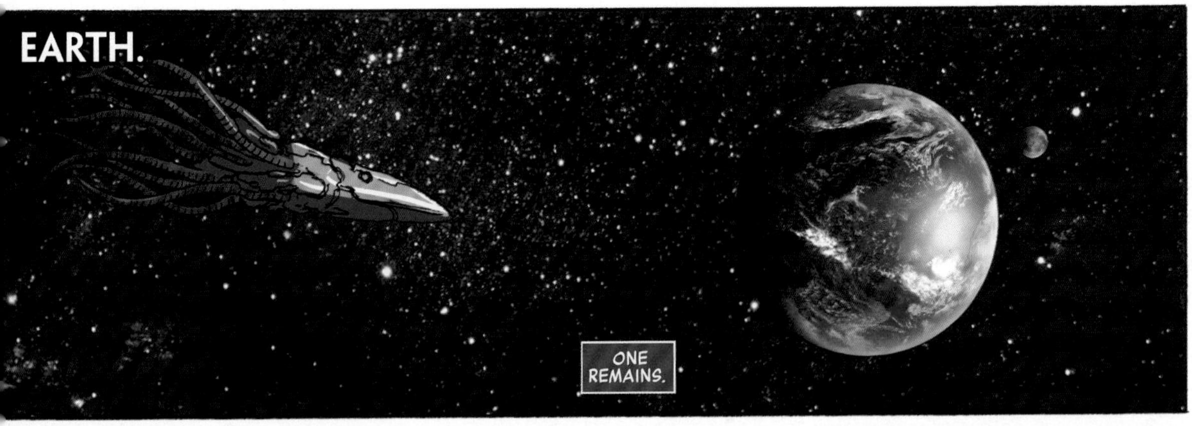
EARTH.
ONE REMAINS.

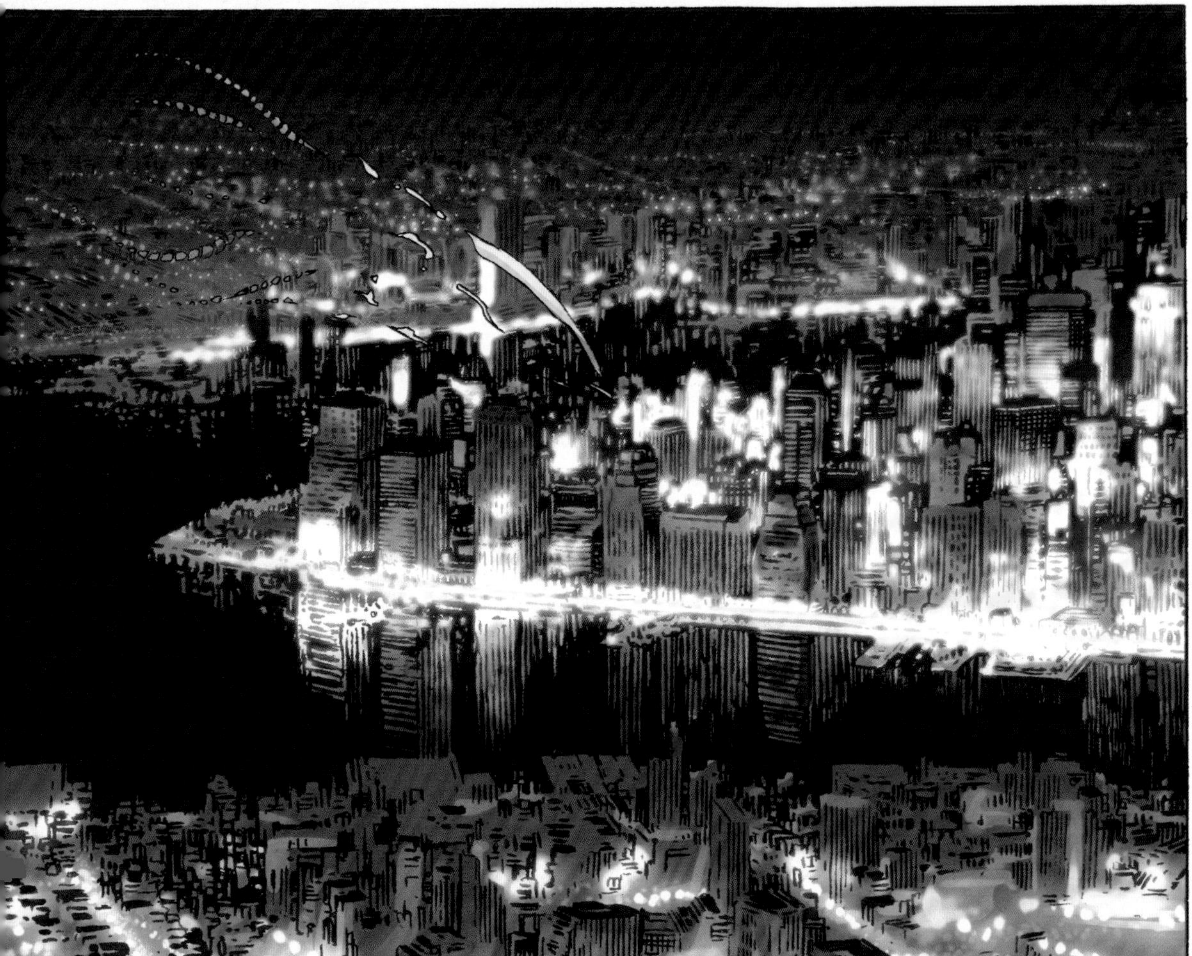

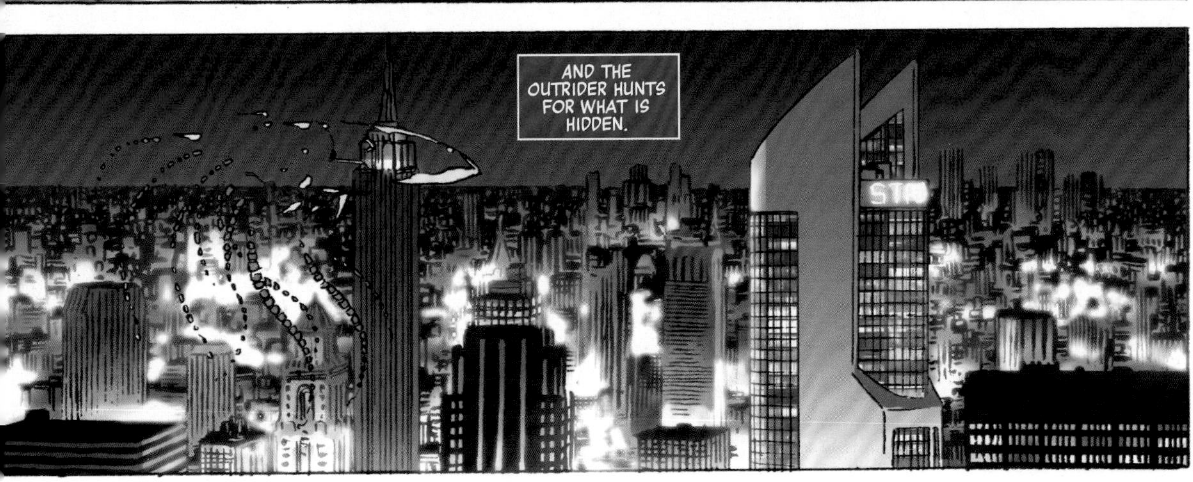
AND THE OUTRIDER HUNTS FOR WHAT IS HIDDEN.

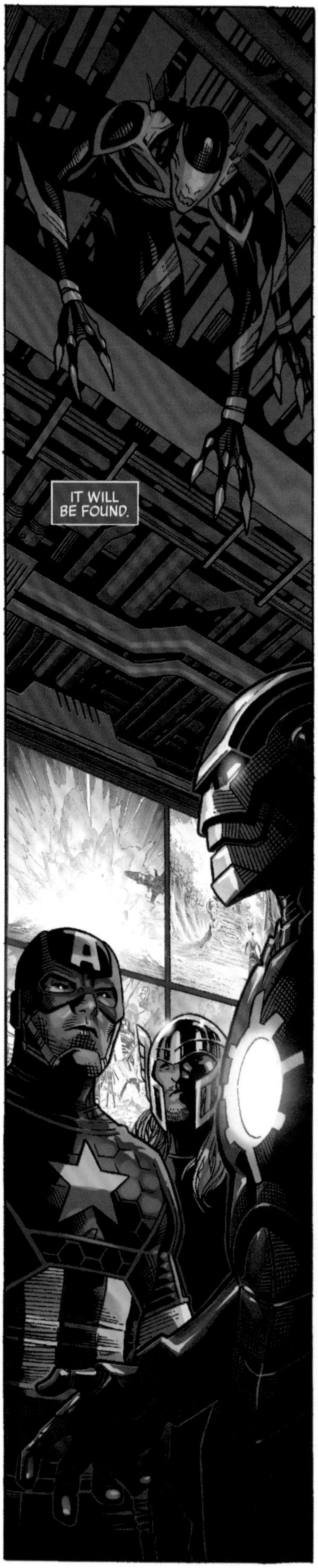
IT WILL
BE FOUND.

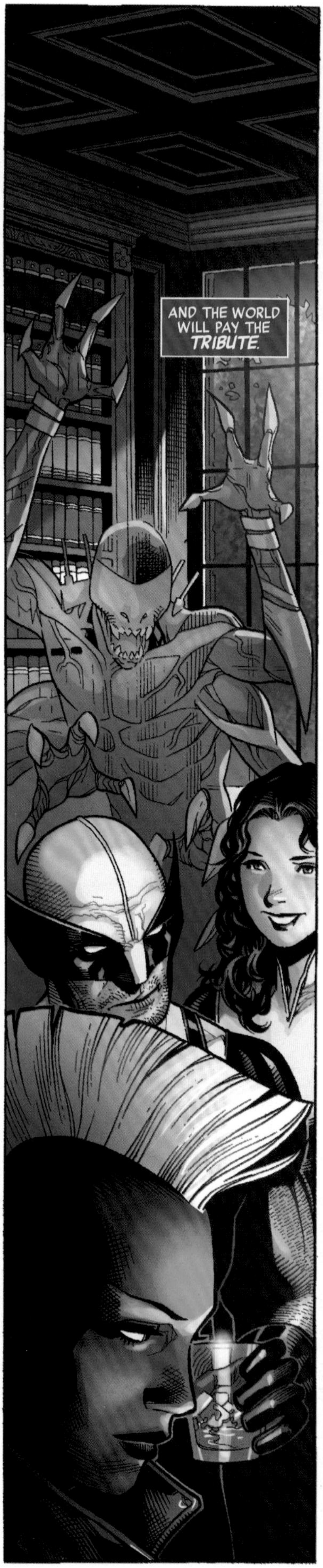
AND THE WORLD
WILL PAY THE
TRIBUTE.

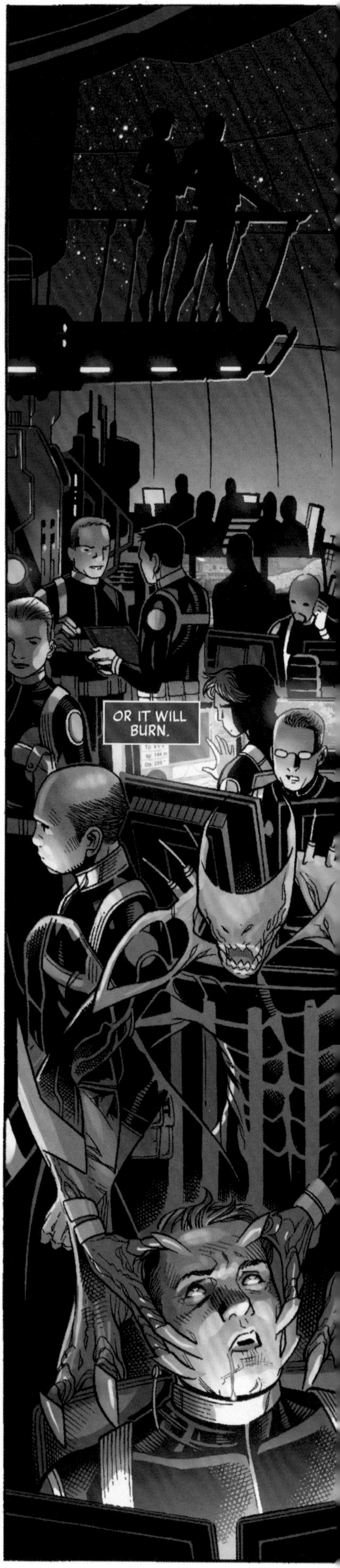
OR IT WILL
BURN.

CONSTRUCTING
APOCALYPSE

◆

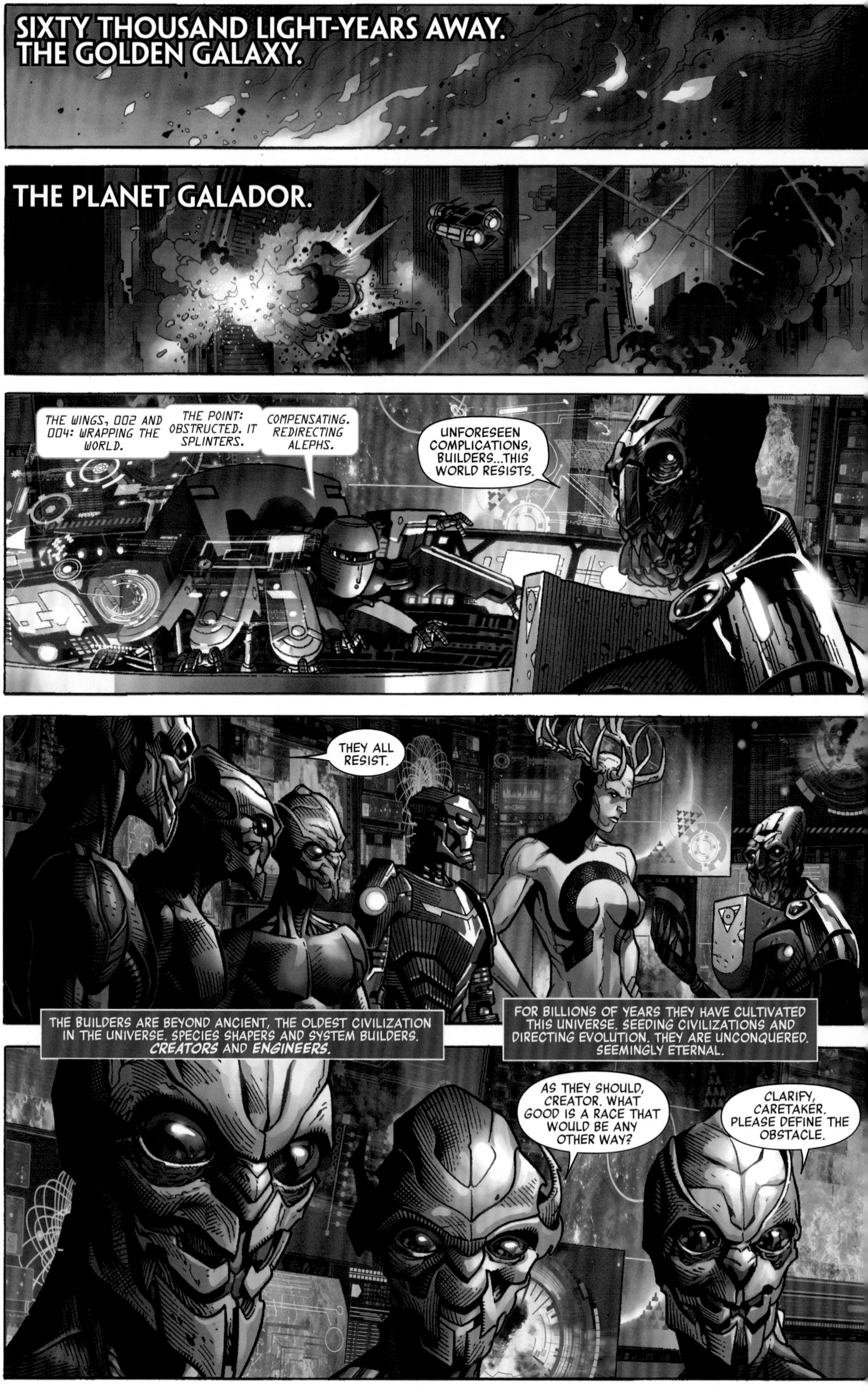
SIXTY THOUSAND LIGHT-YEARS AWAY.
THE GOLDEN GALAXY.
THE PLANET GALADOR.
THE WINGS, 002 AND 004: WRAPPING THE WORLD.
THE POINT: OBSTRUCTED. IT SPLINTERS.
COMPENSATING. REDIRECTING ALEPHS.
UNFORESEEN COMPLICATIONS, BUILDERS...THIS WORLD RESISTS.
THEY ALL RESIST.
THE BUILDERS ARE BEYOND ANCIENT, THE OLDEST CIVILIZATION IN THE UNIVERSE. SPECIES SHAPERS AND SYSTEM BUILDERS. CREATORS AND ENGINEERS.
FOR BILLIONS OF YEARS THEY HAVE CULTIVATED THIS UNIVERSE. SEEDING CIVILIZATIONS AND DIRECTING EVOLUTION. THEY ARE UNCONQUERED. SEEMINGLY ETERNAL.
AS THEY SHOULD, CREATOR. WHAT GOOD IS A RACE THAT WOULD BE ANY OTHER WAY?
CLARIFY, CARETAKER. PLEASE DEFINE THE OBSTACLE.

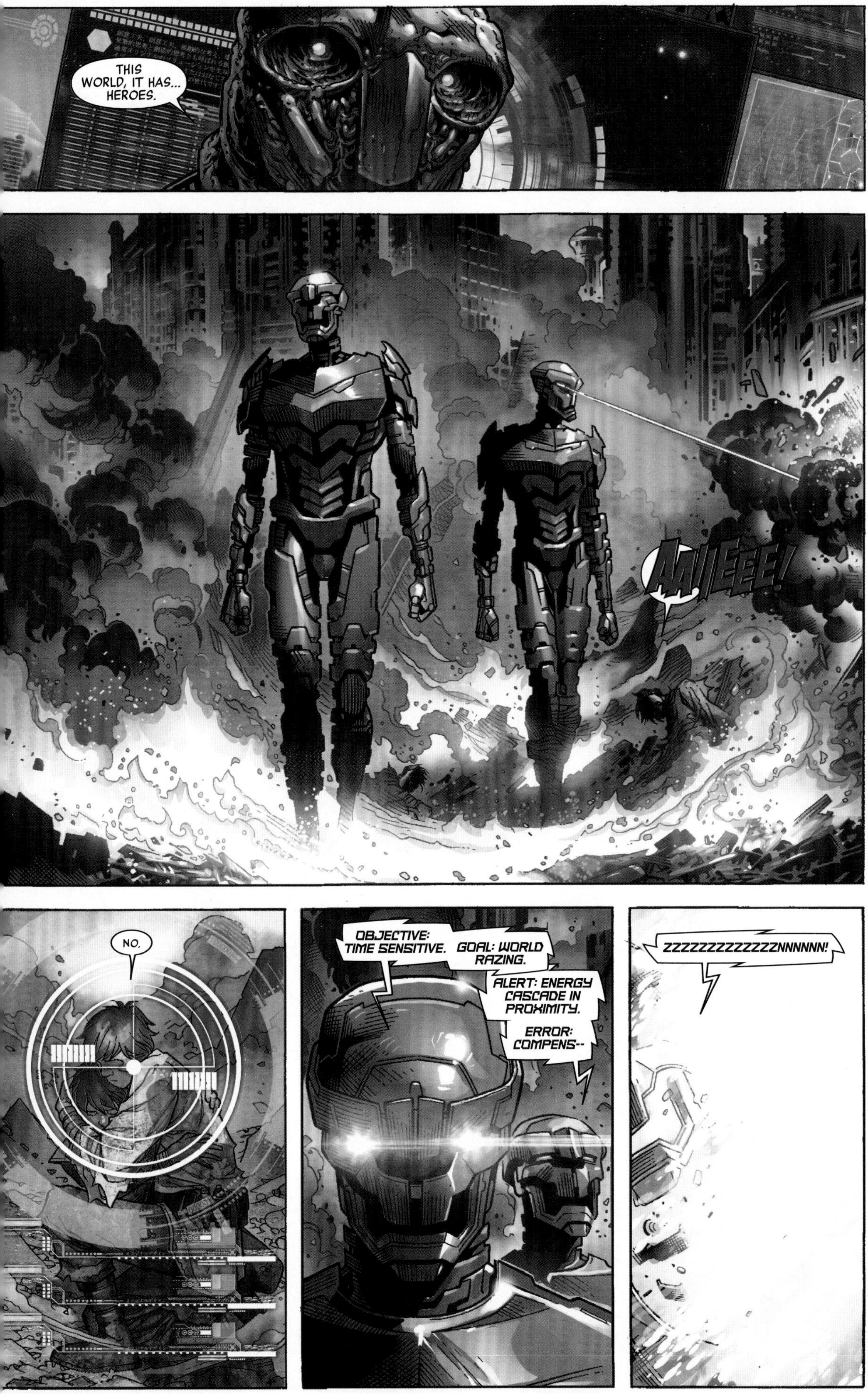
THIS WORLD, IT HAS... HEROES.
AAIIEEE!
NO.
OBJECTIVE: TIME SENSITIVE.
GOAL: WORLD RAZING.
ALERT: ENERGY CASCADE IN PROXIMITY.
ERROR: COMPENS--
ZZZZZZZZZZZZZNNNNNN!

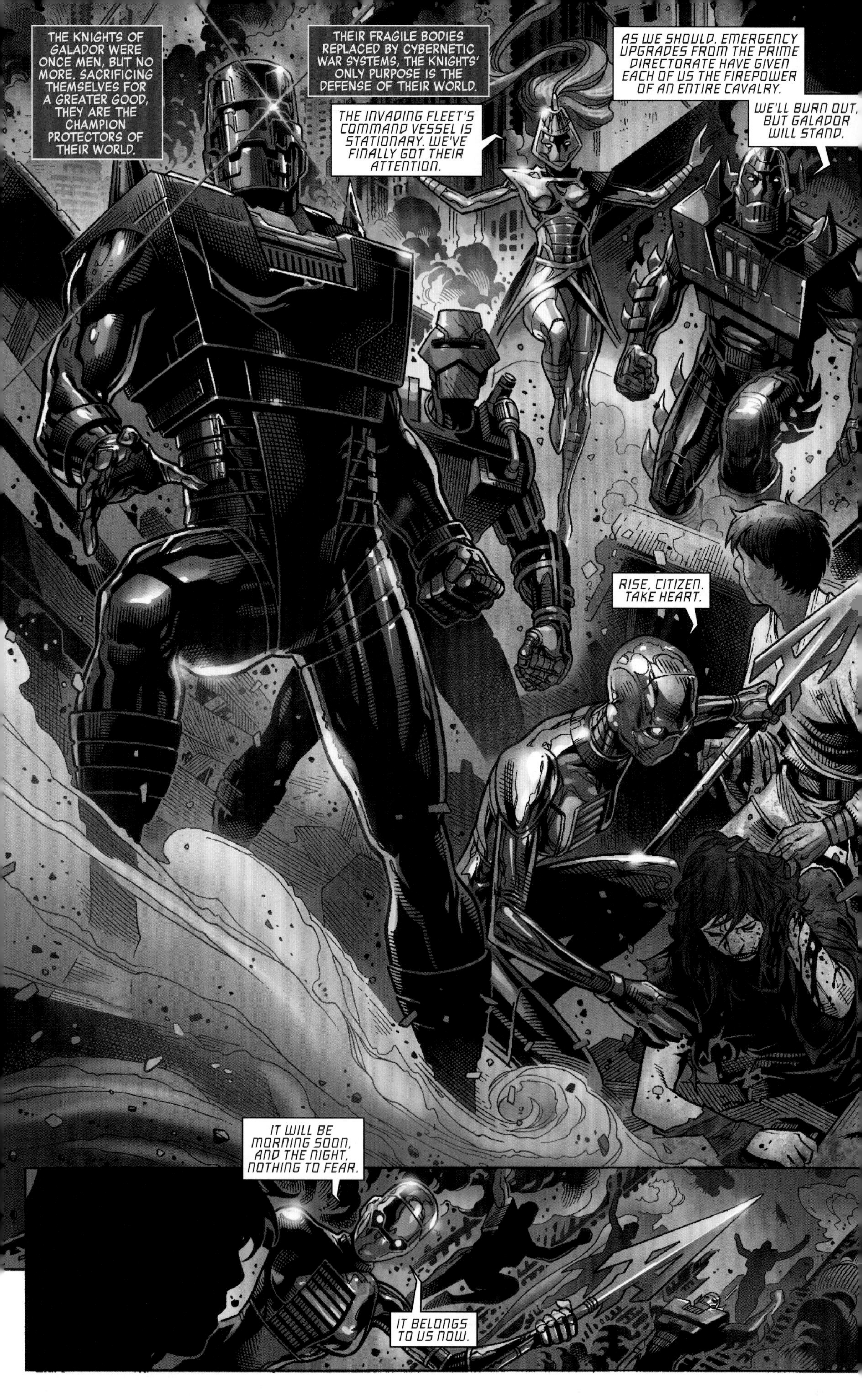
THE KNIGHTS OF GALADOR WERE ONCE MEN, BUT NO MORE. SACRIFICING THEMSELVES FOR A GREATER GOOD, THEY ARE THE CHAMPION PROTECTORS OF THEIR WORLD.
THEIR FRAGILE BODIES REPLACED BY CYBERNETIC WAR SYSTEMS, THE KNIGHTS' ONLY PURPOSE IS THE DEFENSE OF THEIR WORLD.
THE INVADING FLEET'S COMMAND VESSEL IS STATIONARY. WE'VE FINALLY GOT THEIR ATTENTION.
AS WE SHOULD. EMERGENCY UPGRADES FROM THE PRIME DIRECTORATE HAVE GIVEN EACH OF US THE FIREPOWER OF AN ENTIRE CAVALRY.
WE'LL BURN OUT, BUT GALADOR WILL STAND.
RISE, CITIZEN. TAKE HEART.
IT WILL BE MORNING SOON, AND THE NIGHT, NOTHING TO FEAR.
IT BELONGS TO US NOW.

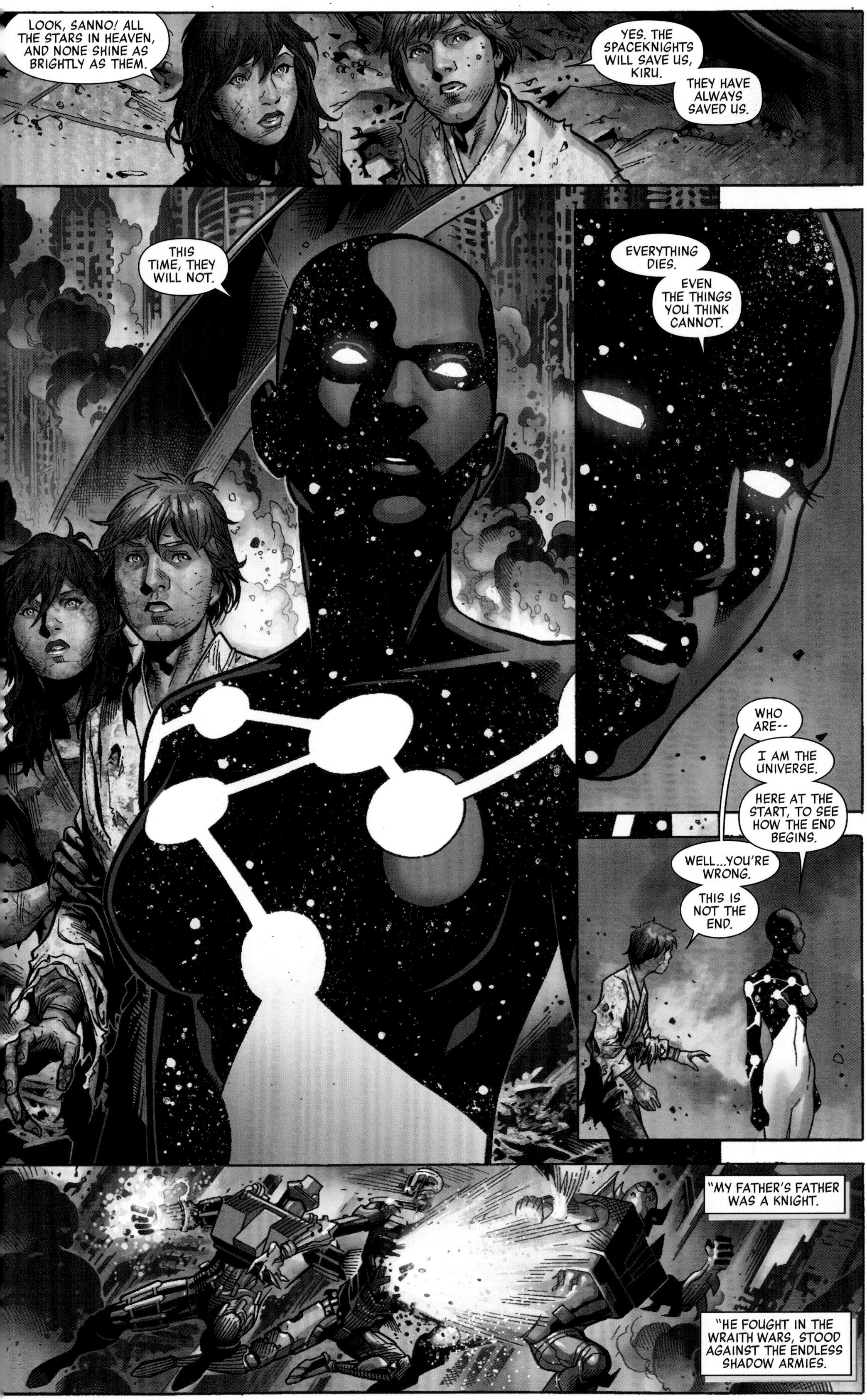
LOOK, SANNO! ALL THE STARS IN HEAVEN, AND NONE SHINE AS BRIGHTLY AS THEM.
YES. THE SPACEKNIGHTS WILL SAVE US, KIRU.
THEY HAVE ALWAYS SAVED US.
THIS TIME, THEY WILL NOT.
EVERYTHING DIES.
EVEN THE THINGS YOU THINK CANNOT.
WHO ARE--
I AM THE UNIVERSE.
HERE AT THE START, TO SEE HOW THE END BEGINS.
WELL...YOU'RE WRONG.
THIS IS NOT THE END.
"MY FATHER'S FATHER WAS A KNIGHT.
"HE FOUGHT IN THE WRAITH WARS, STOOD AGAINST THE ENDLESS SHADOW ARMIES.

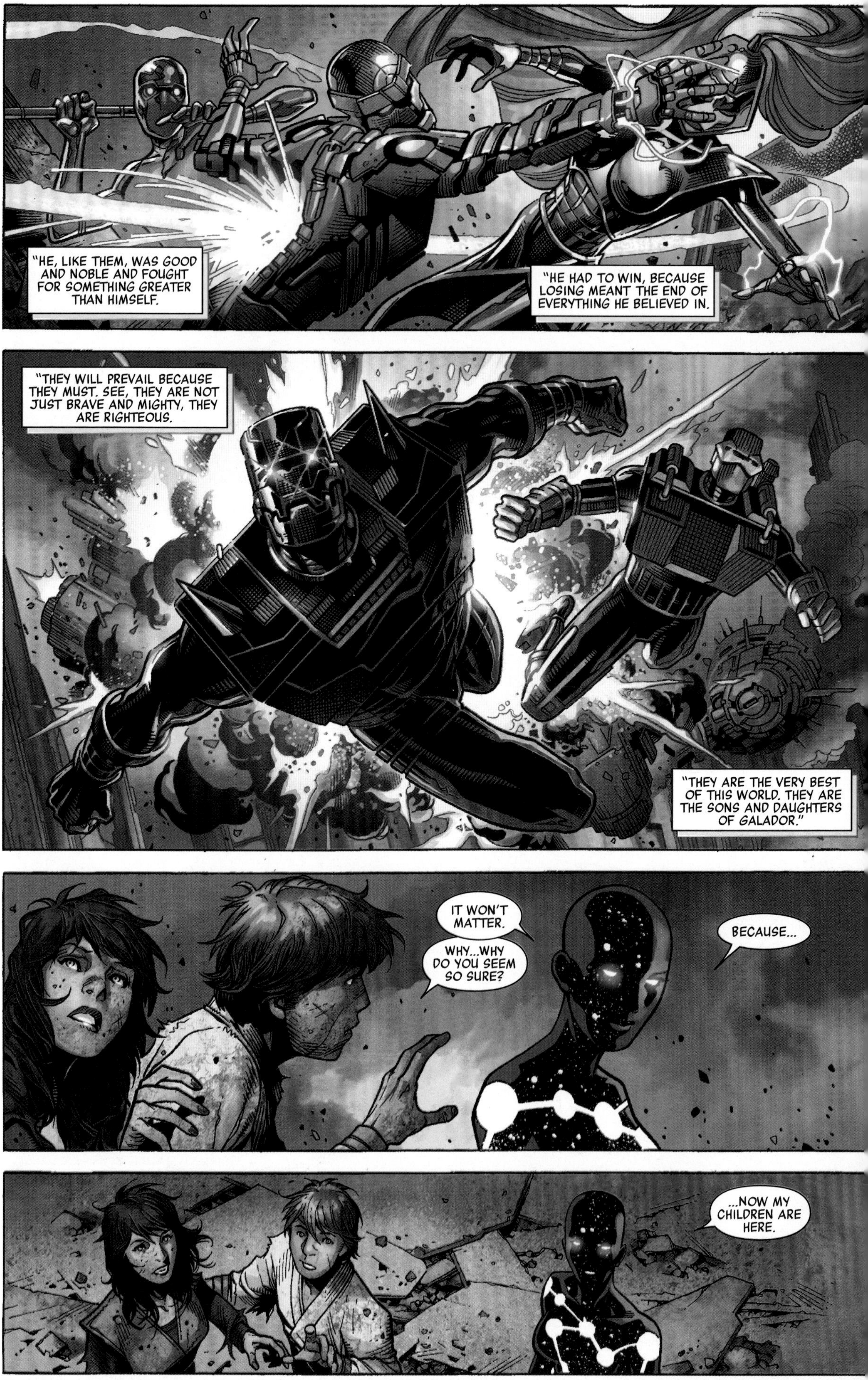
"HE, LIKE THEM, WAS GOOD AND NOBLE AND FOUGHT FOR SOMETHING GREATER THAN HIMSELF.
"HE HAD TO WIN, BECAUSE LOSING MEANT THE END OF EVERYTHING HE BELIEVED IN.
"THEY WILL PREVAIL BECAUSE THEY MUST. SEE, THEY ARE NOT JUST BRAVE AND MIGHTY, THEY ARE RIGHTEOUS.
"THEY ARE THE VERY BEST OF THIS WORLD. THEY ARE THE SONS AND DAUGHTERS OF GALADOR."
IT WON'T MATTER.
WHY...WHY DO YOU SEEM SO SURE?
BECAUSE...
...NOW MY CHILDREN ARE HERE.

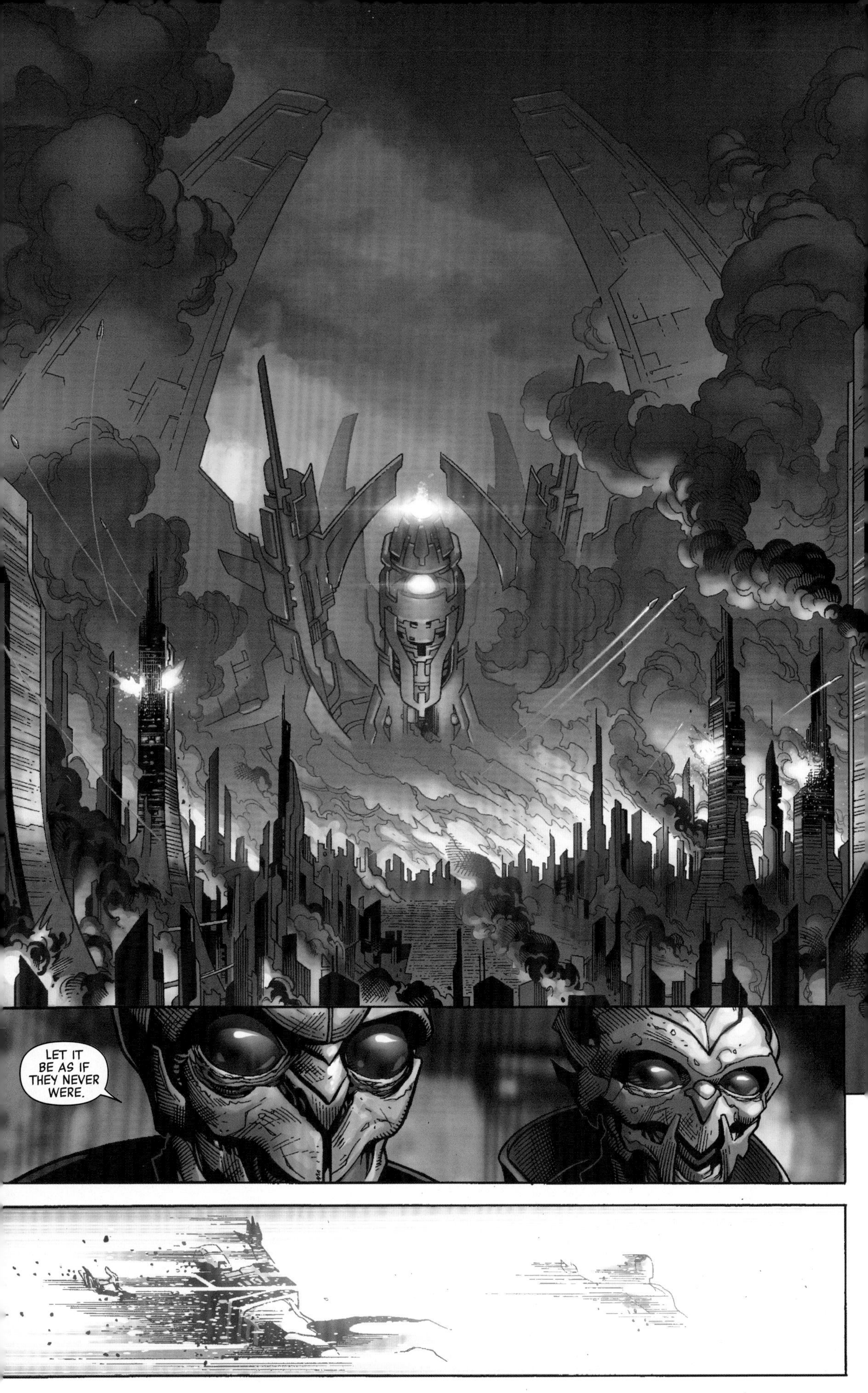
LET IT BE AS IF THEY NEVER WERE.

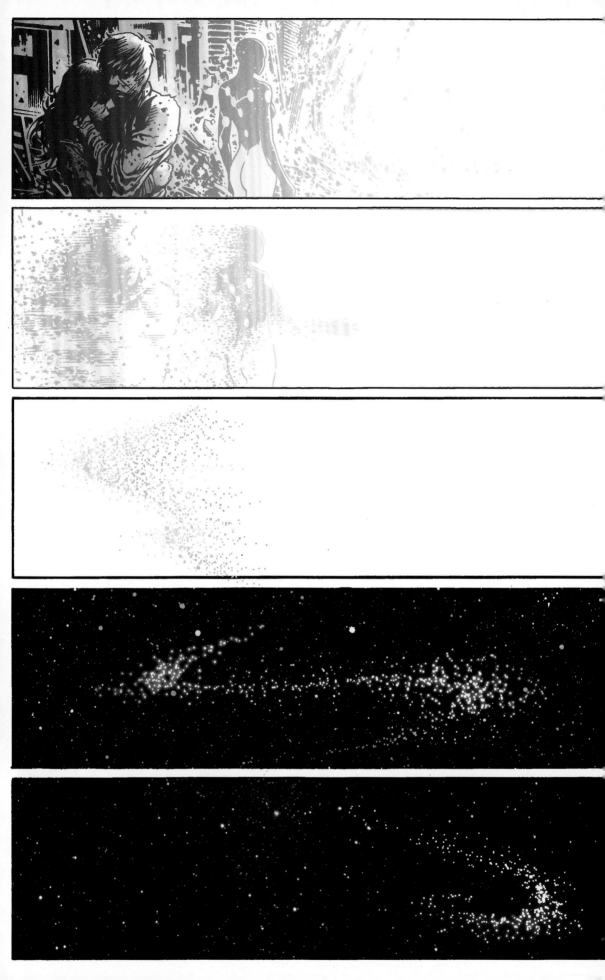

ORBITAL

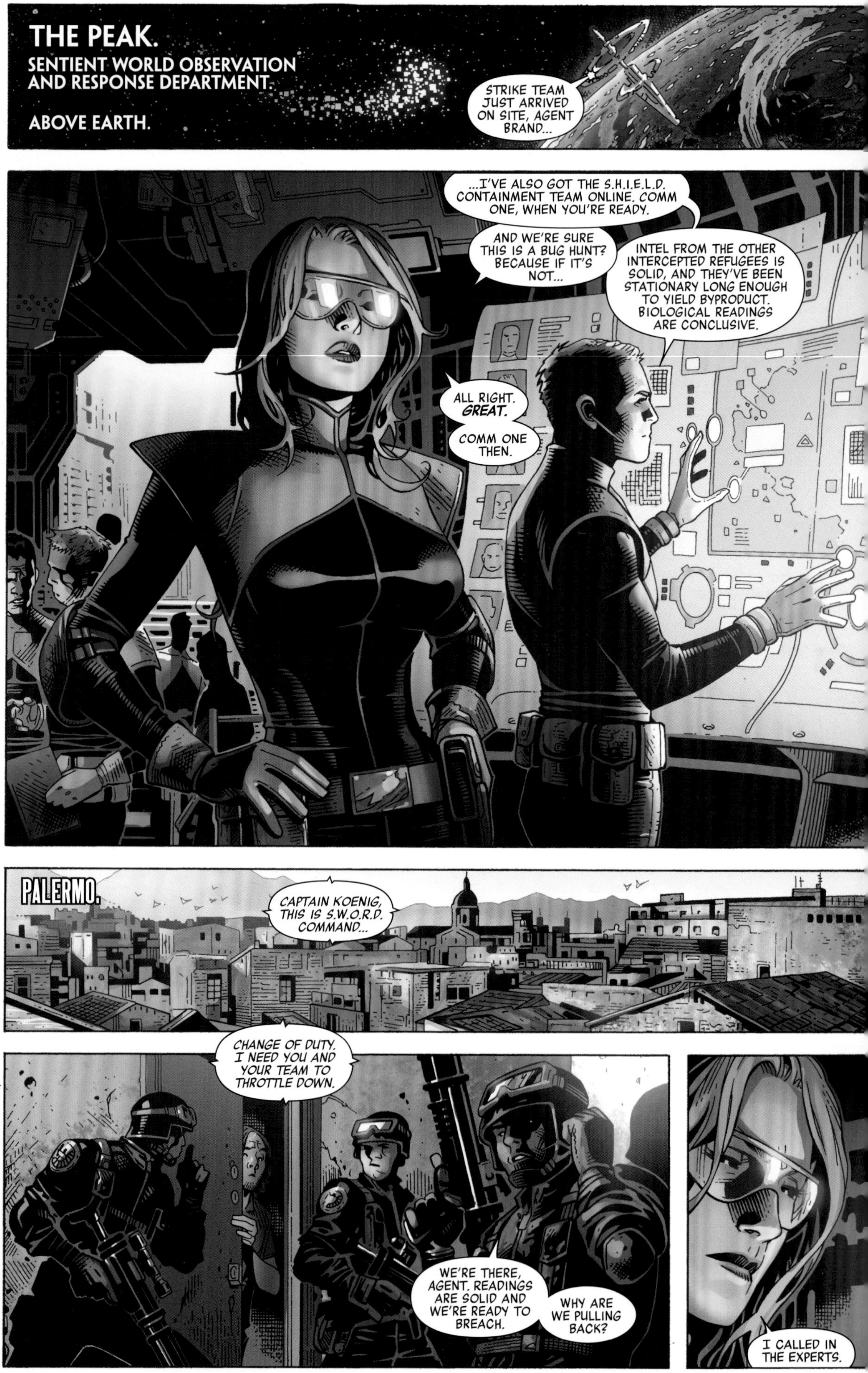
THE PEAK.
SENTIENT WORLD OBSERVATION AND RESPONSE DEPARTMENT.
ABOVE EARTH.
STRIKE TEAM JUST ARRIVED ON SITE, AGENT BRAND...
...I'VE ALSO GOT THE S.H.I.E.L.D. CONTAINMENT TEAM ONLINE. COMM ONE, WHEN YOU'RE READY.
AND WE'RE SURE THIS IS A BUG HUNT? BECAUSE IF IT'S NOT...
INTEL FROM THE OTHER INTERCEPTED REFUGEES IS SOLID, AND THEY'VE BEEN STATIONARY LONG ENOUGH TO YIELD BYPRODUCT. BIOLOGICAL READINGS ARE CONCLUSIVE.
ALL RIGHT. GREAT.
COMM ONE THEN.
PALERMO.
CAPTAIN KOENIG, THIS IS S.W.O.R.D. COMMAND...
CHANGE OF DUTY. I NEED YOU AND YOUR TEAM TO THROTTLE DOWN.
WE'RE THERE, AGENT. READINGS ARE SOLID AND WE'RE READY TO BREACH.
WHY ARE WE PULLING BACK?
I CALLED IN THE EXPERTS.

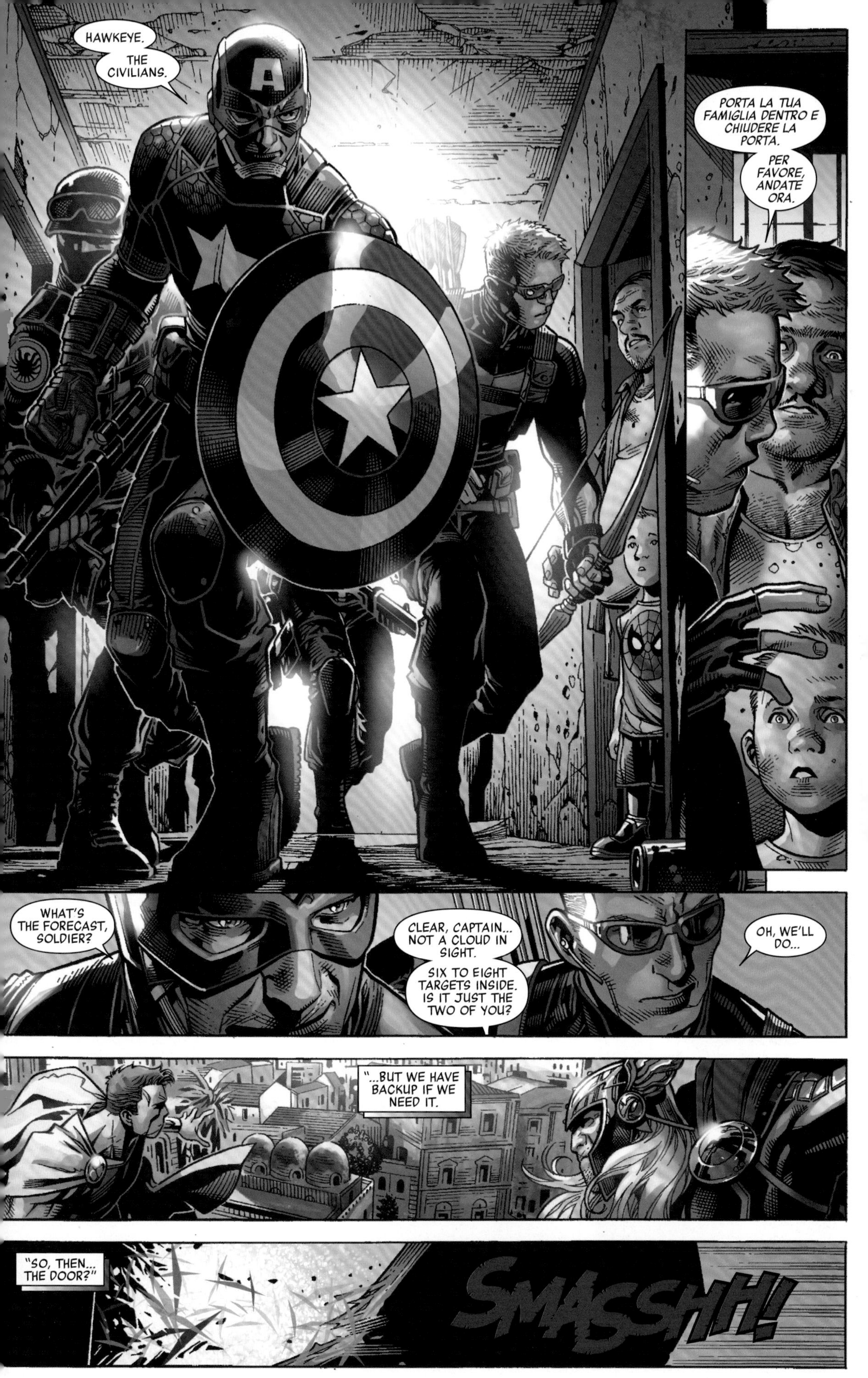
HAWKEYE.
THE CIVILIANS.
PORTA LA TUA FAMIGLIA DENTRO E CHIUDERE LA PORTA.
PER FAVORE, ANDATE ORA.
WHAT'S THE FORECAST, SOLDIER?
CLEAR, CAPTAIN... NOT A CLOUD IN SIGHT.
SIX TO EIGHT TARGETS INSIDE. IS IT JUST THE TWO OF YOU?
OH, WE'LL DO...
"...BUT WE HAVE BACKUP IF WE NEED IT.
"SO, THEN... THE DOOR?"
SMASSHH!

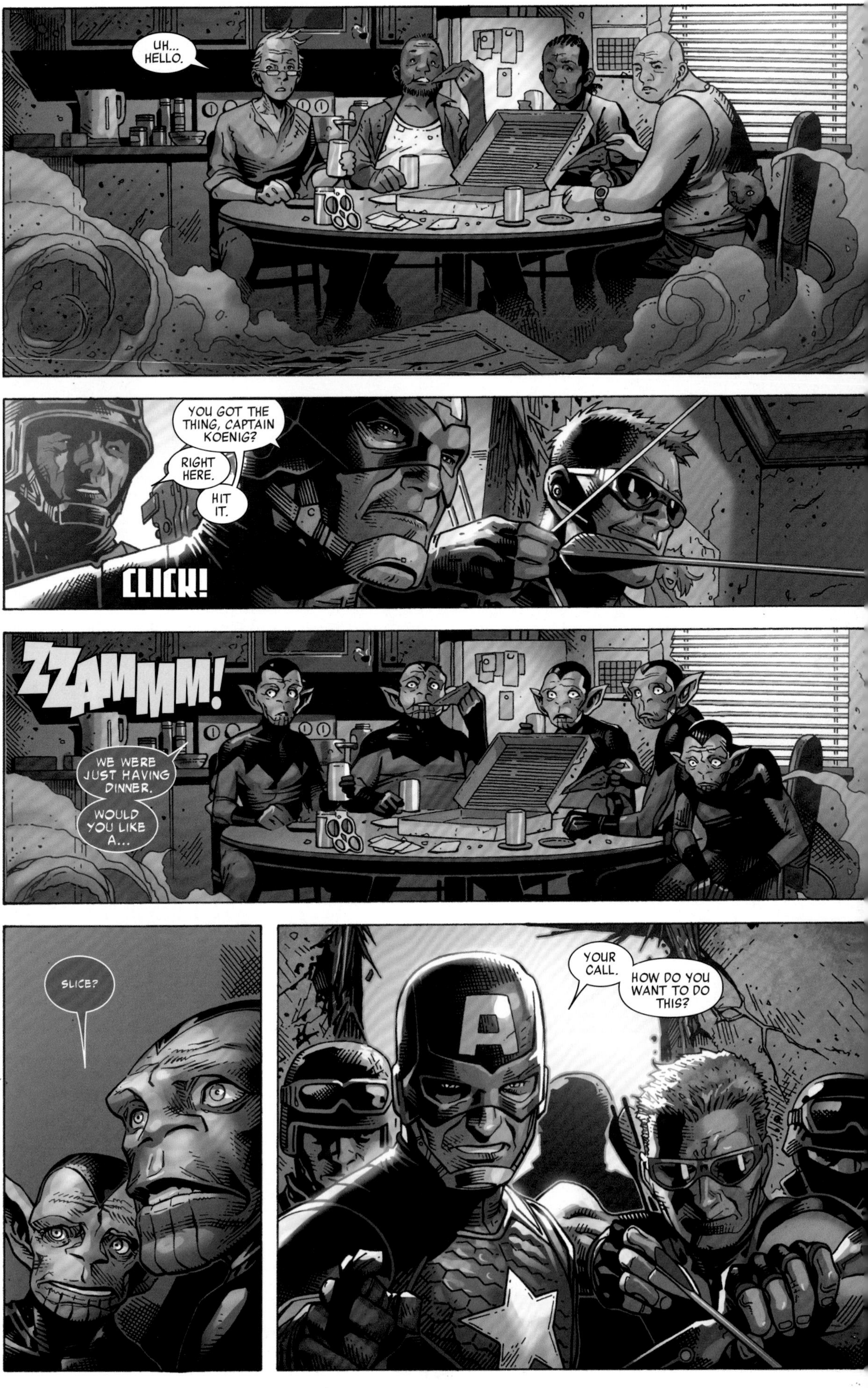
UH... HELLO.
YOU GOT THE THING, CAPTAIN KOENIG?
RIGHT HERE.
HIT IT.
CLICK!
ZZAMMMM!
WE WERE JUST HAVING DINNER.
WOULD YOU LIKE A...
SLICE?
YOUR CALL.
HOW DO YOU WANT TO DO THIS?

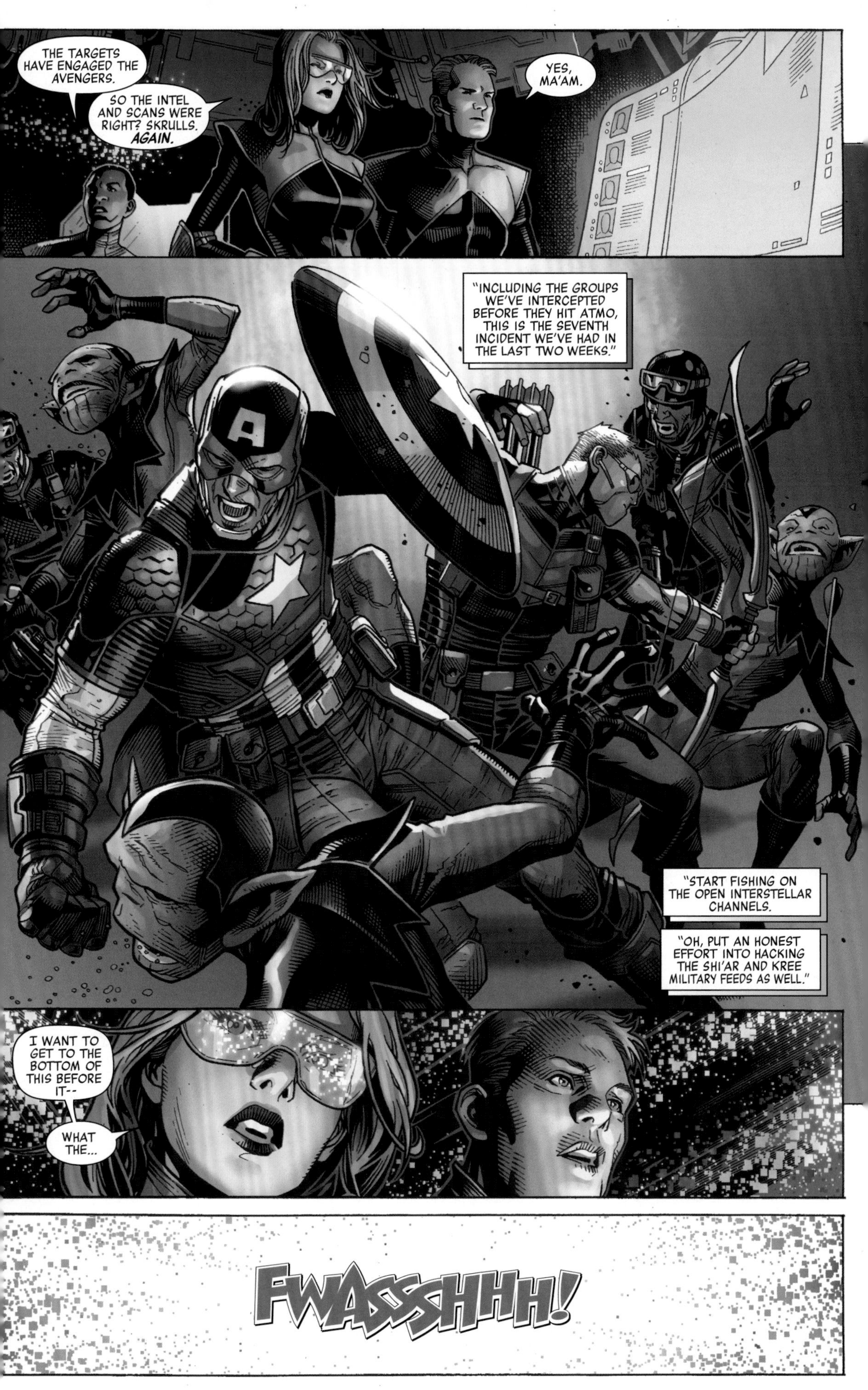
THE TARGETS HAVE ENGAGED THE AVENGERS.
SO THE INTEL AND SCANS WERE RIGHT? SKRULLS. AGAIN.
YES, MA'AM.
"INCLUDING THE GROUPS WE'VE INTERCEPTED BEFORE THEY HIT ATMO, THIS IS THE SEVENTH INCIDENT WE'VE HAD IN THE LAST TWO WEEKS."
"START FISHING ON THE OPEN INTERSTELLAR CHANNELS.
"OH, PUT AN HONEST EFFORT INTO HACKING THE SHI'AR AND KREE MILITARY FEEDS AS WELL."
I WANT TO GET TO THE BOTTOM OF THIS BEFORE IT--
WHAT THE...
FWASSSHHH!

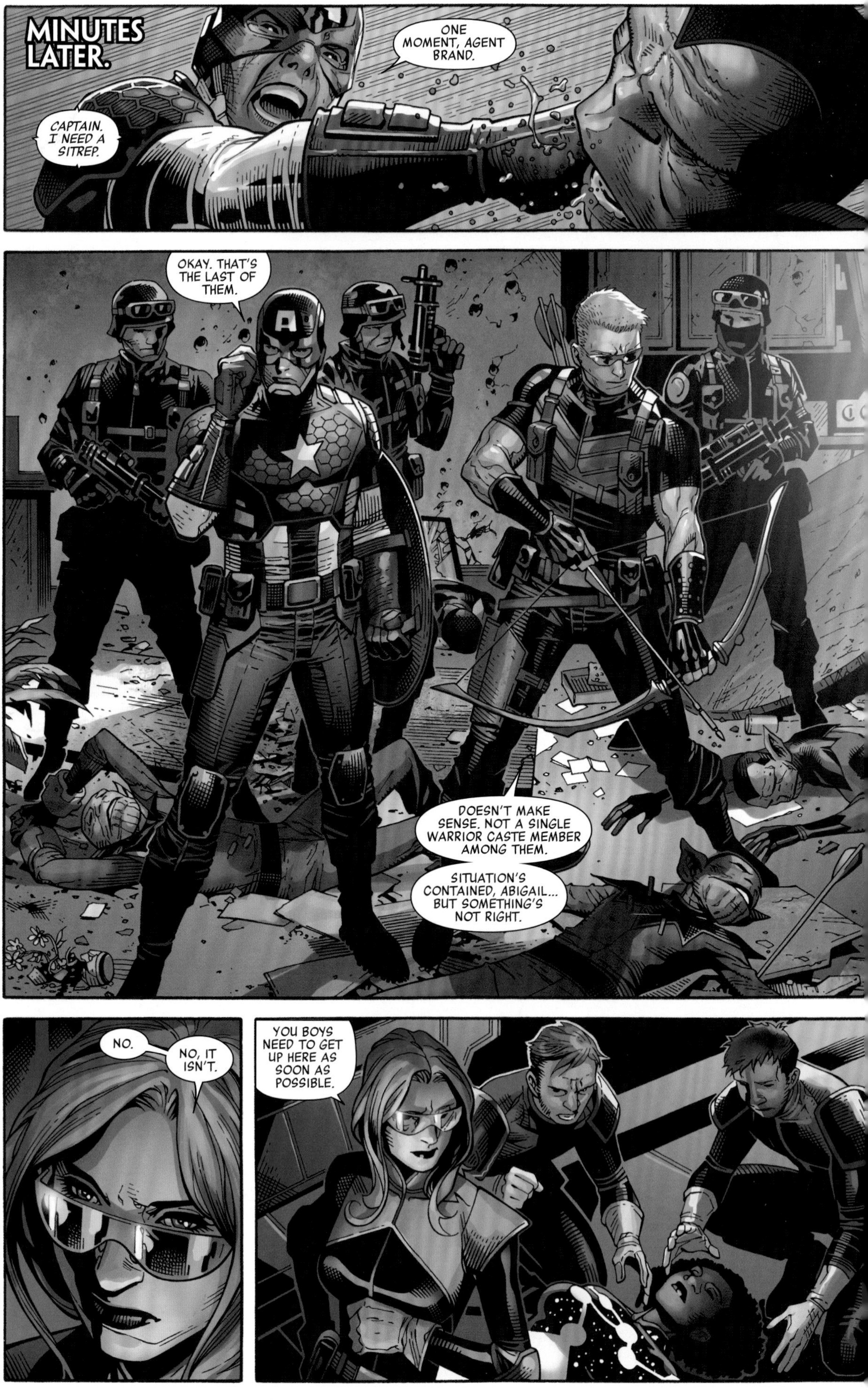
MINUTES LATER.
CAPTAIN. I NEED A SITREP.
ONE MOMENT, AGENT BRAND.
OKAY. THAT'S THE LAST OF THEM.
DOESN'T MAKE SENSE. NOT A SINGLE WARRIOR CASTE MEMBER AMONG THEM.
SITUATION'S CONTAINED, ABIGAIL... BUT SOMETHING'S NOT RIGHT.
NO.
NO, IT ISN'T.
YOU BOYS NEED TO GET UP HERE AS SOON AS POSSIBLE.

WHAT WAS HIDDEN, NOW UNCOVERED

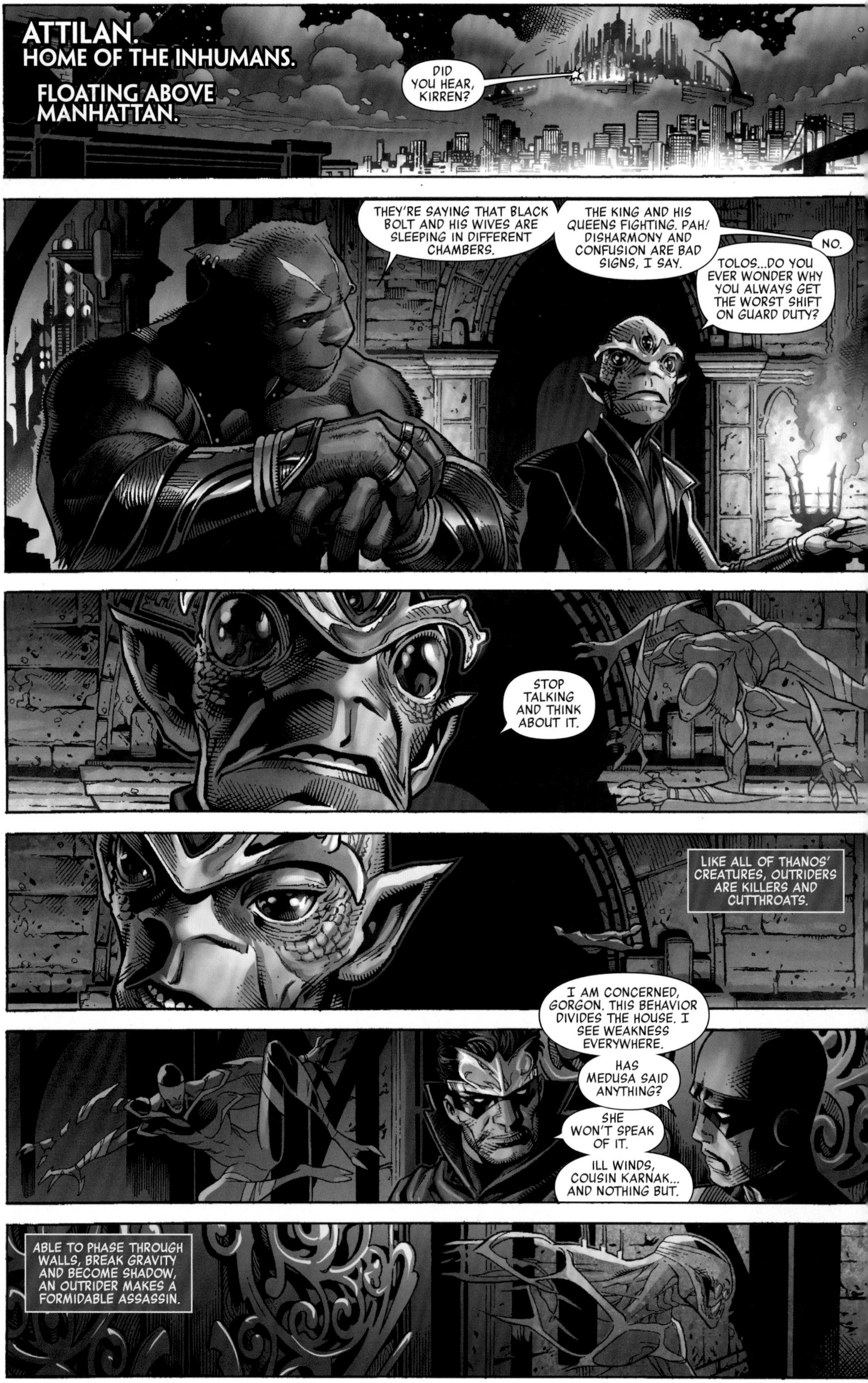
ATTILAN.
HOME OF THE INHUMANS.
FLOATING ABOVE MANHATTAN.
DID YOU HEAR, KIRREN?
THEY'RE SAYING THAT BLACK BOLT AND HIS WIVES ARE SLEEPING IN DIFFERENT CHAMBERS.
THE KING AND HIS QUEENS FIGHTING. PAH! DISHARMONY AND CONFUSION ARE BAD SIGNS, I SAY.
NO.
TOLOS...DO YOU EVER WONDER WHY YOU ALWAYS GET THE WORST SHIFT ON GUARD DUTY?
STOP TALKING AND THINK ABOUT IT.
LIKE ALL OF THANOS' CREATURES, OUTRIDERS ARE KILLERS AND CUTTHROATS.
I AM CONCERNED, GORGON. THIS BEHAVIOR DIVIDES THE HOUSE. I SEE WEAKNESS EVERYWHERE.
HAS MEDUSA SAID ANYTHING?
SHE WON'T SPEAK OF IT.
ILL WINDS, COUSIN KARNAK... AND NOTHING BUT.
ABLE TO PHASE THROUGH WALLS, BREAK GRAVITY AND BECOME SHADOW, AN OUTRIDER MAKES A FORMIDABLE ASSASSIN.

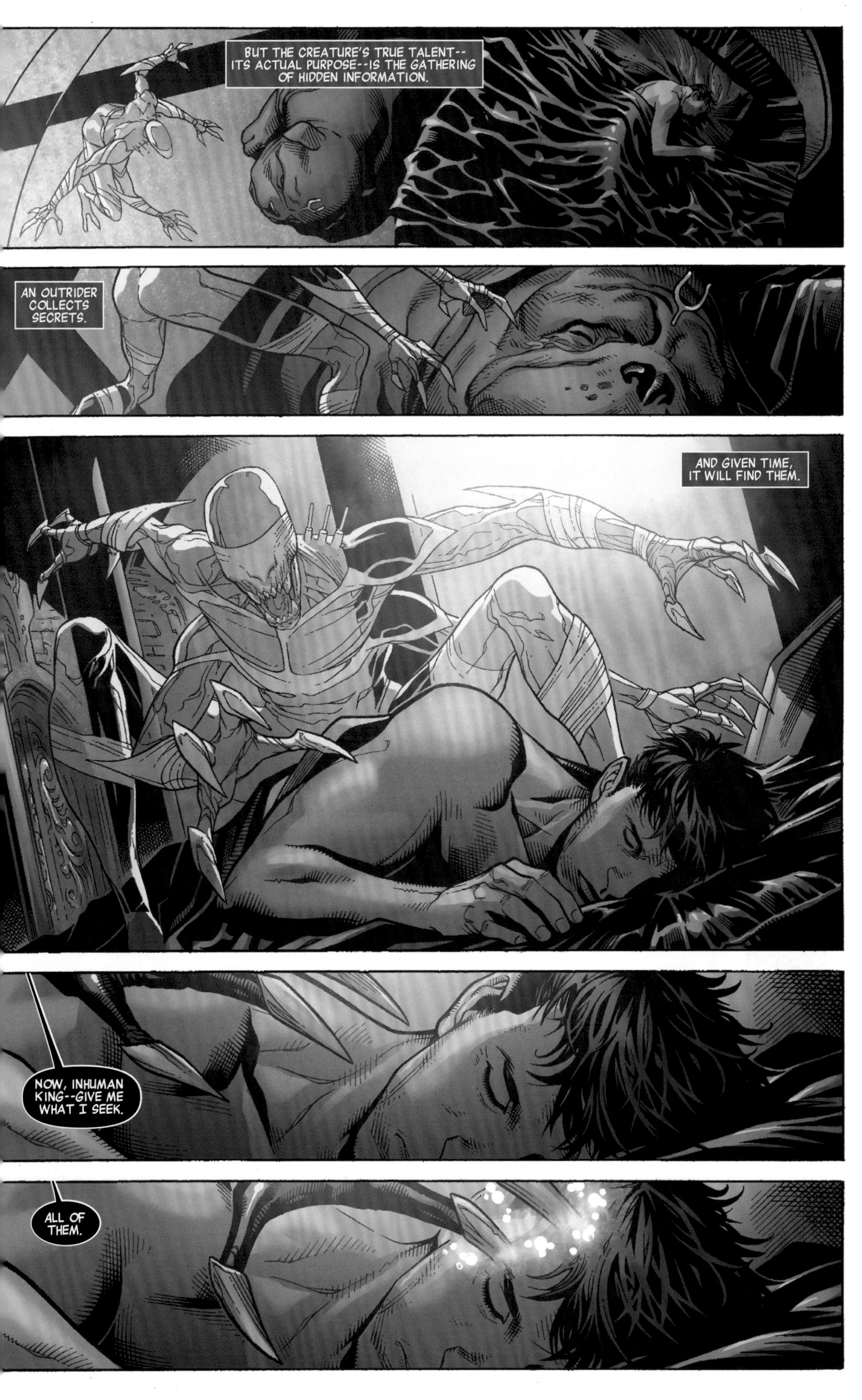
BUT THE CREATURE'S TRUE TALENT--
ITS ACTUAL PURPOSE--IS THE GATHERING
OF HIDDEN INFORMATION.
AN OUTRIDER
COLLECTS
SECRETS.
AND GIVEN TIME,
IT WILL FIND THEM.
NOW, INHUMAN
KING--GIVE ME
WHAT I SEEK.
ALL OF
THEM.

THERE. GENETICALLY IMPRINTED FACTS FORM HIS FIRST MEMORIES.

ONE MILLION YEARS AGO, THE INHUMANS BEGAN AS A KREE EXPERIMENT.

THOSE WILLING, UNDERGOING TERRIGENESIS--TRANSFORMING THEM INTO THEIR TRUE SELVES.

A KING BORN OF A KING-- BLACK BOLT EMERGED FROM THE TERRIGEN MISTS WITH A VOICE THAT COULD SHAKE THE HEAVENS.

A SON OF PROPHECY, THE MIDNIGHT KING TOOK FIVE WIVES. MEDUSA, HIS FIRST, AND THE OTHERS, TO GATHER ALL OF THE UNIVERSAL INHUMAN CASTES UNDER HIS CROWN.

HE LOVES ONE, HATES ONE, AND CARES LITTLE FOR THE REST.

HIS BROTHER, MAXIMUS THE MAD, HAS PLANS. WHEELS WITHIN WHEELS ORCHESTRATED BY BLACK BOLT HIMSELF.

IT DRIVES A WEDGE BETWEEN HIM AND THE REST OF THE ROYAL FAMILY.

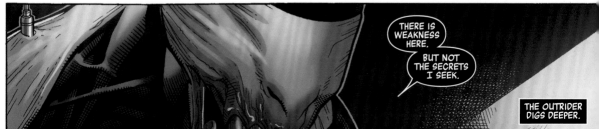

THERE IS WEAKNESS HERE.

BUT NOT THE SECRETS I SEEK.

THE OUTRIDER DIGS DEEPER.

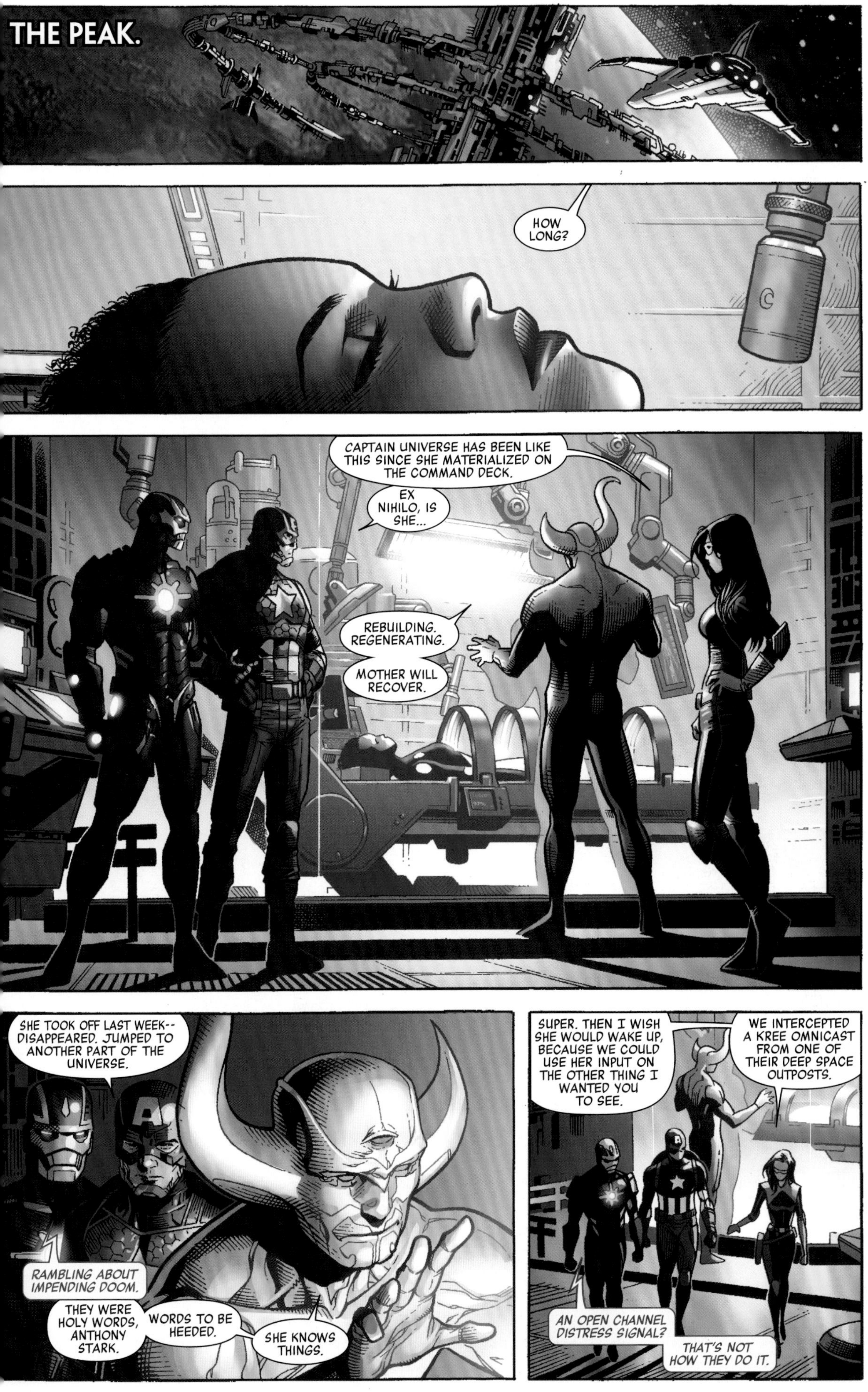
THE PEAK.
HOW LONG?
CAPTAIN UNIVERSE HAS BEEN LIKE THIS SINCE SHE MATERIALIZED ON THE COMMAND DECK.
EX NIHILO, IS SHE...
REBUILDING. REGENERATING.
MOTHER WILL RECOVER.
SHE TOOK OFF LAST WEEK-- DISAPPEARED. JUMPED TO ANOTHER PART OF THE UNIVERSE.
RAMBLING ABOUT IMPENDING DOOM.
THEY WERE HOLY WORDS, ANTHONY STARK.
WORDS TO BE HEEDED.
SHE KNOWS THINGS.
SUPER. THEN I WISH SHE WOULD WAKE UP, BECAUSE WE COULD USE HER INPUT ON THE OTHER THING I WANTED YOU TO SEE.
WE INTERCEPTED A KREE OMNICAST FROM ONE OF THEIR DEEP SPACE OUTPOSTS.
AN OPEN CHANNEL DISTRESS SIGNAL?
THAT'S NOT HOW THEY DO IT.

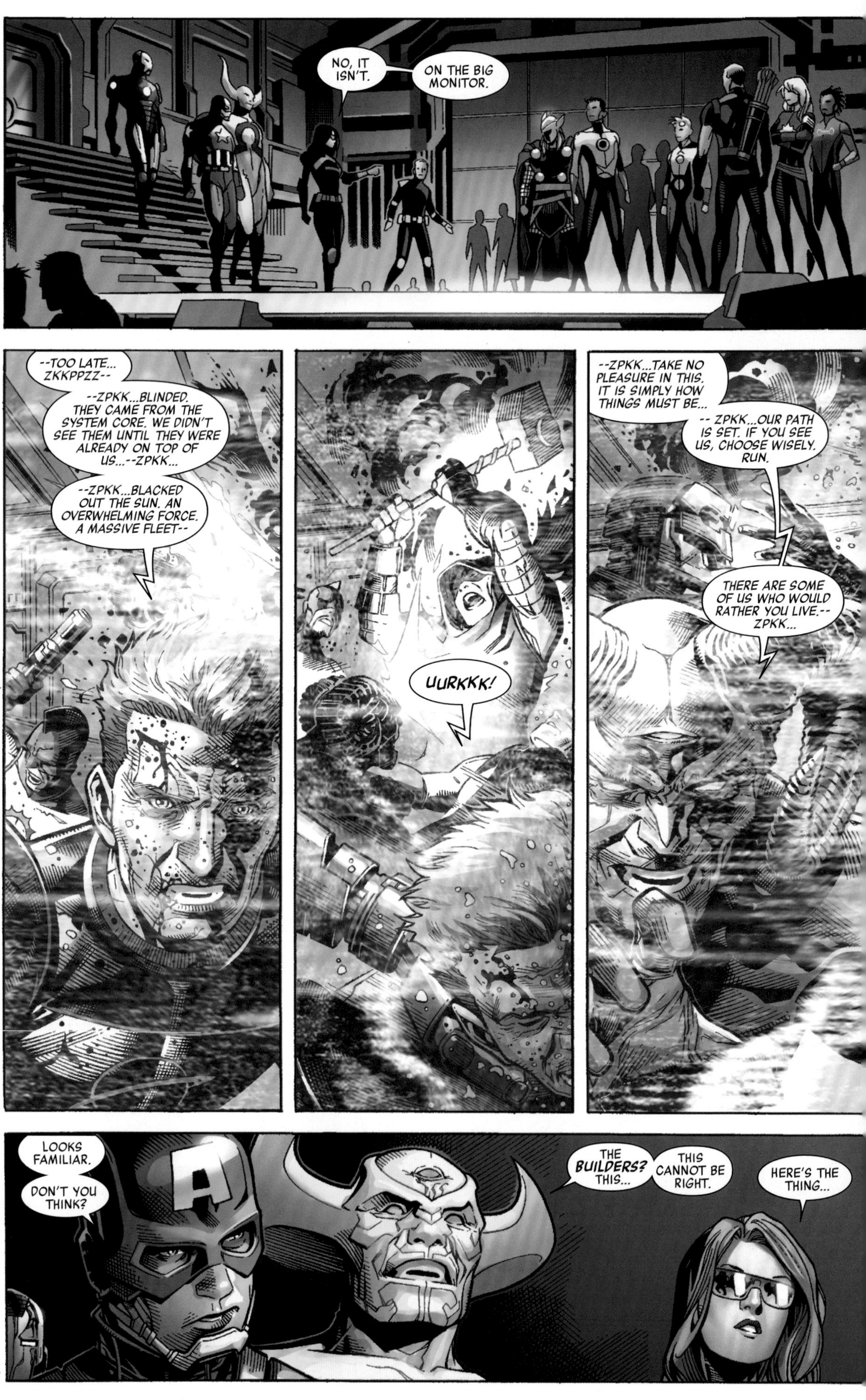
NO, IT ISN'T.
ON THE BIG MONITOR.
--TOO LATE... ZKKPPZZ--
--ZPKK...BLINDED. THEY CAME FROM THE SYSTEM CORE. WE DIDN'T SEE THEM UNTIL THEY WERE ALREADY ON TOP OF US...--ZPKK...
--ZPKK...BLACKED OUT THE SUN. AN OVERWHELMING FORCE. A MASSIVE FLEET--
UURKKK!
--ZPKK...TAKE NO PLEASURE IN THIS. IT IS SIMPLY HOW THINGS MUST BE...
-- ZPKK...OUR PATH IS SET. IF YOU SEE US, CHOOSE WISELY. RUN.
THERE ARE SOME OF US WHO WOULD RATHER YOU LIVE.--ZPKK...
LOOKS FAMILIAR.
DON'T YOU THINK?
THE BUILDERS? THIS...
THIS CANNOT BE RIGHT.
HERE'S THE THING...

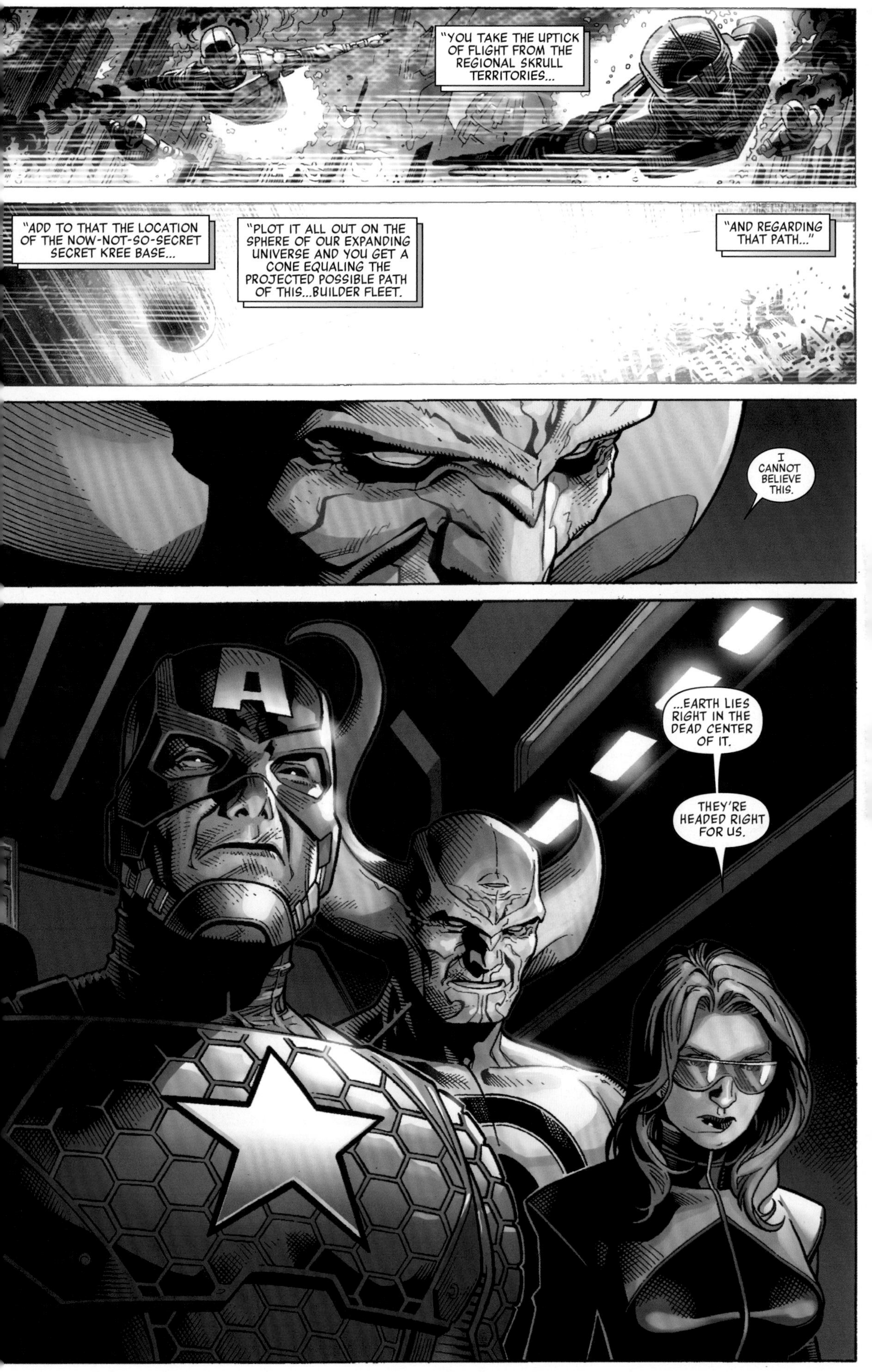
"YOU TAKE THE UPTICK OF FLIGHT FROM THE REGIONAL SKRULL TERRITORIES...
"ADD TO THAT THE LOCATION OF THE NOW-NOT-SO-SECRET SECRET KREE BASE...
"PLOT IT ALL OUT ON THE SPHERE OF OUR EXPANDING UNIVERSE AND YOU GET A CONE EQUALING THE PROJECTED POSSIBLE PATH OF THIS...BUILDER FLEET.
"AND REGARDING THAT PATH..."
I CANNOT BELIEVE THIS.
...EARTH LIES RIGHT IN THE DEAD CENTER OF IT.
THEY'RE HEADED RIGHT FOR US.

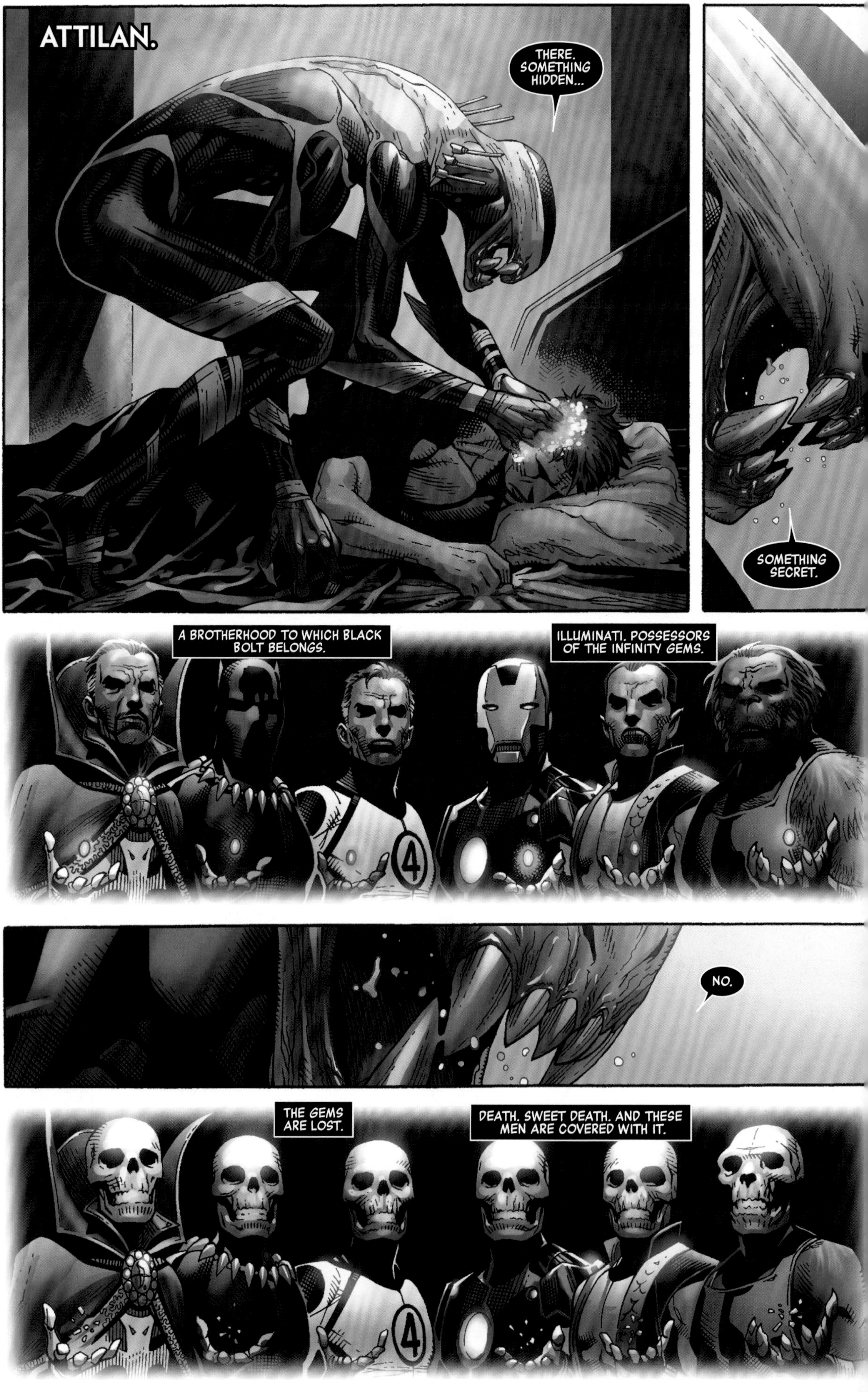
ATTILAN.
THERE. SOMETHING HIDDEN...
SOMETHING SECRET.
A BROTHERHOOD TO WHICH BLACK BOLT BELONGS.
ILLUMINATI. POSSESSORS OF THE INFINITY GEMS.
NO.
THE GEMS ARE LOST.
DEATH. SWEET DEATH. AND THESE MEN ARE COVERED WITH IT.

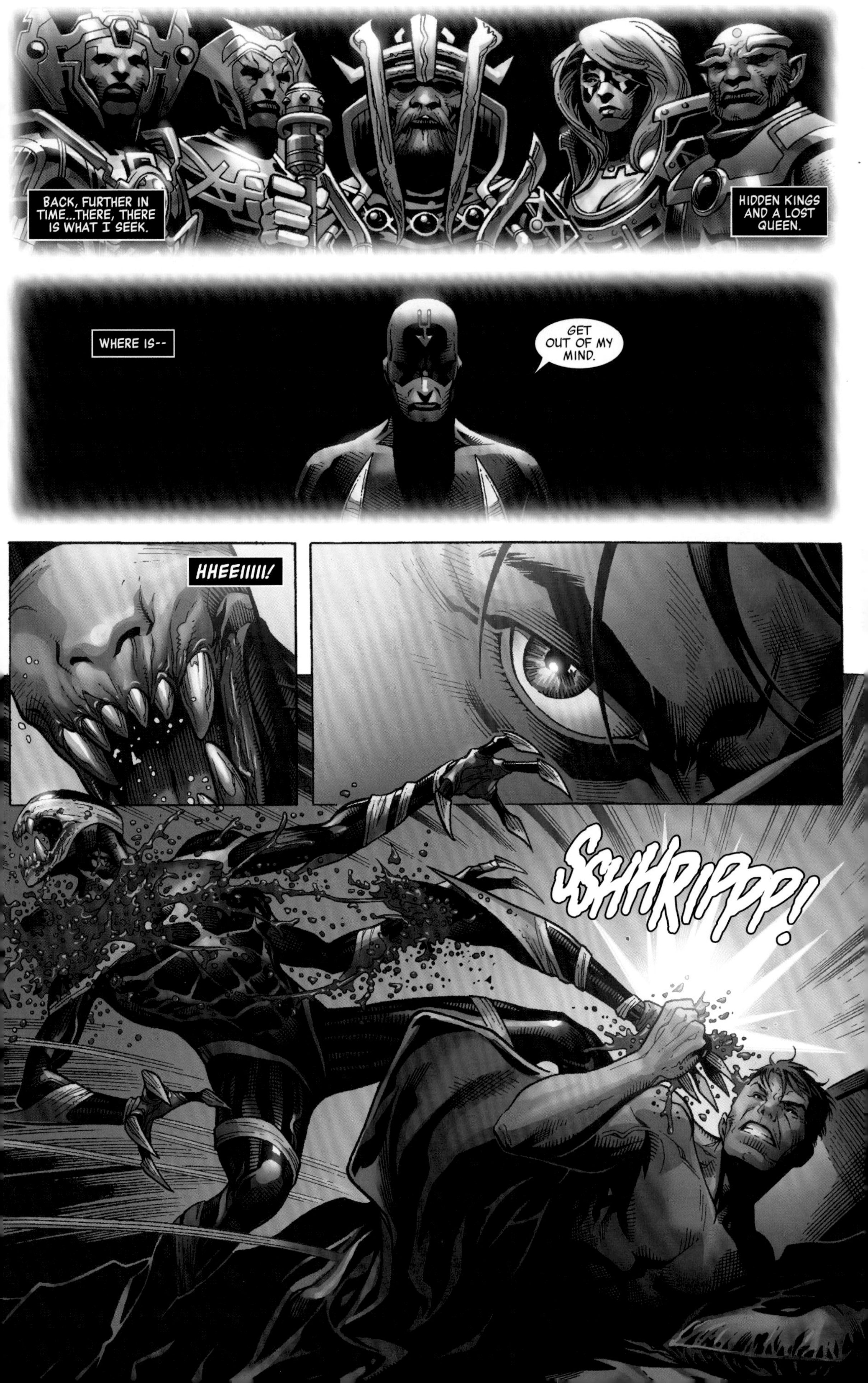
BACK, FURTHER IN TIME...THERE, THERE IS WHAT I SEEK.
HIDDEN KINGS AND A LOST QUEEN.
WHERE IS--
GET OUT OF MY MIND.
HHEEIIIII!
SSHHRIPPP!

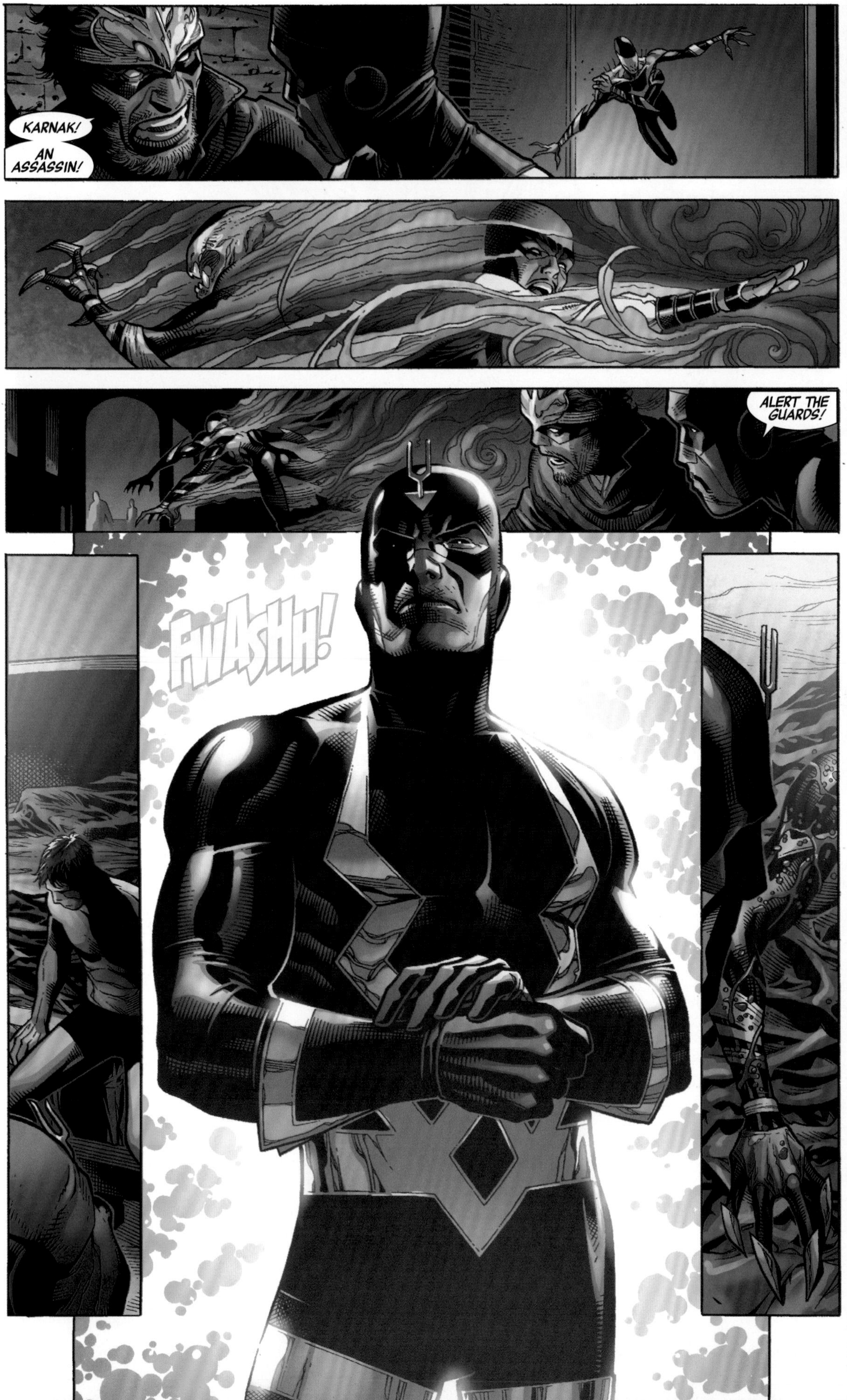
KARNAK!
AN ASSASSIN!
ALERT THE GUARDS!
FWASHH!

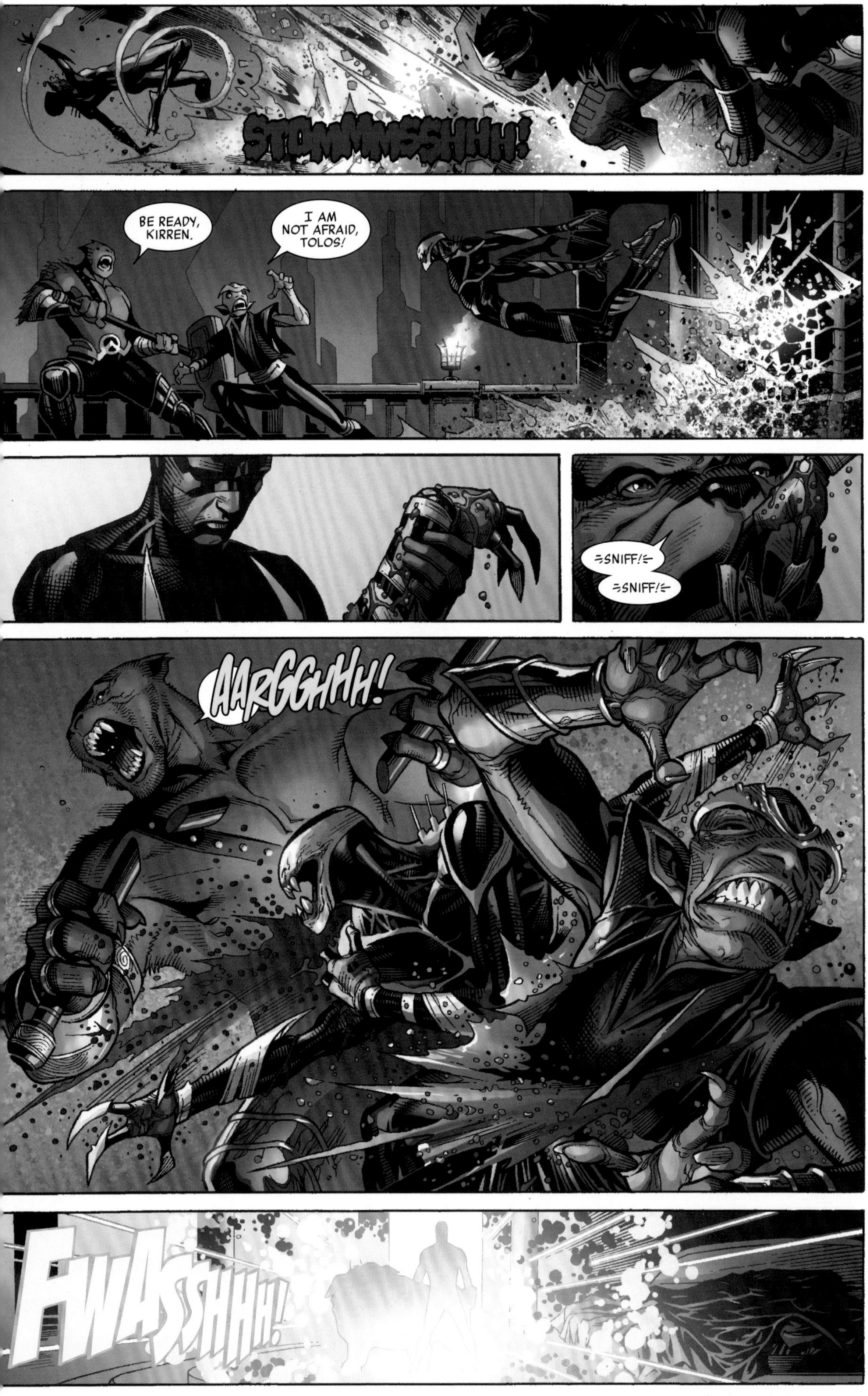
STOMMMSSHHH!
BE READY, KIRREN.
I AM NOT AFRAID, TOLOS!
SNIFF!
SNIFF!
AARGGHHH!
FWASSHHH!

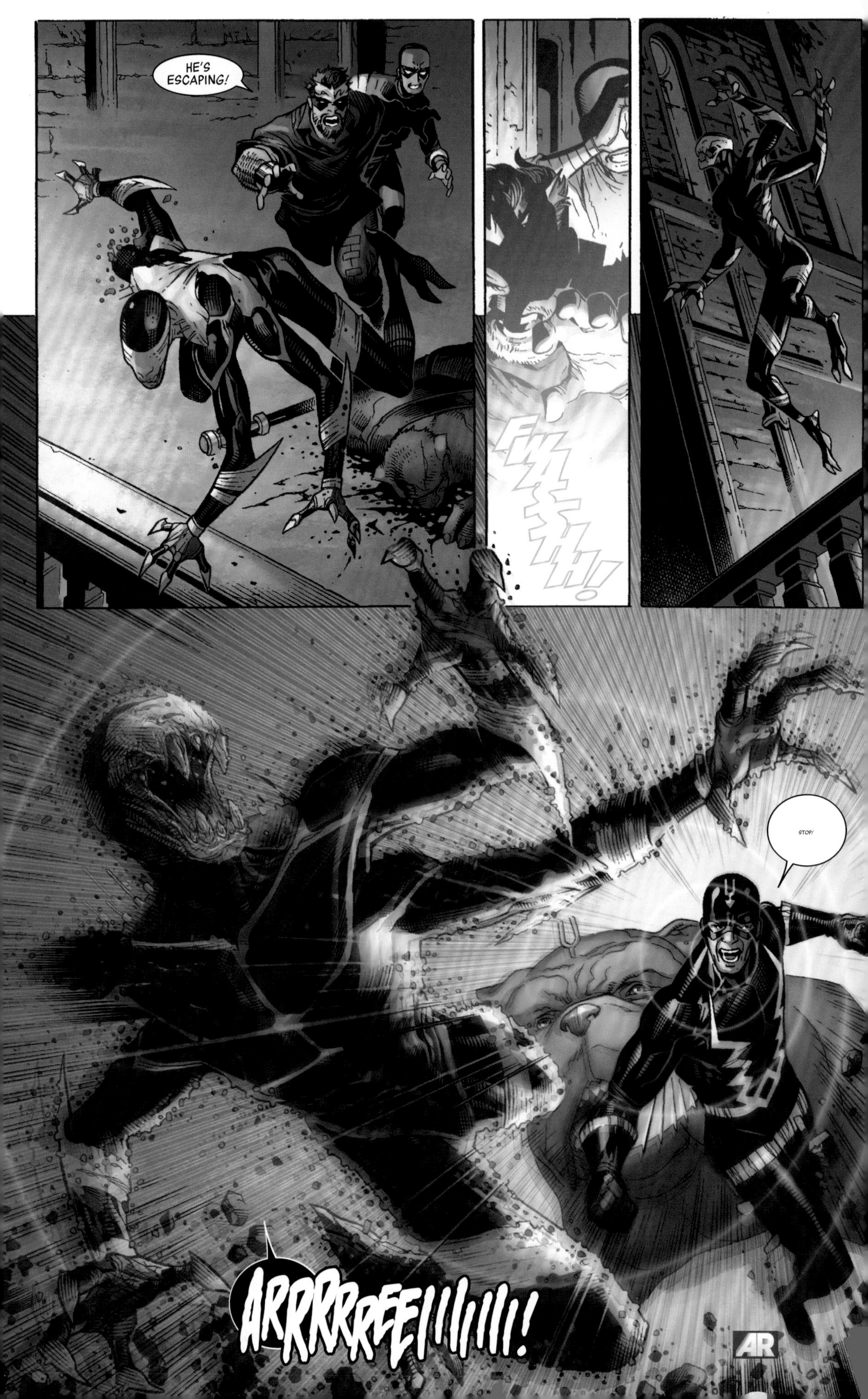
HE'S ESCAPING!
FWASSHH!
STOP!
ARRRRREEIIIIIIIII!

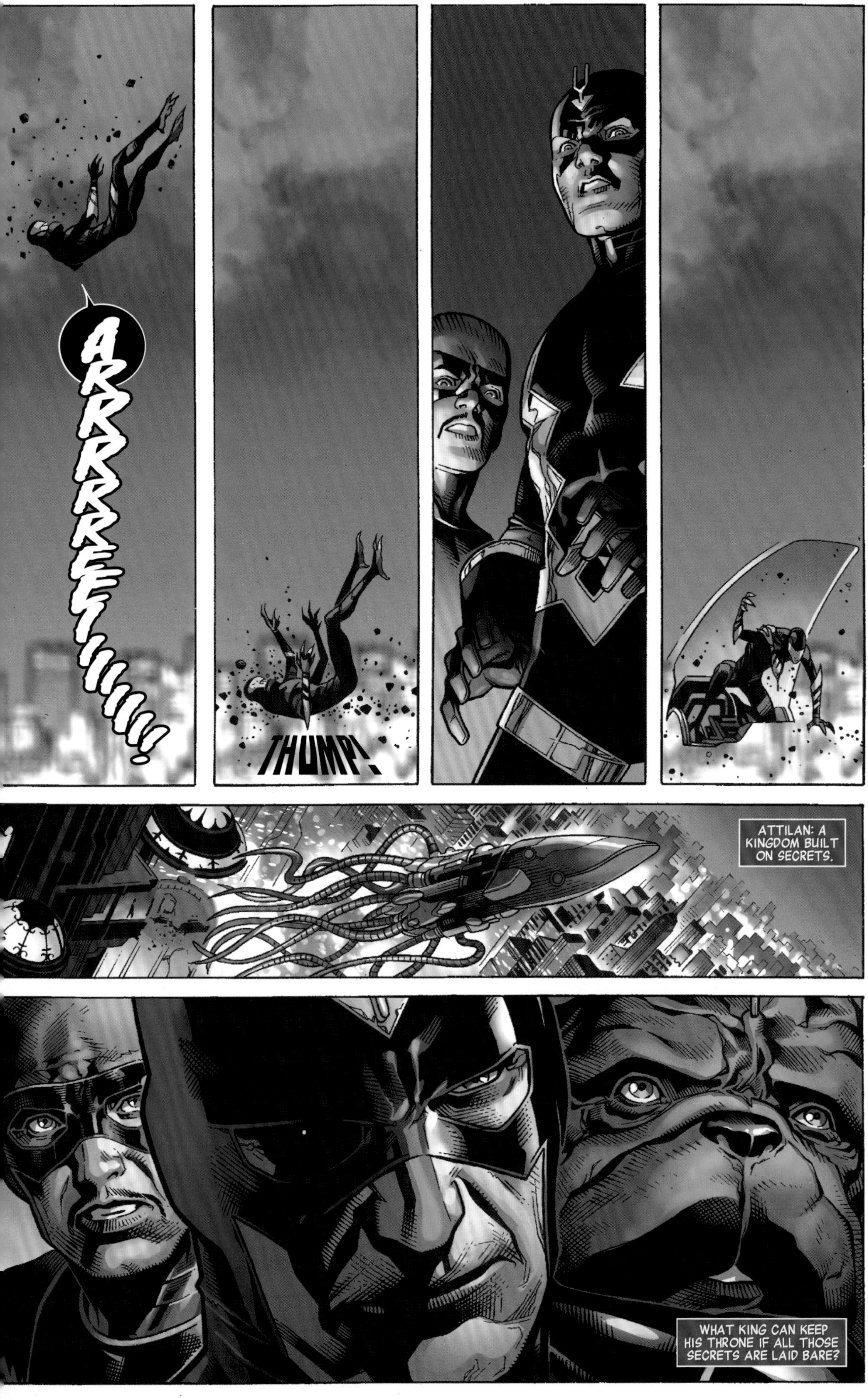
ARRRRREE!!!!!!!
THUMP!
ATTILAN: A KINGDOM BUILT ON SECRETS.
WHAT KING CAN KEEP HIS THRONE IF ALL THOSE SECRETS ARE LAID BARE?

OUTBOUND

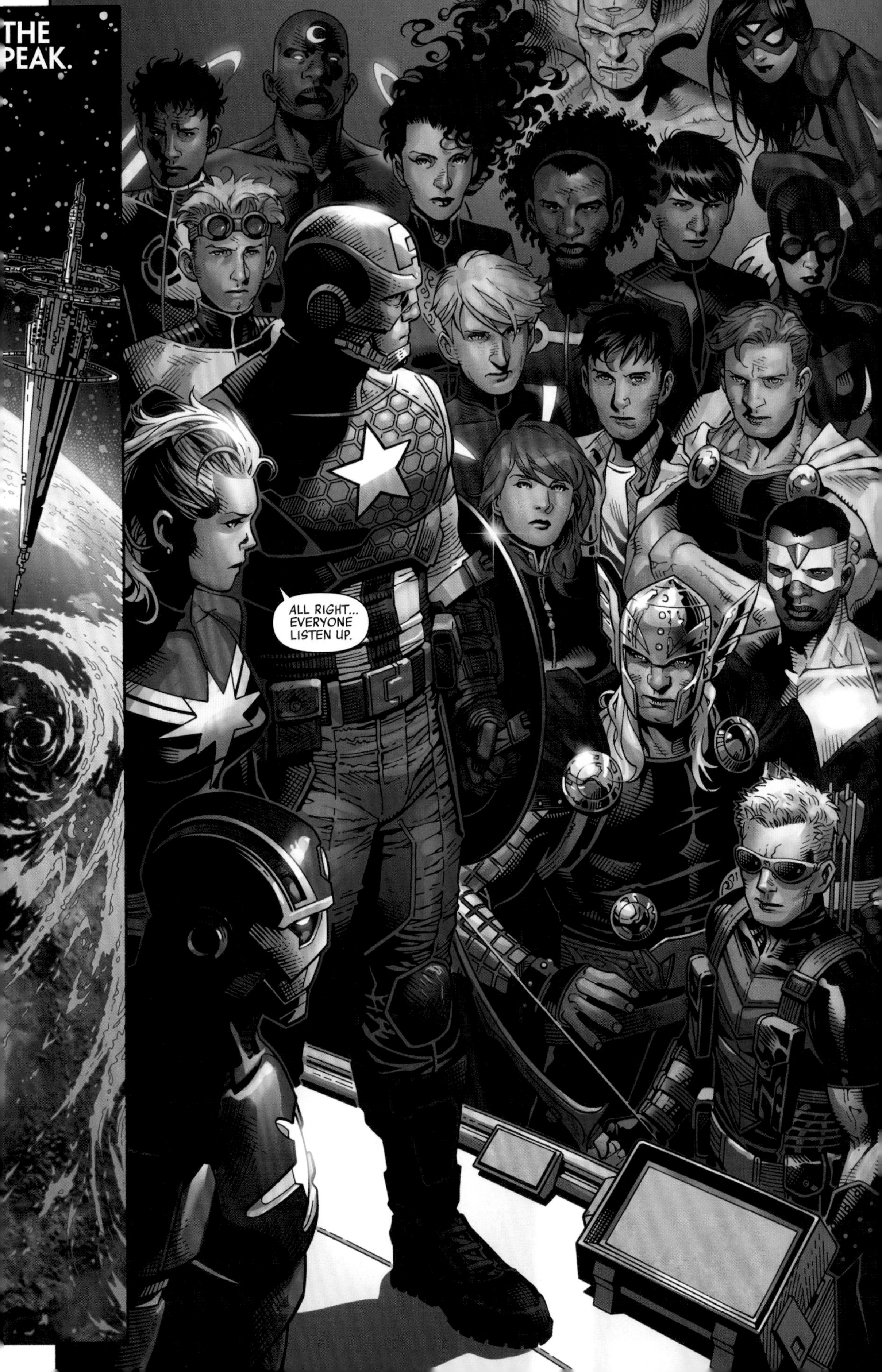
THE PEAK.
ALL RIGHT... EVERYONE LISTEN UP.

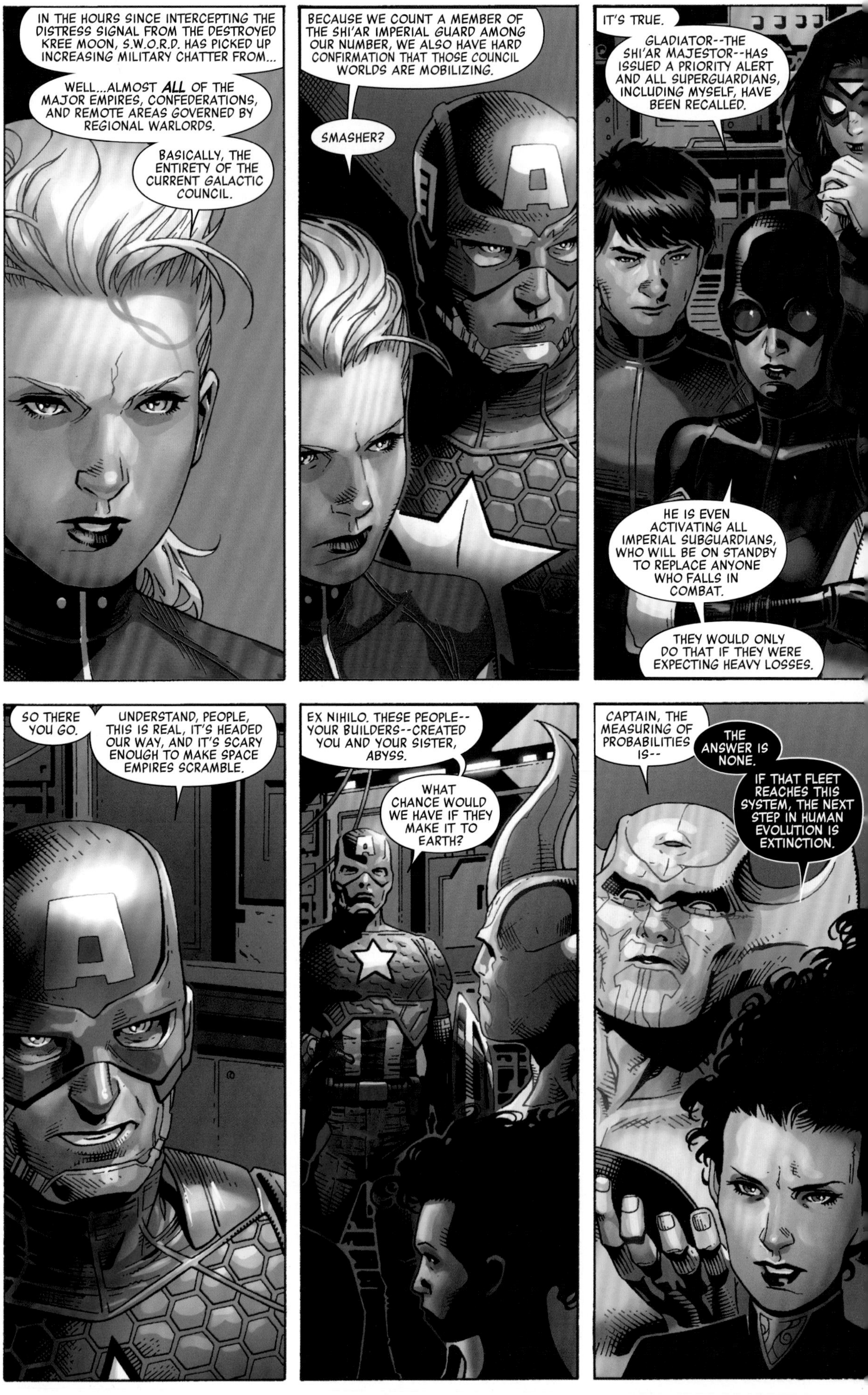
IN THE HOURS SINCE INTERCEPTING THE DISTRESS SIGNAL FROM THE DESTROYED KREE MOON, S.W.O.R.D. HAS PICKED UP INCREASING MILITARY CHATTER FROM...
WELL...ALMOST ALL OF THE MAJOR EMPIRES, CONFEDERATIONS, AND REMOTE AREAS GOVERNED BY REGIONAL WARLORDS.
BASICALLY, THE ENTIRETY OF THE CURRENT GALACTIC COUNCIL.
BECAUSE WE COUNT A MEMBER OF THE SHI'AR IMPERIAL GUARD AMONG OUR NUMBER, WE ALSO HAVE HARD CONFIRMATION THAT THOSE COUNCIL WORLDS ARE MOBILIZING.
SMASHER?
IT'S TRUE.
GLADIATOR--THE SHI'AR MAJESTOR--HAS ISSUED A PRIORITY ALERT AND ALL SUPERGUARDIANS, INCLUDING MYSELF, HAVE BEEN RECALLED.
HE IS EVEN ACTIVATING ALL IMPERIAL SUBGUARDIANS, WHO WILL BE ON STANDBY TO REPLACE ANYONE WHO FALLS IN COMBAT.
THEY WOULD ONLY DO THAT IF THEY WERE EXPECTING HEAVY LOSSES.
SO THERE YOU GO.
UNDERSTAND, PEOPLE, THIS IS REAL, IT'S HEADED OUR WAY, AND IT'S SCARY ENOUGH TO MAKE SPACE EMPIRES SCRAMBLE.
EX NIHILO. THESE PEOPLE--YOUR BUILDERS--CREATED YOU AND YOUR SISTER, ABYSS.
WHAT CHANCE WOULD WE HAVE IF THEY MAKE IT TO EARTH?
CAPTAIN, THE MEASURING OF PROBABILITIES IS--
THE ANSWER IS NONE.
IF THAT FLEET REACHES THIS SYSTEM, THE NEXT STEP IN HUMAN EVOLUTION IS EXTINCTION.

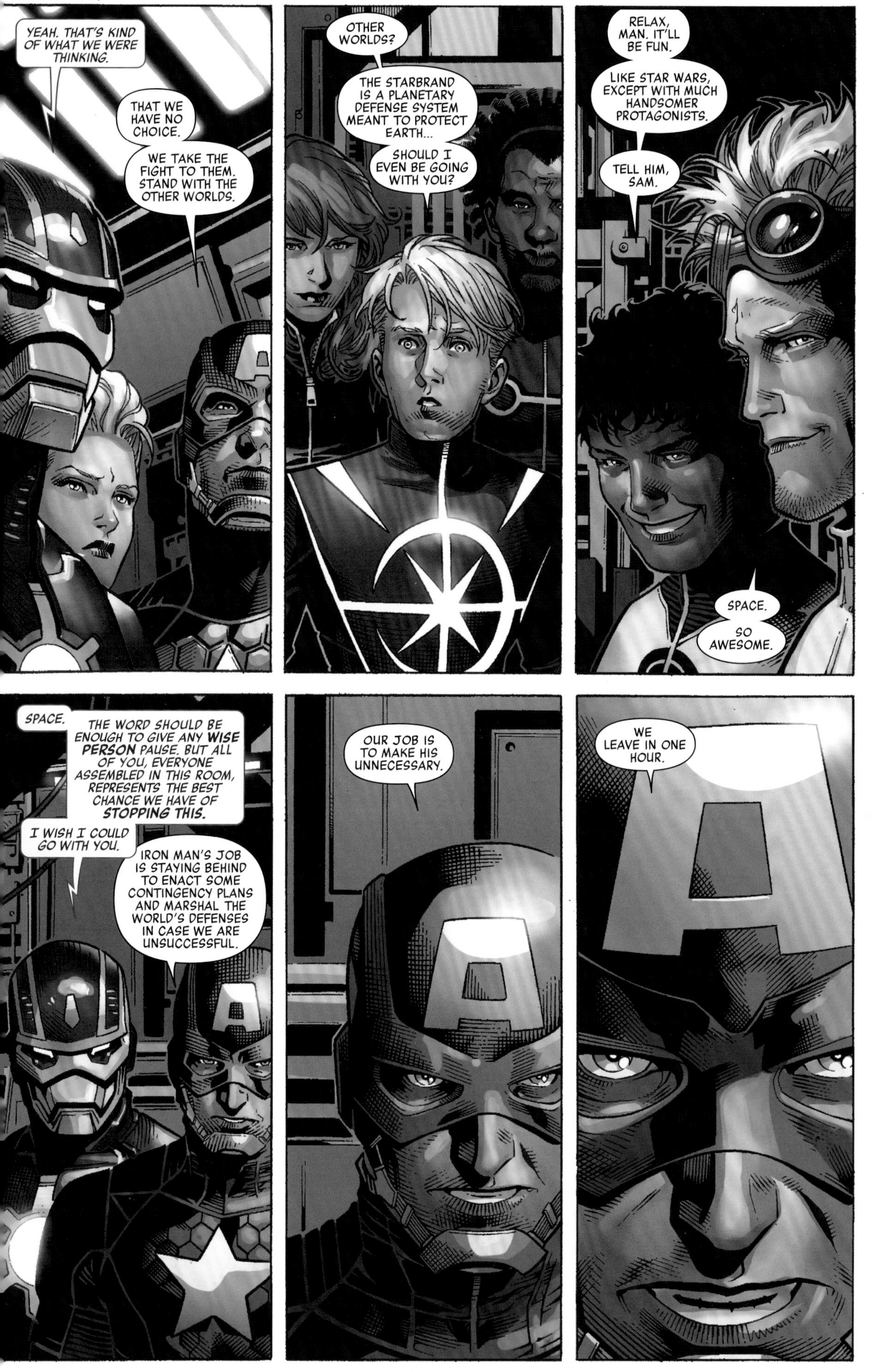
YEAH. THAT'S KIND OF WHAT WE WERE THINKING.
THAT WE HAVE NO CHOICE.
WE TAKE THE FIGHT TO THEM. STAND WITH THE OTHER WORLDS.
OTHER WORLDS?
THE STARBRAND IS A PLANETARY DEFENSE SYSTEM MEANT TO PROTECT EARTH...
SHOULD I EVEN BE GOING WITH YOU?
RELAX, MAN. IT'LL BE FUN.
LIKE STAR WARS, EXCEPT WITH MUCH HANDSOMER PROTAGONISTS.
TELL HIM, SAM.
SPACE.
SO AWESOME.
SPACE.
THE WORD SHOULD BE ENOUGH TO GIVE ANY WISE PERSON PAUSE. BUT ALL OF YOU, EVERYONE ASSEMBLED IN THIS ROOM, REPRESENTS THE BEST CHANCE WE HAVE OF STOPPING THIS.
I WISH I COULD GO WITH YOU.
IRON MAN'S JOB IS STAYING BEHIND TO ENACT SOME CONTINGENCY PLANS AND MARSHAL THE WORLD'S DEFENSES IN CASE WE ARE UNSUCCESSFUL.
OUR JOB IS TO MAKE HIS UNNECESSARY.
WE LEAVE IN ONE HOUR.

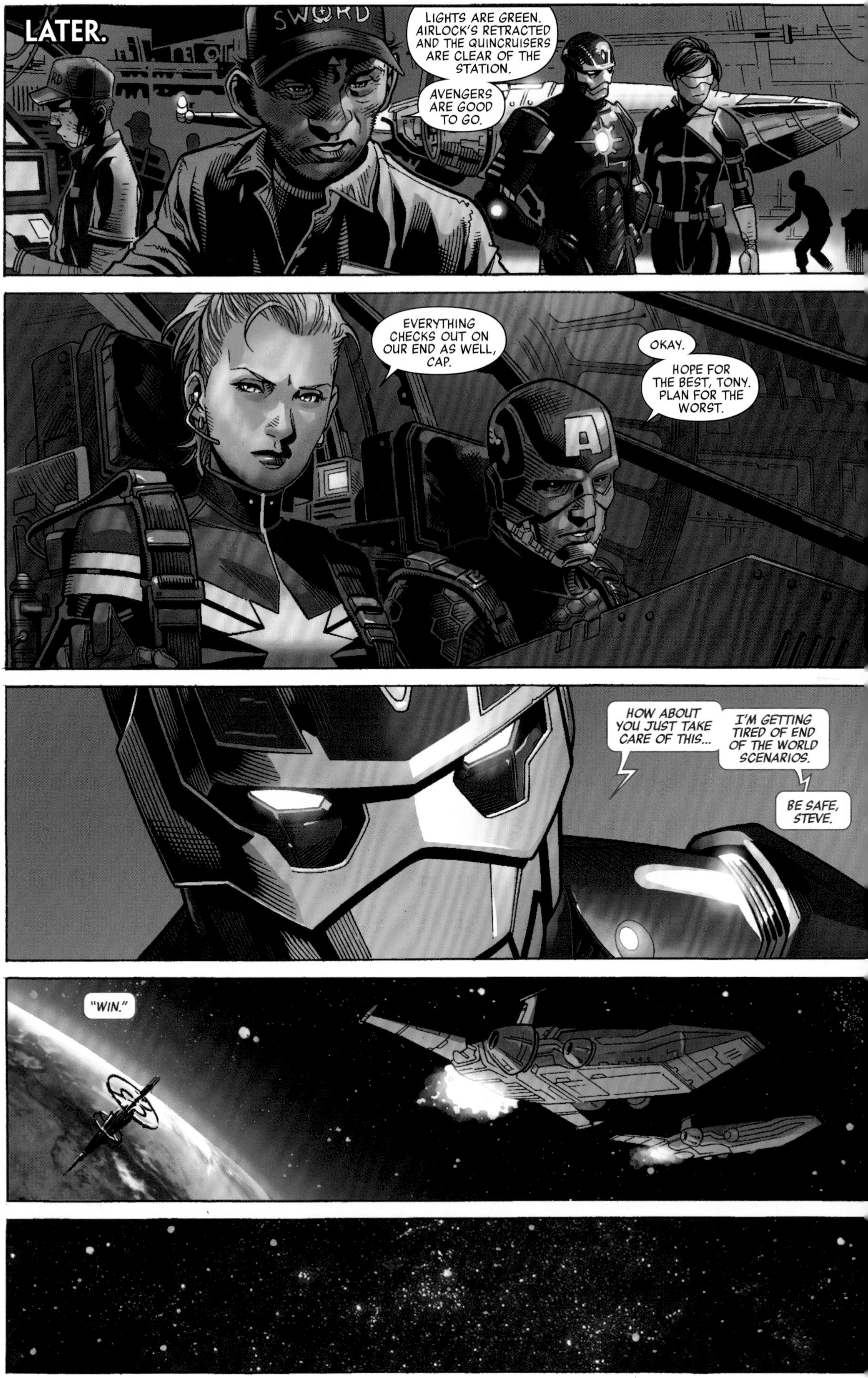
LATER.
LIGHTS ARE GREEN. AIRLOCK'S RETRACTED AND THE QUINCRUISERS ARE CLEAR OF THE STATION.
AVENGERS ARE GOOD TO GO.
SWORD
EVERYTHING CHECKS OUT ON OUR END AS WELL, CAP.
OKAY.
HOPE FOR THE BEST, TONY. PLAN FOR THE WORST.
HOW ABOUT YOU JUST TAKE CARE OF THIS...
I'M GETTING TIRED OF END OF THE WORLD SCENARIOS.
BE SAFE, STEVE.
"WIN."

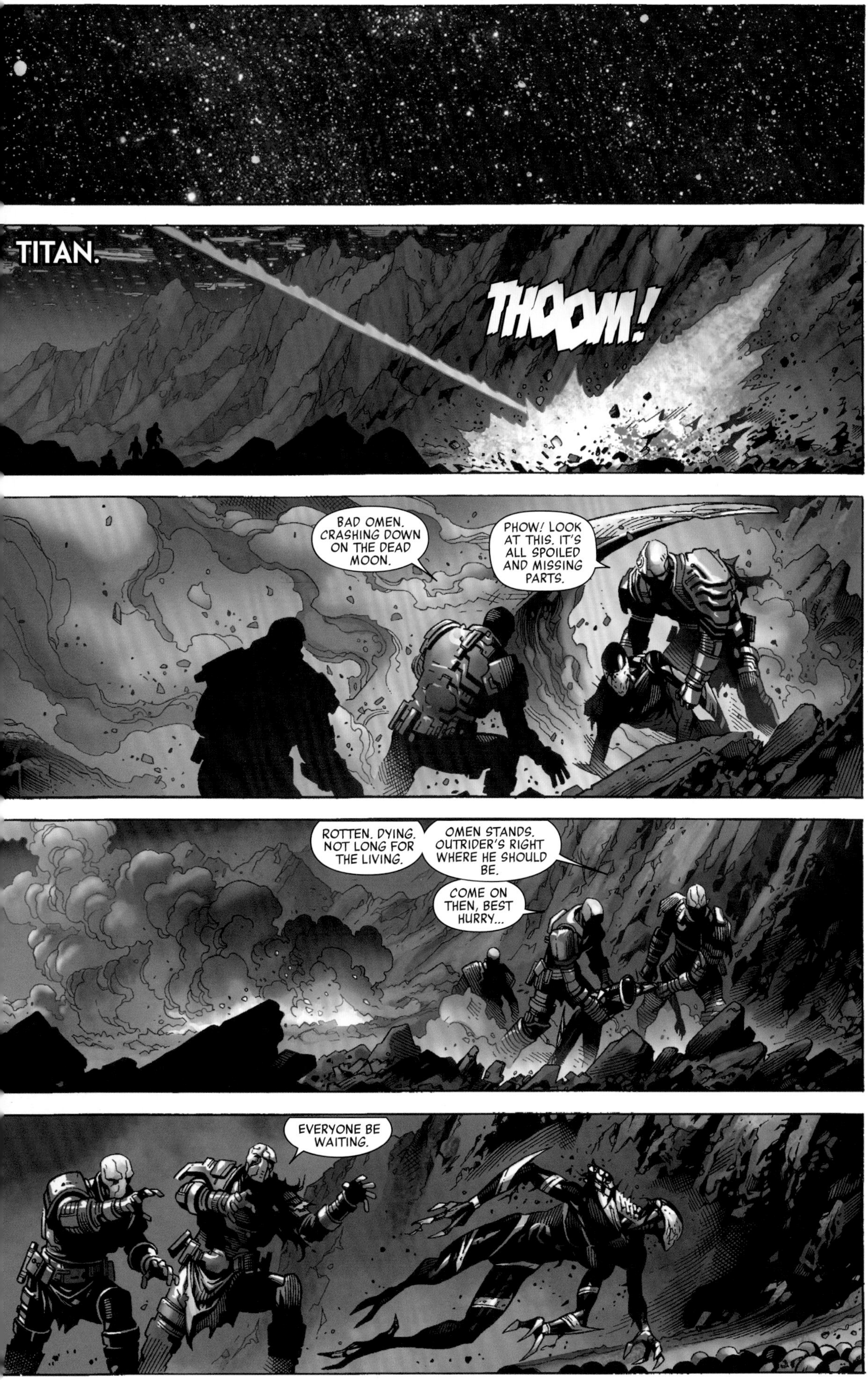
TITAN.
THOOM!
BAD OMEN. CRASHING DOWN ON THE DEAD MOON.
PHOW! LOOK AT THIS. IT'S ALL SPOILED AND MISSING PARTS.
ROTTEN. DYING. NOT LONG FOR THE LIVING.
OMEN STANDS. OUTRIDER'S RIGHT WHERE HE SHOULD BE.
COME ON THEN, BEST HURRY...
EVERYONE BE WAITING.

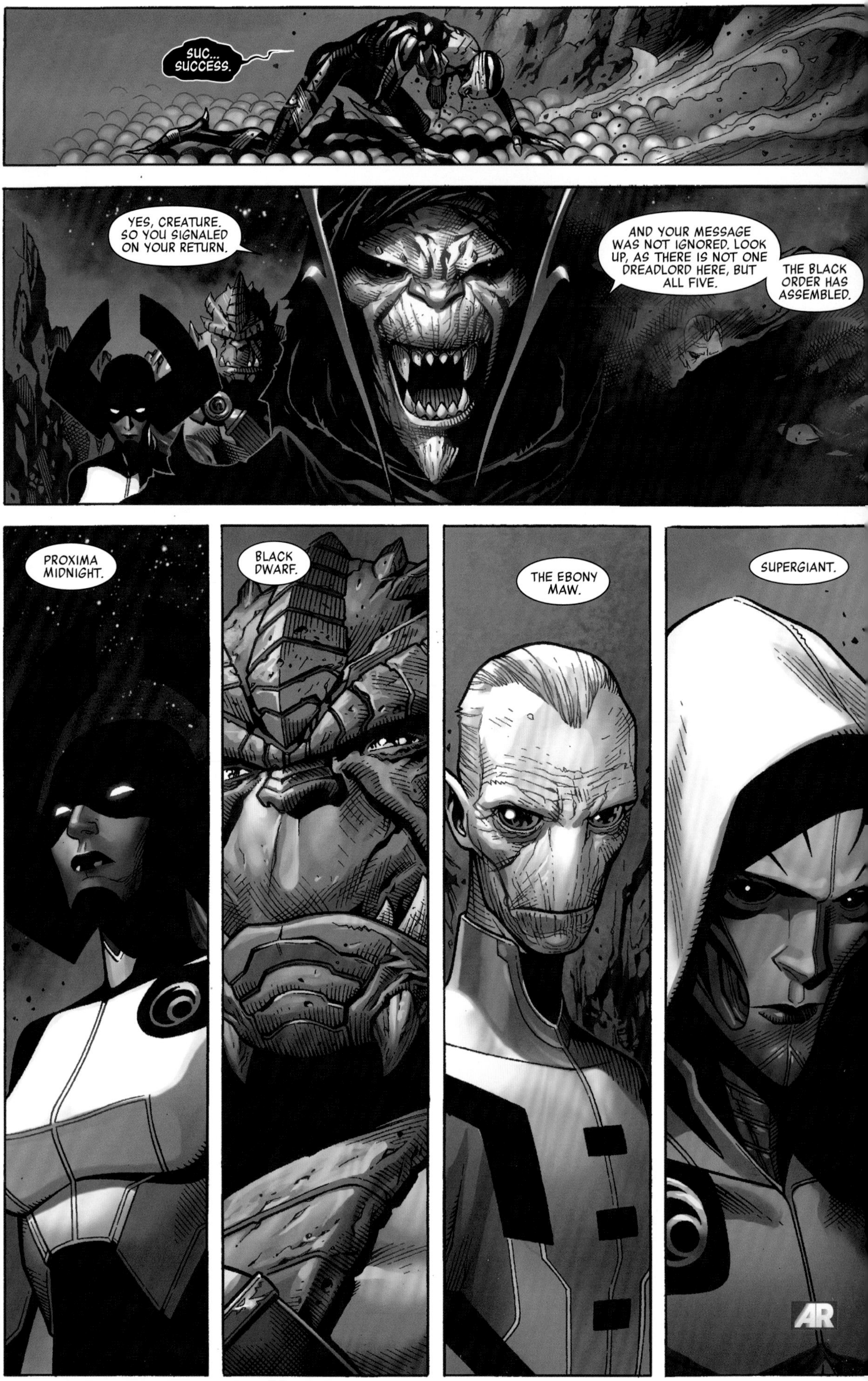
SUC... SUCCESS.
YES, CREATURE. SO YOU SIGNALED ON YOUR RETURN.
AND YOUR MESSAGE WAS NOT IGNORED. LOOK UP, AS THERE IS NOT ONE DREADLORD HERE, BUT ALL FIVE.
THE BLACK ORDER HAS ASSEMBLED.
PROXIMA MIDNIGHT.
BLACK DWARF.
THE EBONY MAW.
SUPERGIANT.

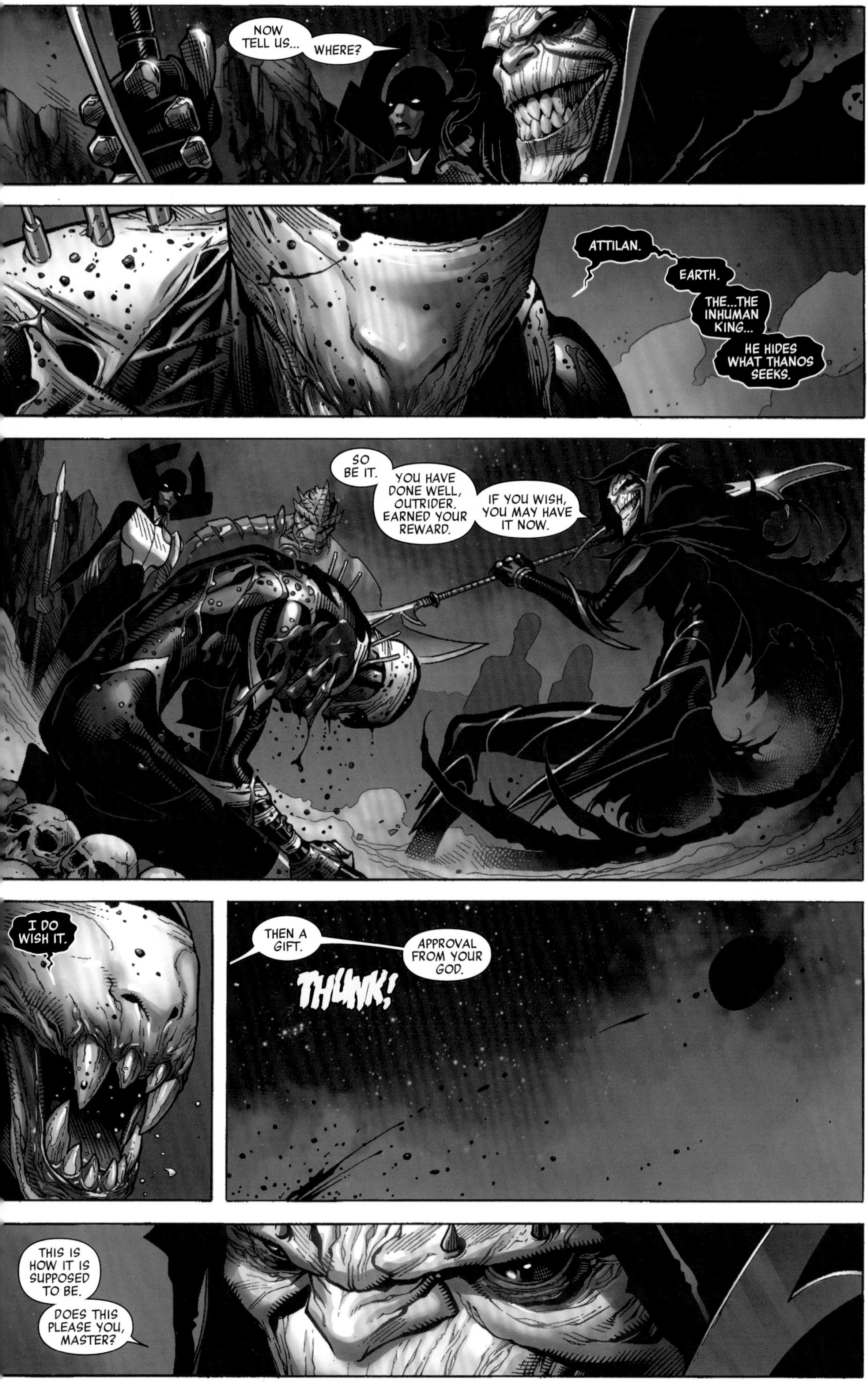
NOW TELL US...
WHERE?
ATTILAN.
EARTH.
THE...THE INHUMAN KING...
HE HIDES WHAT THANOS SEEKS.
SO BE IT.
YOU HAVE DONE WELL, OUTRIDER. EARNED YOUR REWARD.
IF YOU WISH, YOU MAY HAVE IT NOW.
I DO WISH IT.
THEN A GIFT.
APPROVAL FROM YOUR GOD.
THUNK!
THIS IS HOW IT IS SUPPOSED TO BE.
DOES THIS PLEASE YOU, MASTER?

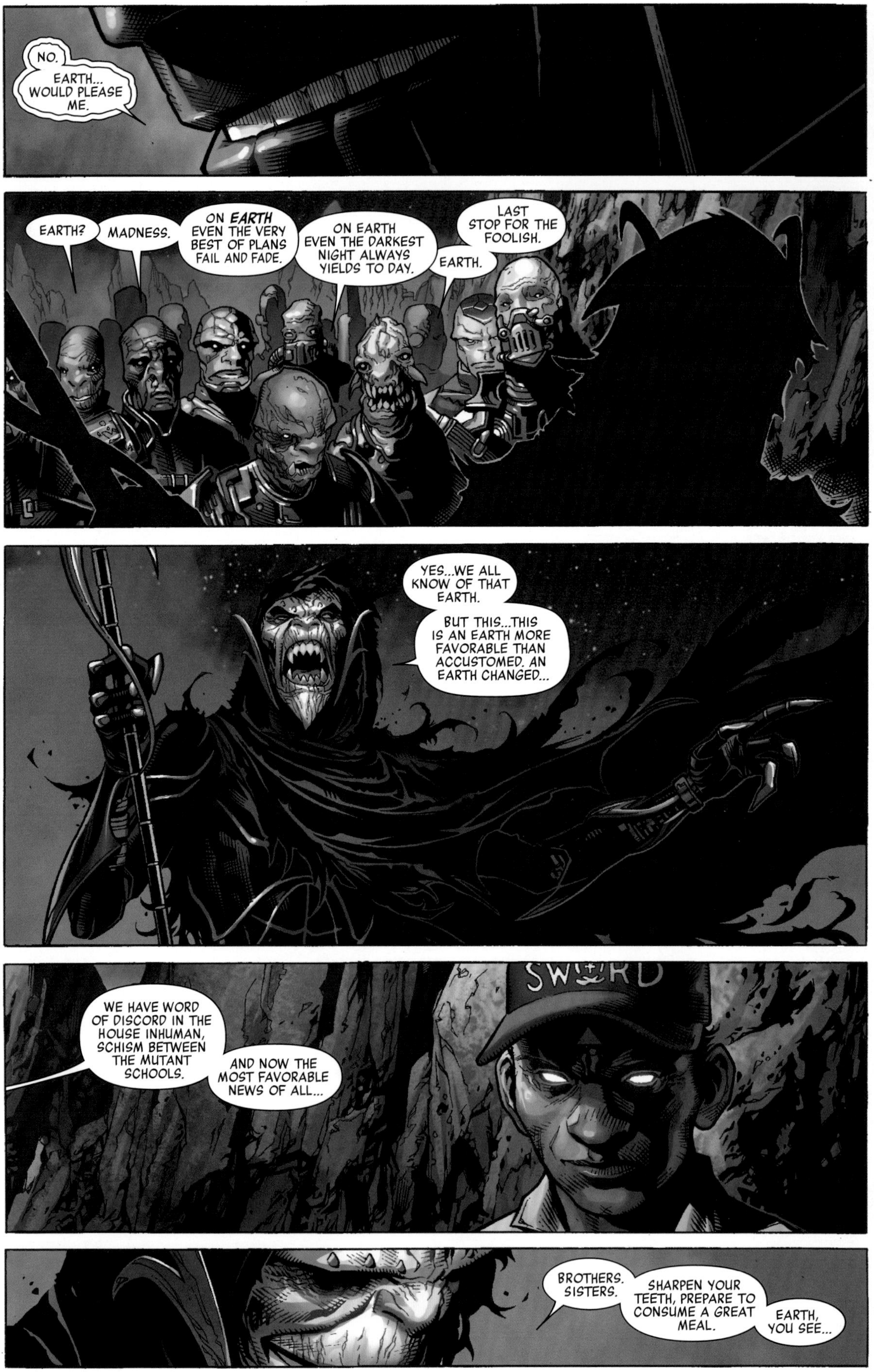
NO.
EARTH... WOULD PLEASE ME.
EARTH?
MADNESS.
ON EARTH EVEN THE VERY BEST OF PLANS FAIL AND FADE.
ON EARTH EVEN THE DARKEST NIGHT ALWAYS YIELDS TO DAY.
EARTH.
LAST STOP FOR THE FOOLISH.
YES...WE ALL KNOW OF THAT EARTH.
BUT THIS...THIS IS AN EARTH MORE FAVORABLE THAN ACCUSTOMED. AN EARTH CHANGED...
SWORD
WE HAVE WORD OF DISCORD IN THE HOUSE INHUMAN, SCHISM BETWEEN THE MUTANT SCHOOLS.
AND NOW THE MOST FAVORABLE NEWS OF ALL...
BROTHERS. SISTERS.
SHARPEN YOUR TEETH, PREPARE TO CONSUME A GREAT MEAL.
EARTH, YOU SEE...

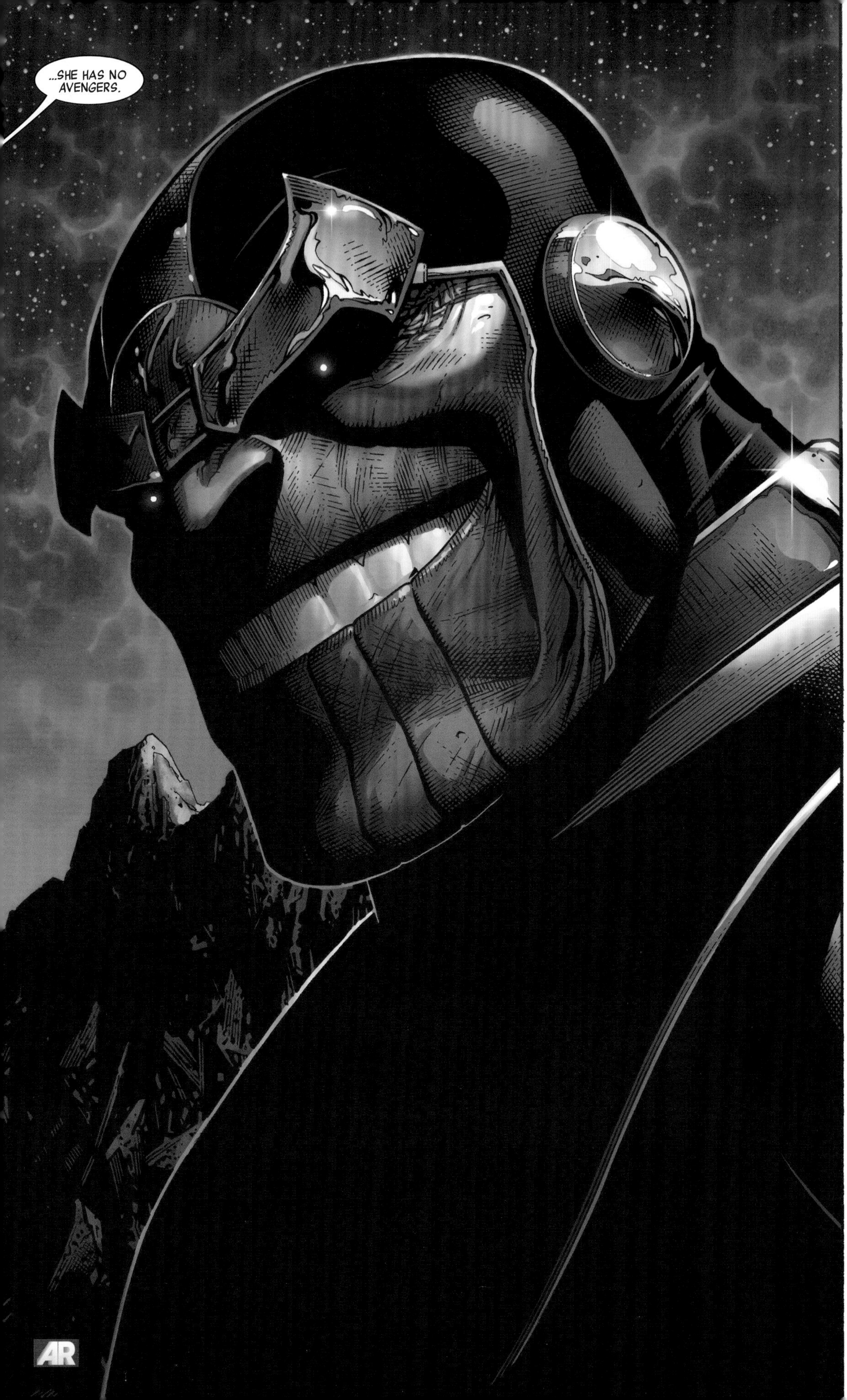
...SHE HAS NO AVENGERS.

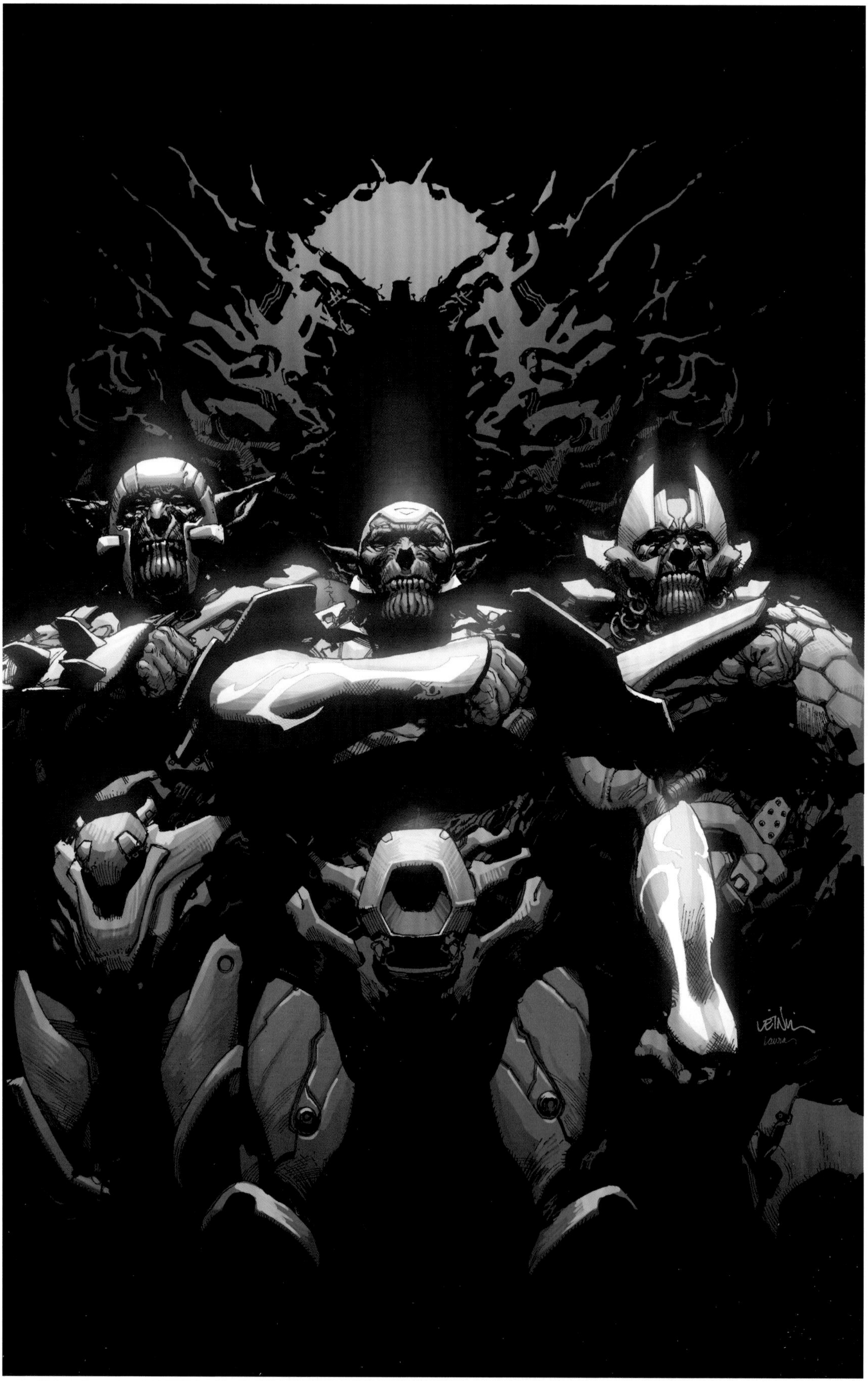

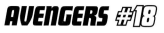

WORLDS RISE

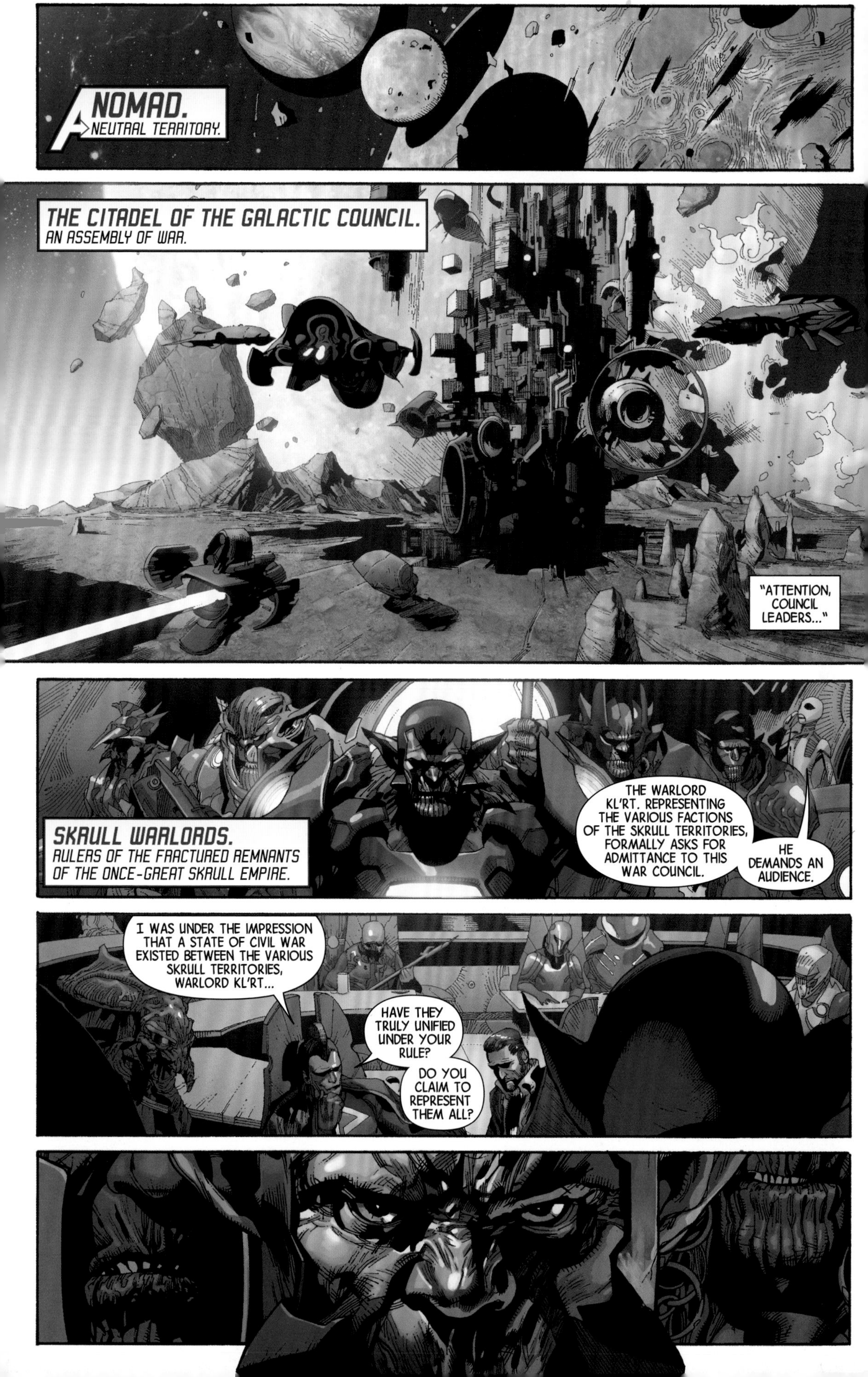
A NOMAD.
NEUTRAL TERRITORY.
THE CITADEL OF THE GALACTIC COUNCIL.
AN ASSEMBLY OF WAR.
"ATTENTION, COUNCIL LEADERS..."
SKRULL WARLORDS.
RULERS OF THE FRACTURED REMNANTS OF THE ONCE-GREAT SKRULL EMPIRE.
THE WARLORD KL'RT. REPRESENTING THE VARIOUS FACTIONS OF THE SKRULL TERRITORIES, FORMALLY ASKS FOR ADMITTANCE TO THIS WAR COUNCIL.
HE DEMANDS AN AUDIENCE.
I WAS UNDER THE IMPRESSION THAT A STATE OF CIVIL WAR EXISTED BETWEEN THE VARIOUS SKRULL TERRITORIES, WARLORD KL'RT...
HAVE THEY TRULY UNIFIED UNDER YOUR RULE?
DO YOU CLAIM TO REPRESENT THEM ALL?

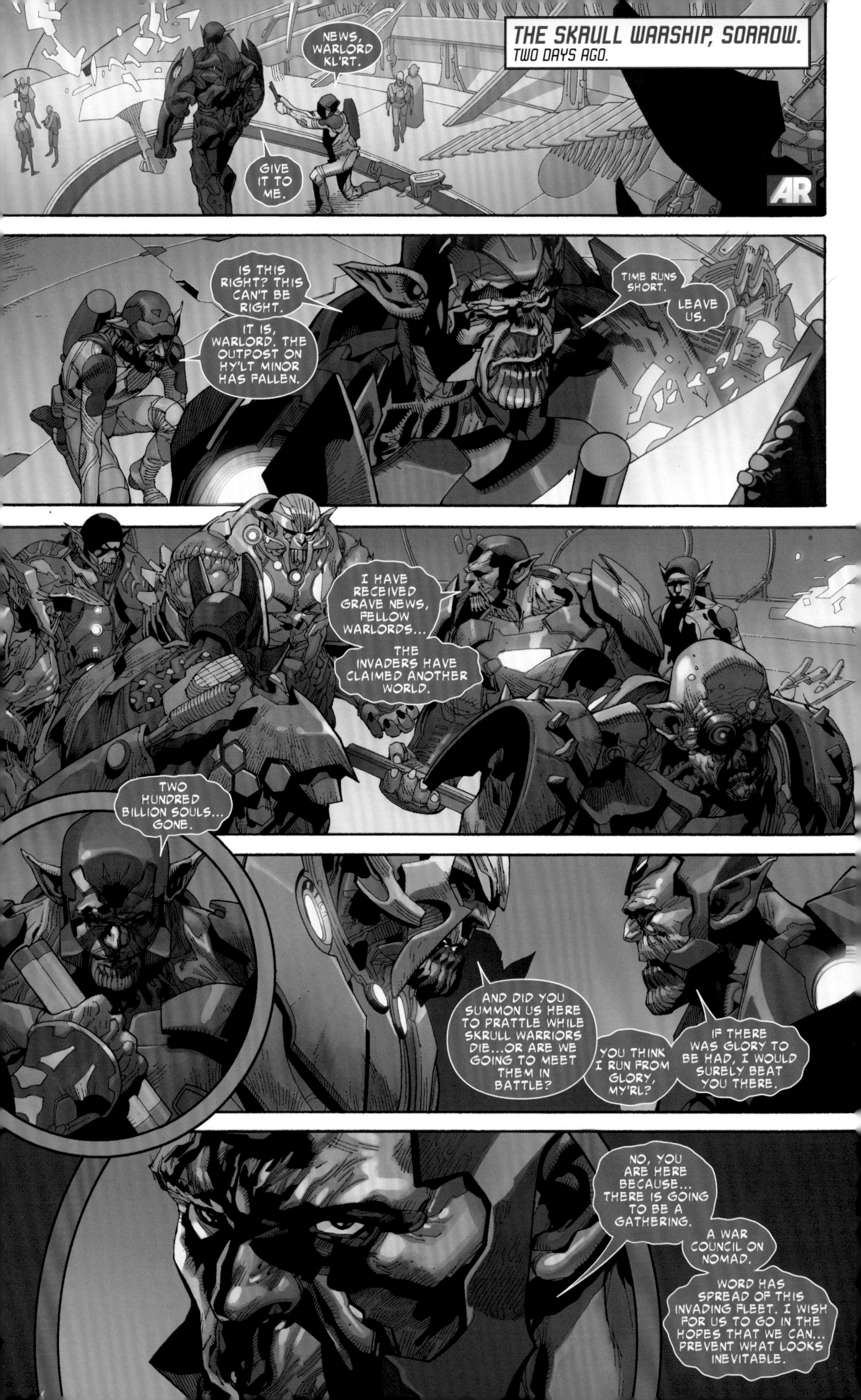
THE SKRULL WARSHIP, SORROW.
TWO DAYS AGO.
NEWS, WARLORD KL'RT.
GIVE IT TO ME.
AR
IS THIS RIGHT? THIS CAN'T BE RIGHT.
IT IS, WARLORD. THE OUTPOST ON HY'LT MINOR HAS FALLEN.
TIME RUNS SHORT.
LEAVE US.
I HAVE RECEIVED GRAVE NEWS, FELLOW WARLORDS...
THE INVADERS HAVE CLAIMED ANOTHER WORLD.
TWO HUNDRED BILLION SOULS... GONE.
AND DID YOU SUMMON US HERE TO PRATTLE WHILE SKRULL WARRIORS DIE...OR ARE WE GOING TO MEET THEM IN BATTLE?
YOU THINK I RUN FROM GLORY, MY'RL?
IF THERE WAS GLORY TO BE HAD, I WOULD SURELY BEAT YOU THERE.
NO, YOU ARE HERE BECAUSE... THERE IS GOING TO BE A GATHERING.
A WAR COUNCIL ON NOMAD.
WORD HAS SPREAD OF THIS INVADING FLEET. I WISH FOR US TO GO IN THE HOPES THAT WE CAN... PREVENT WHAT LOOKS INEVITABLE.

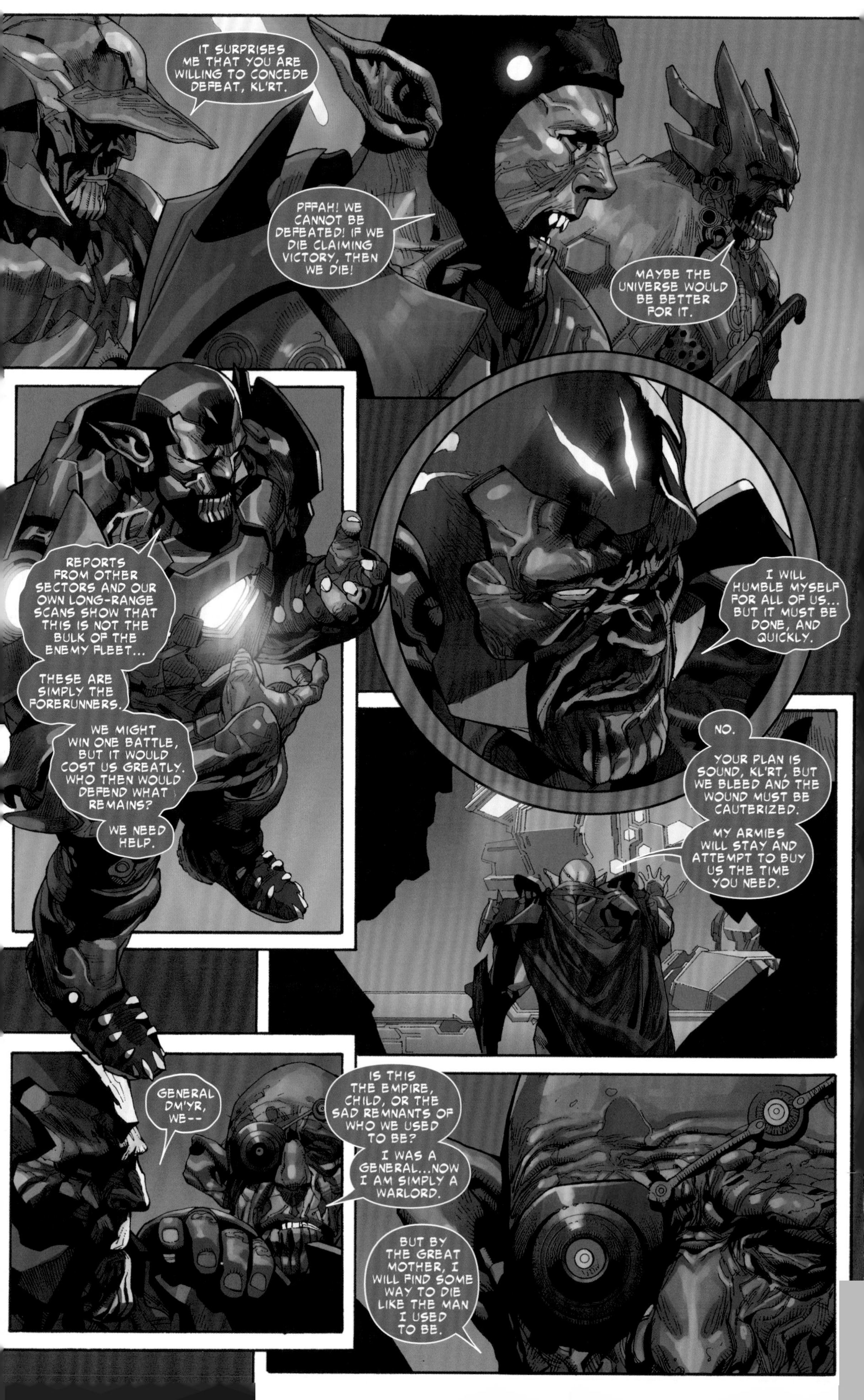
IT SURPRISES ME THAT YOU ARE WILLING TO CONCEDE DEFEAT, KL'RT.
PFFAH! WE CANNOT BE DEFEATED! IF WE DIE CLAIMING VICTORY, THEN WE DIE!
MAYBE THE UNIVERSE WOULD BE BETTER FOR IT.
REPORTS FROM OTHER SECTORS AND OUR OWN LONG-RANGE SCANS SHOW THAT THIS IS NOT THE BULK OF THE ENEMY FLEET...
THESE ARE SIMPLY THE FORERUNNERS.
WE MIGHT WIN ONE BATTLE, BUT IT WOULD COST US GREATLY. WHO THEN WOULD DEFEND WHAT REMAINS?
WE NEED HELP.
I WILL HUMBLE MYSELF FOR ALL OF US... BUT IT MUST BE DONE, AND QUICKLY.
NO.
YOUR PLAN IS SOUND, KL'RT, BUT WE BLEED AND THE WOUND MUST BE CAUTERIZED.
MY ARMIES WILL STAY AND ATTEMPT TO BUY US THE TIME YOU NEED.
GENERAL DM'YR, WE--
IS THIS THE EMPIRE, CHILD, OR THE SAD REMNANTS OF WHO WE USED TO BE?
I WAS A GENERAL...NOW I AM SIMPLY A WARLORD.
BUT BY THE GREAT MOTHER, I WILL FIND SOME WAY TO DIE LIKE THE MAN I USED TO BE.

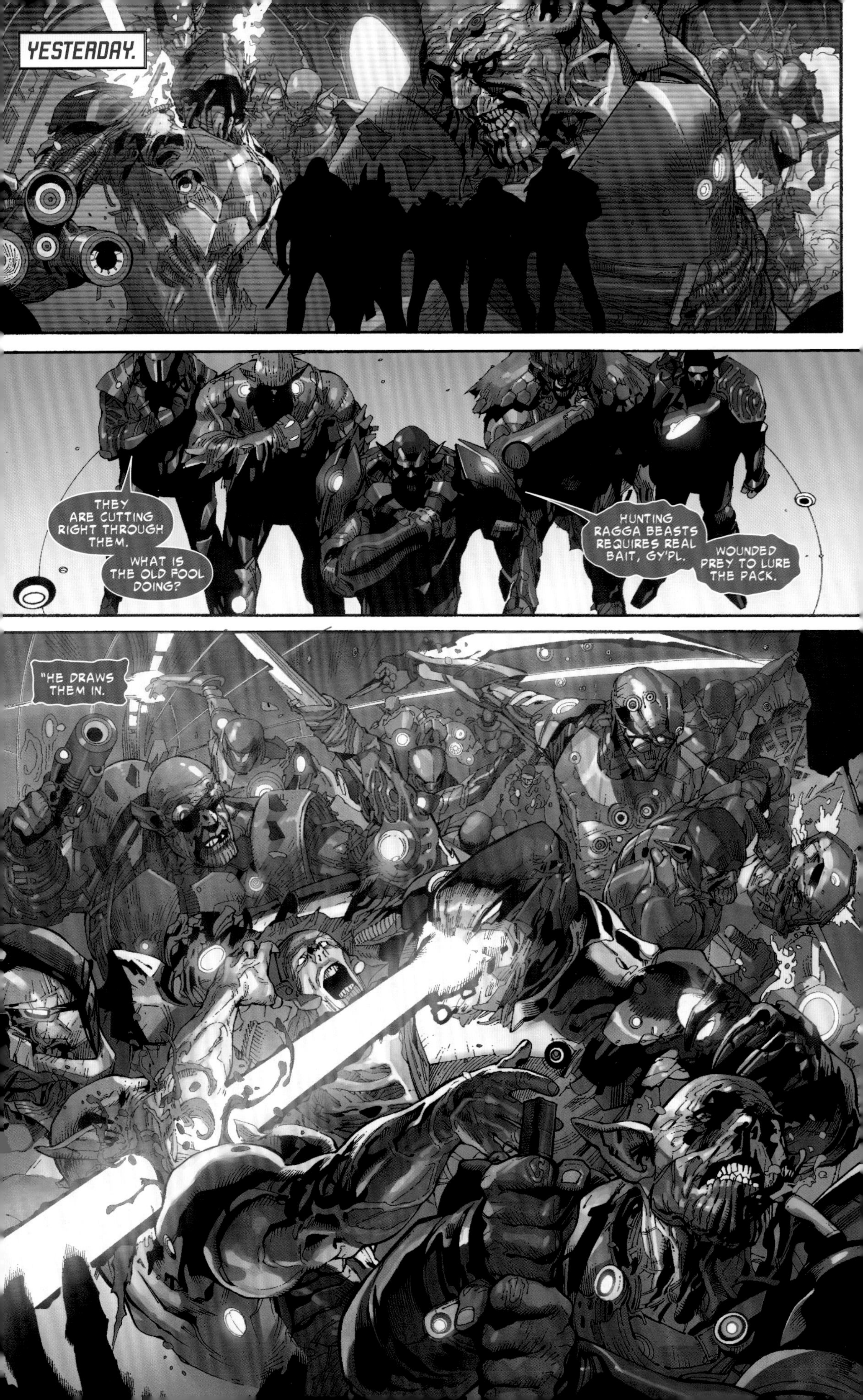
YESTERDAY.
THEY ARE CUTTING RIGHT THROUGH THEM.
WHAT IS THE OLD FOOL DOING?
HUNTING RAGGA BEASTS REQUIRES REAL BAIT, GY'PL.
WOUNDED PREY TO LURE THE PACK.
"HE DRAWS THEM IN.

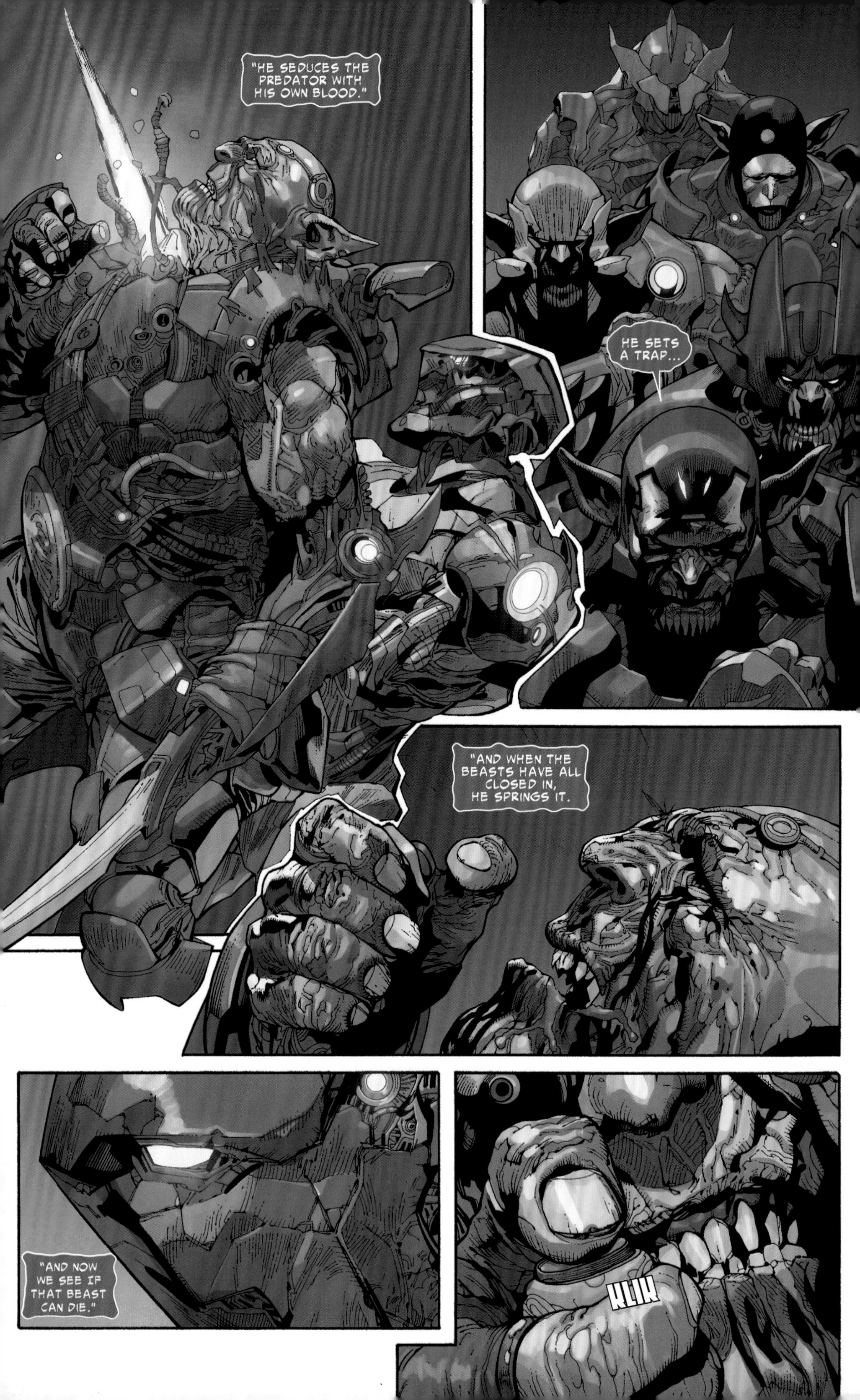
"HE SEDUCES THE PREDATOR WITH HIS OWN BLOOD."
HE SETS A TRAP...
"AND WHEN THE BEASTS HAVE ALL CLOSED IN, HE SPRINGS IT.
"AND NOW WE SEE IF THAT BEAST CAN DIE."
KLIK

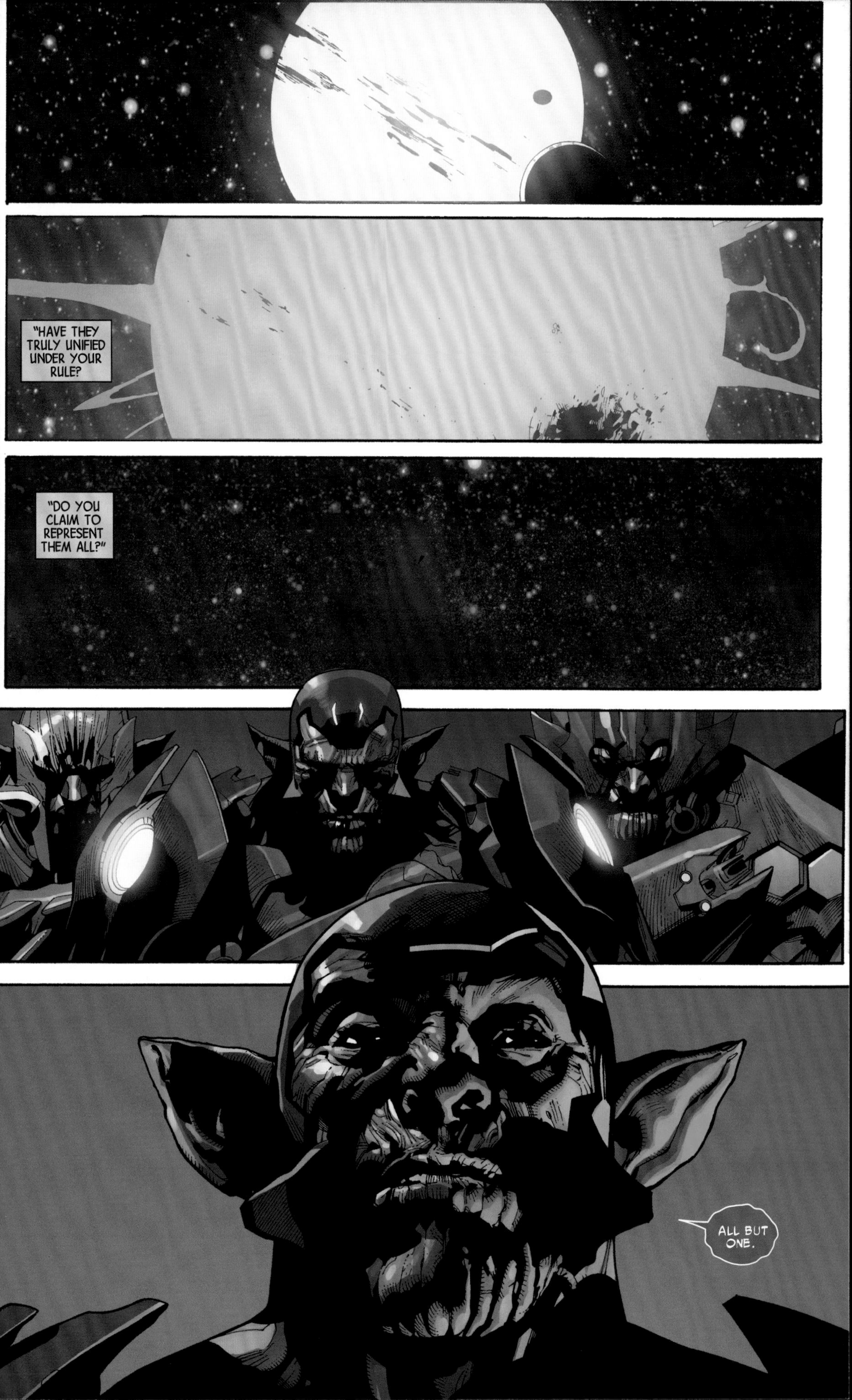
"HAVE THEY TRULY UNIFIED UNDER YOUR RULE?
"DO YOU CLAIM TO REPRESENT THEM ALL?"
ALL BUT ONE.

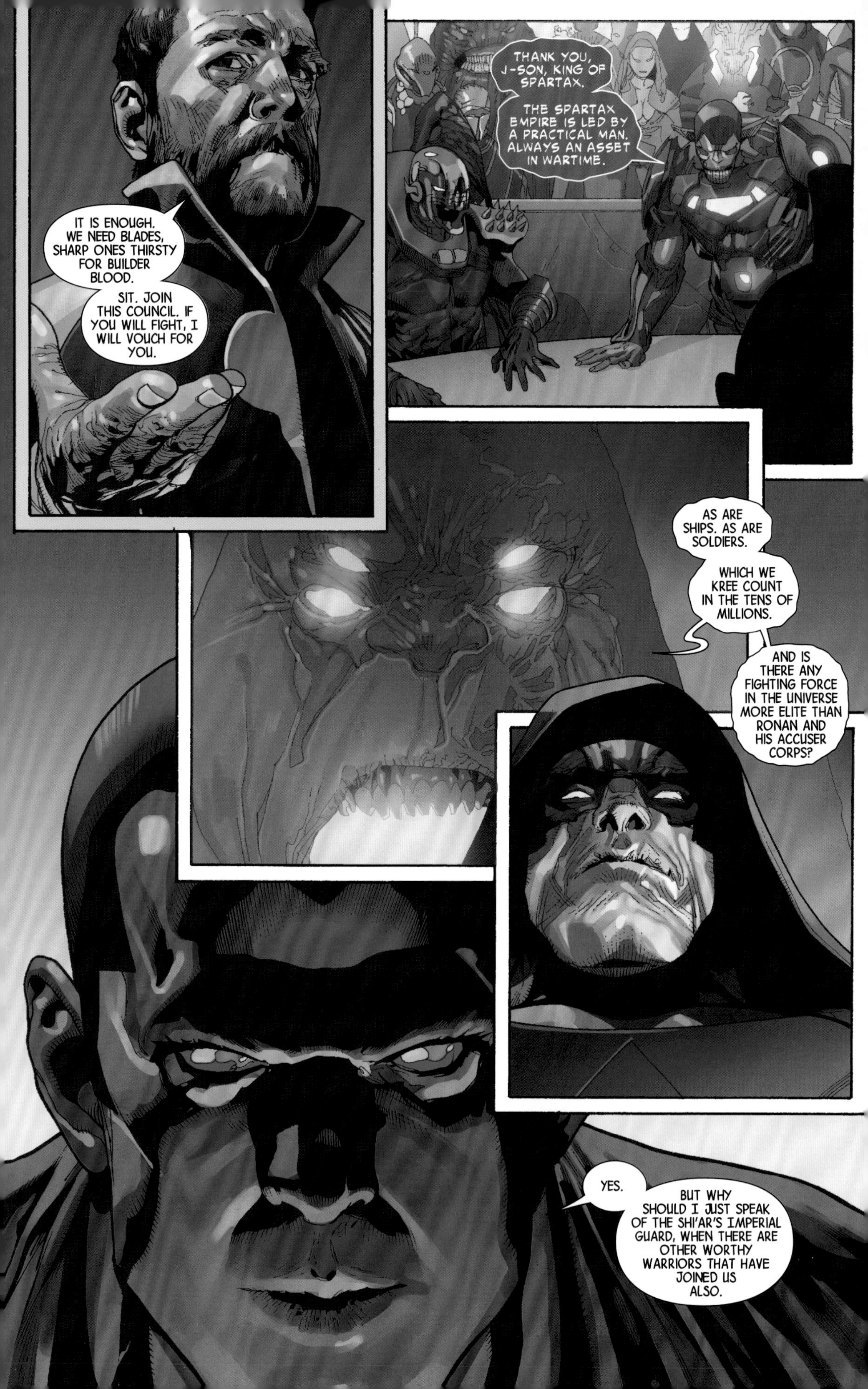

IT IS ENOUGH. WE NEED BLADES, SHARP ONES THIRSTY FOR BUILDER BLOOD.
SIT. JOIN THIS COUNCIL. IF YOU WILL FIGHT, I WILL VOUCH FOR YOU.
THANK YOU, J-SON, KING OF SPARTAX.
THE SPARTAX EMPIRE IS LED BY A PRACTICAL MAN. ALWAYS AN ASSET IN WARTIME.
AS ARE SHIPS. AS ARE SOLDIERS.
WHICH WE KREE COUNT IN THE TENS OF MILLIONS.
AND IS THERE ANY FIGHTING FORCE IN THE UNIVERSE MORE ELITE THAN RONAN AND HIS ACCUSER CORPS?
YES.
BUT WHY SHOULD I JUST SPEAK OF THE SHI'AR'S IMPERIAL GUARD, WHEN THERE ARE OTHER WORTHY WARRIORS THAT HAVE JOINED US ALSO.

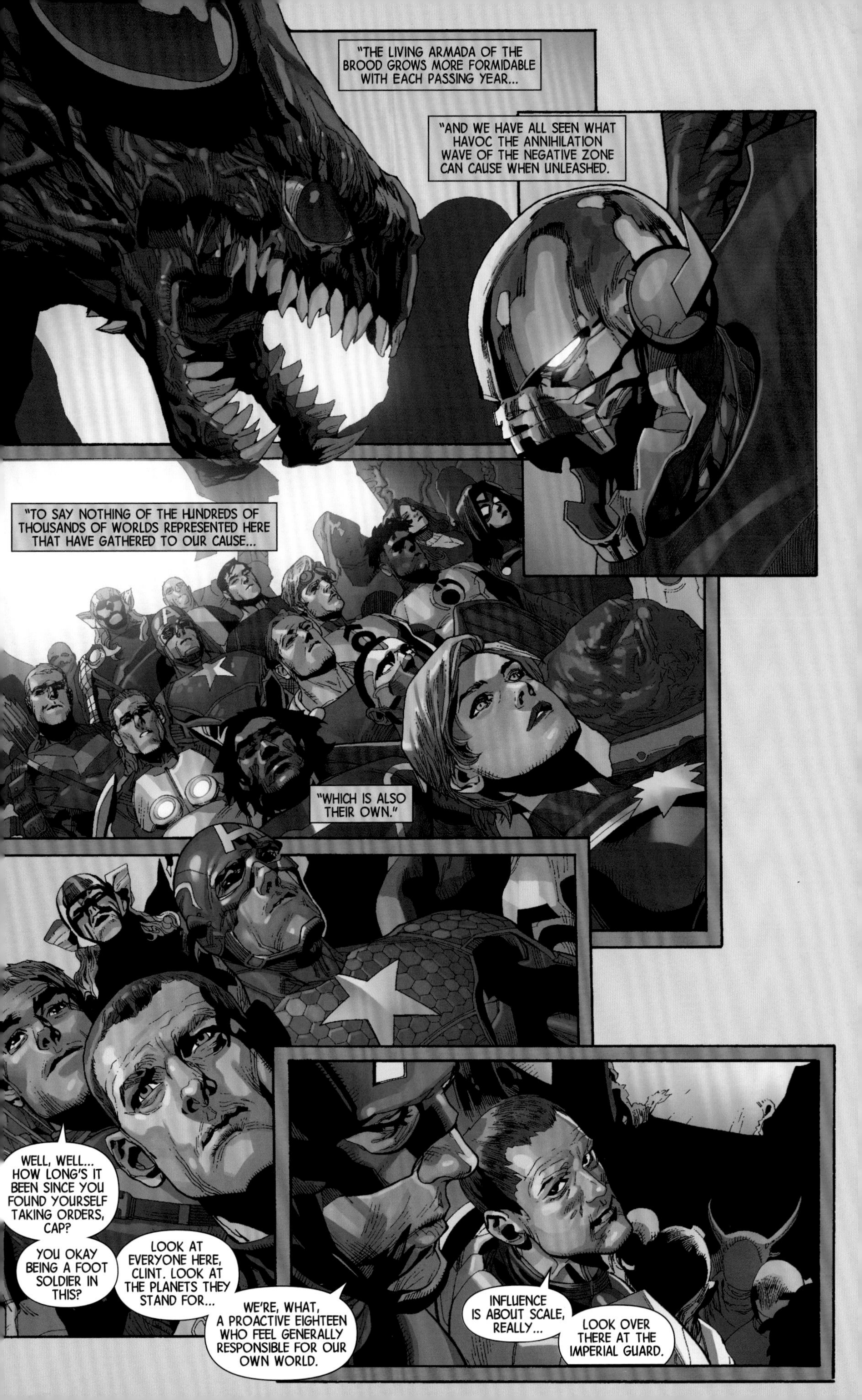
"THE LIVING ARMADA OF THE BROOD GROWS MORE FORMIDABLE WITH EACH PASSING YEAR...
"AND WE HAVE ALL SEEN WHAT HAVOC THE ANNIHILATION WAVE OF THE NEGATIVE ZONE CAN CAUSE WHEN UNLEASHED.
"TO SAY NOTHING OF THE HUNDREDS OF THOUSANDS OF WORLDS REPRESENTED HERE THAT HAVE GATHERED TO OUR CAUSE...
"WHICH IS ALSO THEIR OWN."
WELL, WELL... HOW LONG'S IT BEEN SINCE YOU FOUND YOURSELF TAKING ORDERS, CAP?
YOU OKAY BEING A FOOT SOLDIER IN THIS?
LOOK AT EVERYONE HERE, CLINT. LOOK AT THE PLANETS THEY STAND FOR...
WE'RE, WHAT, A PROACTIVE EIGHTEEN WHO FEEL GENERALLY RESPONSIBLE FOR OUR OWN WORLD.
INFLUENCE IS ABOUT SCALE, REALLY...
LOOK OVER THERE AT THE IMPERIAL GUARD.

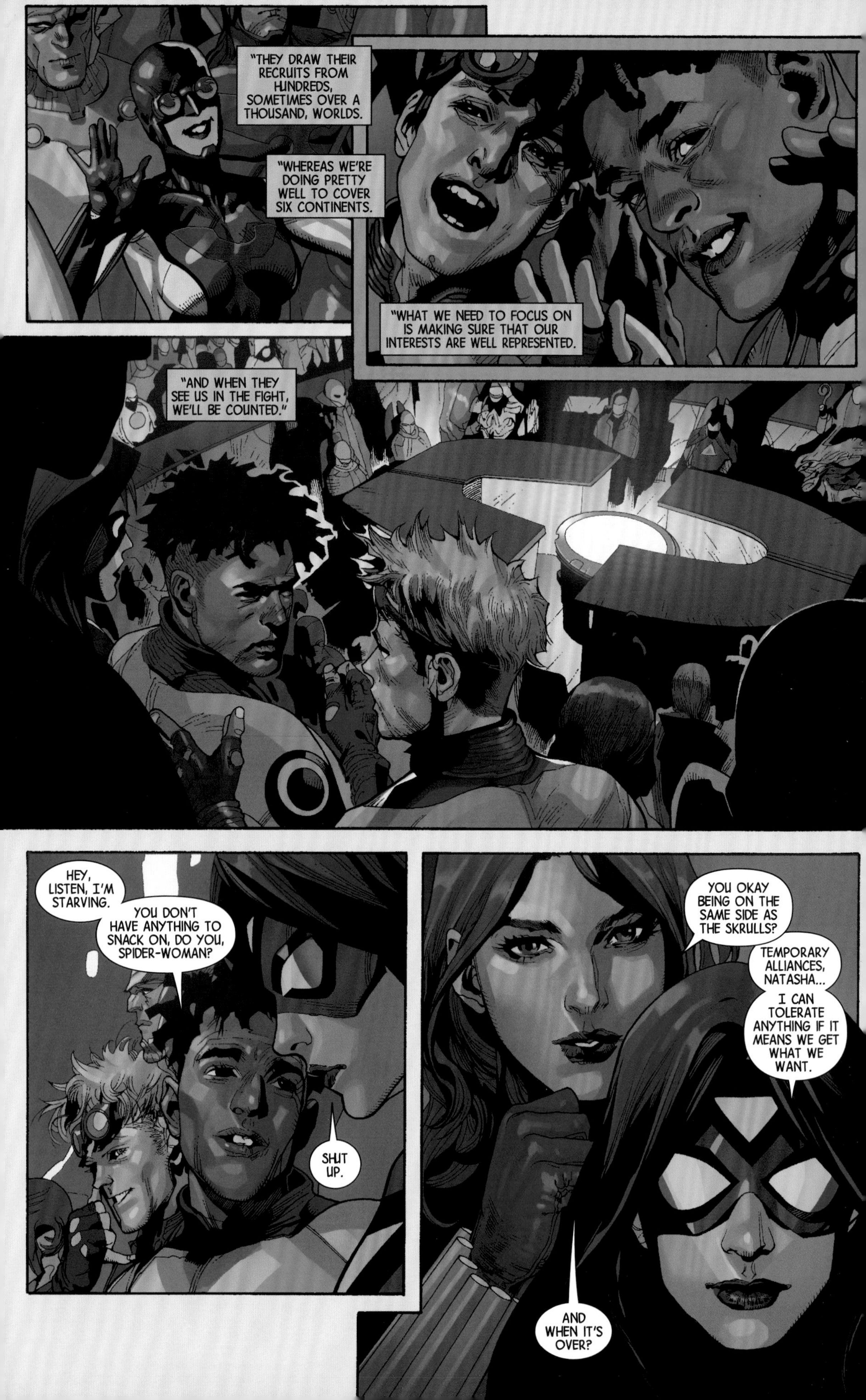
"THEY DRAW THEIR RECRUITS FROM HUNDREDS, SOMETIMES OVER A THOUSAND, WORLDS.
"WHEREAS WE'RE DOING PRETTY WELL TO COVER SIX CONTINENTS.
"WHAT WE NEED TO FOCUS ON IS MAKING SURE THAT OUR INTERESTS ARE WELL REPRESENTED.
"AND WHEN THEY SEE US IN THE FIGHT, WE'LL BE COUNTED."
HEY, LISTEN, I'M STARVING.
YOU DON'T HAVE ANYTHING TO SNACK ON, DO YOU, SPIDER-WOMAN?
SHUT UP.
YOU OKAY BEING ON THE SAME SIDE AS THE SKRULLS?
TEMPORARY ALLIANCES, NATASHA...
I CAN TOLERATE ANYTHING IF IT MEANS WE GET WHAT WE WANT.
AND WHEN IT'S OVER?

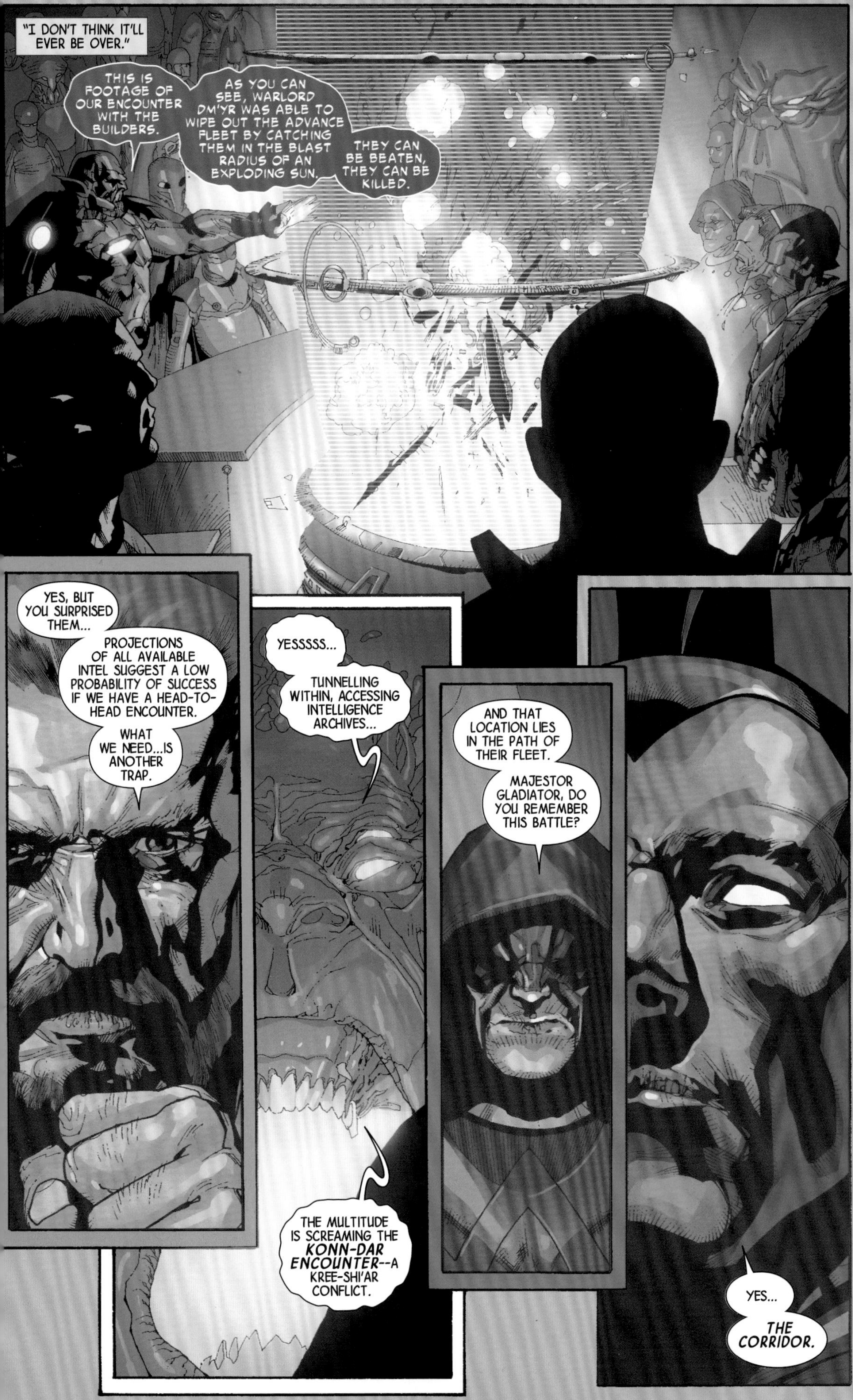
"I DON'T THINK IT'LL EVER BE OVER."
THIS IS FOOTAGE OF OUR ENCOUNTER WITH THE BUILDERS.
AS YOU CAN SEE, WARLORD DM'YR WAS ABLE TO WIPE OUT THE ADVANCE FLEET BY CATCHING THEM IN THE BLAST RADIUS OF AN EXPLODING SUN.
THEY CAN BE BEATEN, THEY CAN BE KILLED.
YES, BUT YOU SURPRISED THEM...
PROJECTIONS OF ALL AVAILABLE INTEL SUGGEST A LOW PROBABILITY OF SUCCESS IF WE HAVE A HEAD-TO-HEAD ENCOUNTER.
WHAT WE NEED...IS ANOTHER TRAP.
YESSSSS...
TUNNELLING WITHIN, ACCESSING INTELLIGENCE ARCHIVES...
THE MULTITUDE IS SCREAMING THE *KONN-DAR ENCOUNTER*--A KREE-SHI'AR CONFLICT.
AND THAT LOCATION LIES IN THE PATH OF THEIR FLEET.
MAJESTOR GLADIATOR, DO YOU REMEMBER THIS BATTLE?
YES...
THE CORRIDOR.

FALL INTO
SINGULARITY

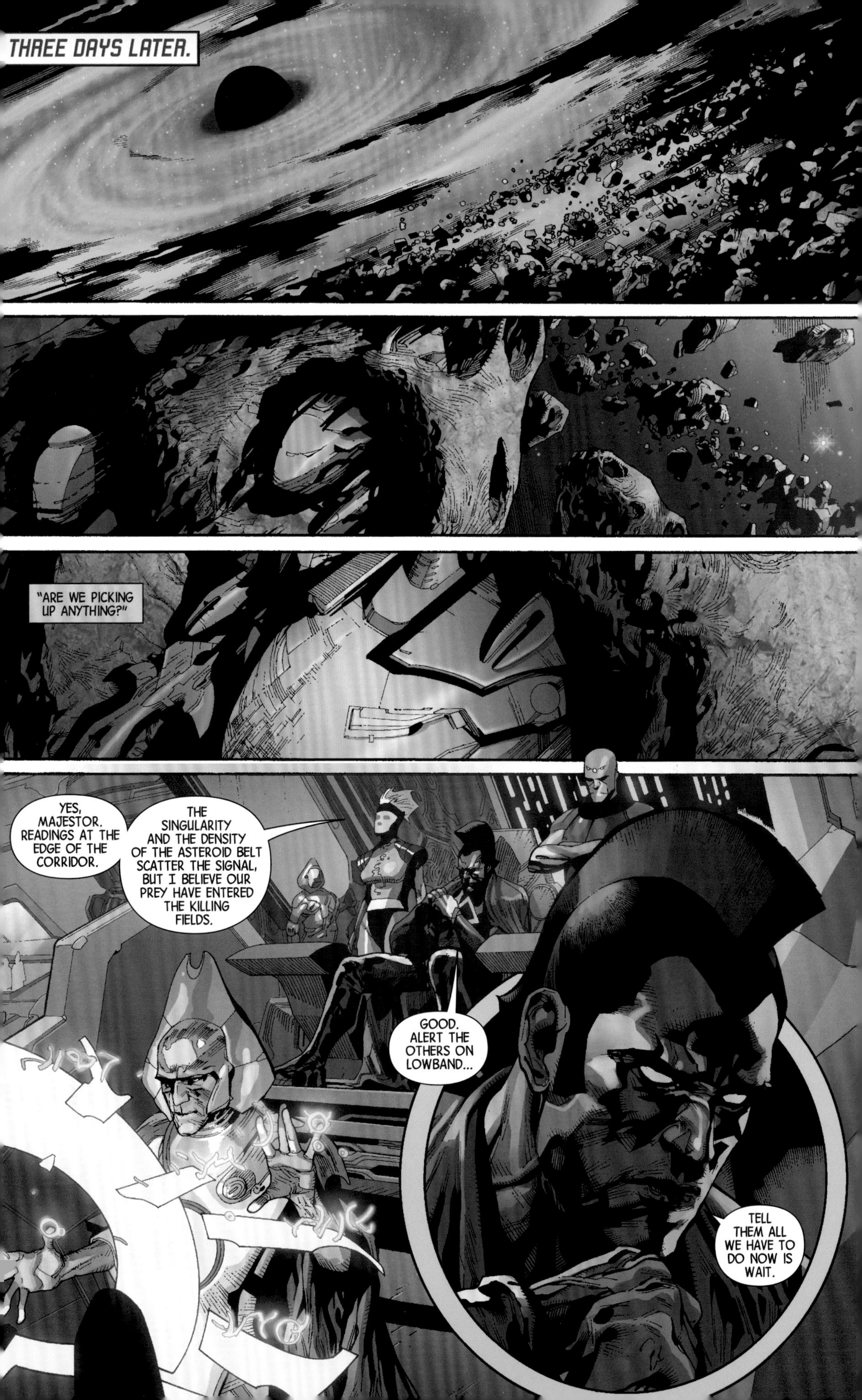
THREE DAYS LATER.
"ARE WE PICKING UP ANYTHING?"
YES, MAJESTOR. READINGS AT THE EDGE OF THE CORRIDOR.
THE SINGULARITY AND THE DENSITY OF THE ASTEROID BELT SCATTER THE SIGNAL, BUT I BELIEVE OUR PREY HAVE ENTERED THE KILLING FIELDS.
GOOD. ALERT THE OTHERS ON LOWBAND...
TELL THEM ALL WE HAVE TO DO NOW IS WAIT.

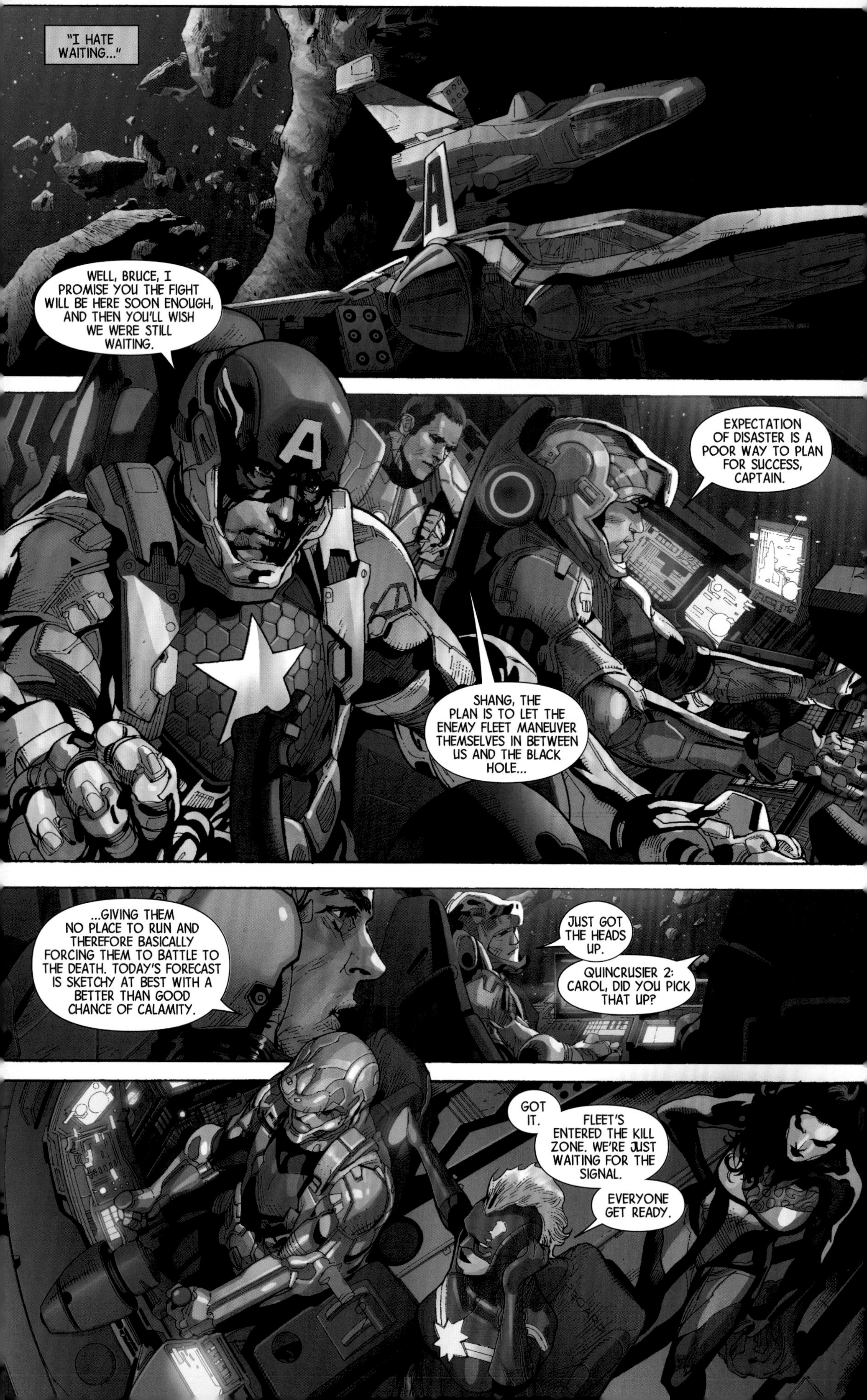
"I HATE WAITING..."
WELL, BRUCE, I PROMISE YOU THE FIGHT WILL BE HERE SOON ENOUGH, AND THEN YOU'LL WISH WE WERE STILL WAITING.
EXPECTATION OF DISASTER IS A POOR WAY TO PLAN FOR SUCCESS, CAPTAIN.
SHANG, THE PLAN IS TO LET THE ENEMY FLEET MANEUVER THEMSELVES IN BETWEEN US AND THE BLACK HOLE...
...GIVING THEM NO PLACE TO RUN AND THEREFORE BASICALLY FORCING THEM TO BATTLE TO THE DEATH. TODAY'S FORECAST IS SKETCHY AT BEST WITH A BETTER THAN GOOD CHANCE OF CALAMITY.
JUST GOT THE HEADS UP.
QUINCRUSIER 2: CAROL, DID YOU PICK THAT UP?
GOT IT.
FLEET'S ENTERED THE KILL ZONE. WE'RE JUST WAITING FOR THE SIGNAL.
EVERYONE GET READY.

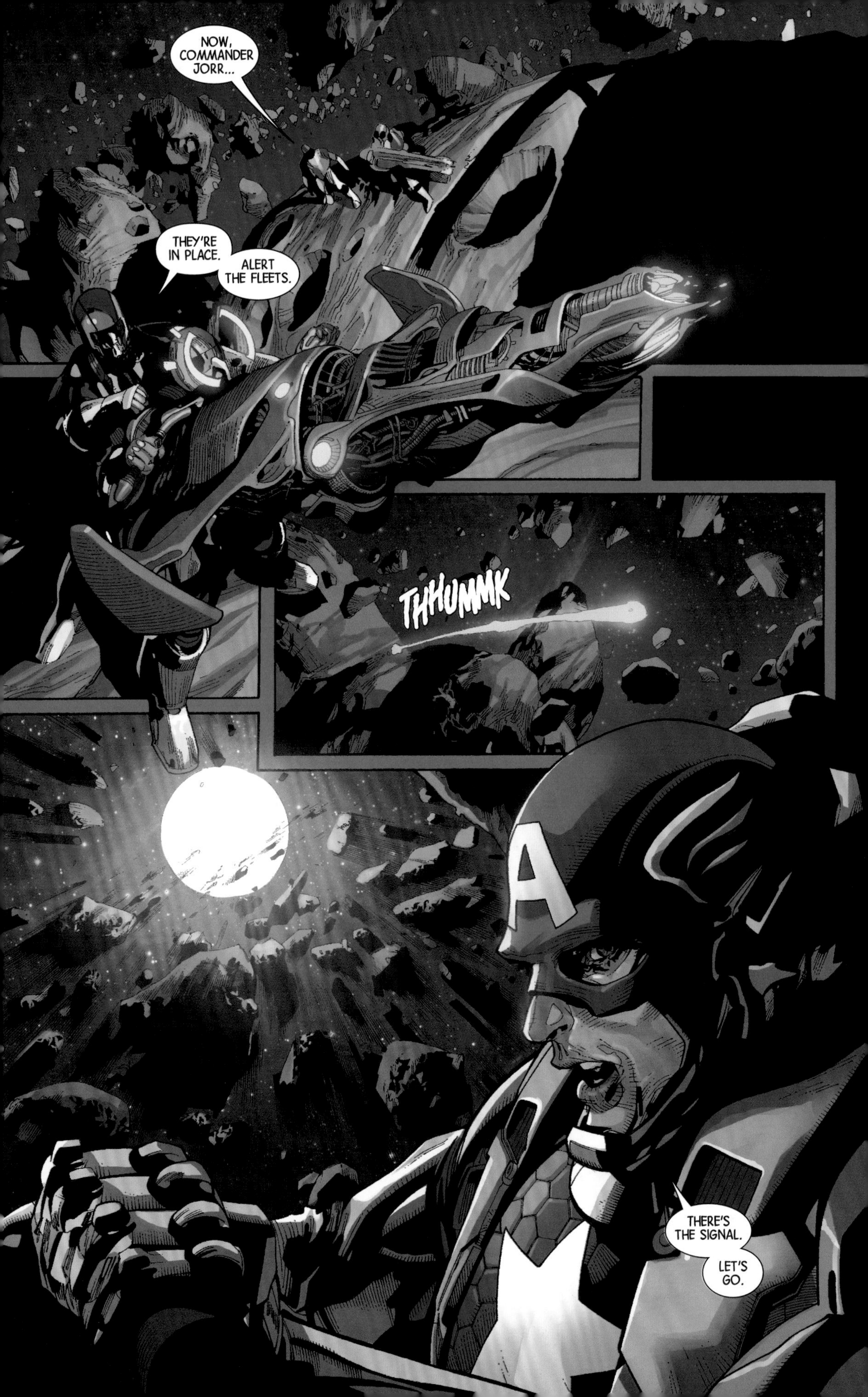
NOW, COMMANDER JORR...
THEY'RE IN PLACE.
ALERT THE FLEETS.
THHUMMK
THERE'S THE SIGNAL.
LET'S GO.

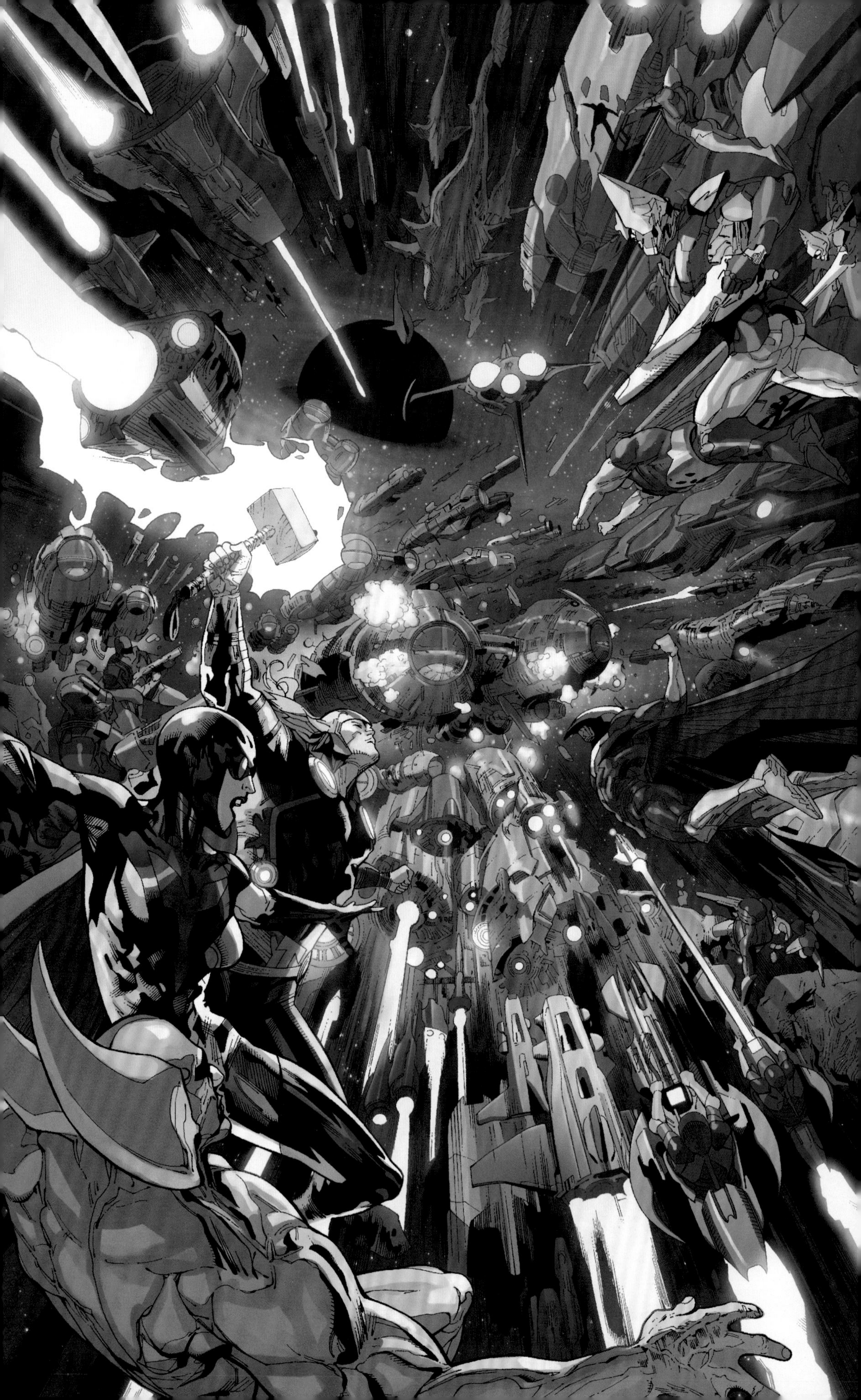

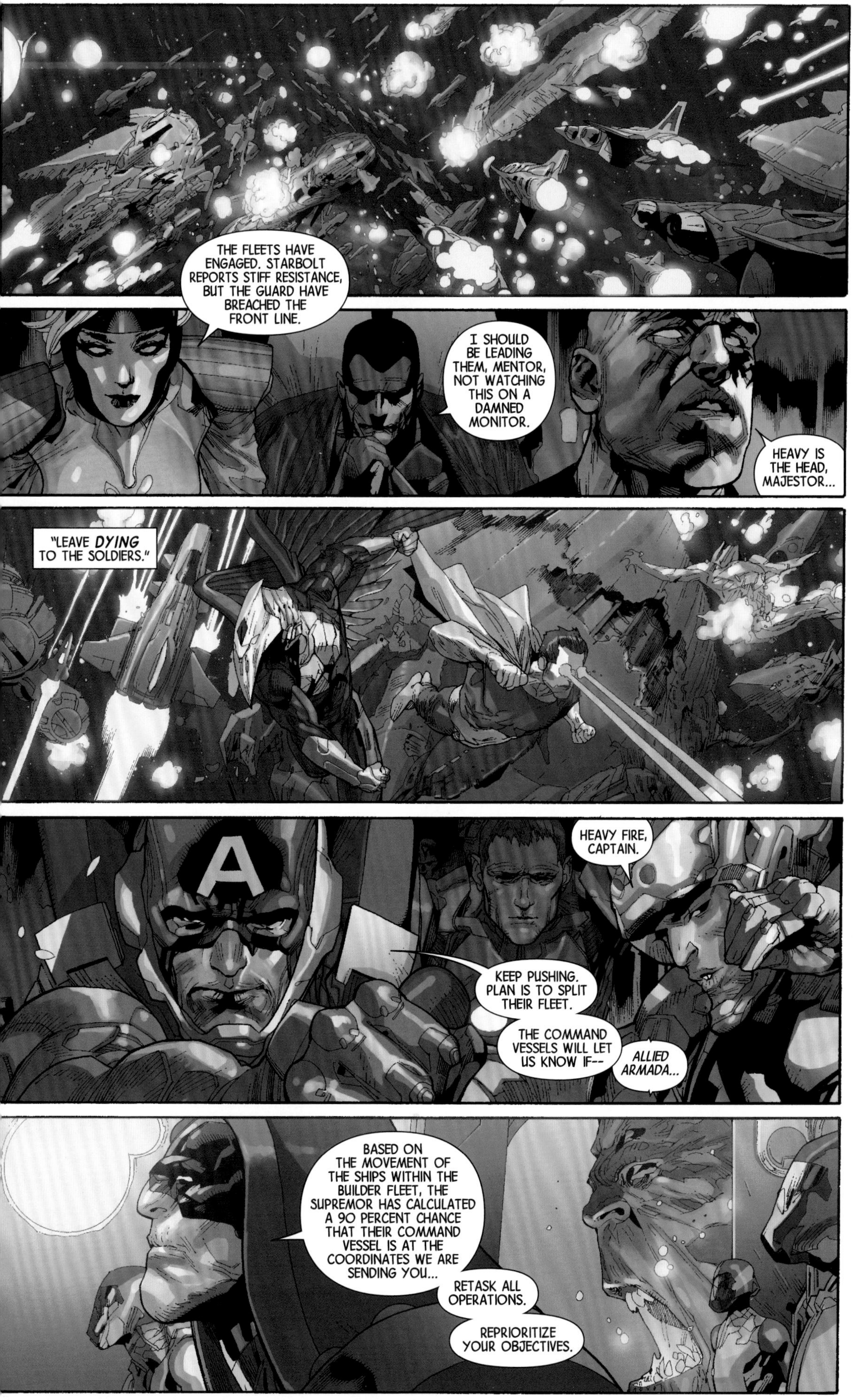
THE FLEETS HAVE ENGAGED. STARBOLT REPORTS STIFF RESISTANCE, BUT THE GUARD HAVE BREACHED THE FRONT LINE.
I SHOULD BE LEADING THEM, MENTOR, NOT WATCHING THIS ON A DAMNED MONITOR.
HEAVY IS THE HEAD, MAJESTOR...
"LEAVE *DYING* TO THE SOLDIERS."
HEAVY FIRE, CAPTAIN.
KEEP PUSHING. PLAN IS TO SPLIT THEIR FLEET.
THE COMMAND VESSELS WILL LET US KNOW IF--
ALLIED ARMADA...
BASED ON THE MOVEMENT OF THE SHIPS WITHIN THE BUILDER FLEET, THE SUPREMOR HAS CALCULATED A 90 PERCENT CHANCE THAT THEIR COMMAND VESSEL IS AT THE COORDINATES WE ARE SENDING YOU...
RETASK ALL OPERATIONS.
REPRIORITIZE YOUR OBJECTIVES.

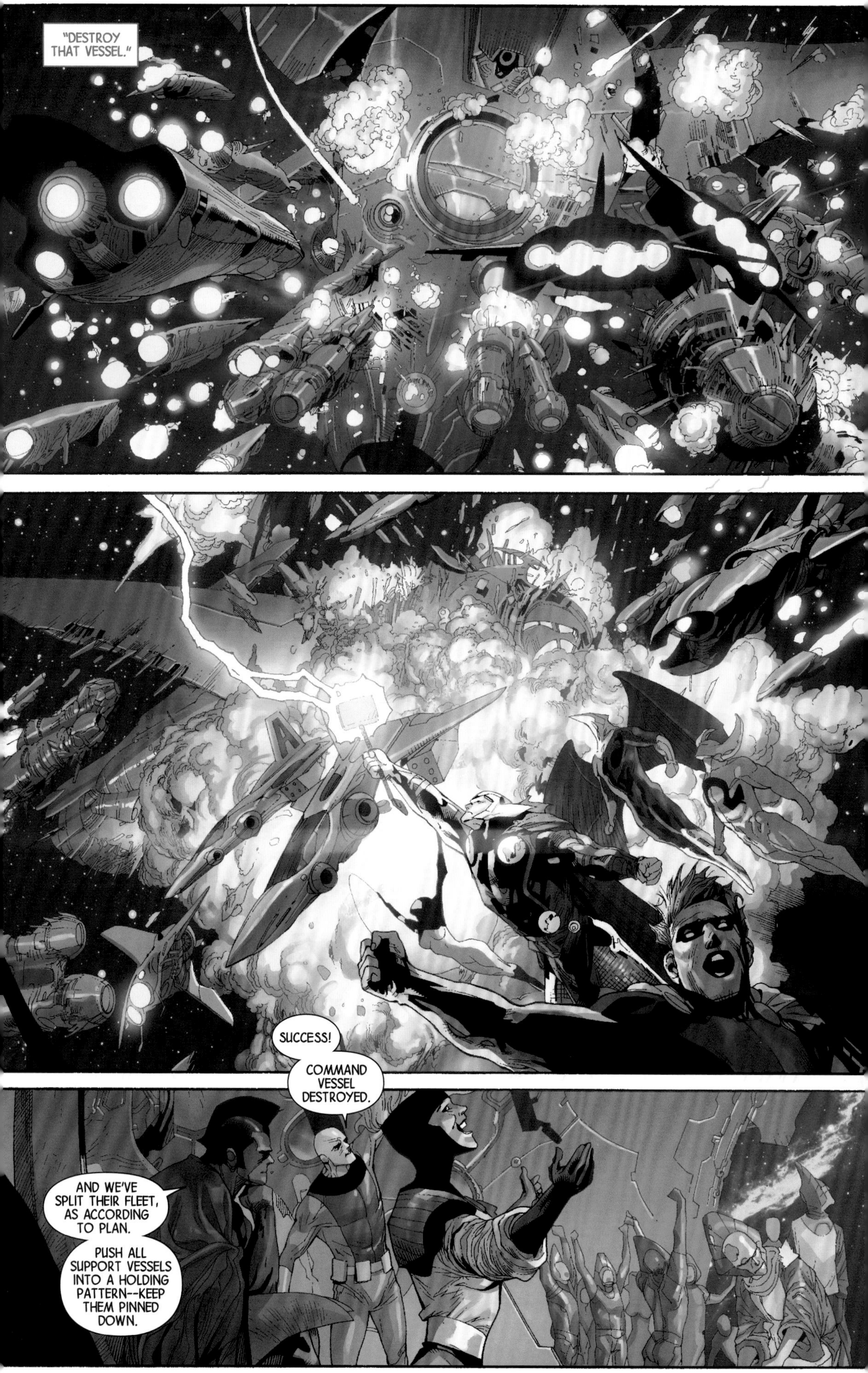
"DESTROY THAT VESSEL."
SUCCESS!
COMMAND VESSEL DESTROYED.
AND WE'VE SPLIT THEIR FLEET, AS ACCORDING TO PLAN.
PUSH ALL SUPPORT VESSELS INTO A HOLDING PATTERN--KEEP THEM PINNED DOWN.

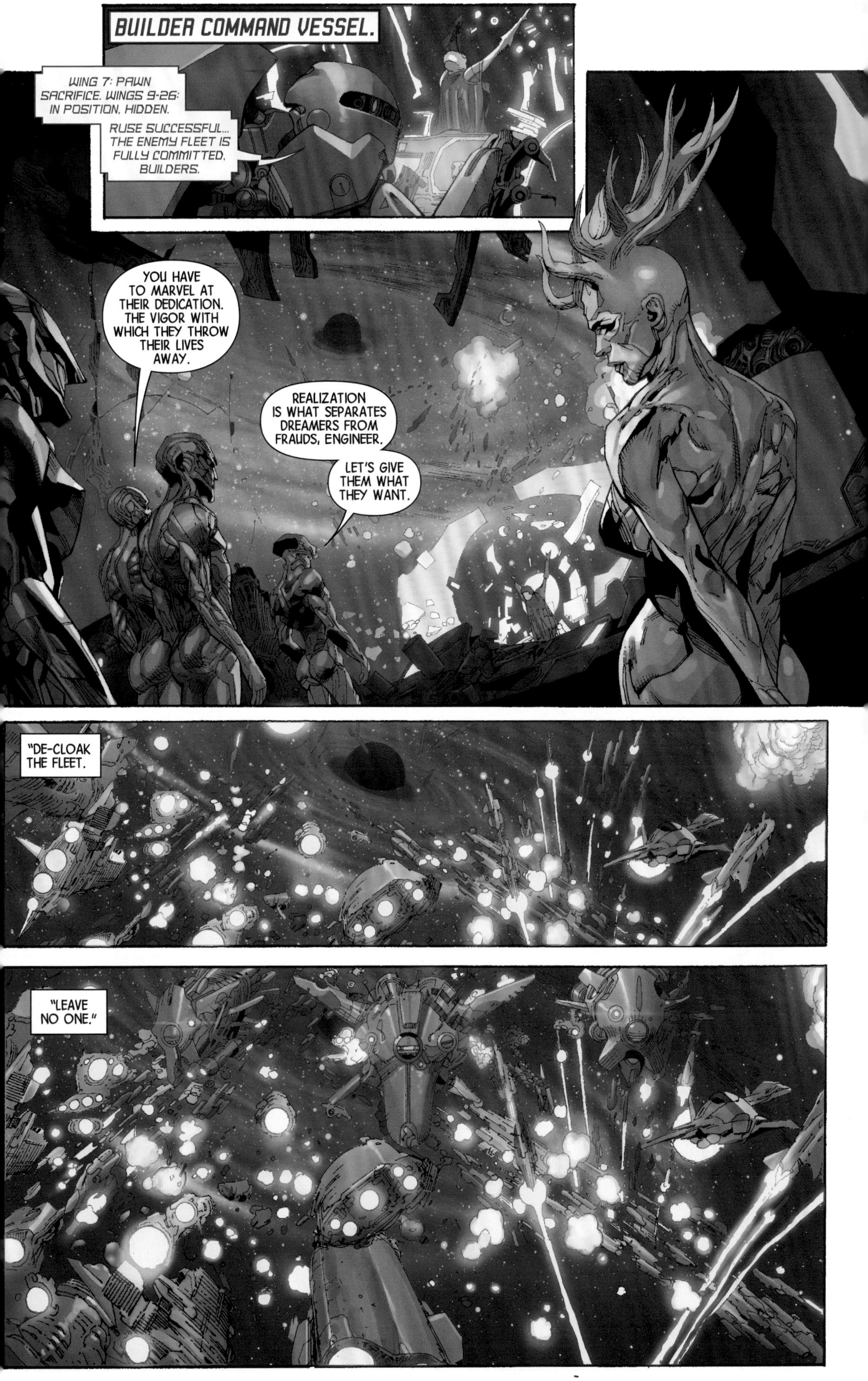
BUILDER COMMAND VESSEL.
WING 7: PAWN SACRIFICE. WINGS 9-26: IN POSITION, HIDDEN.
RUSE SUCCESSFUL... THE ENEMY FLEET IS FULLY COMMITTED, BUILDERS.
YOU HAVE TO MARVEL AT THEIR DEDICATION. THE VIGOR WITH WHICH THEY THROW THEIR LIVES AWAY.
REALIZATION IS WHAT SEPARATES DREAMERS FROM FRAUDS, ENGINEER.
LET'S GIVE THEM WHAT THEY WANT.
"DE-CLOAK THE FLEET.
"LEAVE NO ONE."

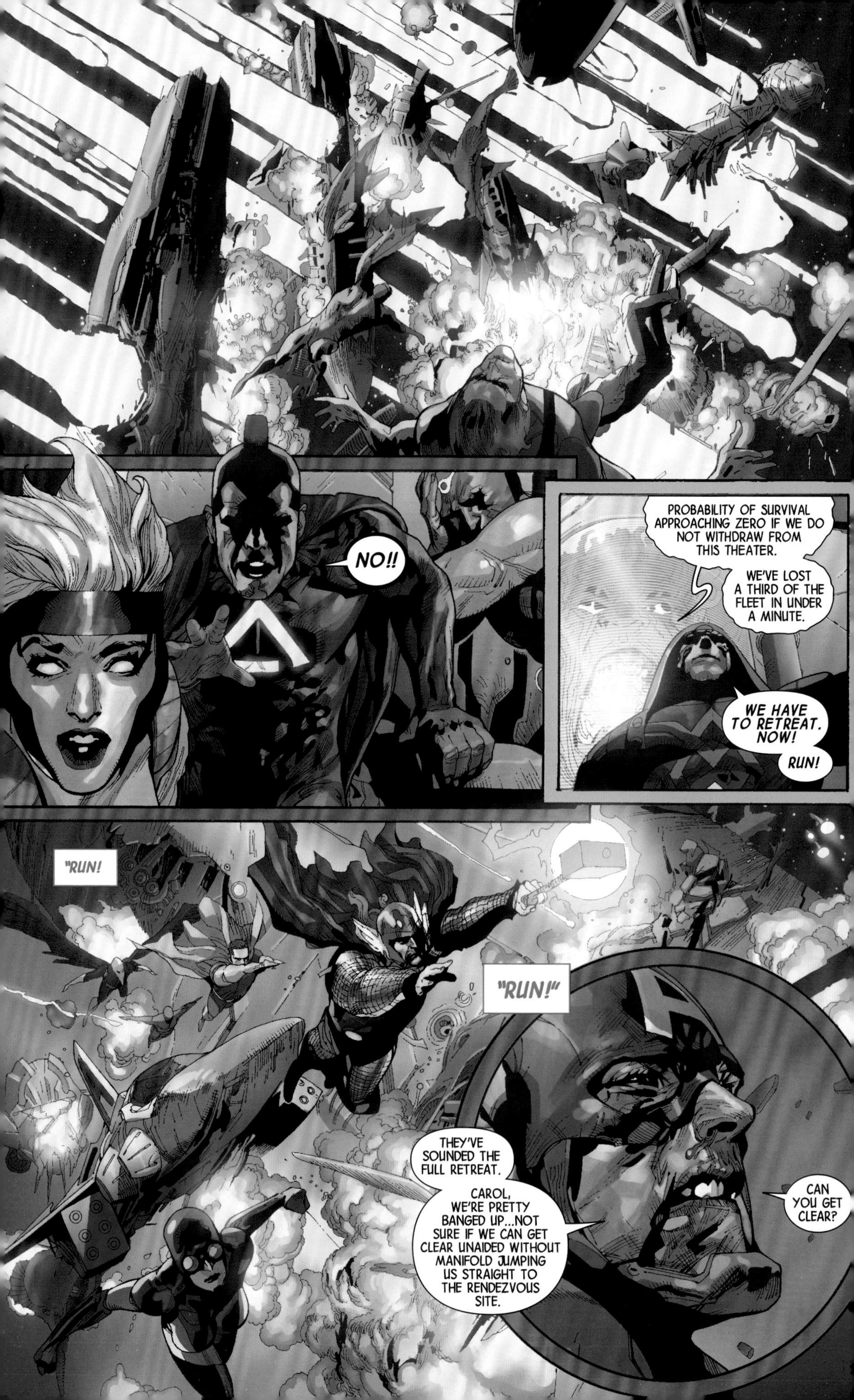
NO!!
PROBABILITY OF SURVIVAL APPROACHING ZERO IF WE DO NOT WITHDRAW FROM THIS THEATER.
WE'VE LOST A THIRD OF THE FLEET IN UNDER A MINUTE.
WE HAVE TO RETREAT. NOW!
RUN!
"RUN!
"RUN!"
THEY'VE SOUNDED THE FULL RETREAT.
CAROL, WE'RE PRETTY BANGED UP...NOT SURE IF WE CAN GET CLEAR UNAIDED WITHOUT MANIFOLD JUMPING US STRAIGHT TO THE RENDEZVOUS SITE.
CAN YOU GET CLEAR?

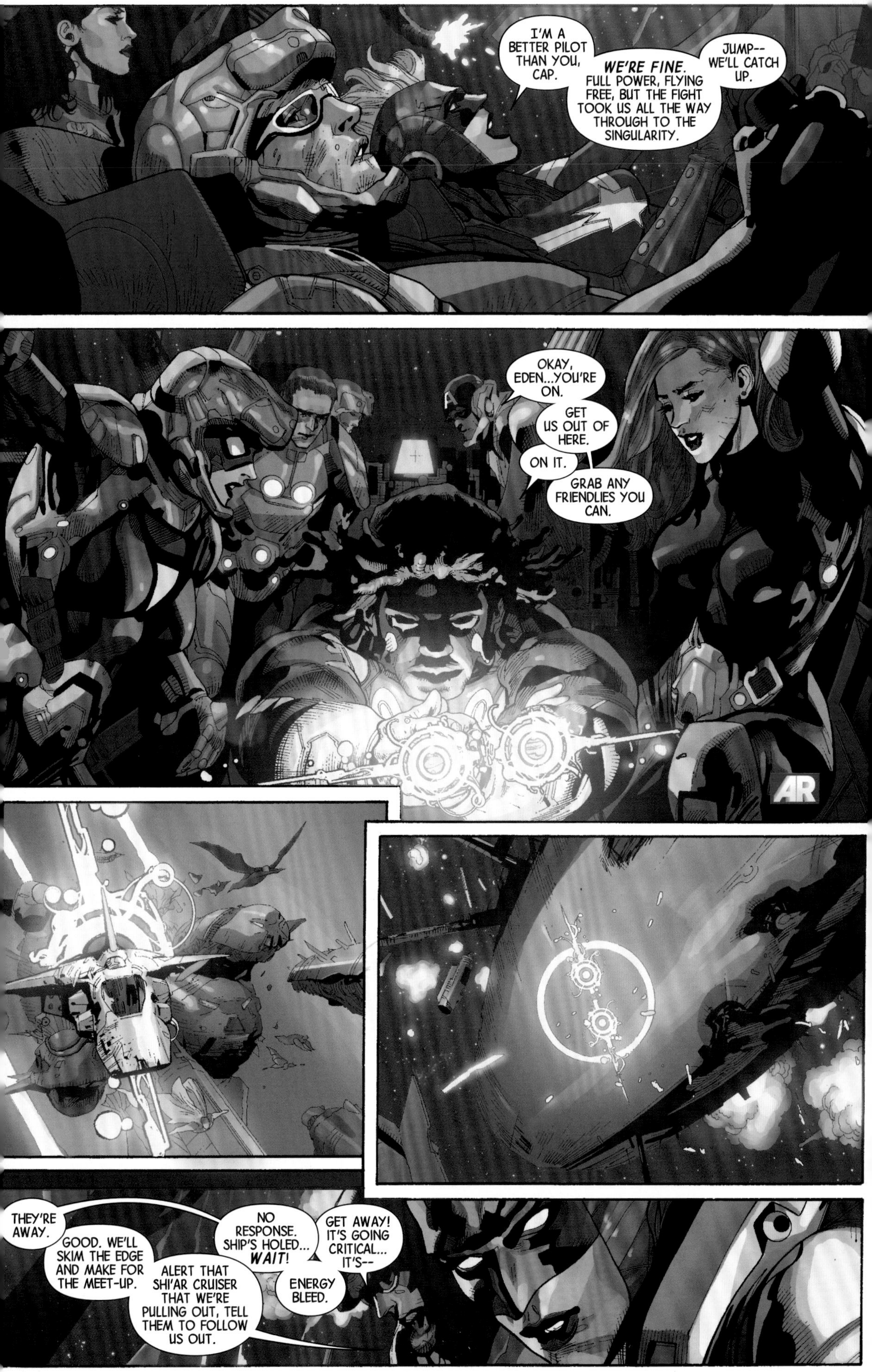
I'M A BETTER PILOT THAN YOU, CAP.
WE'RE FINE. FULL POWER, FLYING FREE, BUT THE FIGHT TOOK US ALL THE WAY THROUGH TO THE SINGULARITY.
JUMP-- WE'LL CATCH UP.
OKAY, EDEN...YOU'RE ON.
GET US OUT OF HERE.
ON IT.
GRAB ANY FRIENDLIES YOU CAN.
THEY'RE AWAY.
GOOD. WE'LL SKIM THE EDGE AND MAKE FOR THE MEET-UP.
ALERT THAT SHI'AR CRUISER THAT WE'RE PULLING OUT, TELL THEM TO FOLLOW US OUT.
NO RESPONSE. SHIP'S HOLED... WAIT!
ENERGY BLEED.
GET AWAY! IT'S GOING CRITICAL... IT'S--

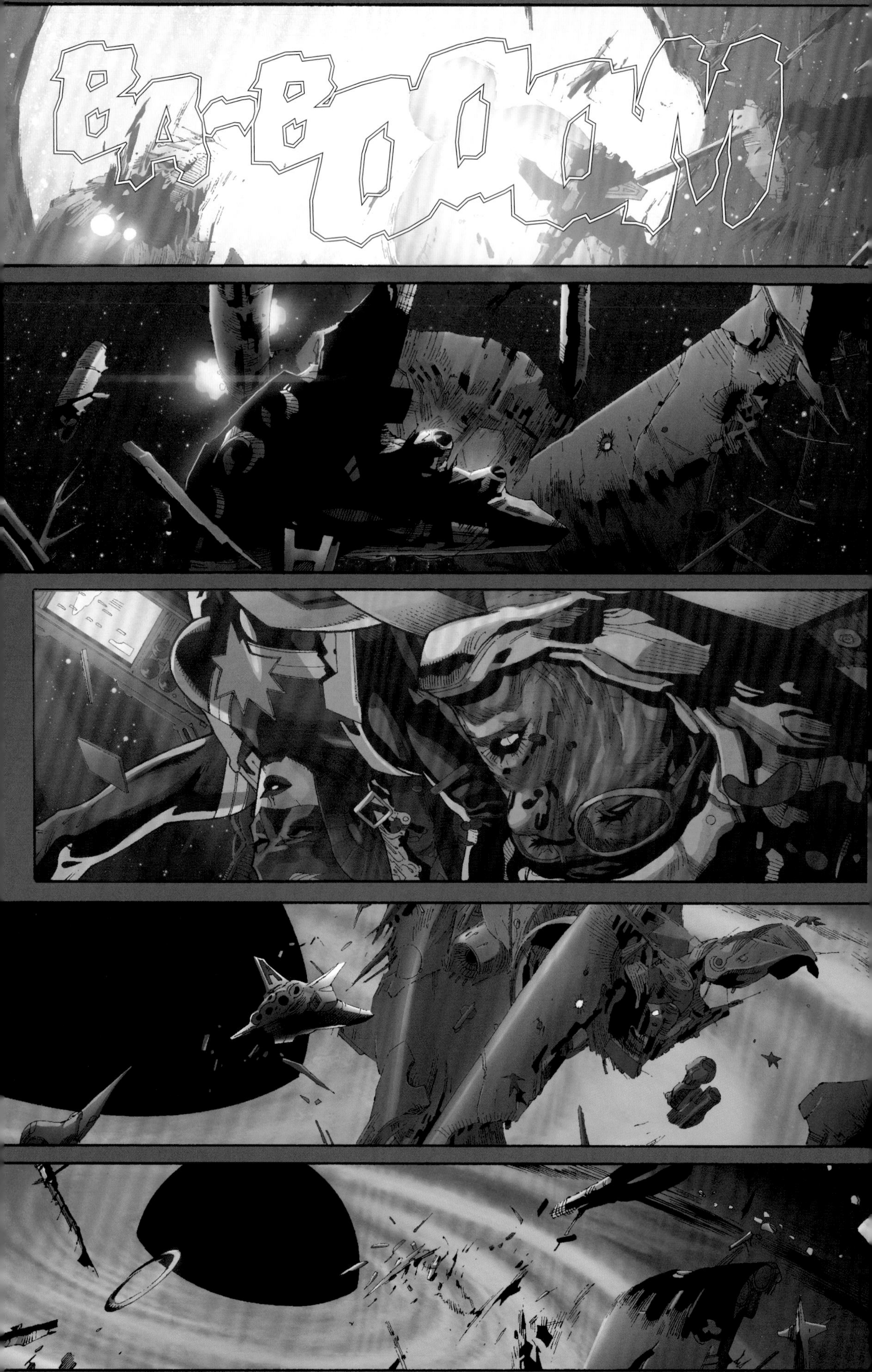
BA-BOOM

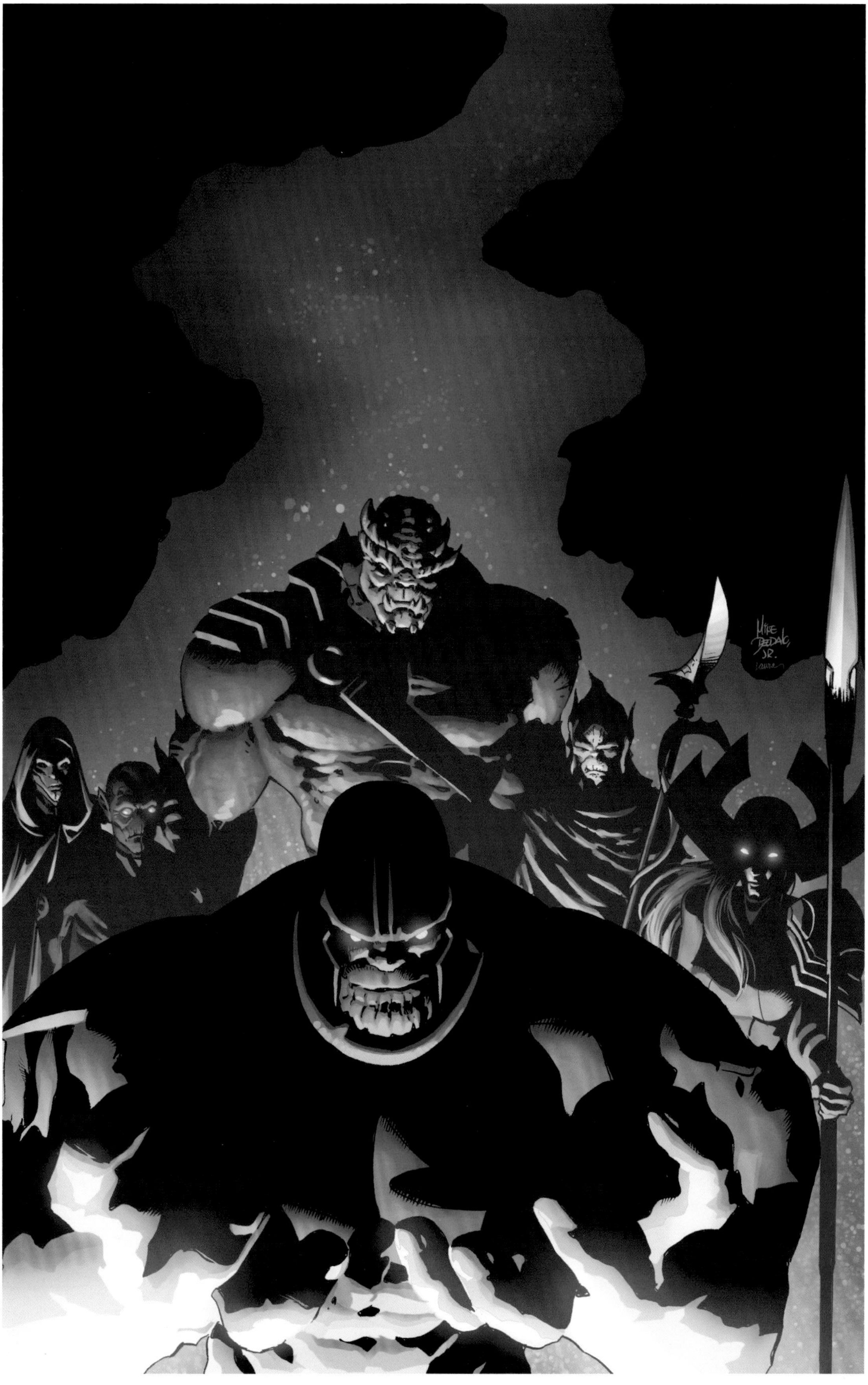

THE STONES,
SHATTERED

◆

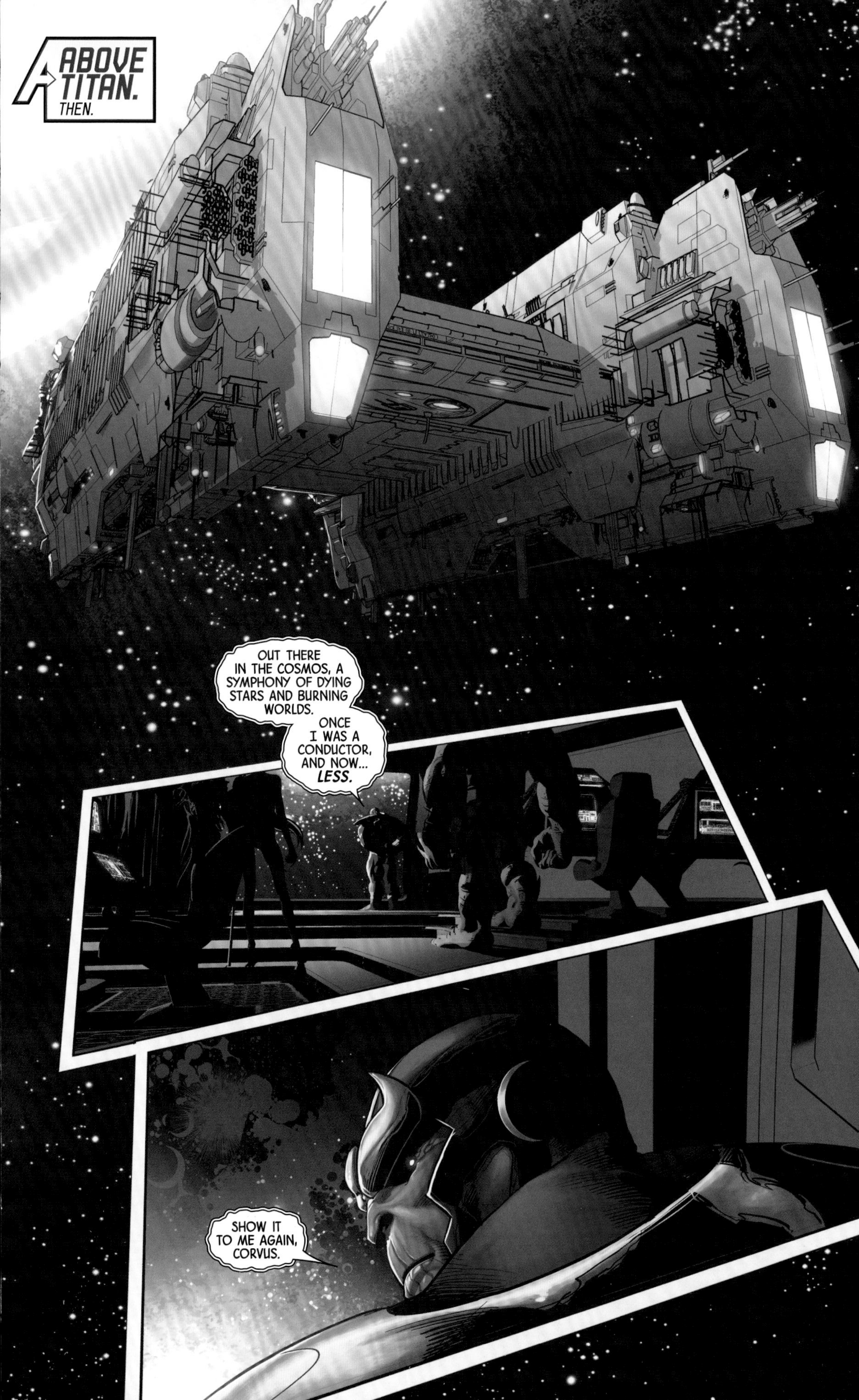
ABOVE TITAN.
THEN.
OUT THERE IN THE COSMOS, A SYMPHONY OF DYING STARS AND BURNING WORLDS.
ONCE I WAS A CONDUCTOR, AND NOW... LESS.
SHOW IT TO ME AGAIN, CORVUS.

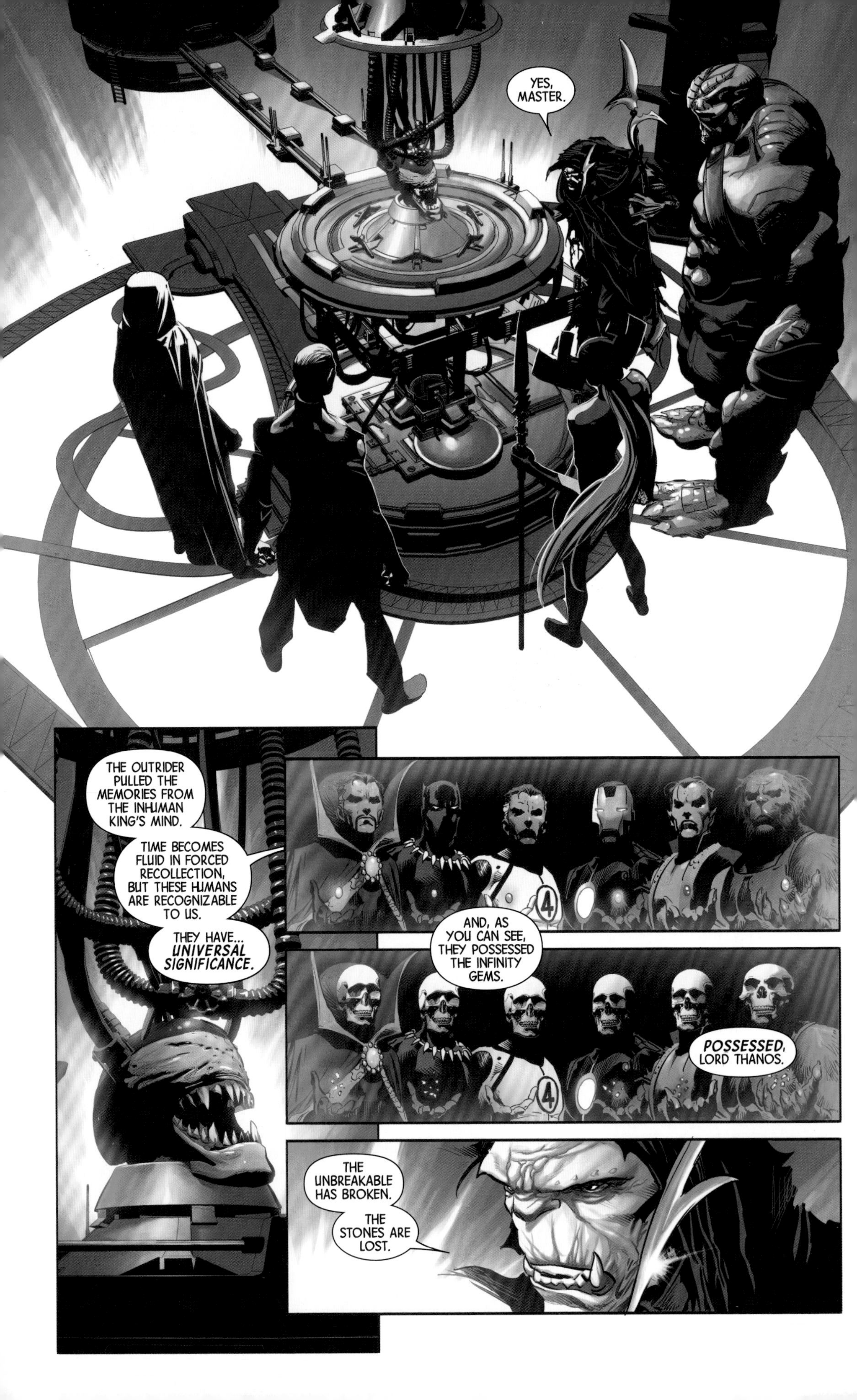
YES, MASTER.
THE OUTRIDER PULLED THE MEMORIES FROM THE INHUMAN KING'S MIND.
TIME BECOMES FLUID IN FORCED RECOLLECTION, BUT THESE HUMANS ARE RECOGNIZABLE TO US.
THEY HAVE... ***UNIVERSAL SIGNIFICANCE.***
AND, AS YOU CAN SEE, THEY POSSESSED THE INFINITY GEMS.
POSSESSED, LORD THANOS.
THE UNBREAKABLE HAS BROKEN.
THE STONES ARE LOST.

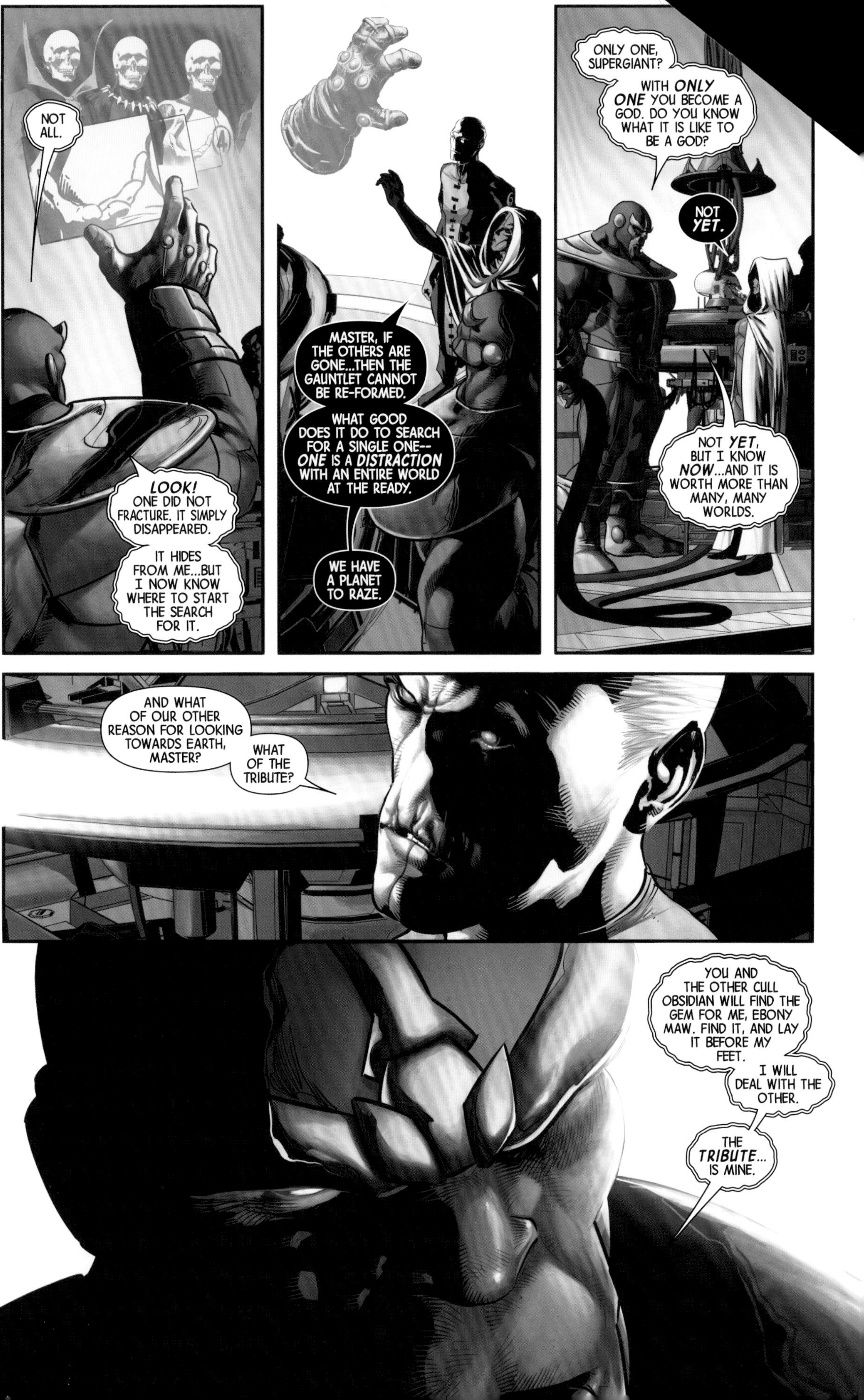
NOT ALL.
LOOK! ONE DID NOT FRACTURE. IT SIMPLY DISAPPEARED.
IT HIDES FROM ME...BUT I NOW KNOW WHERE TO START THE SEARCH FOR IT.
MASTER, IF THE OTHERS ARE GONE...THEN THE GAUNTLET CANNOT BE RE-FORMED.
WHAT GOOD DOES IT DO TO SEARCH FOR A SINGLE ONE--ONE IS A DISTRACTION WITH AN ENTIRE WORLD AT THE READY.
WE HAVE A PLANET TO RAZE.
ONLY ONE, SUPERGIANT?
WITH ONLY ONE YOU BECOME A GOD. DO YOU KNOW WHAT IT IS LIKE TO BE A GOD?
NOT YET.
NOT YET, BUT I KNOW NOW...AND IT IS WORTH MORE THAN MANY, MANY WORLDS.
AND WHAT OF OUR OTHER REASON FOR LOOKING TOWARDS EARTH, MASTER?
WHAT OF THE TRIBUTE?
YOU AND THE OTHER CULL OBSIDIAN WILL FIND THE GEM FOR ME, EBONY MAW. FIND IT, AND LAY IT BEFORE MY FEET.
I WILL DEAL WITH THE OTHER.
THE TRIBUTE... IS MINE.

THE CULL OBSIDIAN

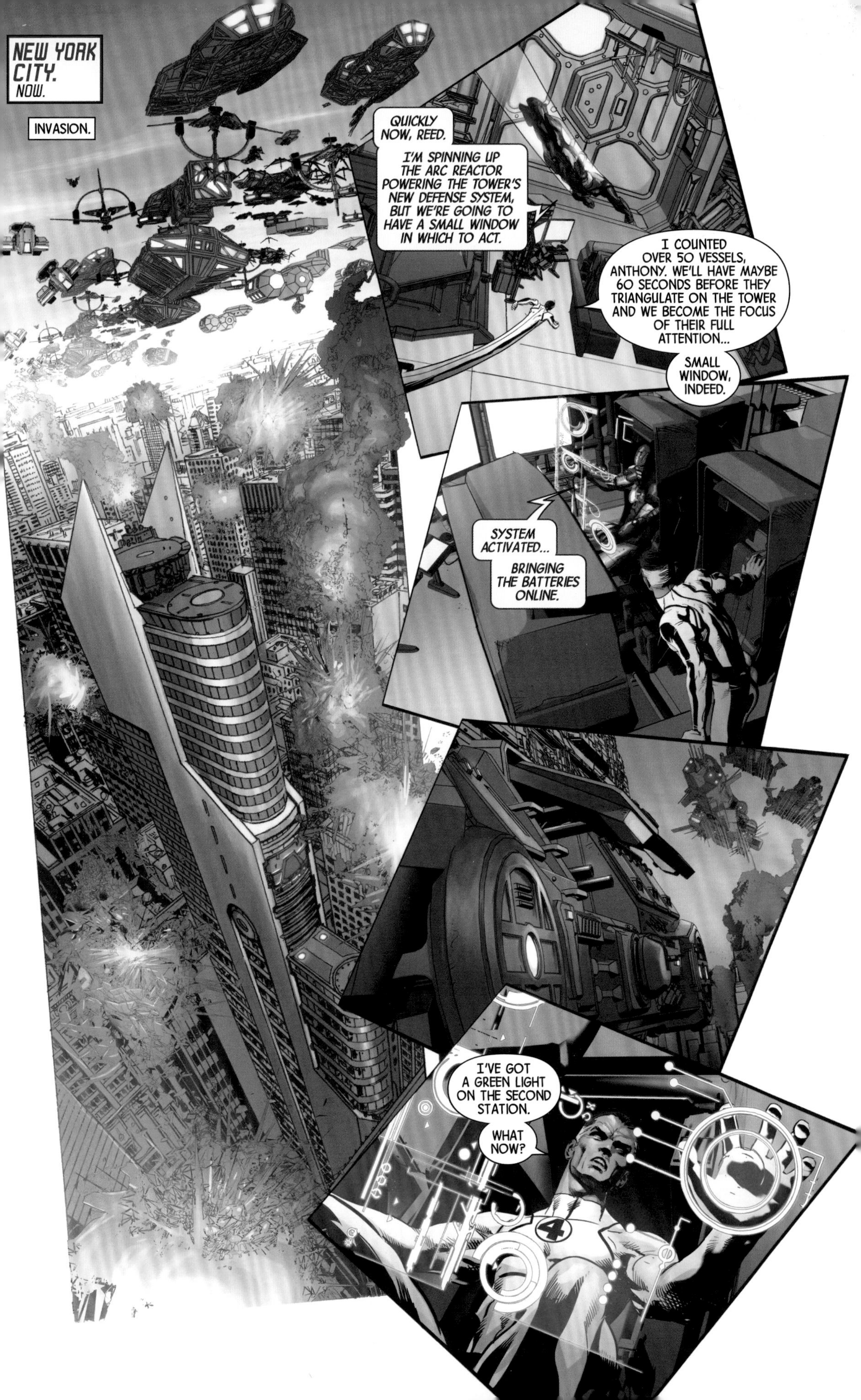
NEW YORK CITY. NOW.
INVASION.
QUICKLY NOW, REED.
I'M SPINNING UP THE ARC REACTOR POWERING THE TOWER'S NEW DEFENSE SYSTEM, BUT WE'RE GOING TO HAVE A SMALL WINDOW IN WHICH TO ACT.
I COUNTED OVER 50 VESSELS, ANTHONY. WE'LL HAVE MAYBE 60 SECONDS BEFORE THEY TRIANGULATE ON THE TOWER AND WE BECOME THE FOCUS OF THEIR FULL ATTENTION...
SMALL WINDOW, INDEED.
SYSTEM ACTIVATED...
BRINGING THE BATTERIES ONLINE.
I'VE GOT A GREEN LIGHT ON THE SECOND STATION.
WHAT NOW?

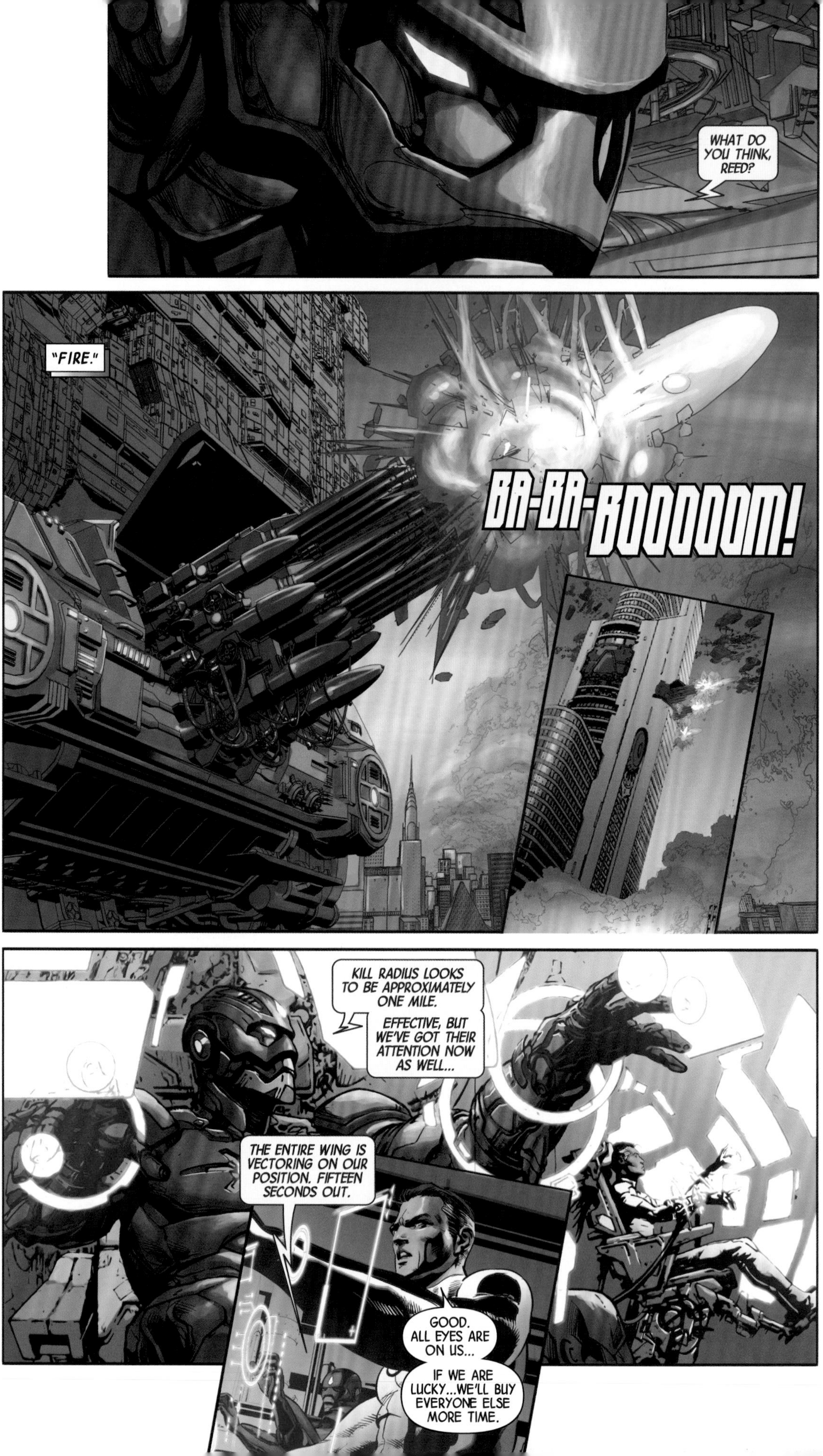
WHAT DO YOU THINK, REED?
"FIRE."
BA-BA-BOOOOOM!
KILL RADIUS LOOKS TO BE APPROXIMATELY ONE MILE.
EFFECTIVE, BUT WE'VE GOT THEIR ATTENTION NOW AS WELL...
THE ENTIRE WING IS VECTORING ON OUR POSITION. FIFTEEN SECONDS OUT.
GOOD. ALL EYES ARE ON US...
IF WE ARE LUCKY...WE'LL BUY EVERYONE ELSE MORE TIME.

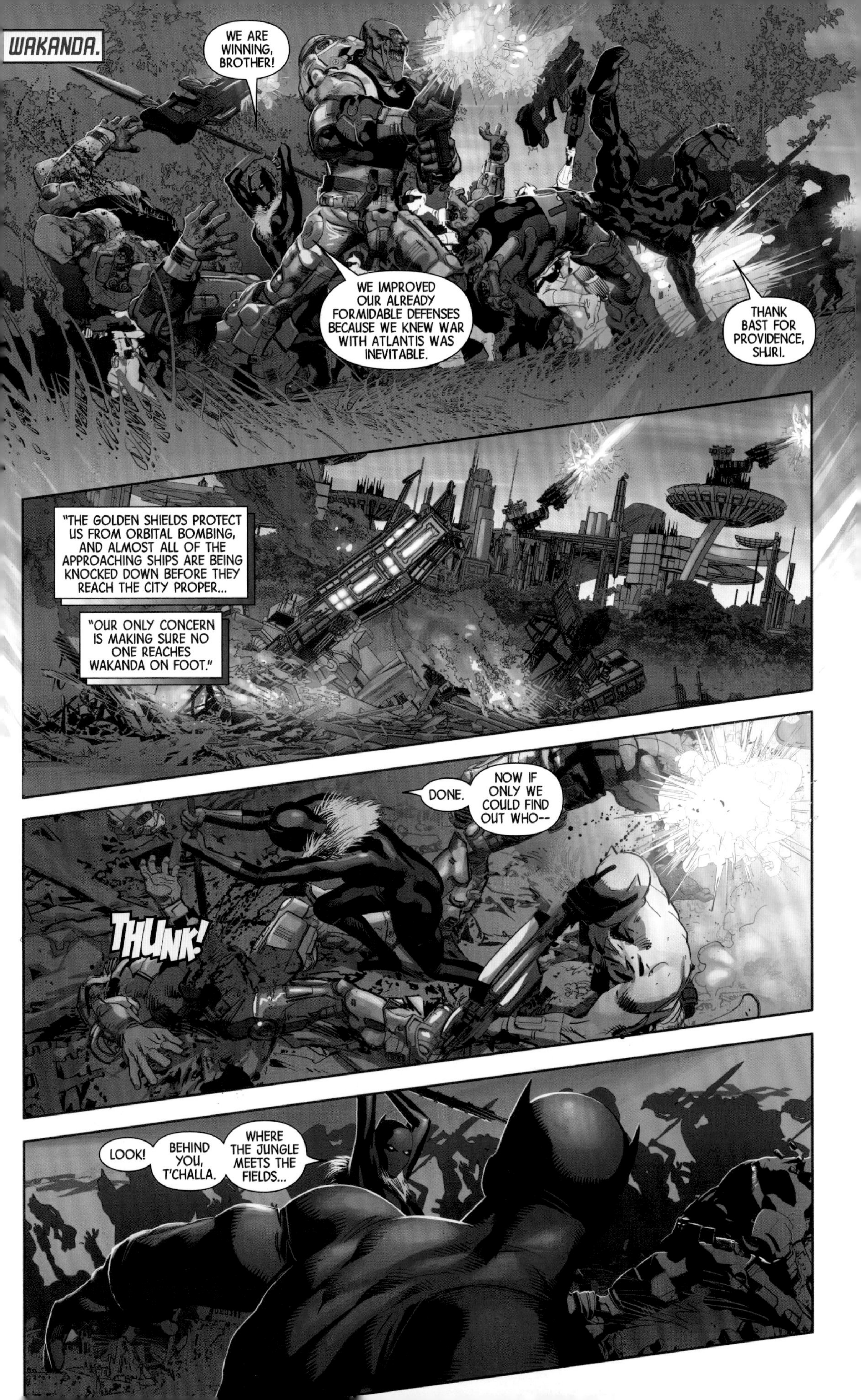
WAKANDA.
WE ARE WINNING, BROTHER!
WE IMPROVED OUR ALREADY FORMIDABLE DEFENSES BECAUSE WE KNEW WAR WITH ATLANTIS WAS INEVITABLE.
THANK BAST FOR PROVIDENCE, SHURI.
"THE GOLDEN SHIELDS PROTECT US FROM ORBITAL BOMBING, AND ALMOST ALL OF THE APPROACHING SHIPS ARE BEING KNOCKED DOWN BEFORE THEY REACH THE CITY PROPER...
"OUR ONLY CONCERN IS MAKING SURE NO ONE REACHES WAKANDA ON FOOT."
DONE.
NOW IF ONLY WE COULD FIND OUT WHO--
THUNK!
LOOK!
BEHIND YOU, T'CHALLA.
WHERE THE JUNGLE MEETS THE FIELDS...

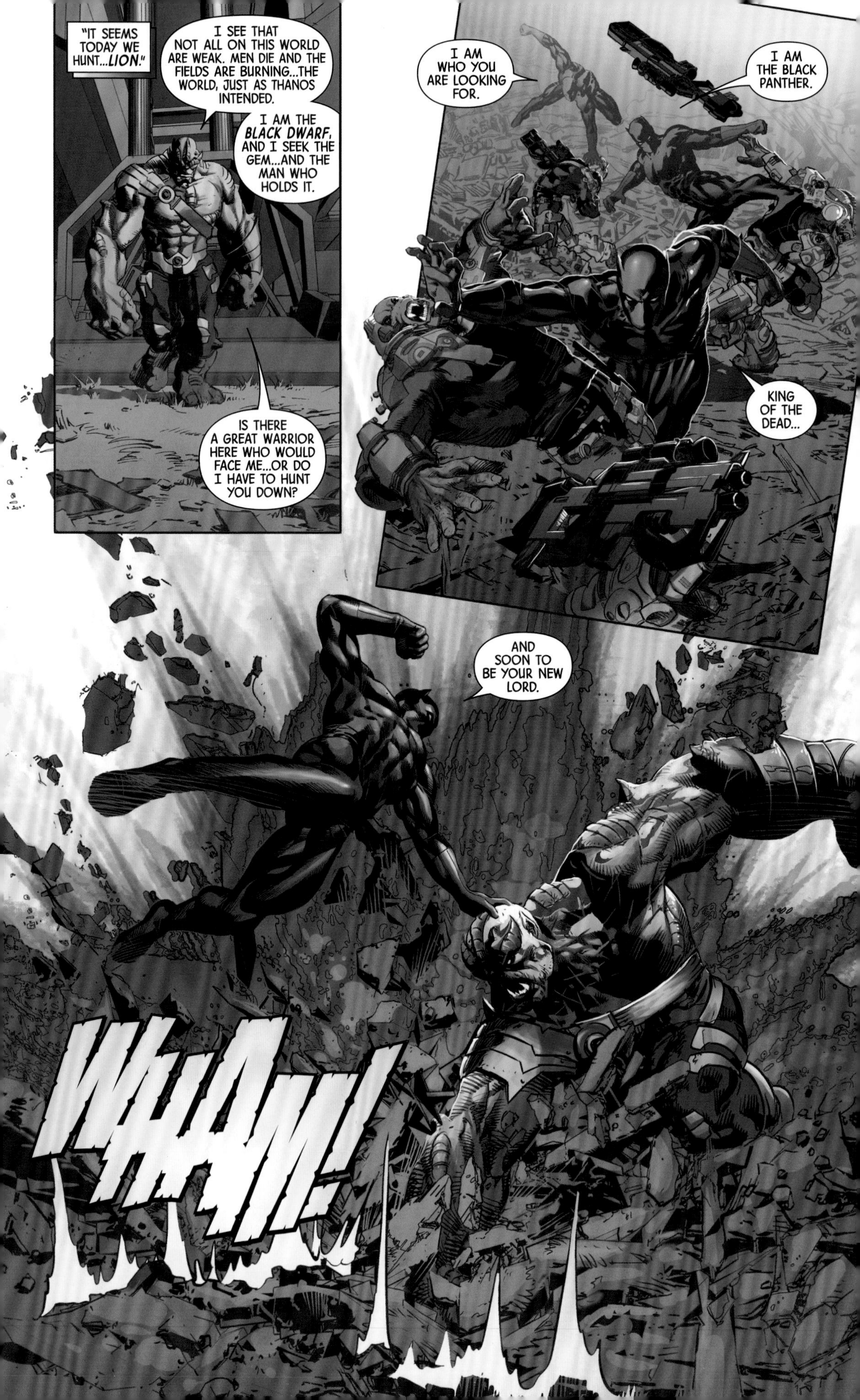
"IT SEEMS TODAY WE HUNT...LION."
I SEE THAT NOT ALL ON THIS WORLD ARE WEAK. MEN DIE AND THE FIELDS ARE BURNING...THE WORLD, JUST AS THANOS INTENDED.
I AM THE BLACK DWARF, AND I SEEK THE GEM...AND THE MAN WHO HOLDS IT.
IS THERE A GREAT WARRIOR HERE WHO WOULD FACE ME...OR DO I HAVE TO HUNT YOU DOWN?
I AM WHO YOU ARE LOOKING FOR.
I AM THE BLACK PANTHER.
KING OF THE DEAD...
AND SOON TO BE YOUR NEW LORD.
WHAM!

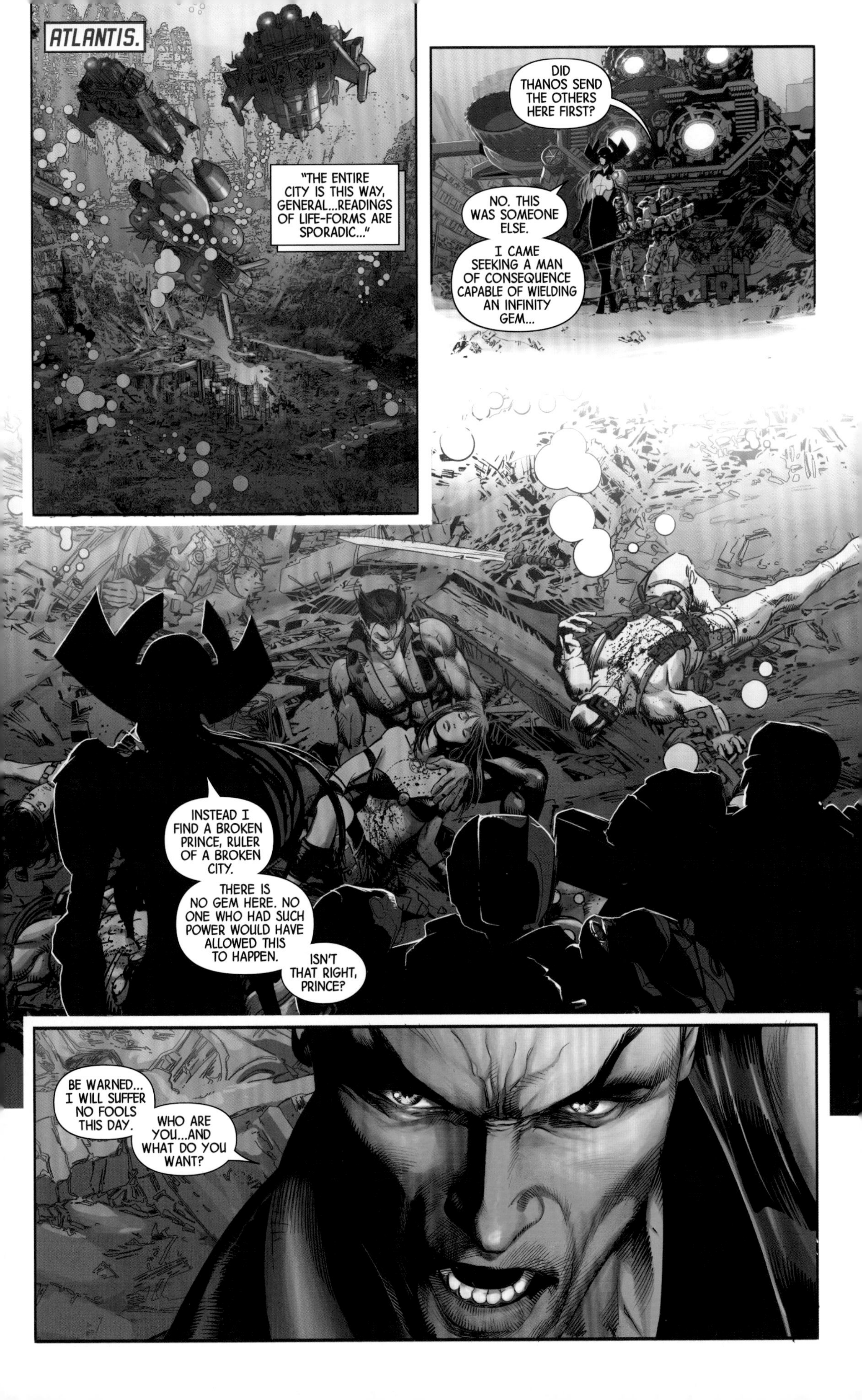
ATLANTIS.
"THE ENTIRE CITY IS THIS WAY, GENERAL...READINGS OF LIFE-FORMS ARE SPORADIC..."
DID THANOS SEND THE OTHERS HERE FIRST?
NO. THIS WAS SOMEONE ELSE.
I CAME SEEKING A MAN OF CONSEQUENCE CAPABLE OF WIELDING AN INFINITY GEM...
INSTEAD I FIND A BROKEN PRINCE, RULER OF A BROKEN CITY.
THERE IS NO GEM HERE. NO ONE WHO HAD SUCH POWER WOULD HAVE ALLOWED THIS TO HAPPEN.
ISN'T THAT RIGHT, PRINCE?
BE WARNED... I WILL SUFFER NO FOOLS THIS DAY.
WHO ARE YOU...AND WHAT DO YOU WANT?

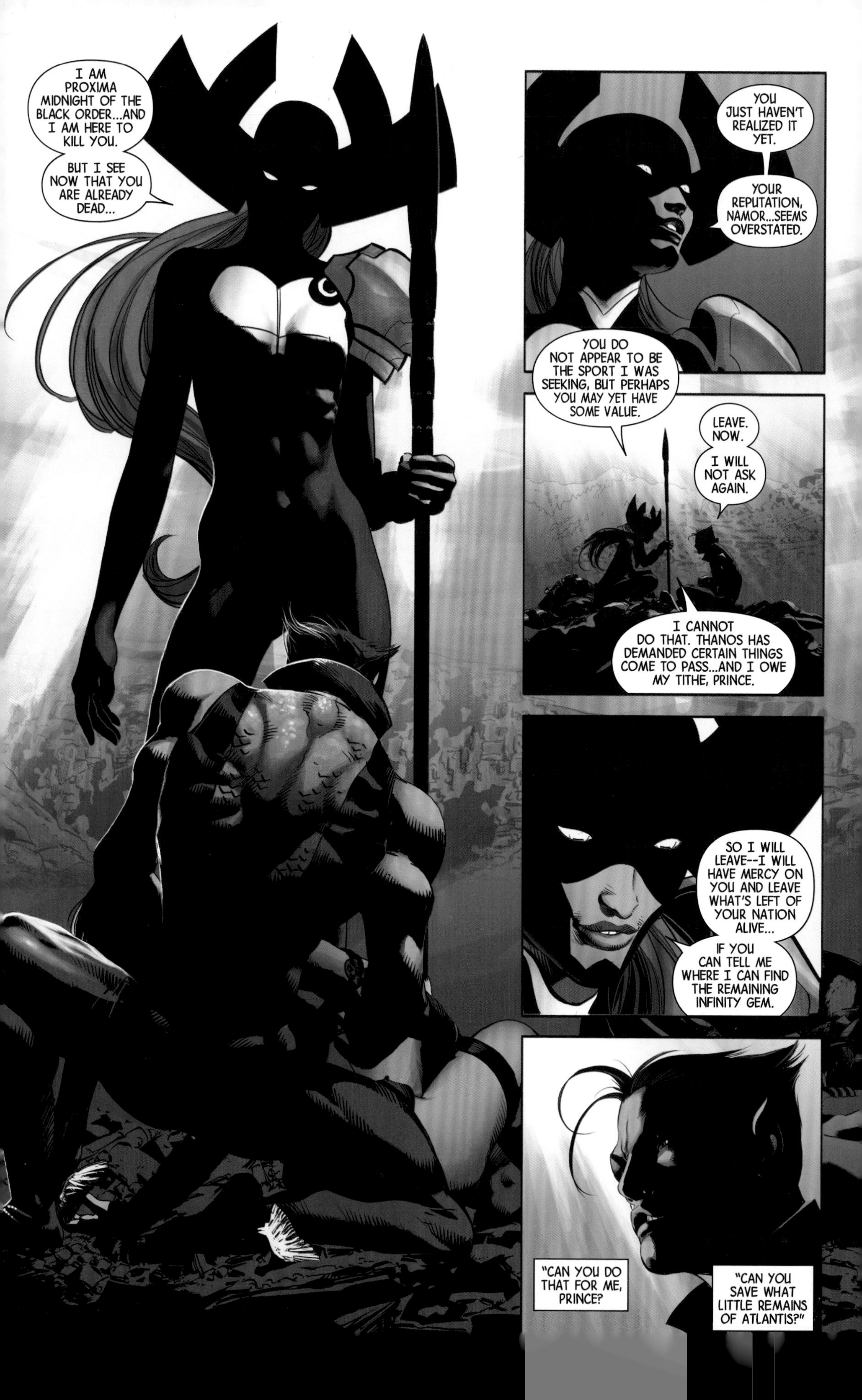
I AM PROXIMA MIDNIGHT OF THE BLACK ORDER...AND I AM HERE TO KILL YOU.
BUT I SEE NOW THAT YOU ARE ALREADY DEAD...
YOU JUST HAVEN'T REALIZED IT YET.
YOUR REPUTATION, NAMOR...SEEMS OVERSTATED.
YOU DO NOT APPEAR TO BE THE SPORT I WAS SEEKING, BUT PERHAPS YOU MAY YET HAVE SOME VALUE.
LEAVE. NOW.
I WILL NOT ASK AGAIN.
I CANNOT DO THAT. THANOS HAS DEMANDED CERTAIN THINGS COME TO PASS...AND I OWE MY TITHE, PRINCE.
SO I WILL LEAVE--I WILL HAVE MERCY ON YOU AND LEAVE WHAT'S LEFT OF YOUR NATION ALIVE...
IF YOU CAN TELL ME WHERE I CAN FIND THE REMAINING INFINITY GEM.
"CAN YOU DO THAT FOR ME, PRINCE?
"CAN YOU SAVE WHAT LITTLE REMAINS OF ATLANTIS?"

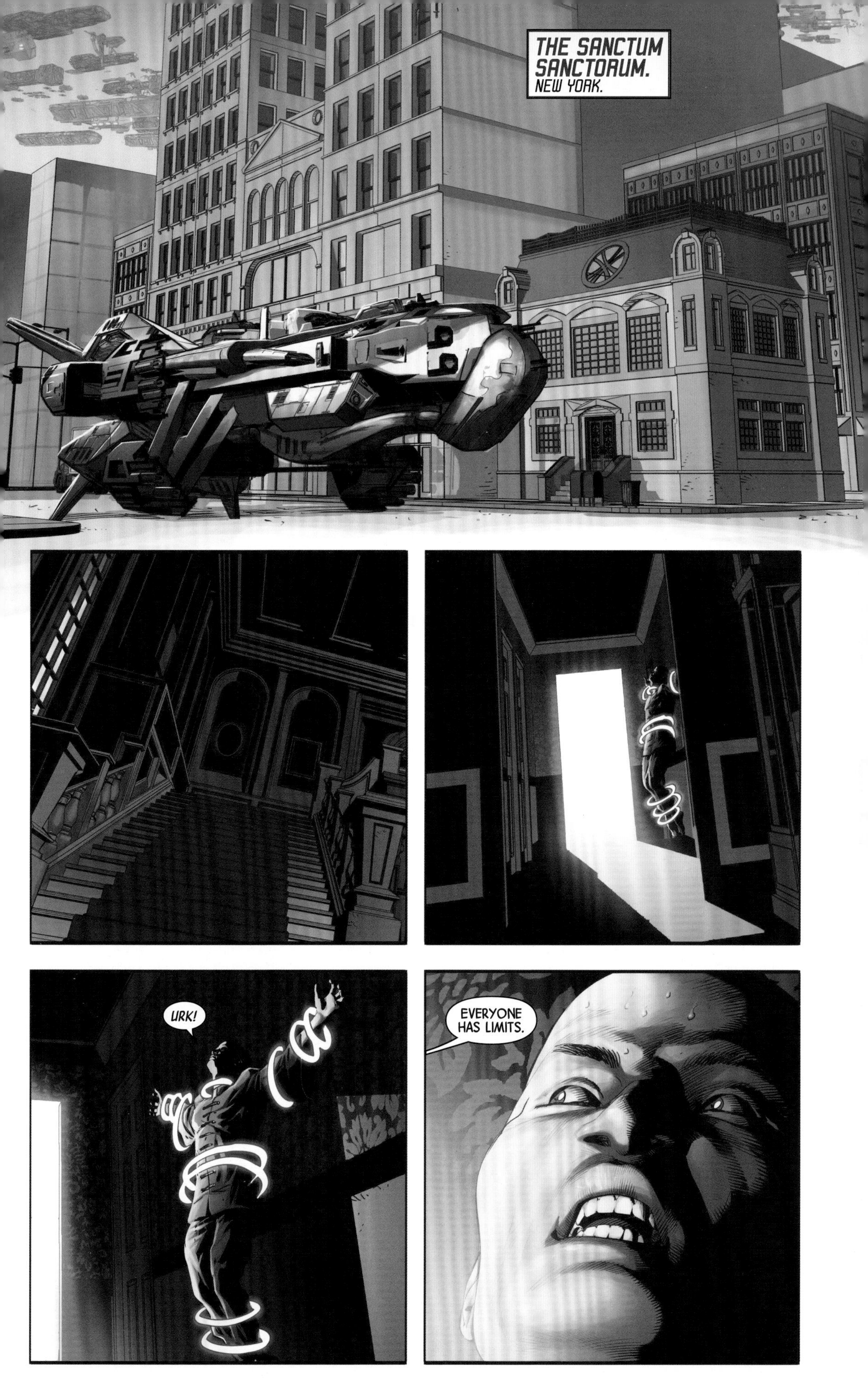
THE SANCTUM SANCTORUM.
NEW YORK.
URK!
EVERYONE HAS LIMITS.

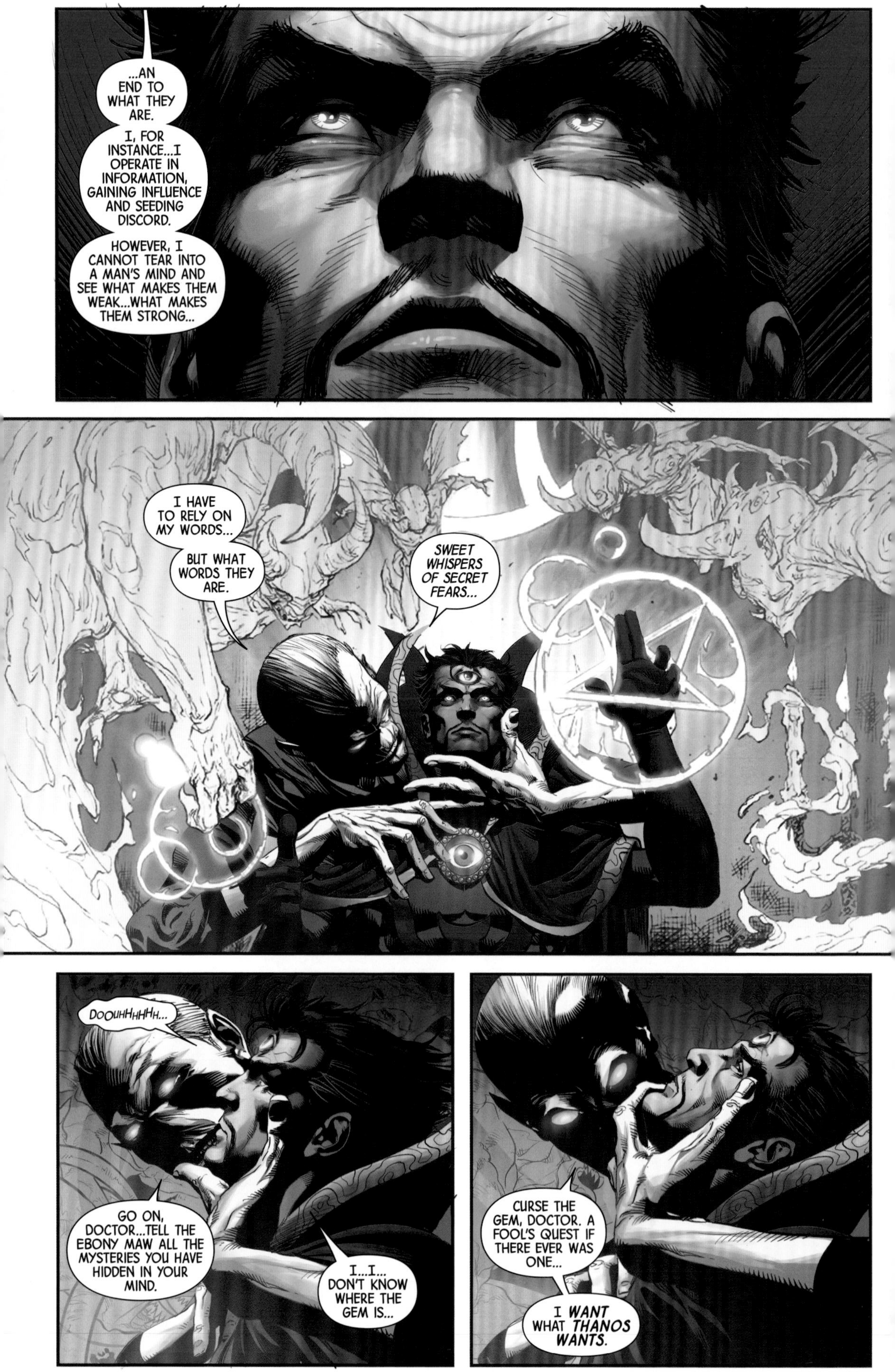
...AN END TO WHAT THEY ARE.
I, FOR INSTANCE...I OPERATE IN INFORMATION, GAINING INFLUENCE AND SEEDING DISCORD.
HOWEVER, I CANNOT TEAR INTO A MAN'S MIND AND SEE WHAT MAKES THEM WEAK...WHAT MAKES THEM STRONG...
I HAVE TO RELY ON MY WORDS...
BUT WHAT WORDS THEY ARE.
SWEET WHISPERS OF SECRET FEARS...
DOOUHHHHHH...
GO ON, DOCTOR...TELL THE EBONY MAW ALL THE MYSTERIES YOU HAVE HIDDEN IN YOUR MIND.
I...I... DON'T KNOW WHERE THE GEM IS...
CURSE THE GEM, DOCTOR. A FOOL'S QUEST IF THERE EVER WAS ONE...
I WANT WHAT THANOS WANTS.

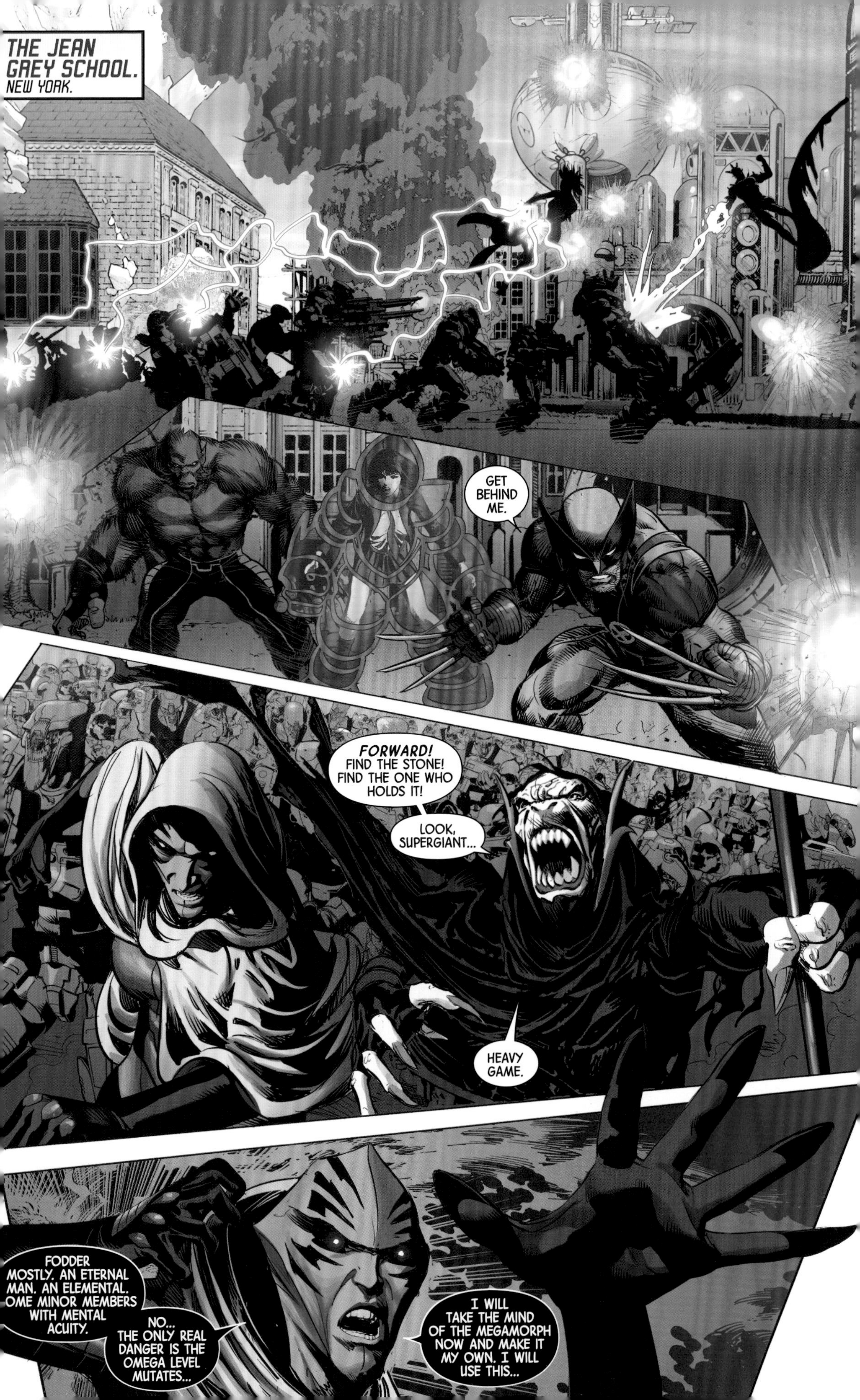
THE JEAN GREY SCHOOL. NEW YORK.
GET BEHIND ME.
FORWARD! FIND THE STONE! FIND THE ONE WHO HOLDS IT!
LOOK, SUPERGIANT...
HEAVY GAME.
FODDER MOSTLY. AN ETERNAL MAN. AN ELEMENTAL. OME MINOR MEMBERS WITH MENTAL ACUITY.
NO... THE ONLY REAL DANGER IS THE OMEGA LEVEL MUTATES...
I WILL TAKE THE MIND OF THE MEGAMORPH NOW AND MAKE IT MY OWN. I WILL USE THIS...

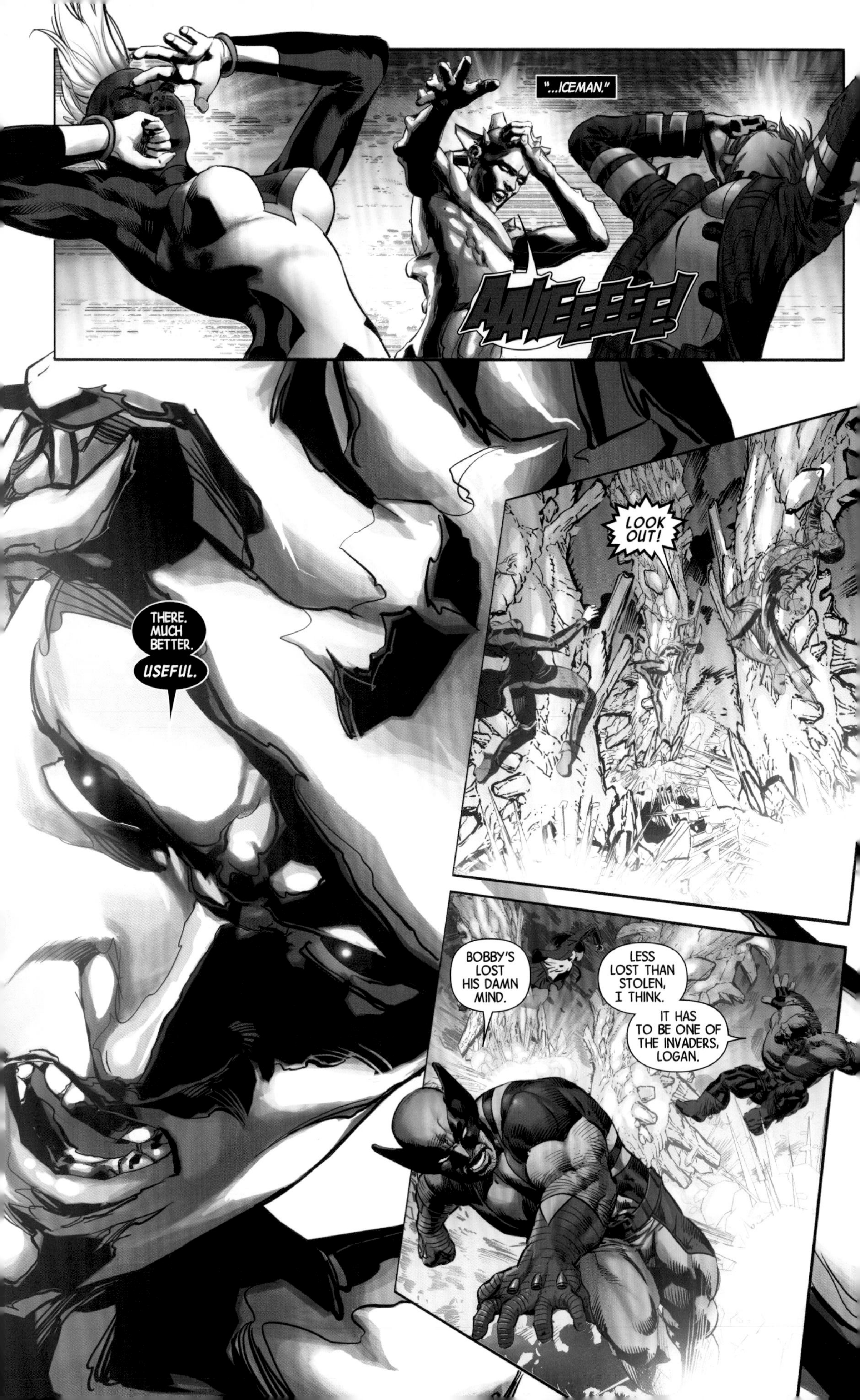
"...ICEMAN."
AAIIEEEEEE!
THERE. MUCH BETTER.
USEFUL.
LOOK OUT!
BOBBY'S LOST HIS DAMN MIND.
LESS LOST THAN STOLEN, I THINK.
IT HAS TO BE ONE OF THE INVADERS, LOGAN.

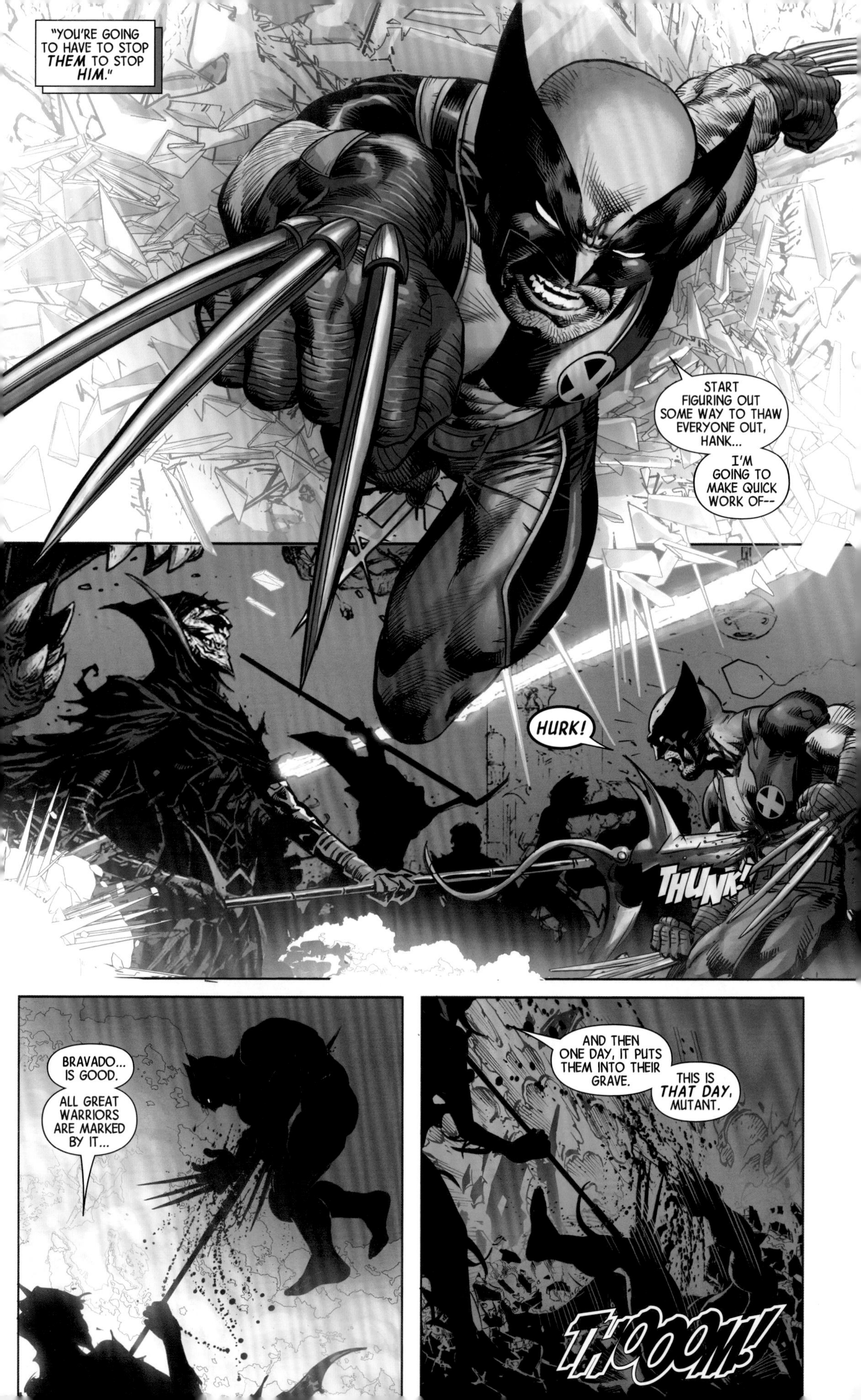
"YOU'RE GOING TO HAVE TO STOP *THEM* TO STOP *HIM*."
START FIGURING OUT SOME WAY TO THAW EVERYONE OUT, HANK...
I'M GOING TO MAKE QUICK WORK OF--
HURK!
THUNK!
BRAVADO... IS GOOD.
ALL GREAT WARRIORS ARE MARKED BY IT...
AND THEN ONE DAY, IT PUTS THEM INTO THEIR GRAVE.
THIS IS *THAT DAY*, MUTANT.
THOOOM!

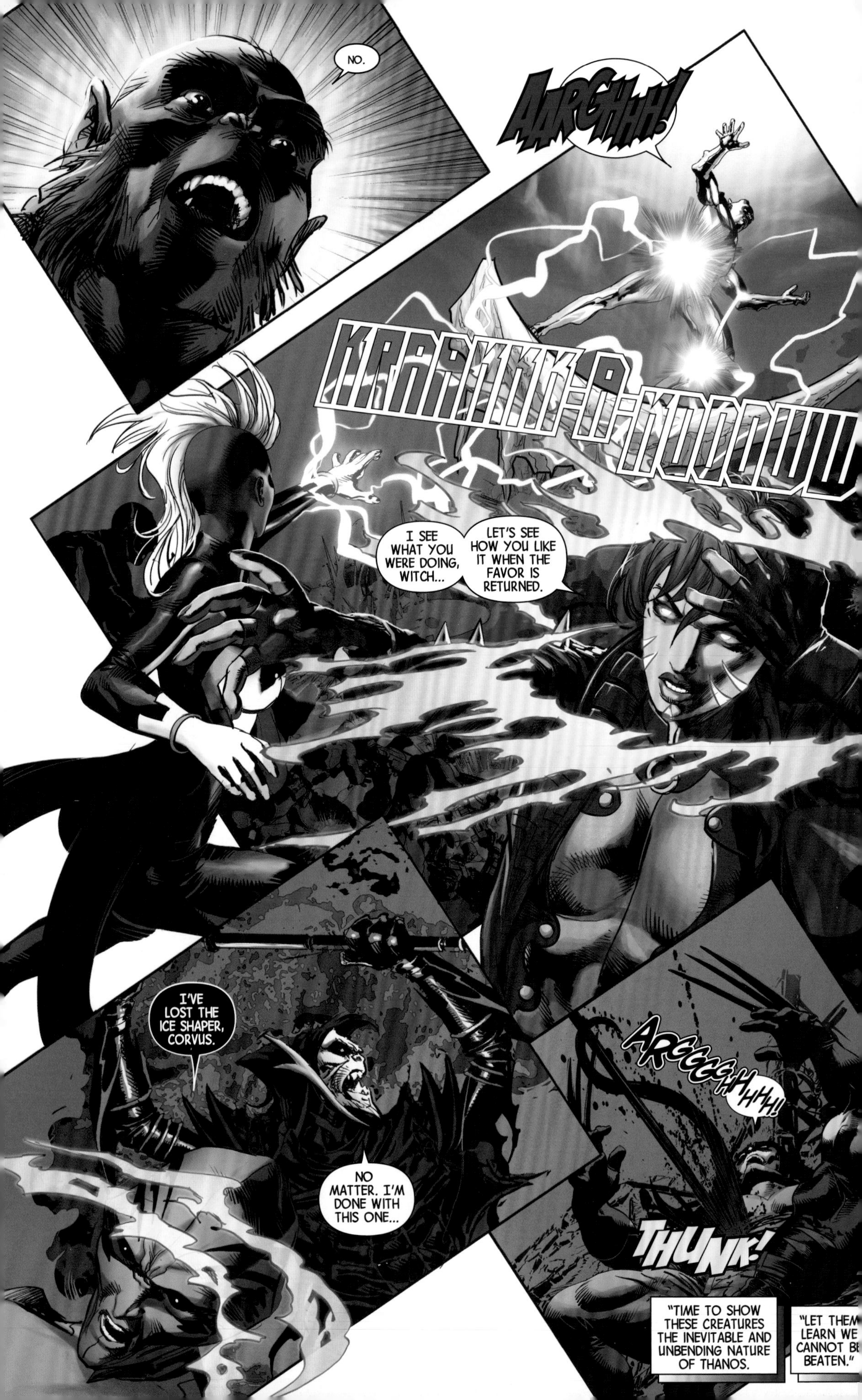

NO.
AARGHHH!
KRAAKKK-A-KOOOOWW
I SEE WHAT YOU WERE DOING, WITCH...
LET'S SEE HOW YOU LIKE IT WHEN THE FAVOR IS RETURNED.
I'VE LOST THE ICE SHAPER, CORVUS.
NO MATTER. I'M DONE WITH THIS ONE...
ARGGGGHHHH!
THUNK!
"TIME TO SHOW THESE CREATURES THE INEVITABLE AND UNBENDING NATURE OF THANOS.

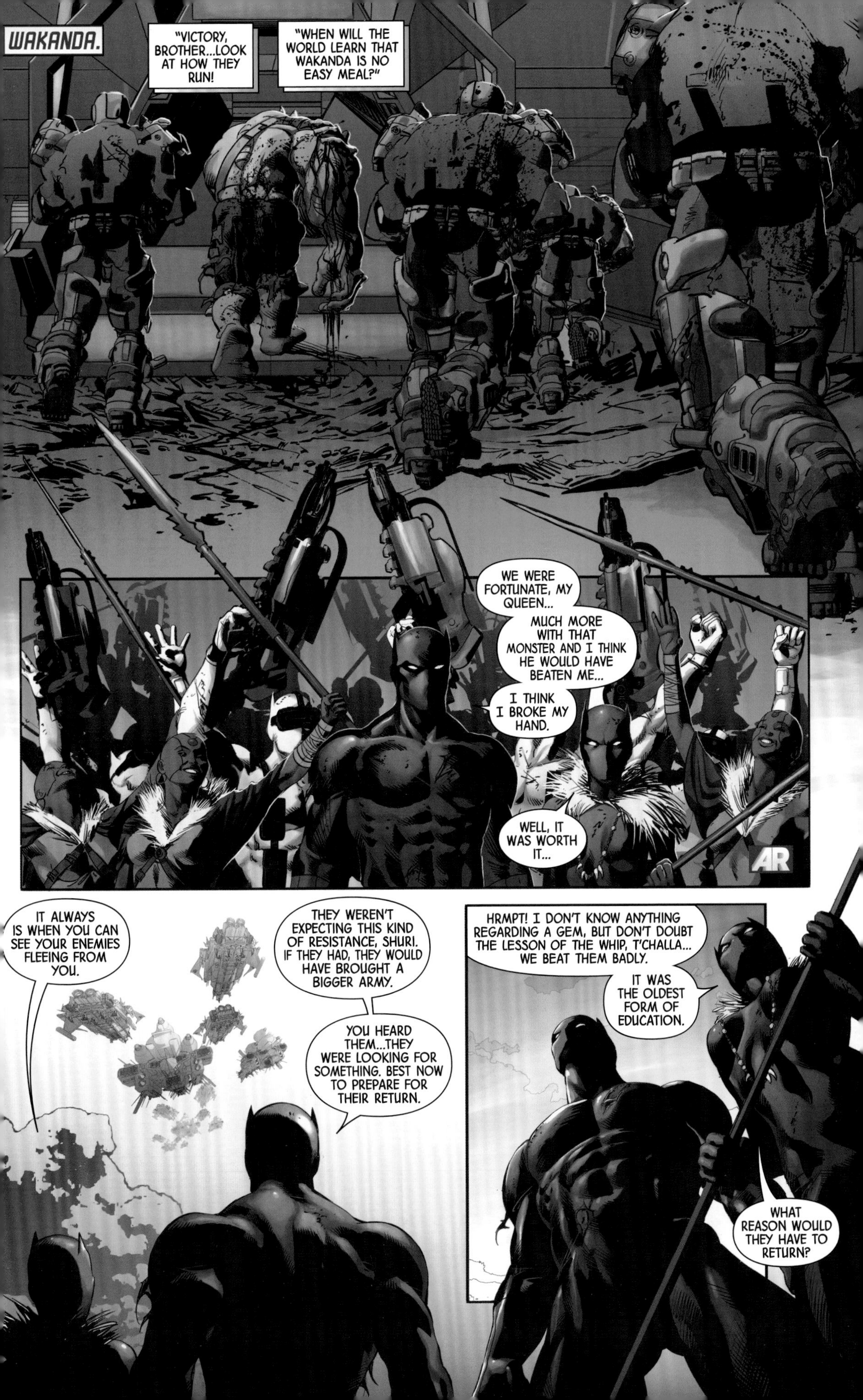
WAKANDA.
"VICTORY, BROTHER...LOOK AT HOW THEY RUN!
"WHEN WILL THE WORLD LEARN THAT WAKANDA IS NO EASY MEAL?"
WE WERE FORTUNATE, MY QUEEN...
MUCH MORE WITH THAT MONSTER AND I THINK HE WOULD HAVE BEATEN ME...
I THINK I BROKE MY HAND.
WELL, IT WAS WORTH IT...
IT ALWAYS IS WHEN YOU CAN SEE YOUR ENEMIES FLEEING FROM YOU.
THEY WEREN'T EXPECTING THIS KIND OF RESISTANCE, SHURI. IF THEY HAD, THEY WOULD HAVE BROUGHT A BIGGER ARMY.
YOU HEARD THEM...THEY WERE LOOKING FOR SOMETHING. BEST NOW TO PREPARE FOR THEIR RETURN.
HRMPT! I DON'T KNOW ANYTHING REGARDING A GEM, BUT DON'T DOUBT THE LESSON OF THE WHIP, T'CHALLA... WE BEAT THEM BADLY.
IT WAS THE OLDEST FORM OF EDUCATION.
WHAT REASON WOULD THEY HAVE TO RETURN?

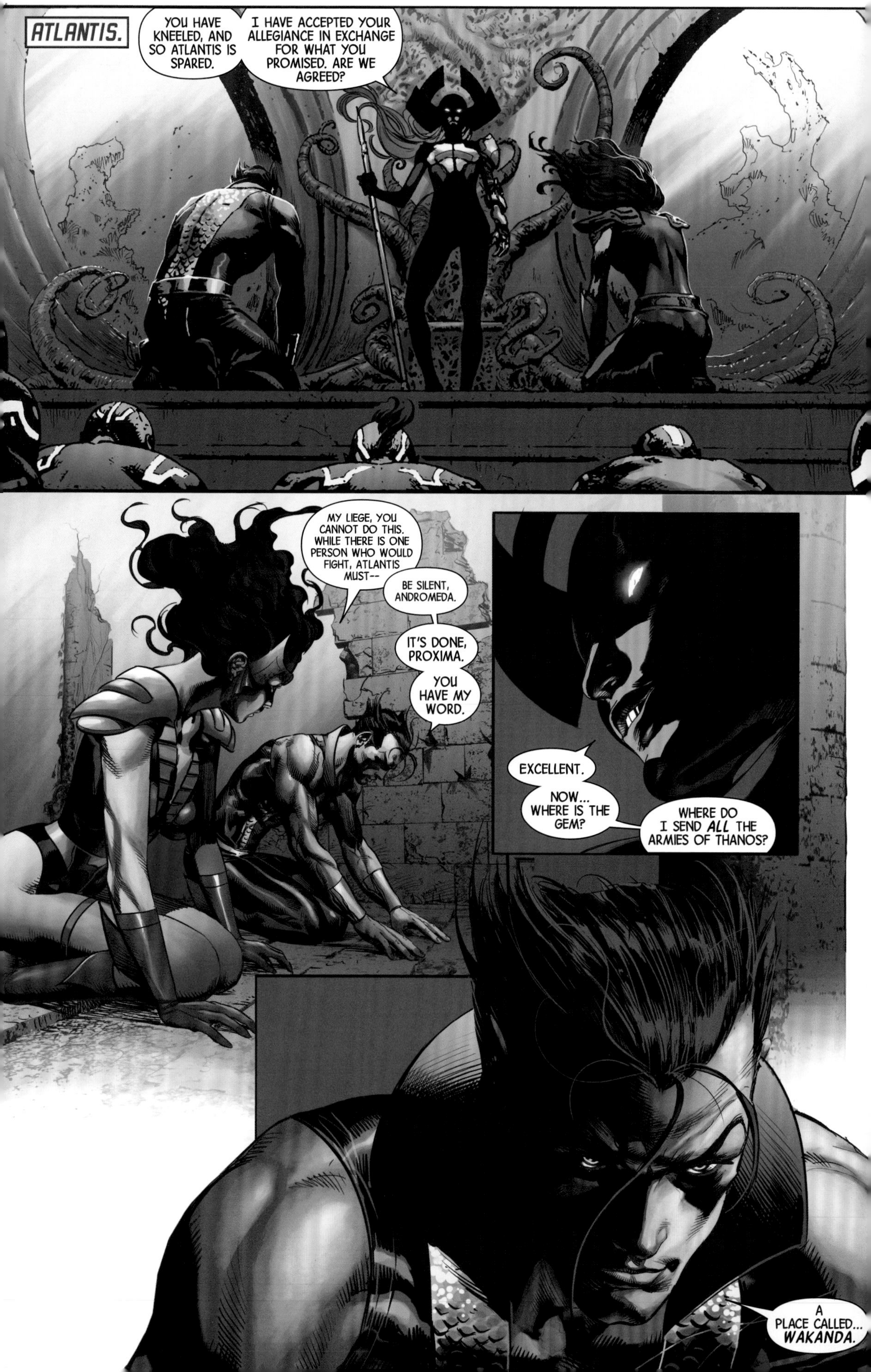
ATLANTIS.
YOU HAVE KNEELED, AND SO ATLANTIS IS SPARED.
I HAVE ACCEPTED YOUR ALLEGIANCE IN EXCHANGE FOR WHAT YOU PROMISED. ARE WE AGREED?
MY LIEGE, YOU CANNOT DO THIS. WHILE THERE IS ONE PERSON WHO WOULD FIGHT, ATLANTIS MUST--
BE SILENT, ANDROMEDA.
IT'S DONE, PROXIMA.
YOU HAVE MY WORD.
EXCELLENT.
NOW... WHERE IS THE GEM?
WHERE DO I SEND ALL THE ARMIES OF THANOS?
A PLACE CALLED... WAKANDA.

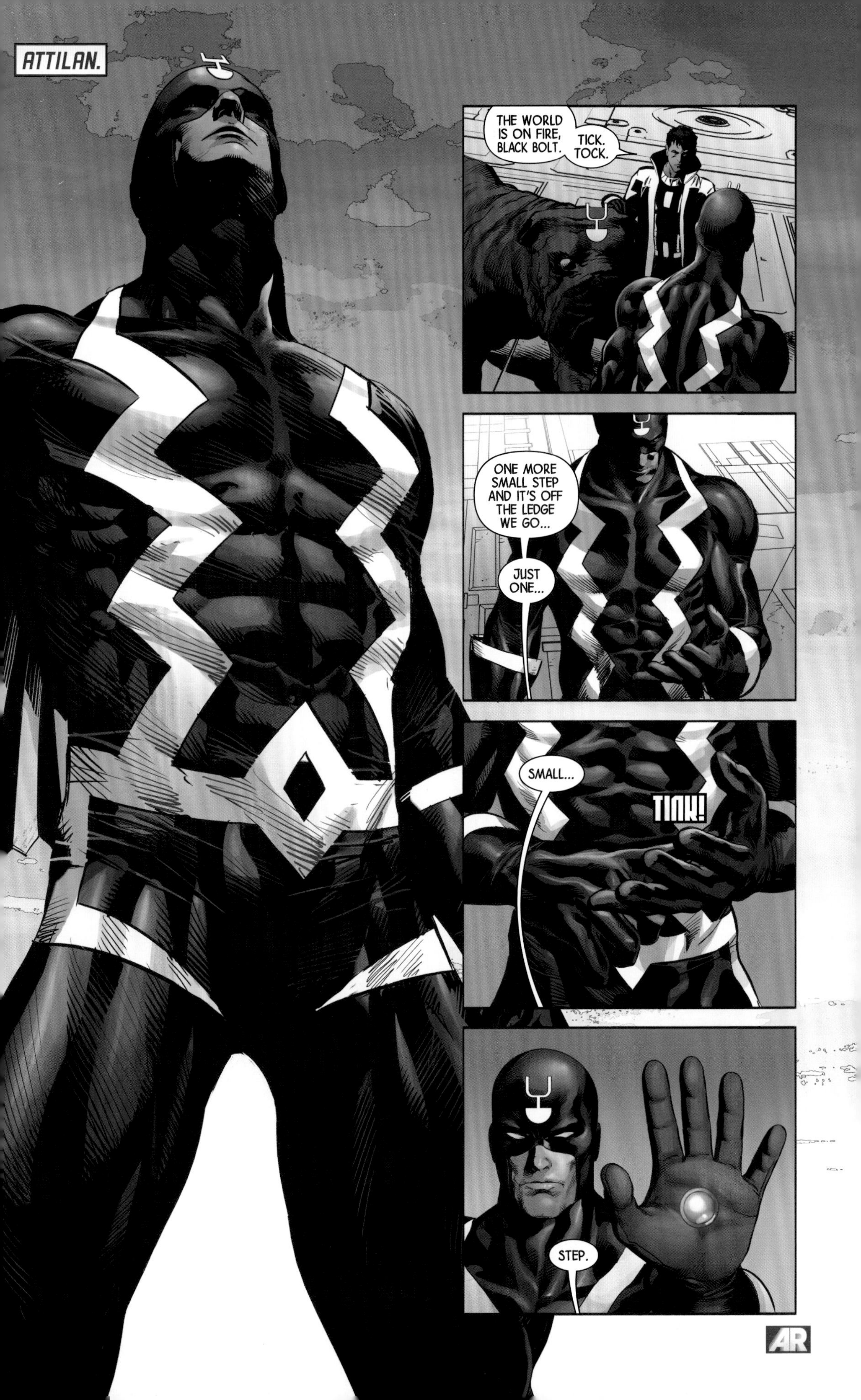
ATTILAN.
THE WORLD IS ON FIRE, BLACK BOLT.
TICK. TOCK.
ONE MORE SMALL STEP AND IT'S OFF THE LEDGE WE GO...
JUST ONE...
SMALL...
TINK!
STEP.
AR

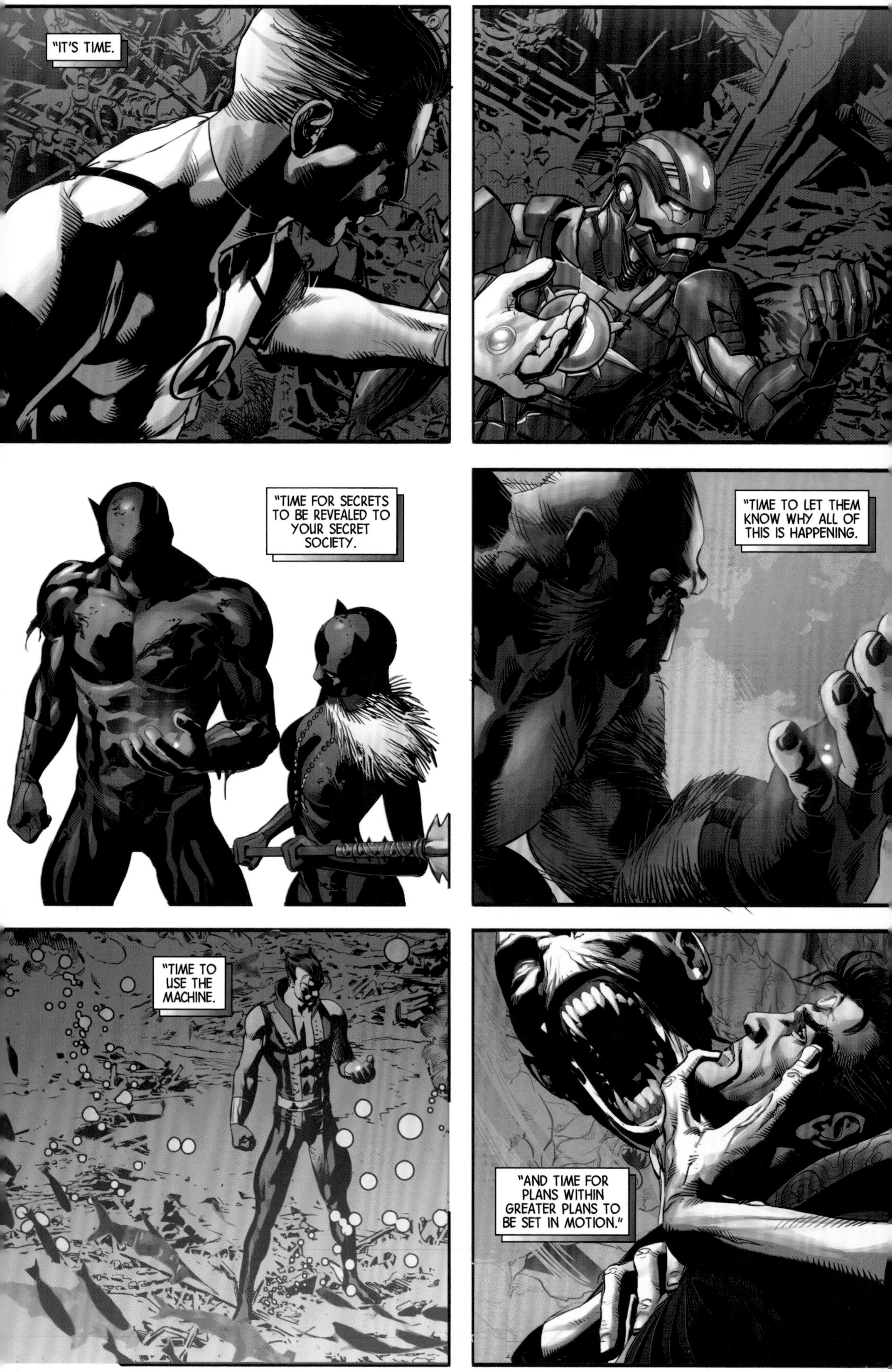
"IT'S TIME.
"TIME FOR SECRETS TO BE REVEALED TO YOUR SECRET SOCIETY.
"TIME TO LET THEM KNOW WHY ALL OF THIS IS HAPPENING.
"TIME TO USE THE MACHINE.
"AND TIME FOR PLANS WITHIN GREATER PLANS TO BE SET IN MOTION."

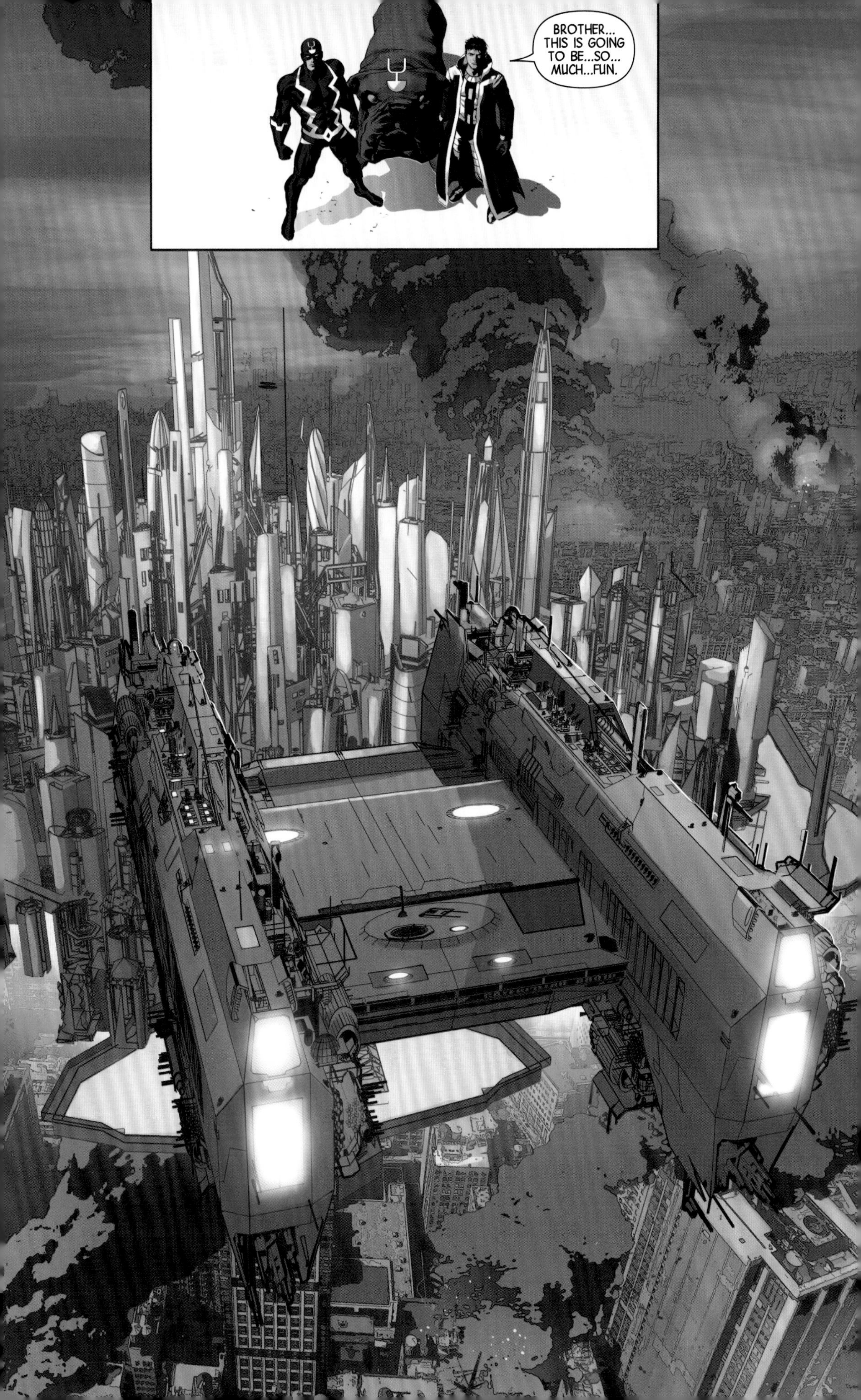
BROTHER... THIS IS GOING TO BE...SO... MUCH...FUN.

CULL OBSIDIAN
(THE BLACK ORDER)

CORVUS GLAIVE: The first of the five. Thanos' most favored. Corvus is cruel, arrogant and the most loyal of the Black Order. A warrior who betrayed his people and sold his soul to Thanos to pursue a different kind of glory.

POWERS: Strength, speed…As long as his otherworldly blade remains whole, he cannot die.

PROXIMA MIDNIGHT: The cruelest of Thanos' generals. A predator in every sense of the word, Proxima Midnight is the greatest warrior in Thanos' army.

POWERS: Savage hand-to-hand fighter. Her spear, when thrown, transforms into three tracers of black light that never miss. These beams are lethal to most creatures.

BLACK DWARF: When compared to the others of the Black Order, Black Dwarf seems almost normal. Feigning joy and contentment, in reality this celestial nihilist is simply more at peace with the oblivion Thanos seeks than the others of the Black Order.

POWERS: Super-strength. Super-dense, unbreakable skin.

SUPERGIANT: History unknown. An mentally unstable omnipath and telepathic parasite, Supergiant seeks out intellect and devours it. What she knows, Thanos knows.

POWERS: Mental parasite. Controls, steals or devours the minds of her victims.

THE EBONY MAW: A thin razor of a man. Not a fighter, a thinker. A black tongue that spreads mischief and evil wherever he goes. He seems to be the weakest of the Black Order, but in truth, he is the most dangerous of them all.

POWERS: Believed to be none, but that, like most things about him could be a lie.

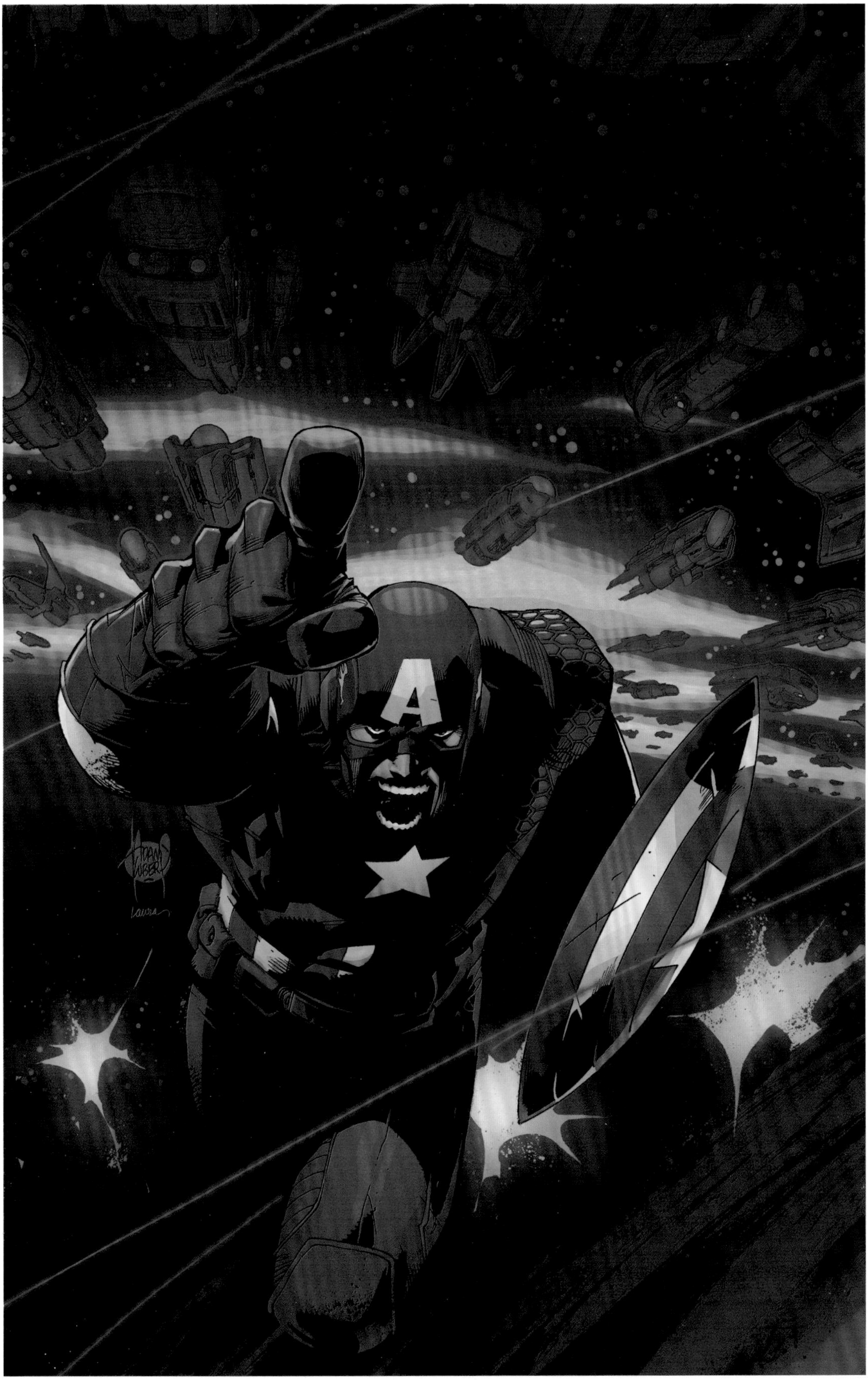

FROM TITAN,
THE HORDE

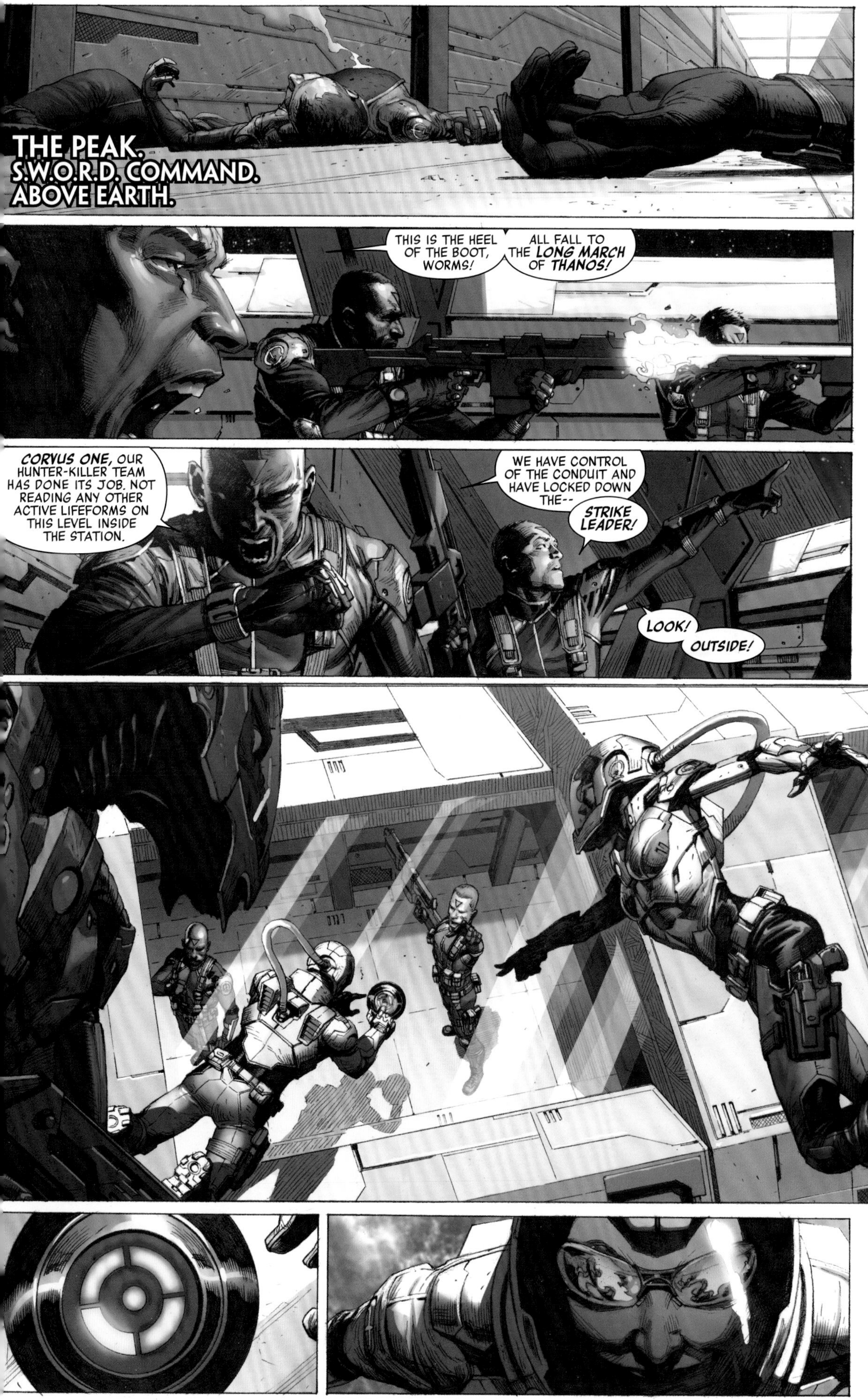
THE PEAK.
S.W.O.R.D. COMMAND.
ABOVE EARTH.
THIS IS THE HEEL OF THE BOOT, WORMS!
ALL FALL TO THE LONG MARCH OF THANOS!
CORVUS ONE, OUR HUNTER-KILLER TEAM HAS DONE ITS JOB. NOT READING ANY OTHER ACTIVE LIFEFORMS ON THIS LEVEL INSIDE THE STATION.
WE HAVE CONTROL OF THE CONDUIT AND HAVE LOCKED DOWN THE--
STRIKE LEADER!
LOOK!
OUTSIDE!

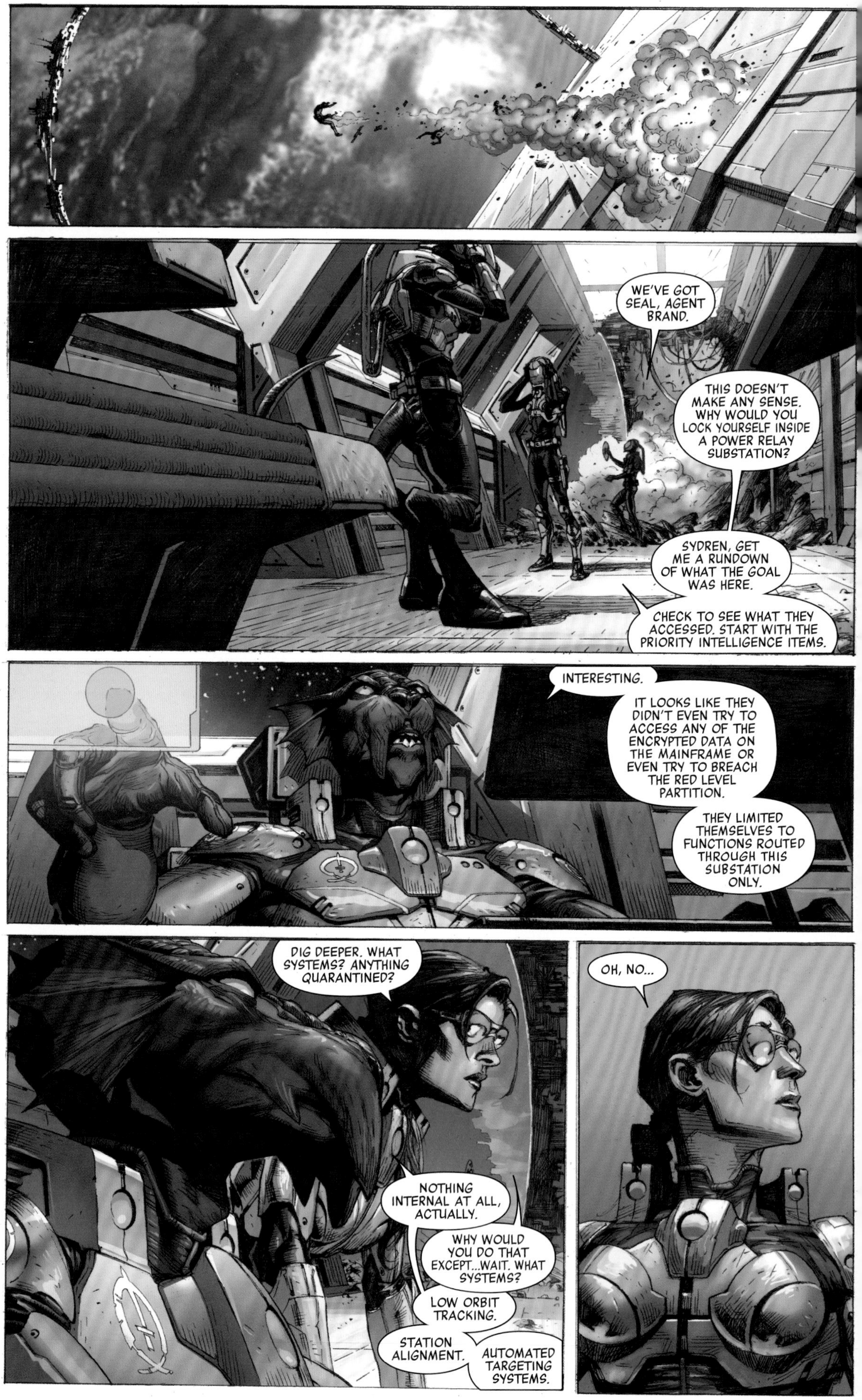
WE'VE GOT SEAL, AGENT BRAND.
THIS DOESN'T MAKE ANY SENSE. WHY WOULD YOU LOCK YOURSELF INSIDE A POWER RELAY SUBSTATION?
SYDREN, GET ME A RUNDOWN OF WHAT THE GOAL WAS HERE.
CHECK TO SEE WHAT THEY ACCESSED. START WITH THE PRIORITY INTELLIGENCE ITEMS.
INTERESTING.
IT LOOKS LIKE THEY DIDN'T EVEN TRY TO ACCESS ANY OF THE ENCRYPTED DATA ON THE MAINFRAME OR EVEN TRY TO BREACH THE RED LEVEL PARTITION.
THEY LIMITED THEMSELVES TO FUNCTIONS ROUTED THROUGH THIS SUBSTATION ONLY.
DIG DEEPER. WHAT SYSTEMS? ANYTHING QUARANTINED?
NOTHING INTERNAL AT ALL, ACTUALLY.
WHY WOULD YOU DO THAT EXCEPT...WAIT. WHAT SYSTEMS?
LOW ORBIT TRACKING.
STATION ALIGNMENT.
AUTOMATED TARGETING SYSTEMS.
OH, NO...

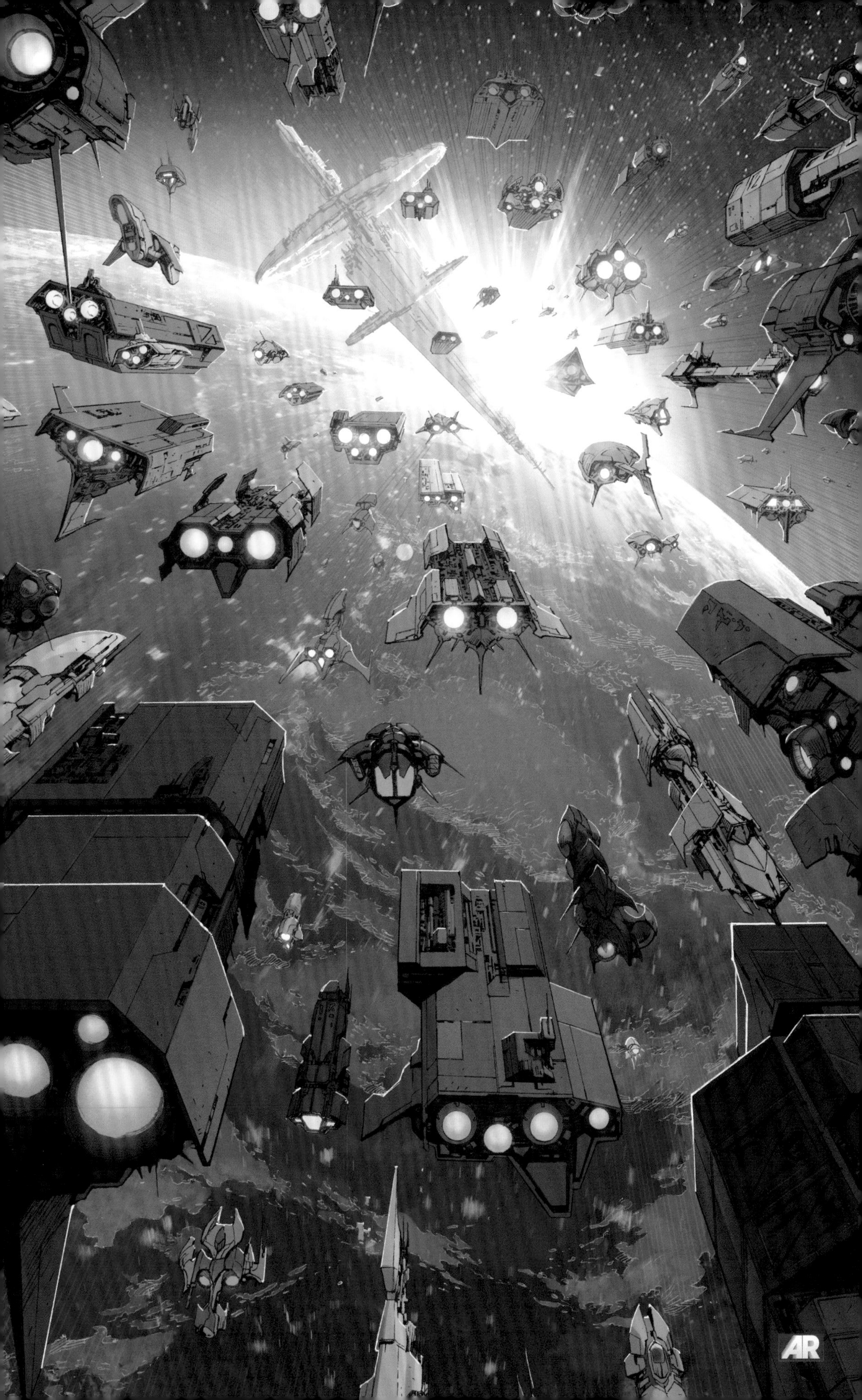

THE GAUNTLET

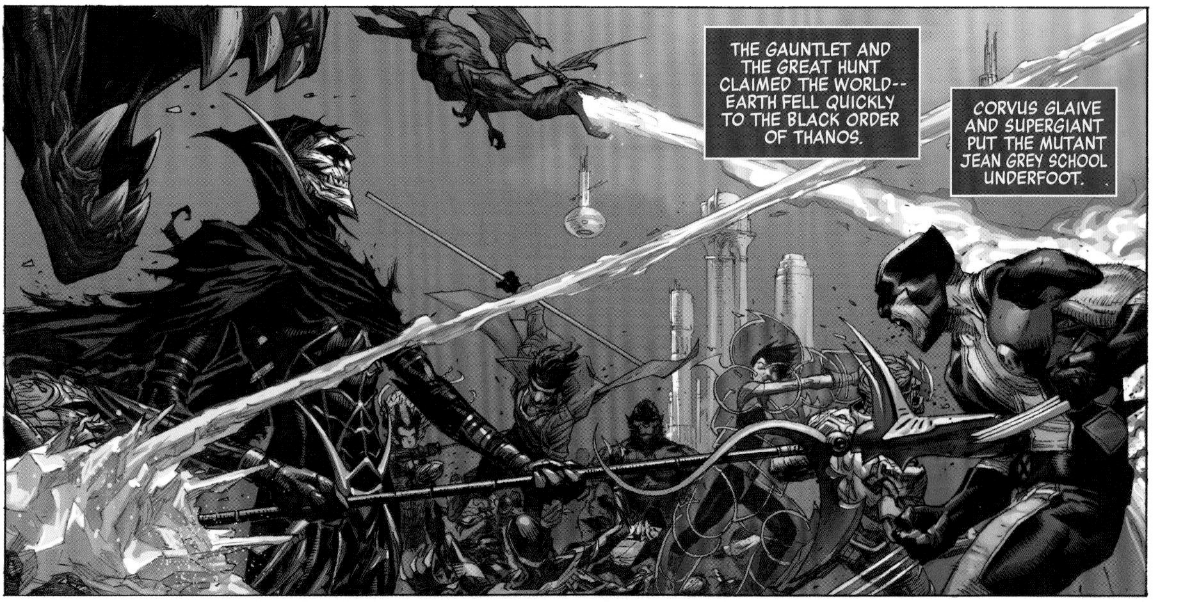
THE GAUNTLET AND THE GREAT HUNT CLAIMED THE WORLD-- EARTH FELL QUICKLY TO THE BLACK ORDER OF THANOS.
CORVUS GLAIVE AND SUPERGIANT PUT THE MUTANT JEAN GREY SCHOOL UNDERFOOT.

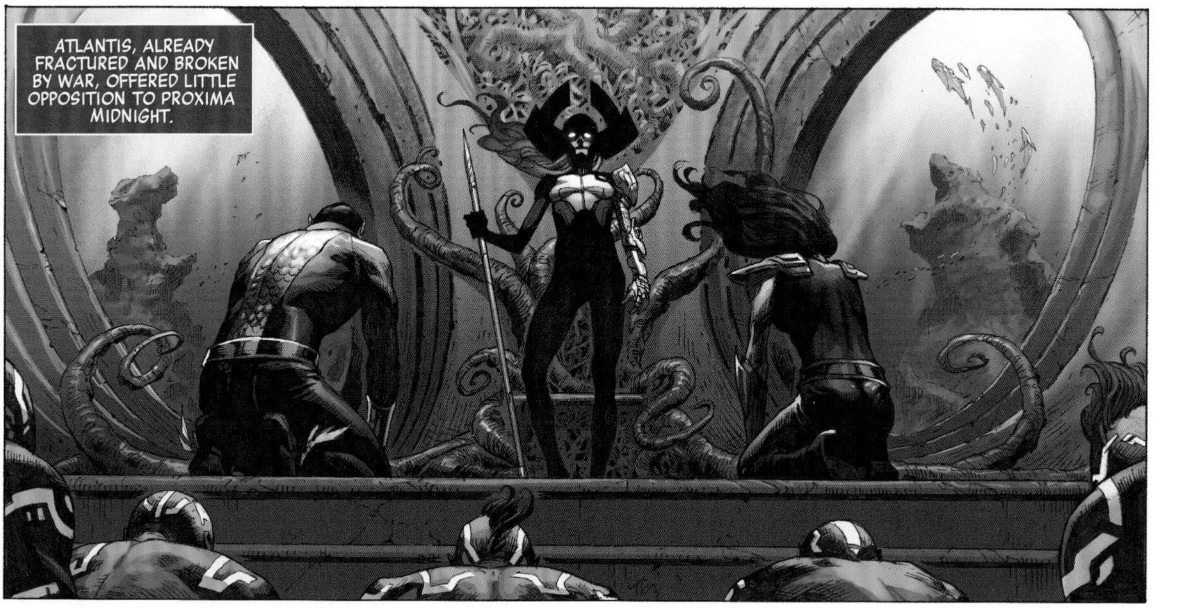
ATLANTIS, ALREADY FRACTURED AND BROKEN BY WAR, OFFERED LITTLE OPPOSITION TO PROXIMA MIDNIGHT.

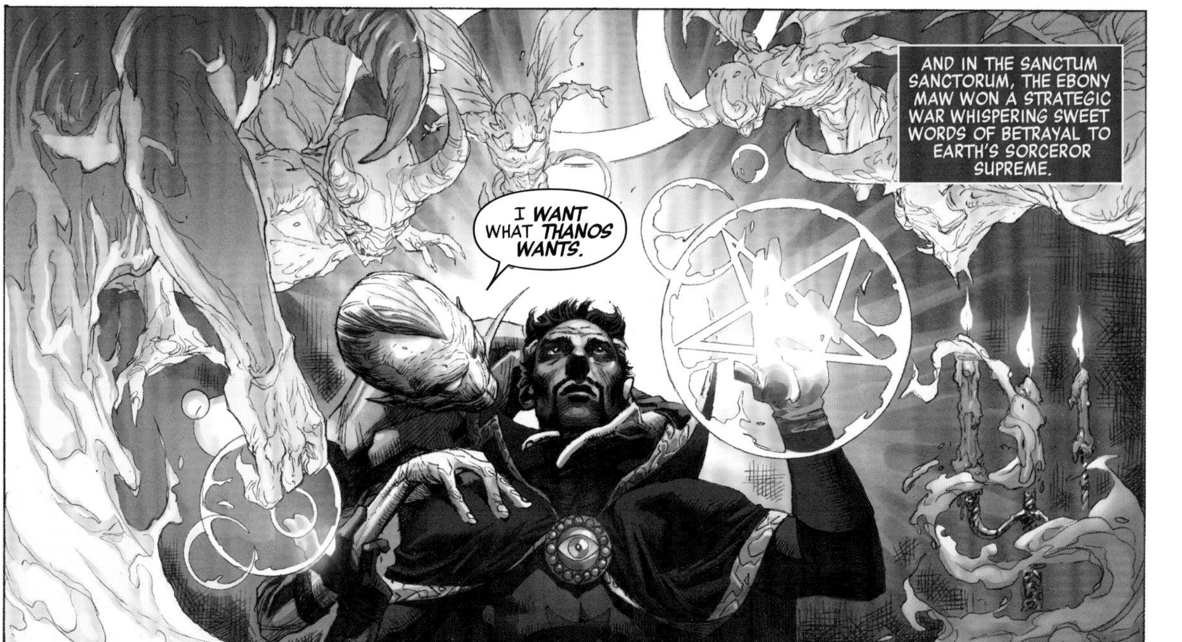
AND IN THE SANCTUM SANCTORUM, THE EBONY MAW WON A STRATEGIC WAR WHISPERING SWEET WORDS OF BETRAYAL TO EARTH'S SORCEROR SUPREME.
I WANT WHAT THANOS WANTS.

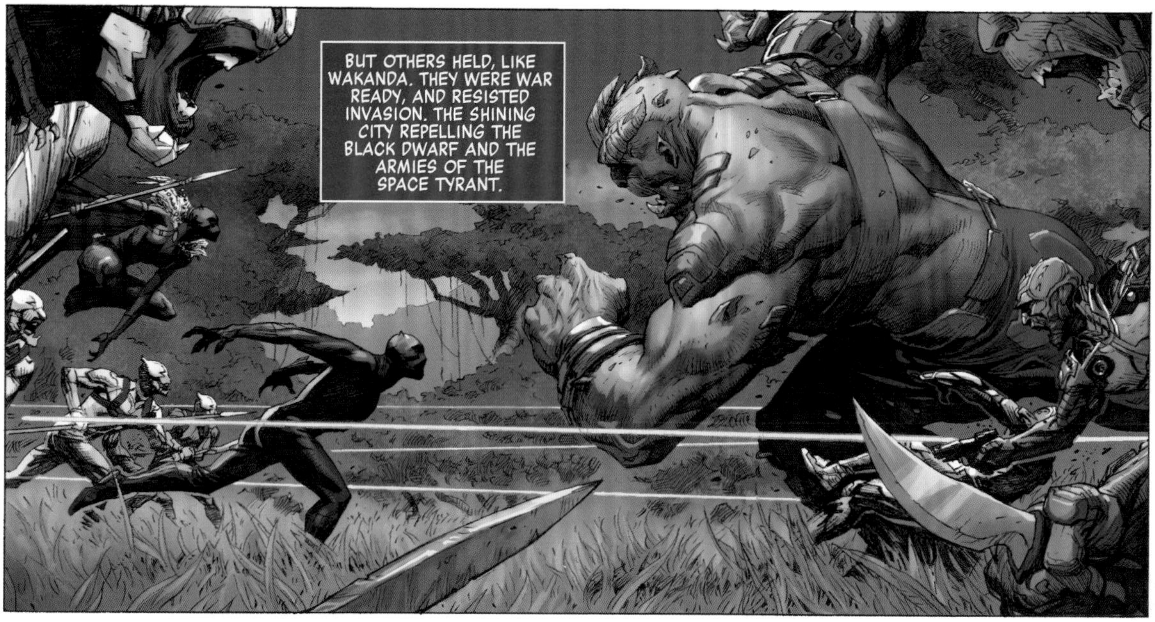
BUT OTHERS HELD, LIKE WAKANDA. THEY WERE WAR READY, AND RESISTED INVASION. THE SHINING CITY REPELLING THE BLACK DWARF AND THE ARMIES OF THE SPACE TYRANT.

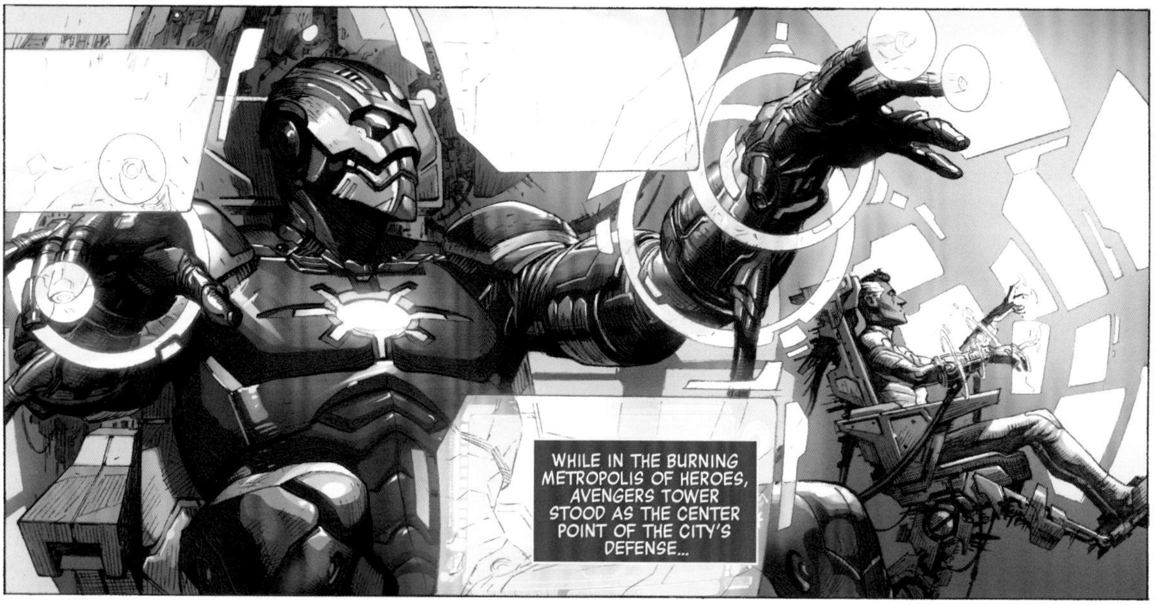
WHILE IN THE BURNING METROPOLIS OF HEROES, AVENGERS TOWER STOOD AS THE CENTER POINT OF THE CITY'S DEFENSE...

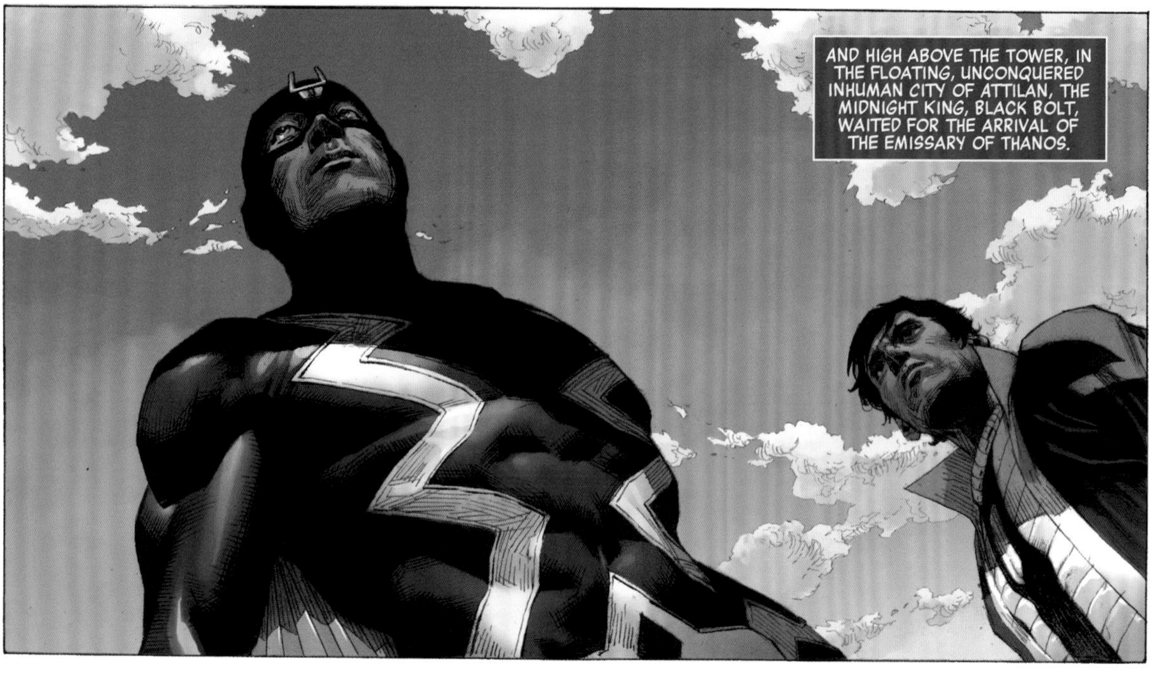
AND HIGH ABOVE THE TOWER, IN THE FLOATING, UNCONQUERED INHUMAN CITY OF ATTILAN, THE MIDNIGHT KING, BLACK BOLT, WAITED FOR THE ARRIVAL OF THE EMISSARY OF THANOS.

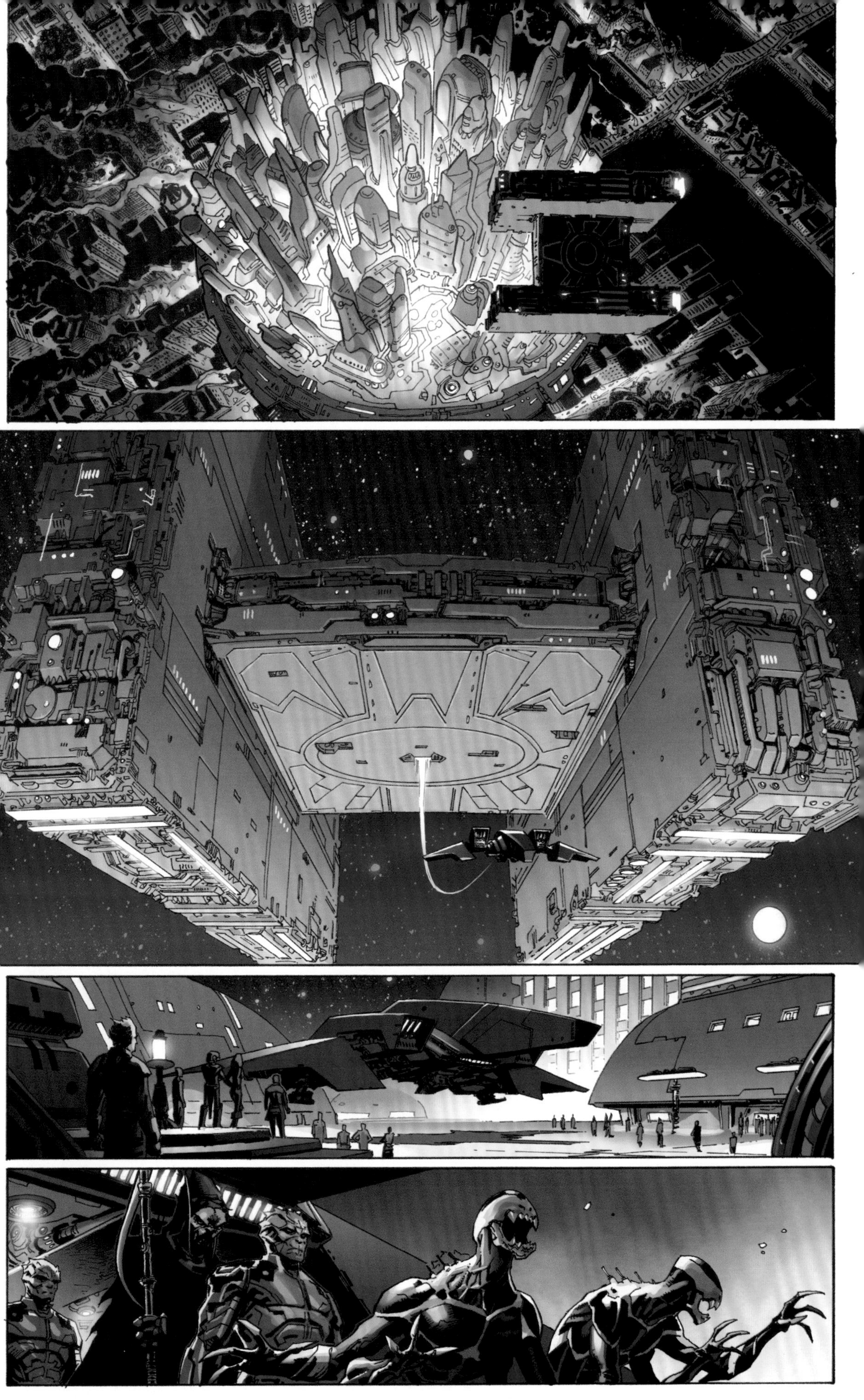

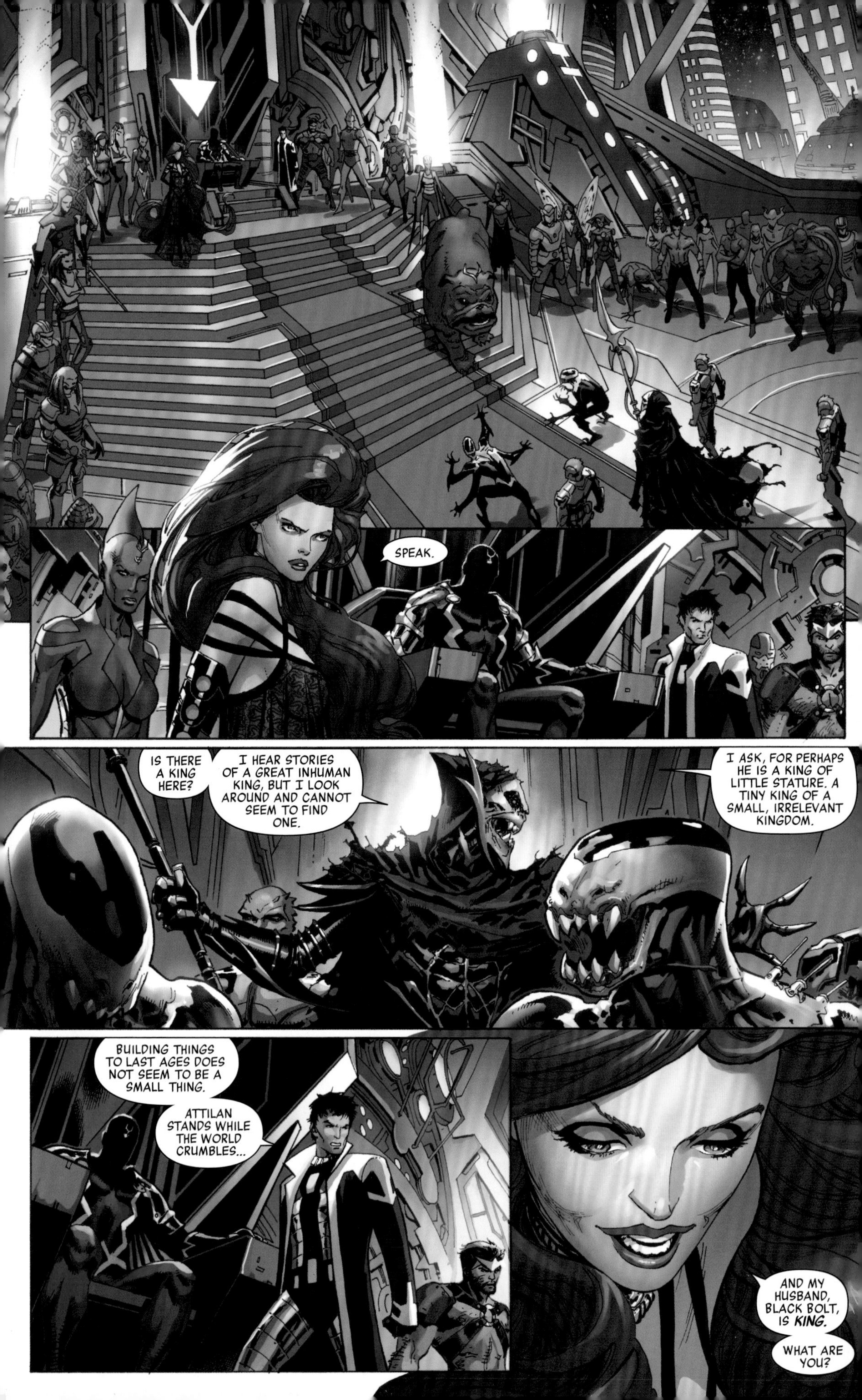
SPEAK.
IS THERE A KING HERE?
I HEAR STORIES OF A GREAT INHUMAN KING, BUT I LOOK AROUND AND CANNOT SEEM TO FIND ONE.
I ASK, FOR PERHAPS HE IS A KING OF LITTLE STATURE. A TINY KING OF A SMALL, IRRELEVANT KINGDOM.
BUILDING THINGS TO LAST AGES DOES NOT SEEM TO BE A SMALL THING.
ATTILAN STANDS WHILE THE WORLD CRUMBLES...
AND MY HUSBAND, BLACK BOLT, IS ***KING.***
WHAT ARE YOU?

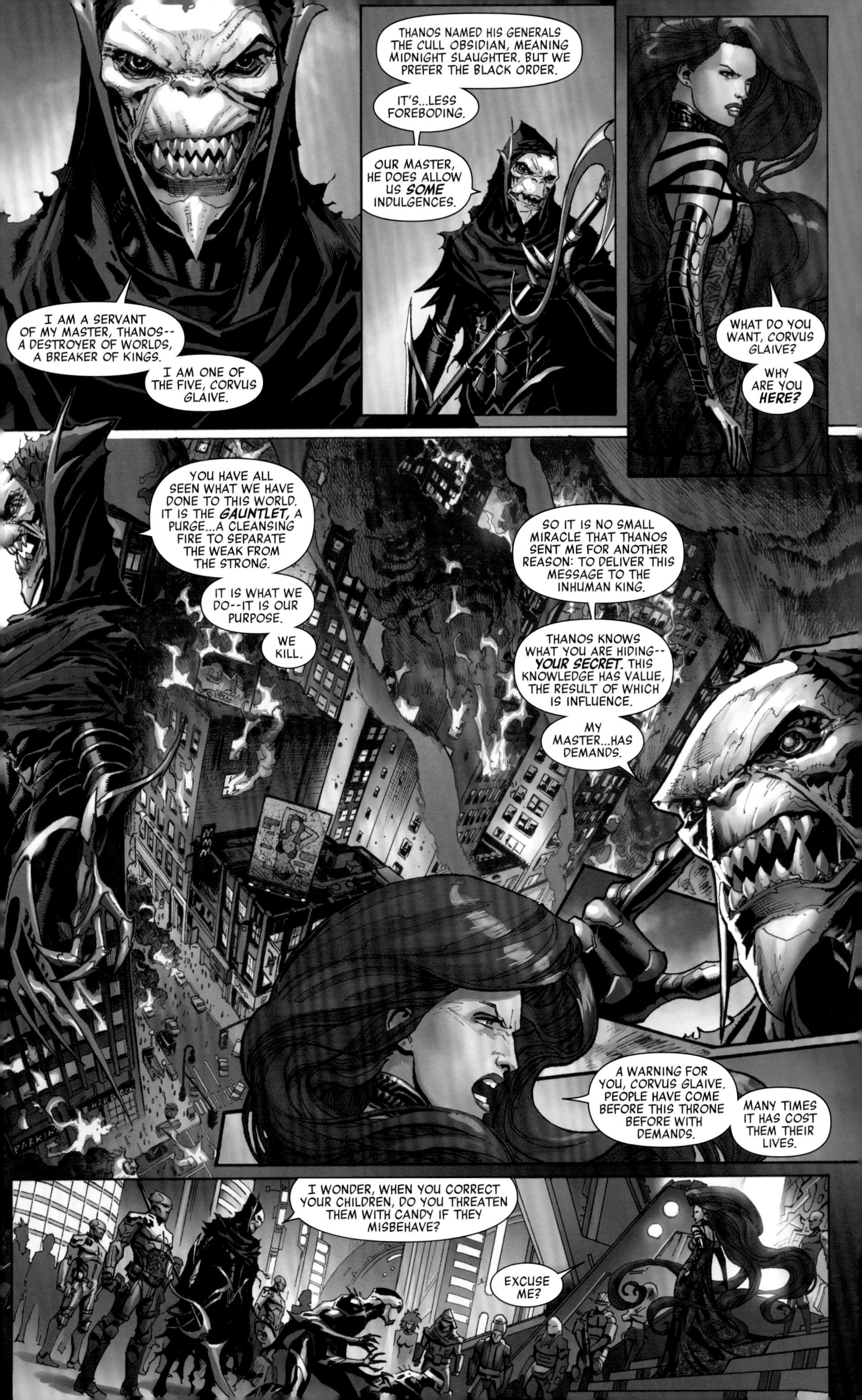
I AM A SERVANT OF MY MASTER, THANOS-- A DESTROYER OF WORLDS, A BREAKER OF KINGS.
I AM ONE OF THE FIVE, CORVUS GLAIVE.
THANOS NAMED HIS GENERALS THE CULL OBSIDIAN, MEANING MIDNIGHT SLAUGHTER. BUT WE PREFER THE BLACK ORDER.
IT'S...LESS FOREBODING.
OUR MASTER, HE DOES ALLOW US SOME INDULGENCES.
WHAT DO YOU WANT, CORVUS GLAIVE?
WHY ARE YOU HERE?
YOU HAVE ALL SEEN WHAT WE HAVE DONE TO THIS WORLD. IT IS THE GAUNTLET, A PURGE...A CLEANSING FIRE TO SEPARATE THE WEAK FROM THE STRONG.
IT IS WHAT WE DO--IT IS OUR PURPOSE.
WE KILL.
SO IT IS NO SMALL MIRACLE THAT THANOS SENT ME FOR ANOTHER REASON: TO DELIVER THIS MESSAGE TO THE INHUMAN KING.
THANOS KNOWS WHAT YOU ARE HIDING-- YOUR SECRET. THIS KNOWLEDGE HAS VALUE, THE RESULT OF WHICH IS INFLUENCE.
MY MASTER...HAS DEMANDS.
A WARNING FOR YOU, CORVUS GLAIVE. PEOPLE HAVE COME BEFORE THIS THRONE BEFORE WITH DEMANDS.
MANY TIMES IT HAS COST THEM THEIR LIVES.
I WONDER, WHEN YOU CORRECT YOUR CHILDREN, DO YOU THREATEN THEM WITH CANDY IF THEY MISBEHAVE?
EXCUSE ME?

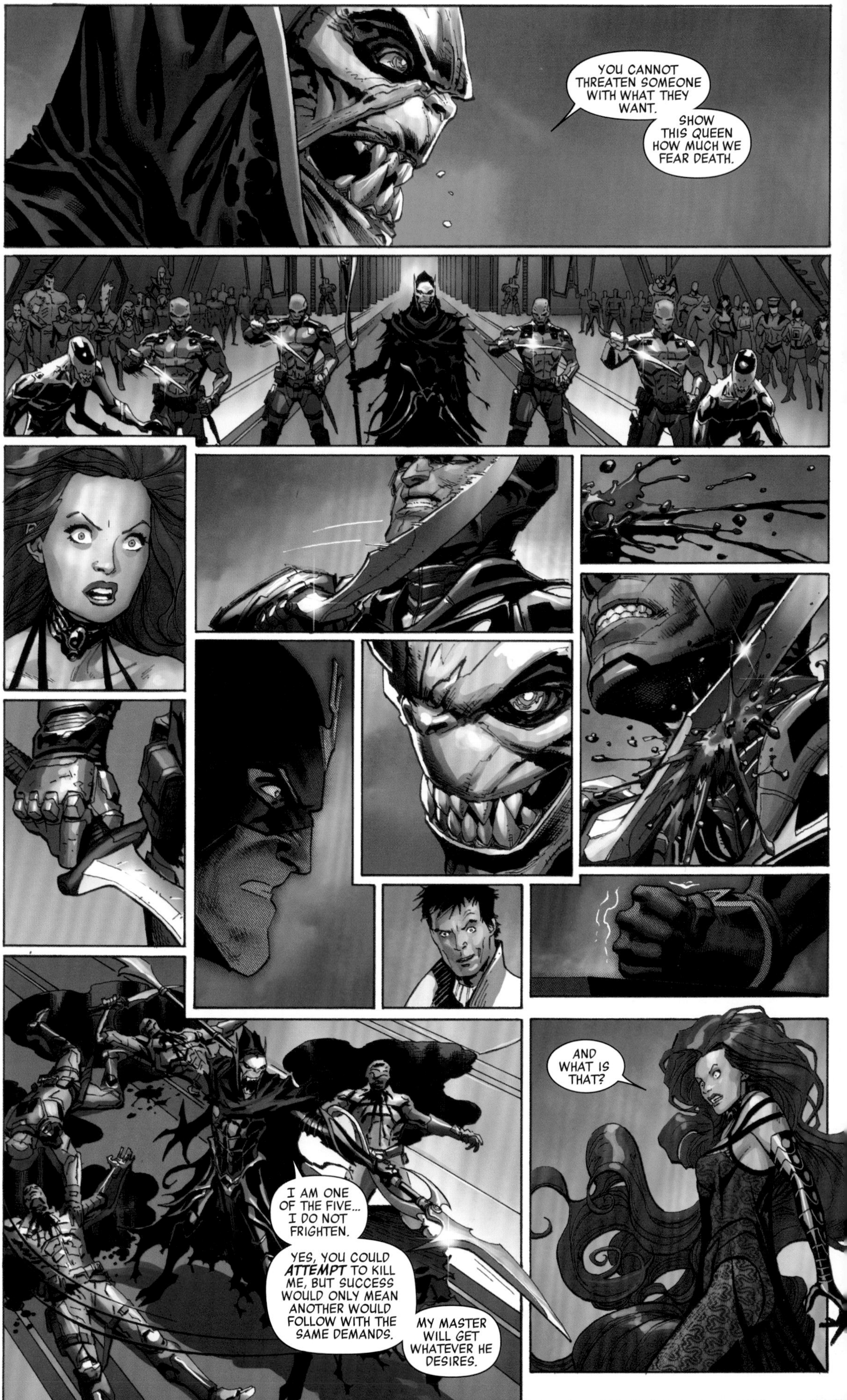
YOU CANNOT THREATEN SOMEONE WITH WHAT THEY WANT.
SHOW THIS QUEEN HOW MUCH WE FEAR DEATH.
AND WHAT IS THAT?
I AM ONE OF THE FIVE... I DO NOT FRIGHTEN.
YES, YOU COULD ATTEMPT TO KILL ME, BUT SUCCESS WOULD ONLY MEAN ANOTHER WOULD FOLLOW WITH THE SAME DEMANDS.
MY MASTER WILL GET WHATEVER HE DESIRES.

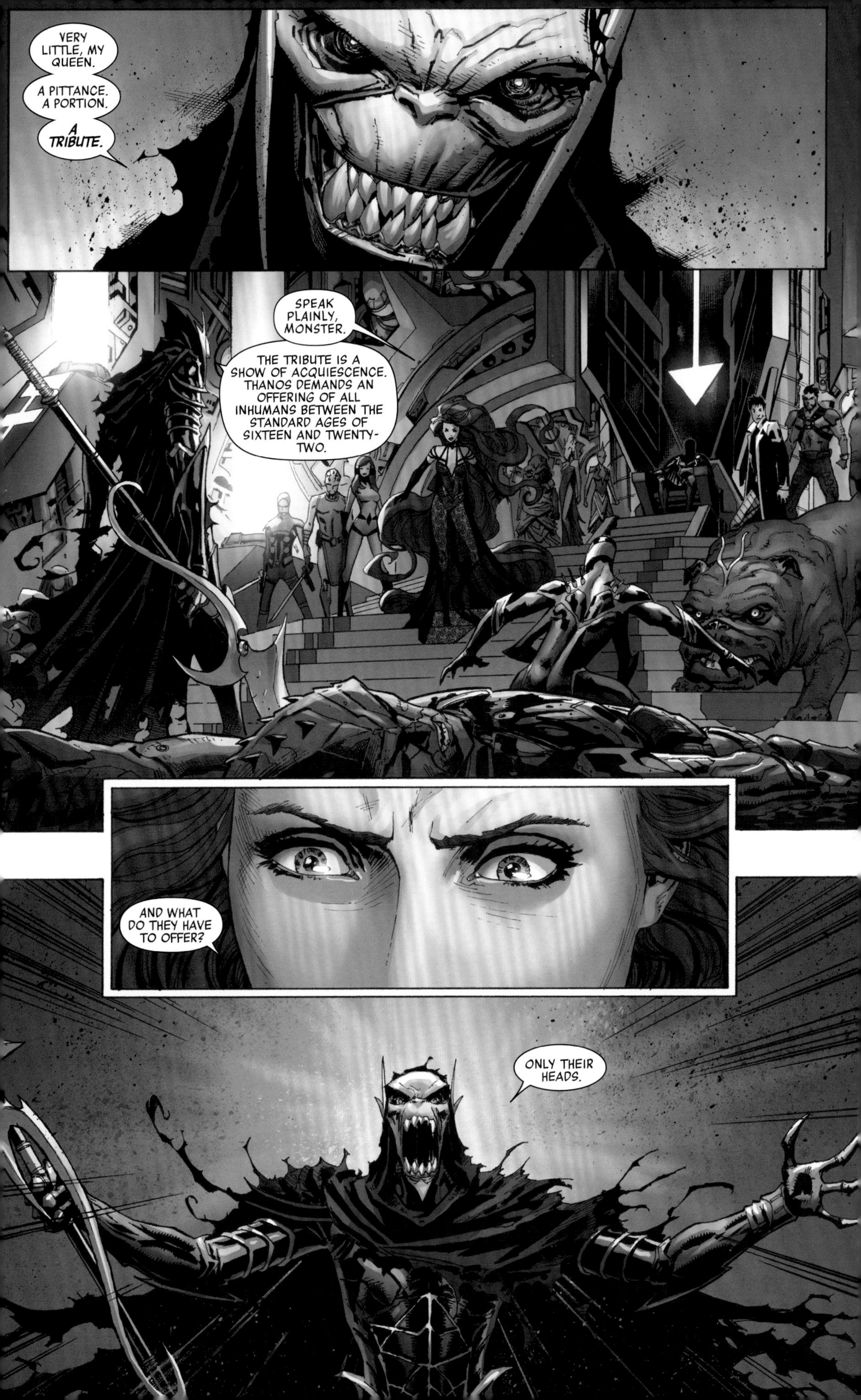
VERY LITTLE, MY QUEEN.
A PITTANCE. A PORTION.
A *TRIBUTE.*
SPEAK PLAINLY, MONSTER.
THE TRIBUTE IS A SHOW OF ACQUIESCENCE. THANOS DEMANDS AN OFFERING OF ALL INHUMANS BETWEEN THE STANDARD AGES OF SIXTEEN AND TWENTY-TWO.
AND WHAT DO THEY HAVE TO OFFER?
ONLY THEIR HEADS.

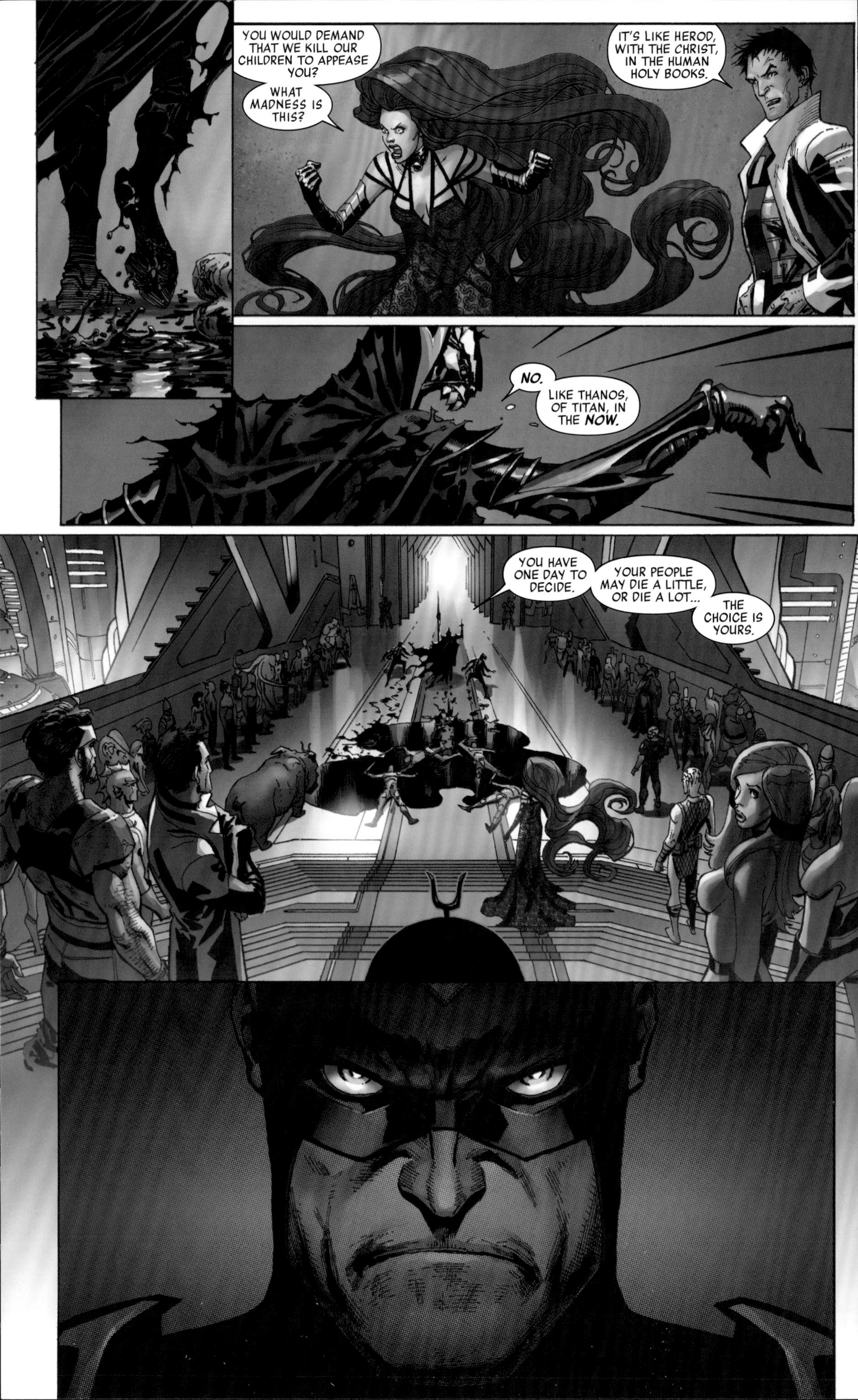
YOU WOULD DEMAND THAT WE KILL OUR CHILDREN TO APPEASE YOU?
WHAT MADNESS IS THIS?
IT'S LIKE HEROD, WITH THE CHRIST, IN THE HUMAN HOLY BOOKS.
NO.
LIKE THANOS, OF TITAN, IN THE NOW.
YOU HAVE ONE DAY TO DECIDE.
YOUR PEOPLE MAY DIE A LITTLE, OR DIE A LOT...
THE CHOICE IS YOURS.

A WAR
IN THE HEAVENS

◆

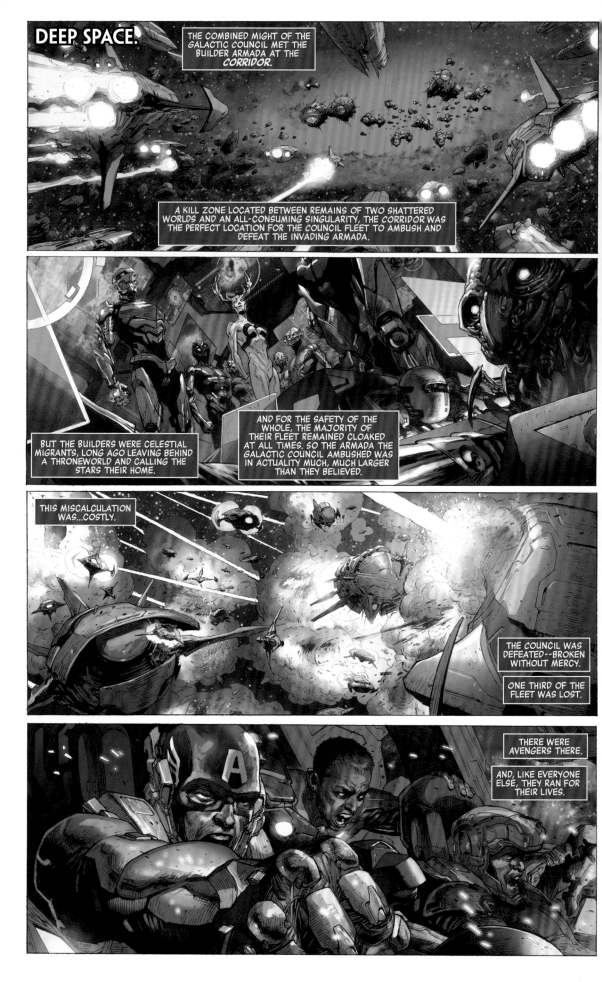

DEEP SPACE.

THE COMBINED MIGHT OF THE GALACTIC COUNCIL MET THE BUILDER ARMADA AT THE *CORRIDOR*.

A KILL ZONE LOCATED BETWEEN REMAINS OF TWO SHATTERED WORLDS AND AN ALL-CONSUMING SINGULARITY, THE CORRIDOR WAS THE PERFECT LOCATION FOR THE COUNCIL FLEET TO AMBUSH AND DEFEAT THE INVADING ARMADA.

BUT THE BUILDERS WERE CELESTIAL MIGRANTS, LONG AGO LEAVING BEHIND A THRONEWORLD AND CALLING THE STARS THEIR HOME.

AND FOR THE SAFETY OF THE WHOLE, THE MAJORITY OF THEIR FLEET REMAINED CLOAKED AT ALL TIMES. SO THE ARMADA THE GALACTIC COUNCIL AMBUSHED WAS IN ACTUALITY MUCH, MUCH LARGER THAN THEY BELIEVED.

THIS MISCALCULATION WAS...COSTLY.

THE COUNCIL WAS DEFEATED--BROKEN WITHOUT MERCY.

ONE THIRD OF THE FLEET WAS LOST.

THERE WERE AVENGERS THERE.

AND, LIKE EVERYONE ELSE, THEY RAN FOR THEIR LIVES.

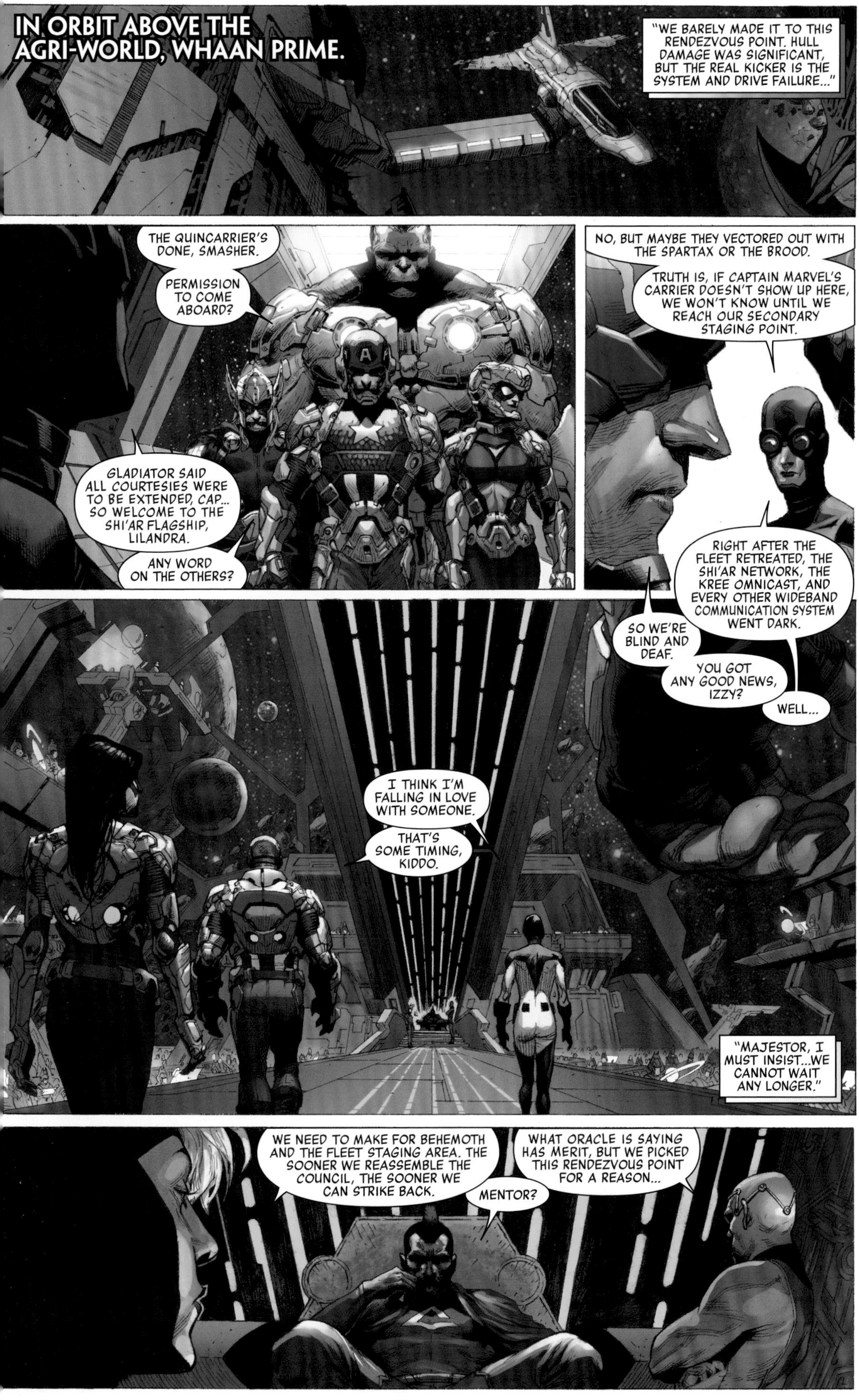
IN ORBIT ABOVE THE AGRI-WORLD, WHAAN PRIME.
"WE BARELY MADE IT TO THIS RENDEZVOUS POINT. HULL DAMAGE WAS SIGNIFICANT, BUT THE REAL KICKER IS THE SYSTEM AND DRIVE FAILURE..."
THE QUINCARRIER'S DONE, SMASHER.
PERMISSION TO COME ABOARD?
GLADIATOR SAID ALL COURTESIES WERE TO BE EXTENDED, CAP... SO WELCOME TO THE SHI'AR FLAGSHIP, LILANDRA.
ANY WORD ON THE OTHERS?
NO, BUT MAYBE THEY VECTORED OUT WITH THE SPARTAX OR THE BROOD.
TRUTH IS, IF CAPTAIN MARVEL'S CARRIER DOESN'T SHOW UP HERE, WE WON'T KNOW UNTIL WE REACH OUR SECONDARY STAGING POINT.
RIGHT AFTER THE FLEET RETREATED, THE SHI'AR NETWORK, THE KREE OMNICAST, AND EVERY OTHER WIDEBAND COMMUNICATION SYSTEM WENT DARK.
SO WE'RE BLIND AND DEAF.
YOU GOT ANY GOOD NEWS, IZZY?
WELL...
I THINK I'M FALLING IN LOVE WITH SOMEONE.
THAT'S SOME TIMING, KIDDO.
"MAJESTOR, I MUST INSIST...WE CANNOT WAIT ANY LONGER."
WE NEED TO MAKE FOR BEHEMOTH AND THE FLEET STAGING AREA. THE SOONER WE REASSEMBLE THE COUNCIL, THE SOONER WE CAN STRIKE BACK.
MENTOR?
WHAT ORACLE IS SAYING HAS MERIT, BUT WE PICKED THIS RENDEZVOUS POINT FOR A REASON...

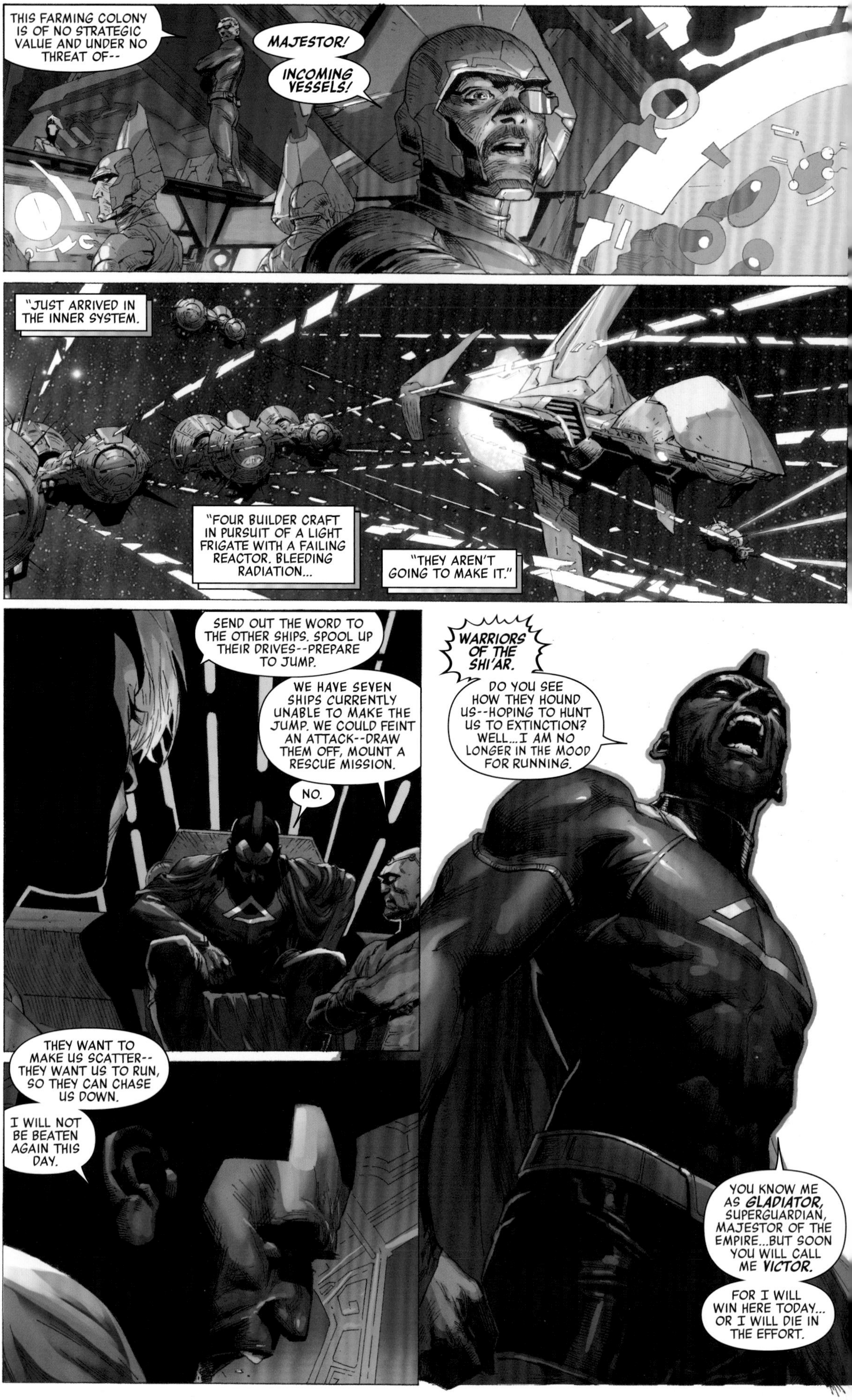

THIS FARMING COLONY IS OF NO STRATEGIC VALUE AND UNDER NO THREAT OF--
MAJESTOR!
INCOMING VESSELS!
"JUST ARRIVED IN THE INNER SYSTEM.
"FOUR BUILDER CRAFT IN PURSUIT OF A LIGHT FRIGATE WITH A FAILING REACTOR. BLEEDING RADIATION...
"THEY AREN'T GOING TO MAKE IT."
SEND OUT THE WORD TO THE OTHER SHIPS. SPOOL UP THEIR DRIVES--PREPARE TO JUMP.
WE HAVE SEVEN SHIPS CURRENTLY UNABLE TO MAKE THE JUMP. WE COULD FEINT AN ATTACK--DRAW THEM OFF, MOUNT A RESCUE MISSION.
NO.
THEY WANT TO MAKE US SCATTER--THEY WANT US TO RUN, SO THEY CAN CHASE US DOWN.
I WILL NOT BE BEATEN AGAIN THIS DAY.
WARRIORS OF THE SHI'AR.
DO YOU SEE HOW THEY HOUND US--HOPING TO HUNT US TO EXTINCTION? WELL...I AM NO LONGER IN THE MOOD FOR RUNNING.
YOU KNOW ME AS GLADIATOR, SUPERGUARDIAN, MAJESTOR OF THE EMPIRE...BUT SOON YOU WILL CALL ME VICTOR.
FOR I WILL WIN HERE TODAY... OR I WILL DIE IN THE EFFORT.

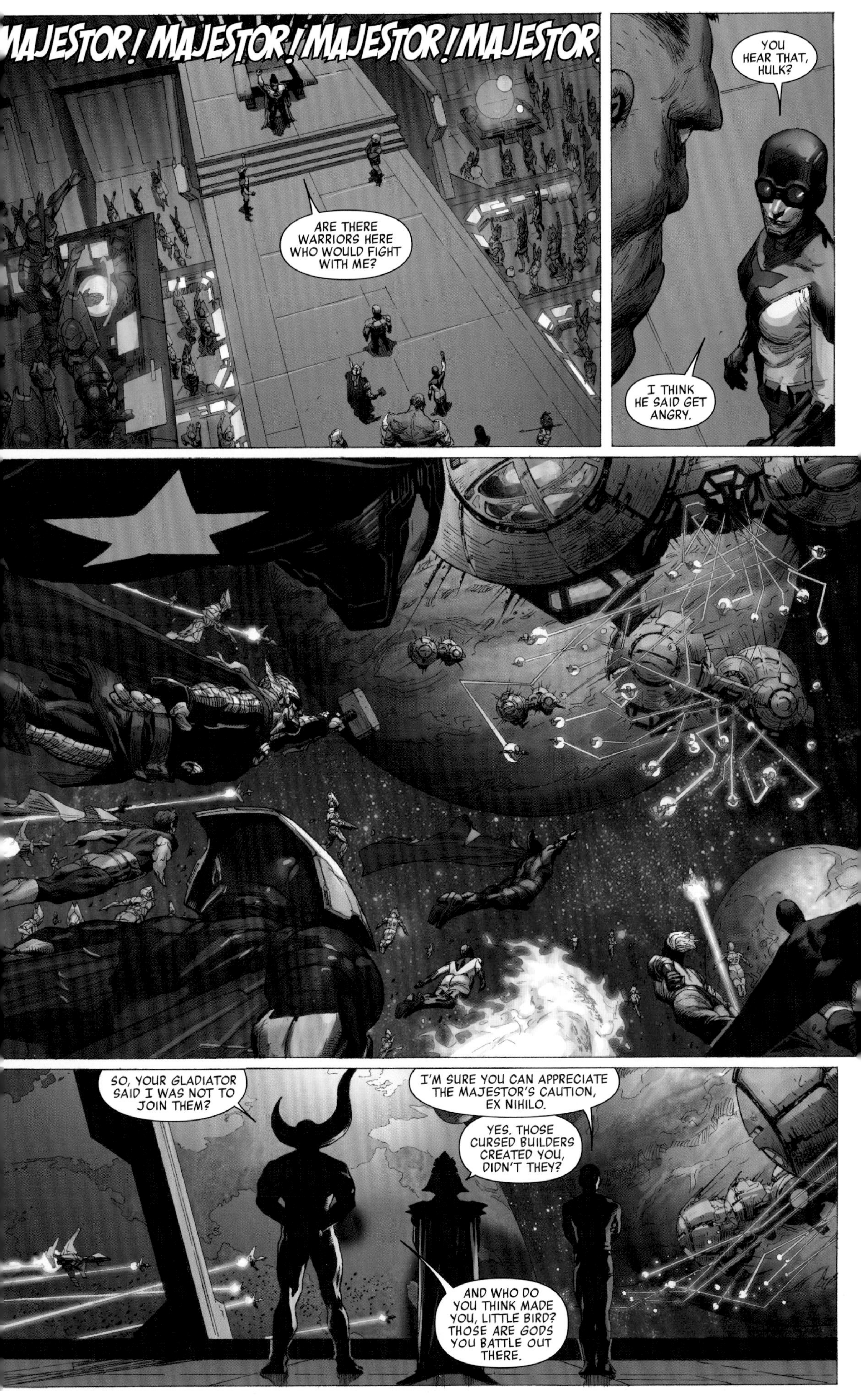
MAJESTOR! MAJESTOR! MAJESTOR! MAJESTOR!
ARE THERE WARRIORS HERE WHO WOULD FIGHT WITH ME?
YOU HEAR THAT, HULK?
I THINK HE SAID GET ANGRY.
SO, YOUR GLADIATOR SAID I WAS NOT TO JOIN THEM?
I'M SURE YOU CAN APPRECIATE THE MAJESTOR'S CAUTION, EX NIHILO.
YES. THOSE CURSED BUILDERS CREATED YOU, DIDN'T THEY?
AND WHO DO YOU THINK MADE YOU, LITTLE BIRD? THOSE ARE GODS YOU BATTLE OUT THERE.

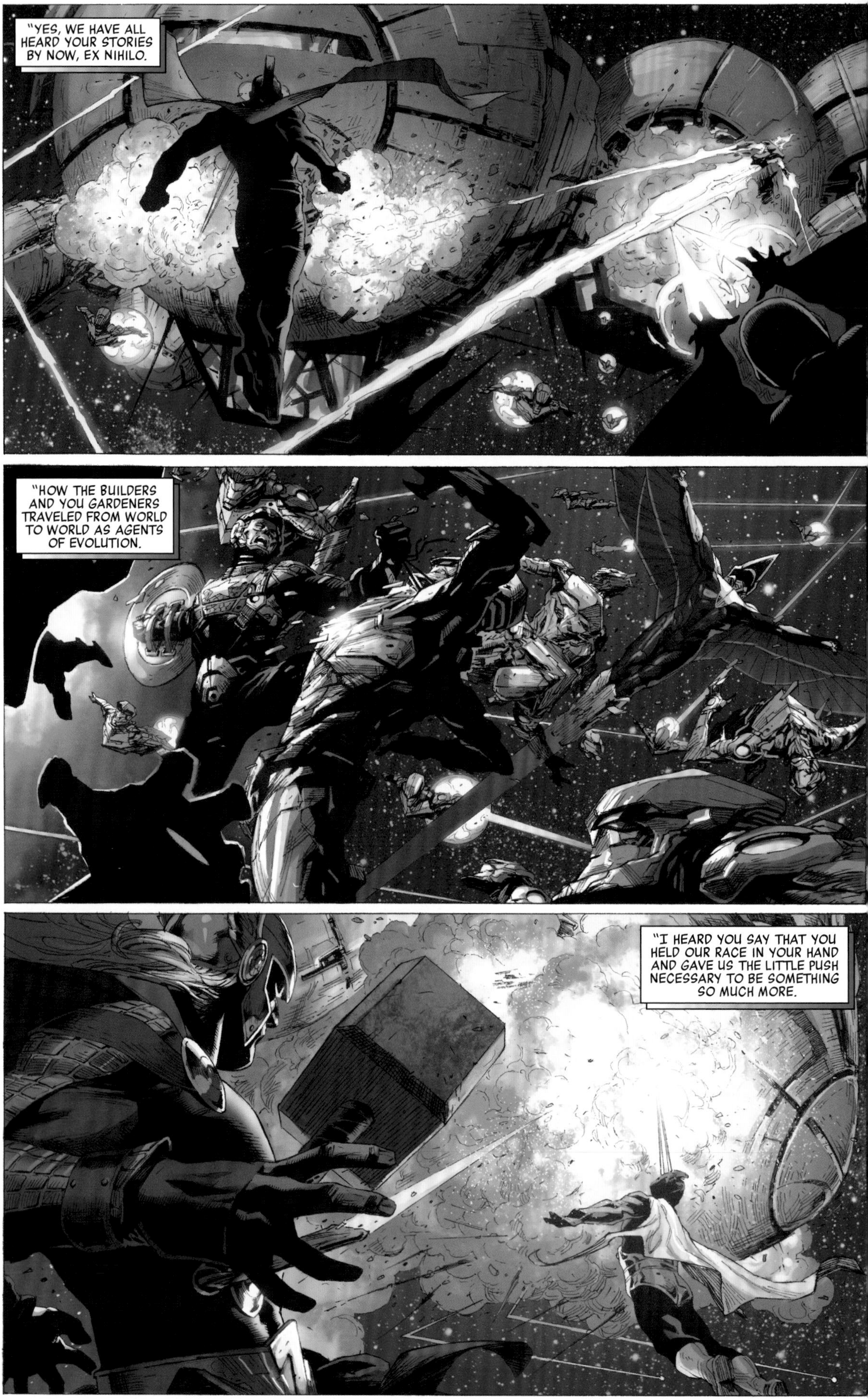
"YES, WE HAVE ALL HEARD YOUR STORIES BY NOW, EX NIHILO.
"HOW THE BUILDERS AND YOU GARDENERS TRAVELED FROM WORLD TO WORLD AS AGENTS OF EVOLUTION.
"I HEARD YOU SAY THAT YOU HELD OUR RACE IN YOUR HAND AND GAVE US THE LITTLE PUSH NECESSARY TO BE SOMETHING SO MUCH MORE.

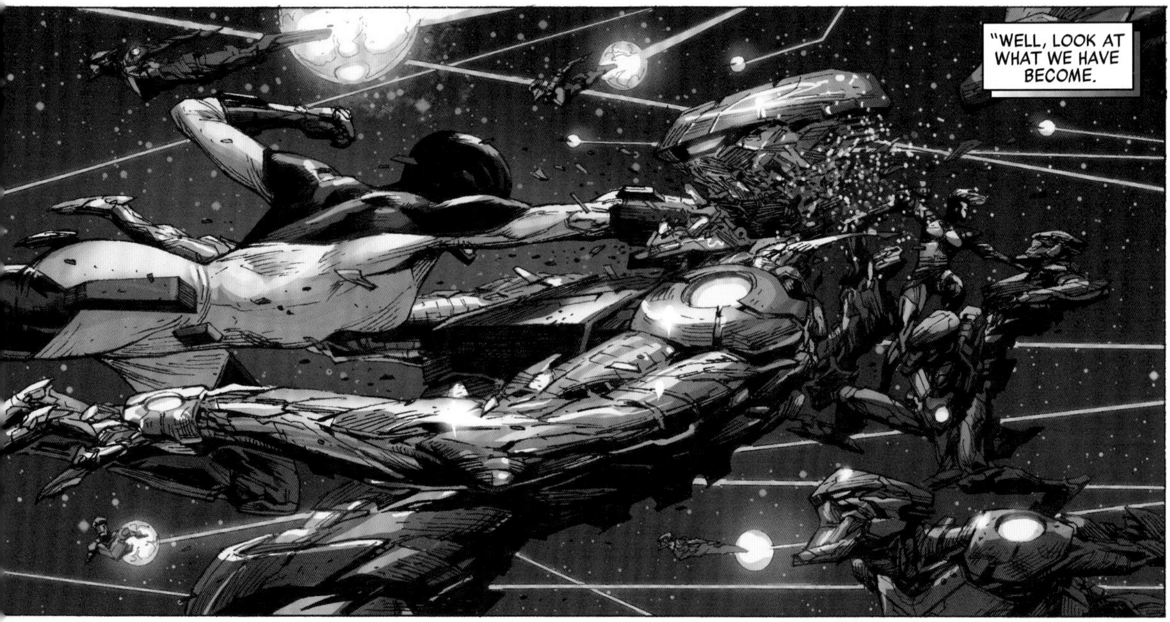
"WELL, LOOK AT WHAT WE HAVE BECOME.

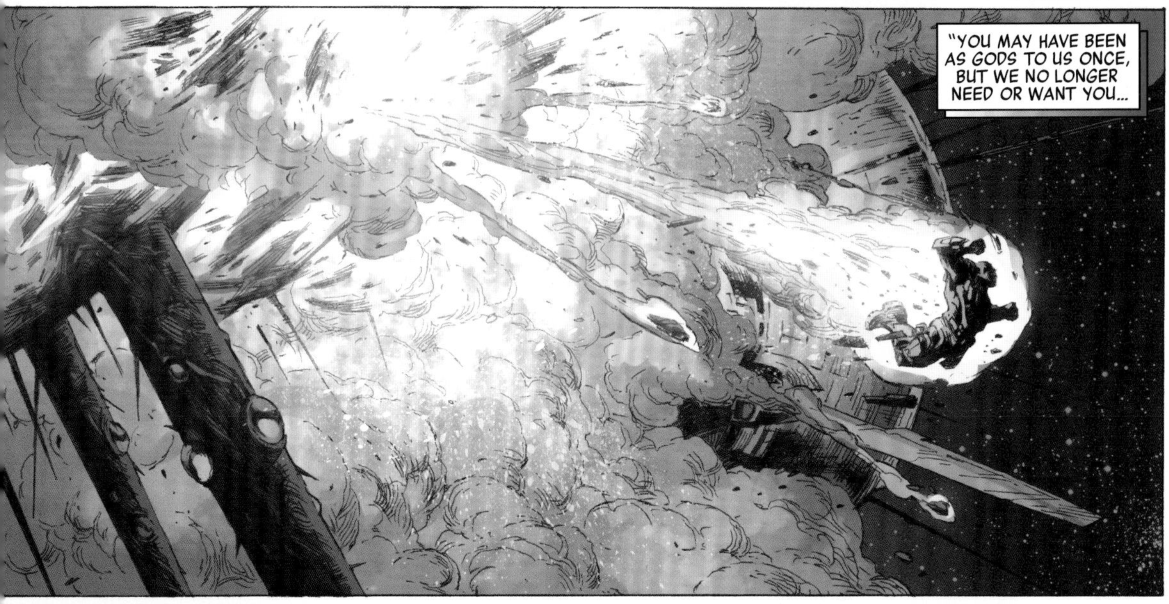
"YOU MAY HAVE BEEN AS GODS TO US ONCE, BUT WE NO LONGER NEED OR WANT YOU...

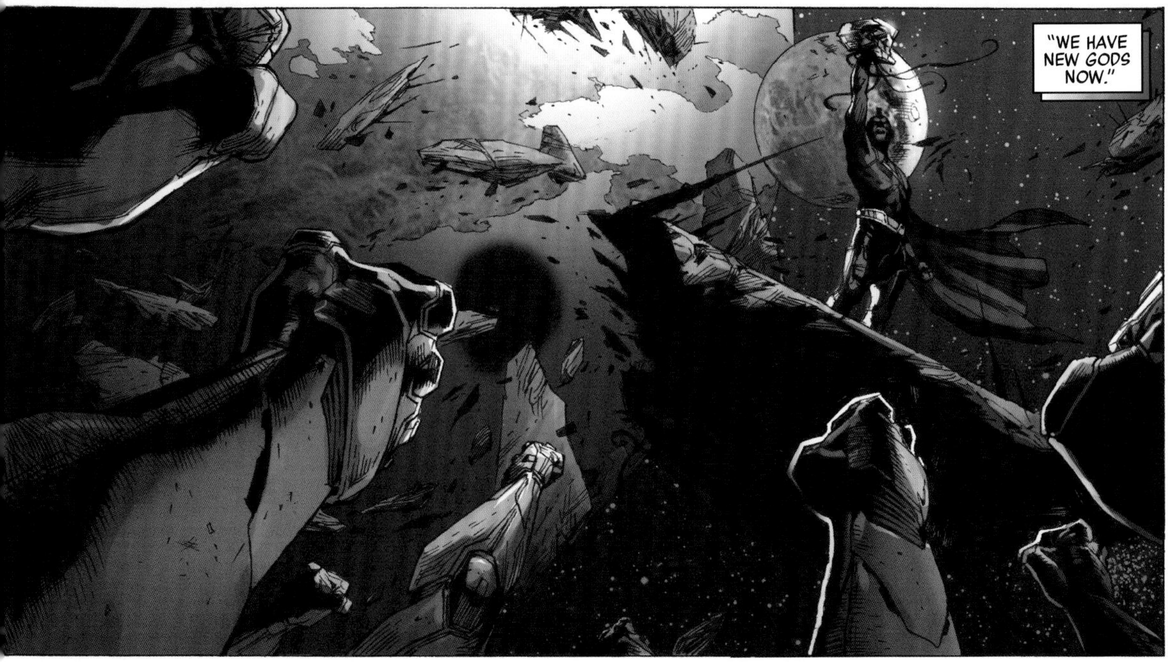
"WE HAVE NEW GODS NOW."

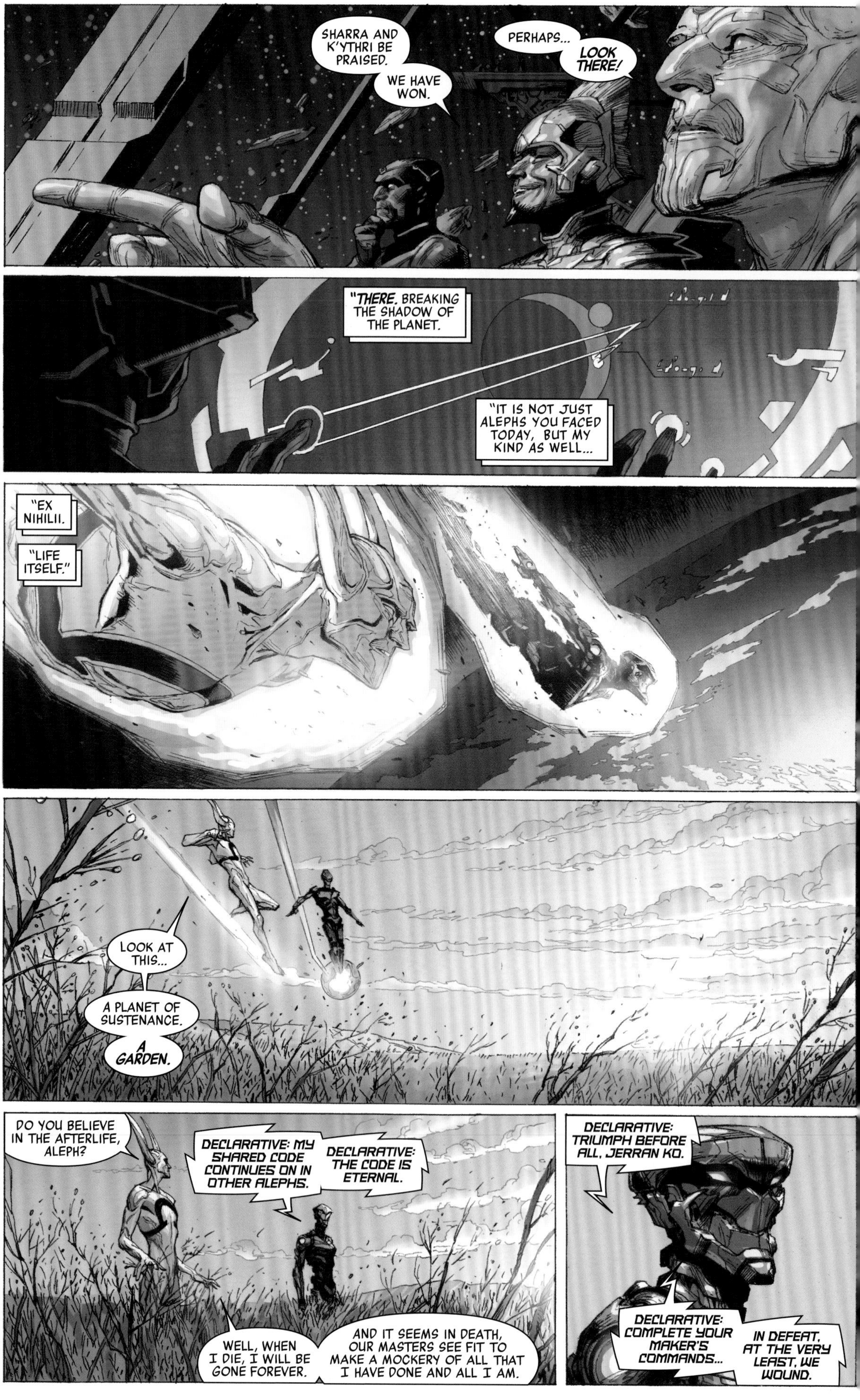
SHARRA AND K'YTHRI BE PRAISED.
WE HAVE WON.
PERHAPS...
LOOK THERE!
"THERE. BREAKING THE SHADOW OF THE PLANET.
"IT IS NOT JUST ALEPHS YOU FACED TODAY, BUT MY KIND AS WELL...
"EX NIHILII.
"LIFE ITSELF."
LOOK AT THIS...
A PLANET OF SUSTENANCE.
A GARDEN.
DO YOU BELIEVE IN THE AFTERLIFE, ALEPH?
DECLARATIVE: MY SHARED CODE CONTINUES ON IN OTHER ALEPHS.
DECLARATIVE: THE CODE IS ETERNAL.
WELL, WHEN I DIE, I WILL BE GONE FOREVER.
AND IT SEEMS IN DEATH, OUR MASTERS SEE FIT TO MAKE A MOCKERY OF ALL THAT I HAVE DONE AND ALL I AM.
DECLARATIVE: TRIUMPH BEFORE ALL, JERRAN KO.
DECLARATIVE: COMPLETE YOUR MAKER'S COMMANDS...
IN DEFEAT, AT THE VERY LEAST, WE WOUND.

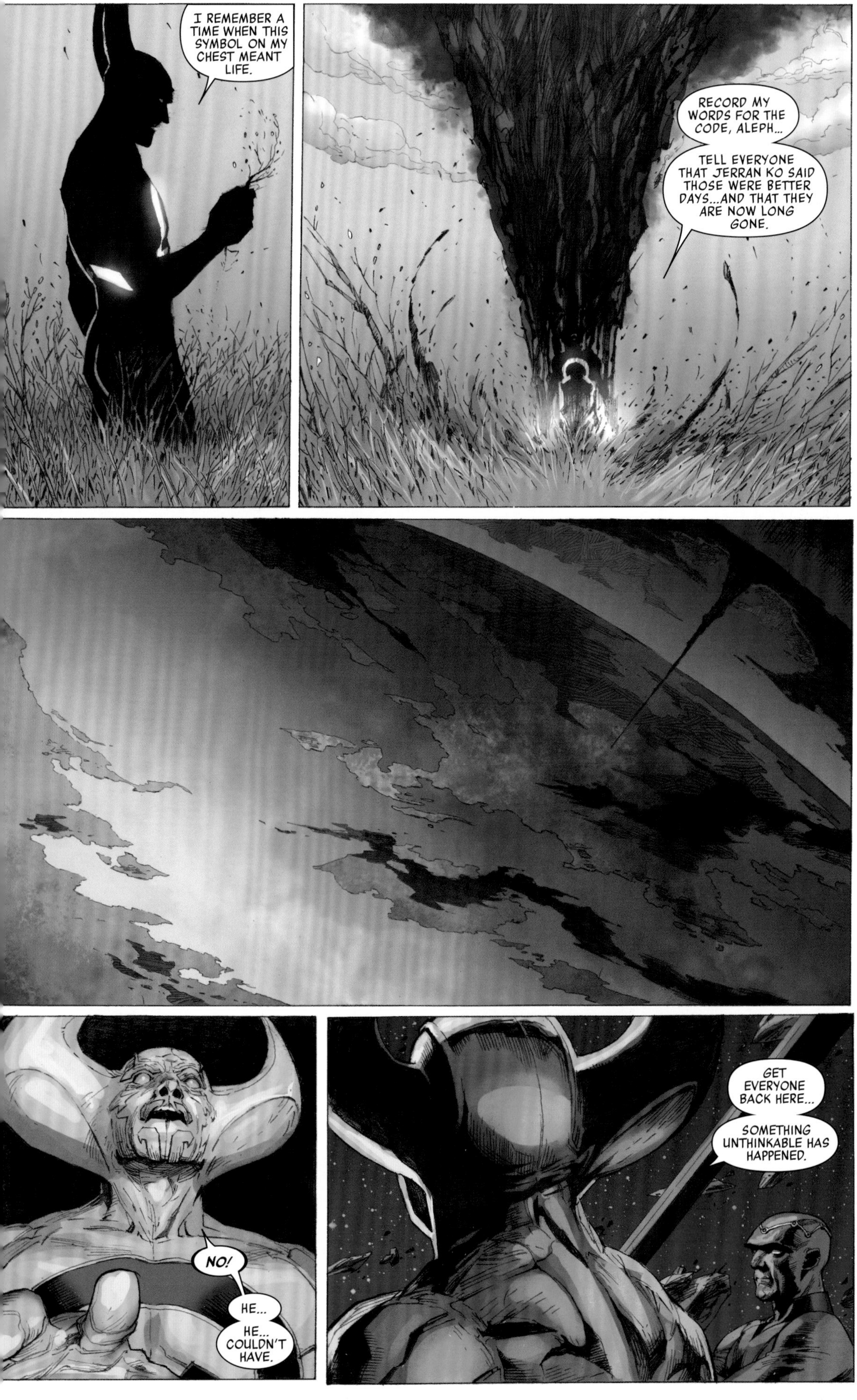
I REMEMBER A TIME WHEN THIS SYMBOL ON MY CHEST MEANT LIFE.
RECORD MY WORDS FOR THE CODE, ALEPH...
TELL EVERYONE THAT JERRAN KO SAID THOSE WERE BETTER DAYS...AND THAT THEY ARE NOW LONG GONE.
NO!
HE...
HE... COULDN'T HAVE.
GET EVERYONE BACK HERE...
SOMETHING UNTHINKABLE HAS HAPPENED.

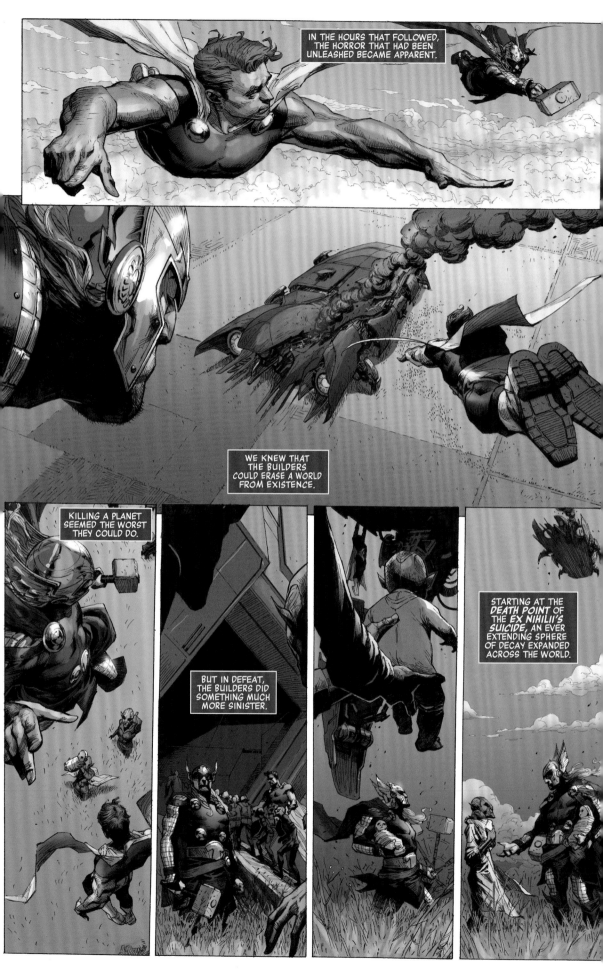

IN THE HOURS THAT FOLLOWED, THE HORROR THAT HAD BEEN UNLEASHED BECAME APPARENT.

WE KNEW THAT THE BUILDERS COULD ERASE A WORLD FROM EXISTENCE.

KILLING A PLANET SEEMED THE WORST THEY COULD DO.

BUT IN DEFEAT, THE BUILDERS DID SOMETHING MUCH MORE SINISTER.

STARTING AT THE *DEATH POINT* OF THE *EX NIHILII'S SUICIDE,* AN EVER EXTENDING SPHERE OF DECAY EXPANDED ACROSS THE WORLD.

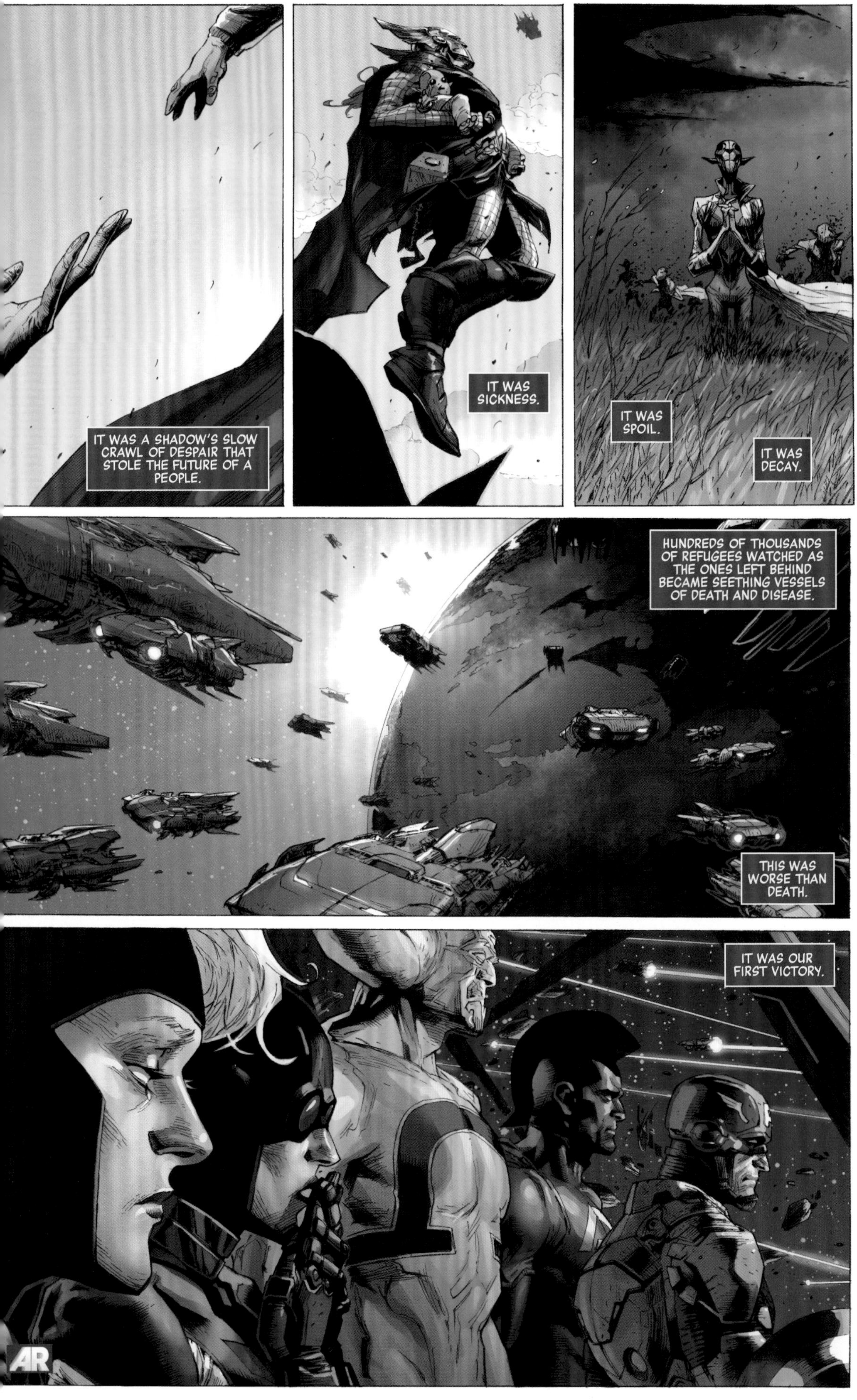
IT WAS A SHADOW'S SLOW CRAWL OF DESPAIR THAT STOLE THE FUTURE OF A PEOPLE.
IT WAS SICKNESS.
IT WAS SPOIL.
IT WAS DECAY.
HUNDREDS OF THOUSANDS OF REFUGEES WATCHED AS THE ONES LEFT BEHIND BECAME SEETHING VESSELS OF DEATH AND DISEASE.
THIS WAS WORSE THAN DEATH.
IT WAS OUR FIRST VICTORY.

A CONVENIENT LIE

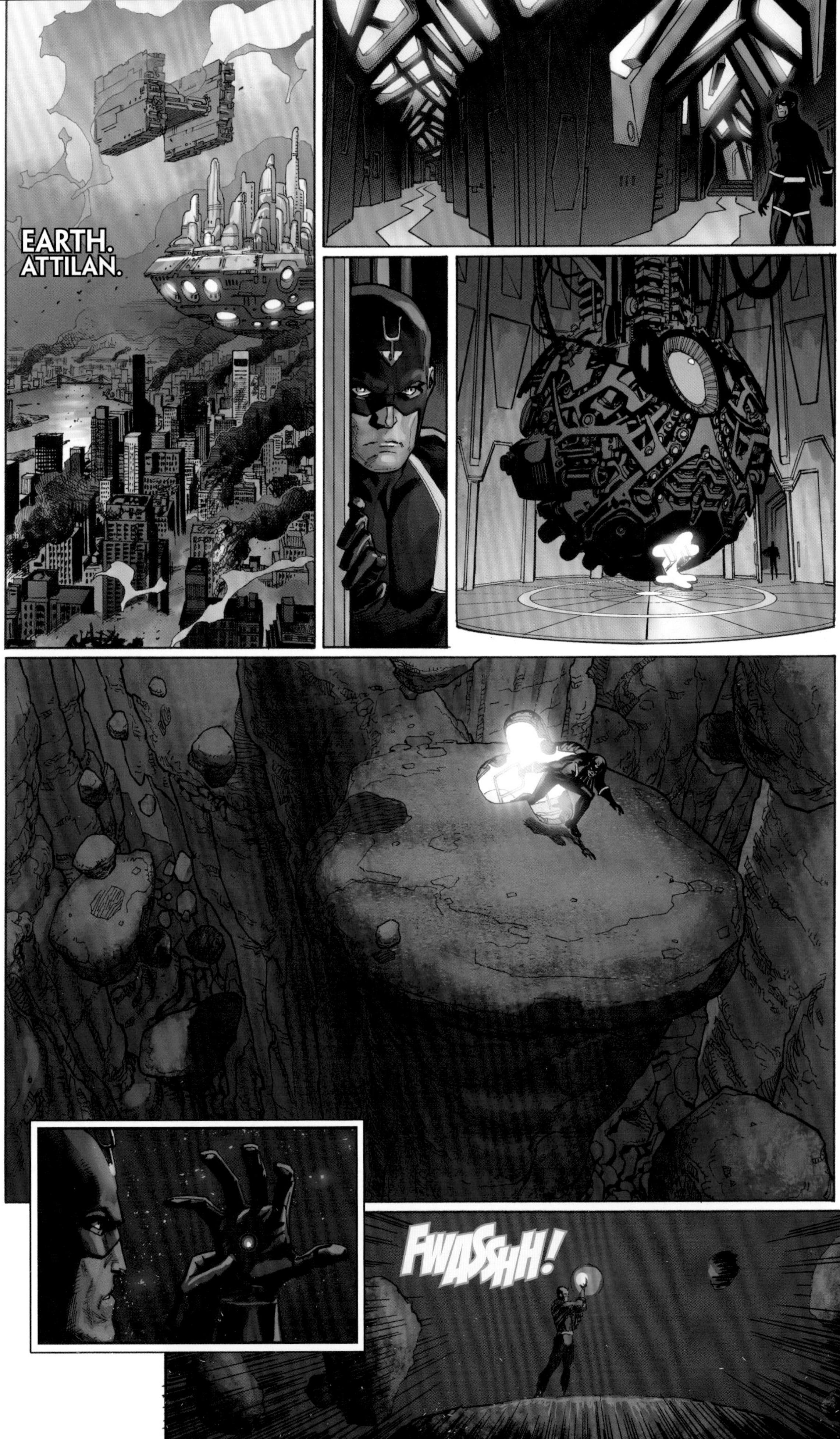
EARTH.
ATTILAN.
FWASSHH!

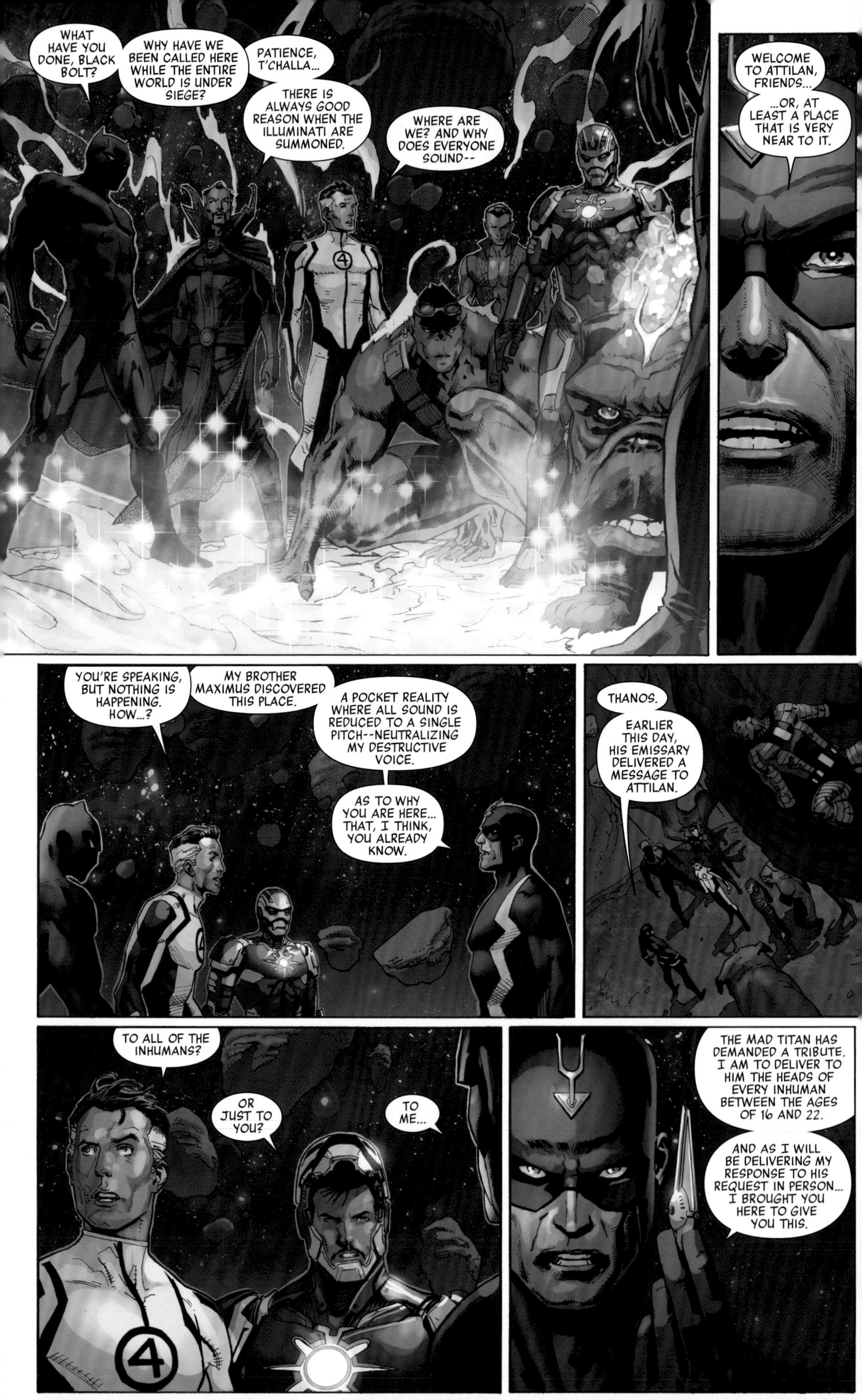

WHAT HAVE YOU DONE, BLACK BOLT?
WHY HAVE WE BEEN CALLED HERE WHILE THE ENTIRE WORLD IS UNDER SIEGE?
PATIENCE, T'CHALLA...
THERE IS ALWAYS GOOD REASON WHEN THE ILLUMINATI ARE SUMMONED.
WHERE ARE WE? AND WHY DOES EVERYONE SOUND--
WELCOME TO ATTILAN, FRIENDS...
...OR, AT LEAST A PLACE THAT IS VERY NEAR TO IT.
YOU'RE SPEAKING, BUT NOTHING IS HAPPENING. HOW...?
MY BROTHER MAXIMUS DISCOVERED THIS PLACE.
A POCKET REALITY WHERE ALL SOUND IS REDUCED TO A SINGLE PITCH--NEUTRALIZING MY DESTRUCTIVE VOICE.
AS TO WHY YOU ARE HERE... THAT, I THINK, YOU ALREADY KNOW.
THANOS.
EARLIER THIS DAY, HIS EMISSARY DELIVERED A MESSAGE TO ATTILAN.
TO ALL OF THE INHUMANS?
OR JUST TO YOU?
TO ME...
THE MAD TITAN HAS DEMANDED A TRIBUTE. I AM TO DELIVER TO HIM THE HEADS OF EVERY INHUMAN BETWEEN THE AGES OF 16 AND 22.
AND AS I WILL BE DELIVERING MY RESPONSE TO HIS REQUEST IN PERSON... I BROUGHT YOU HERE TO GIVE YOU THIS.

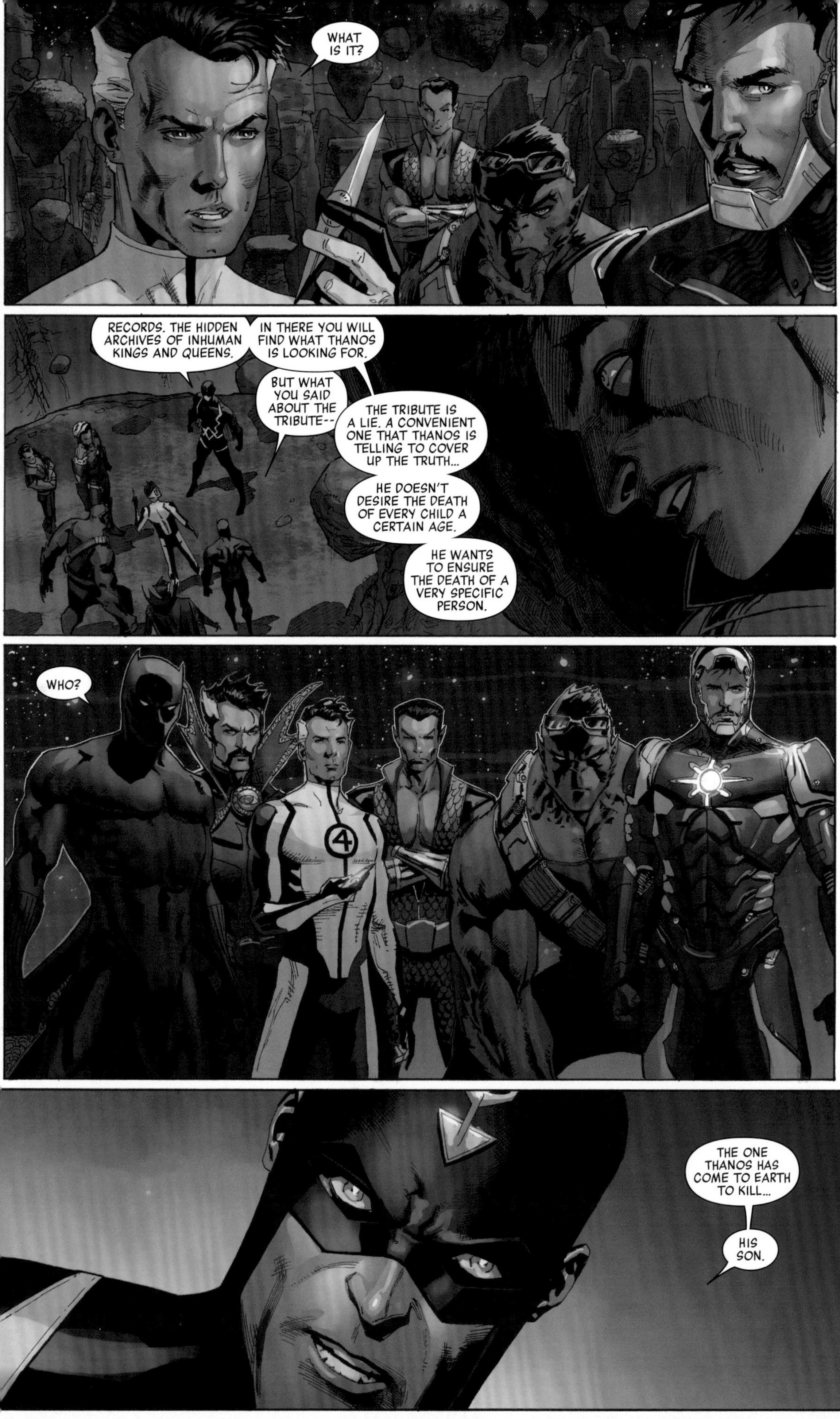
WHAT IS IT?
RECORDS. THE HIDDEN ARCHIVES OF INHUMAN KINGS AND QUEENS.
IN THERE YOU WILL FIND WHAT THANOS IS LOOKING FOR.
BUT WHAT YOU SAID ABOUT THE TRIBUTE--
THE TRIBUTE IS A LIE. A CONVENIENT ONE THAT THANOS IS TELLING TO COVER UP THE TRUTH...
HE DOESN'T DESIRE THE DEATH OF EVERY CHILD A CERTAIN AGE.
HE WANTS TO ENSURE THE DEATH OF A VERY SPECIFIC PERSON.
WHO?
THE ONE THANOS HAS COME TO EARTH TO KILL...
HIS SON.

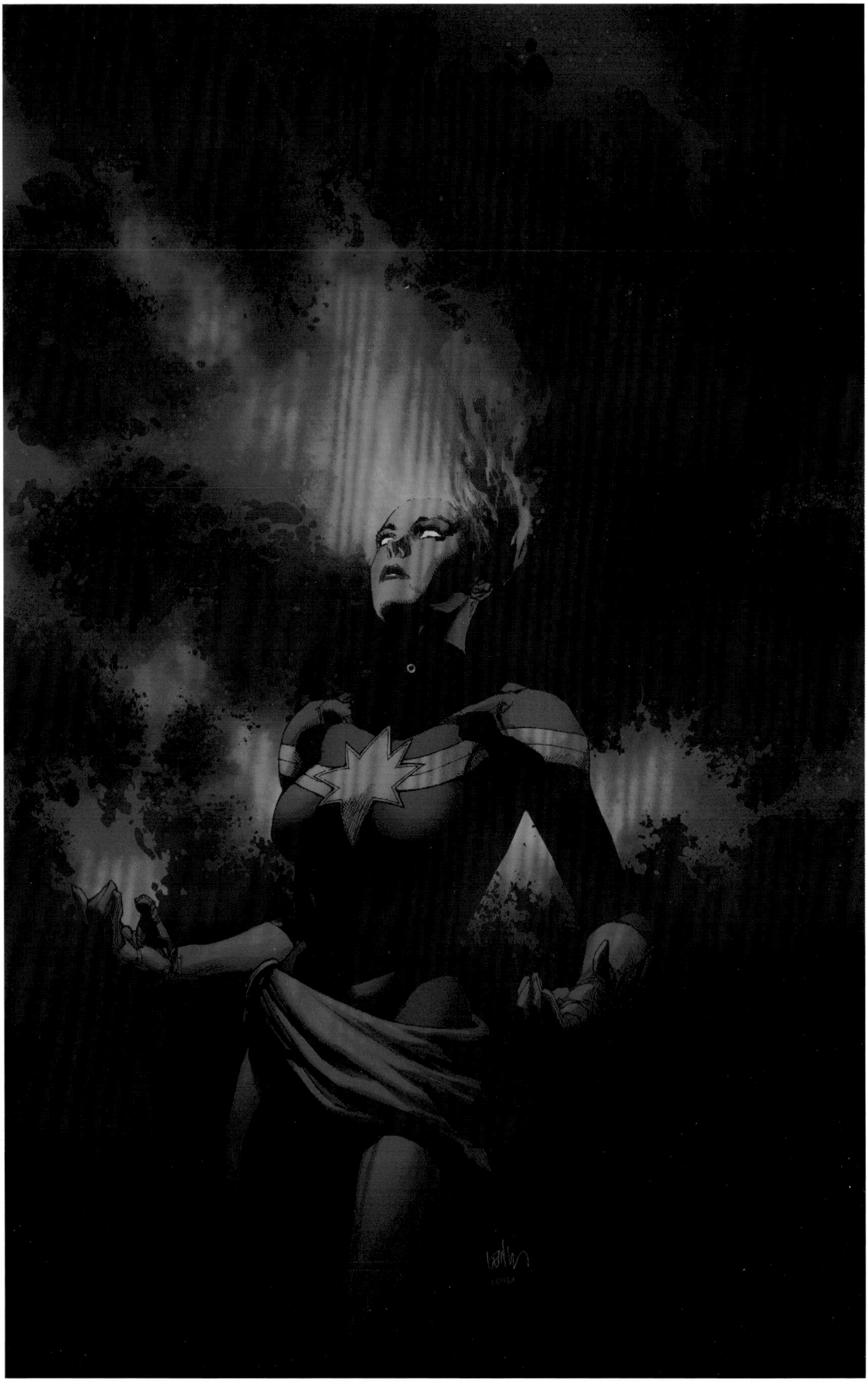

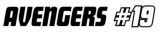

BINARY COLLAPSE

◆

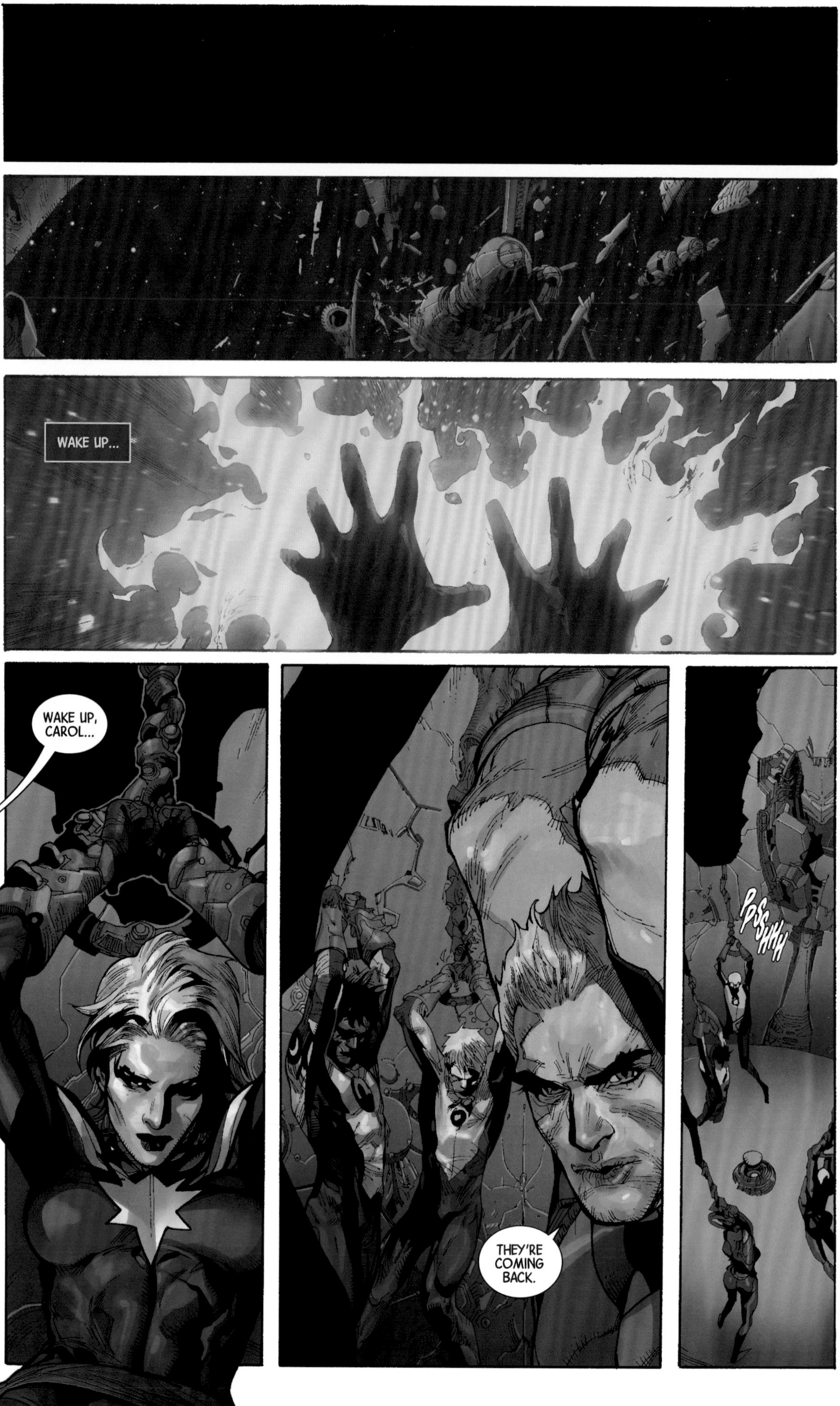
WAKE UP...
WAKE UP, CAROL...
THEY'RE COMING BACK.
PPSSHHH

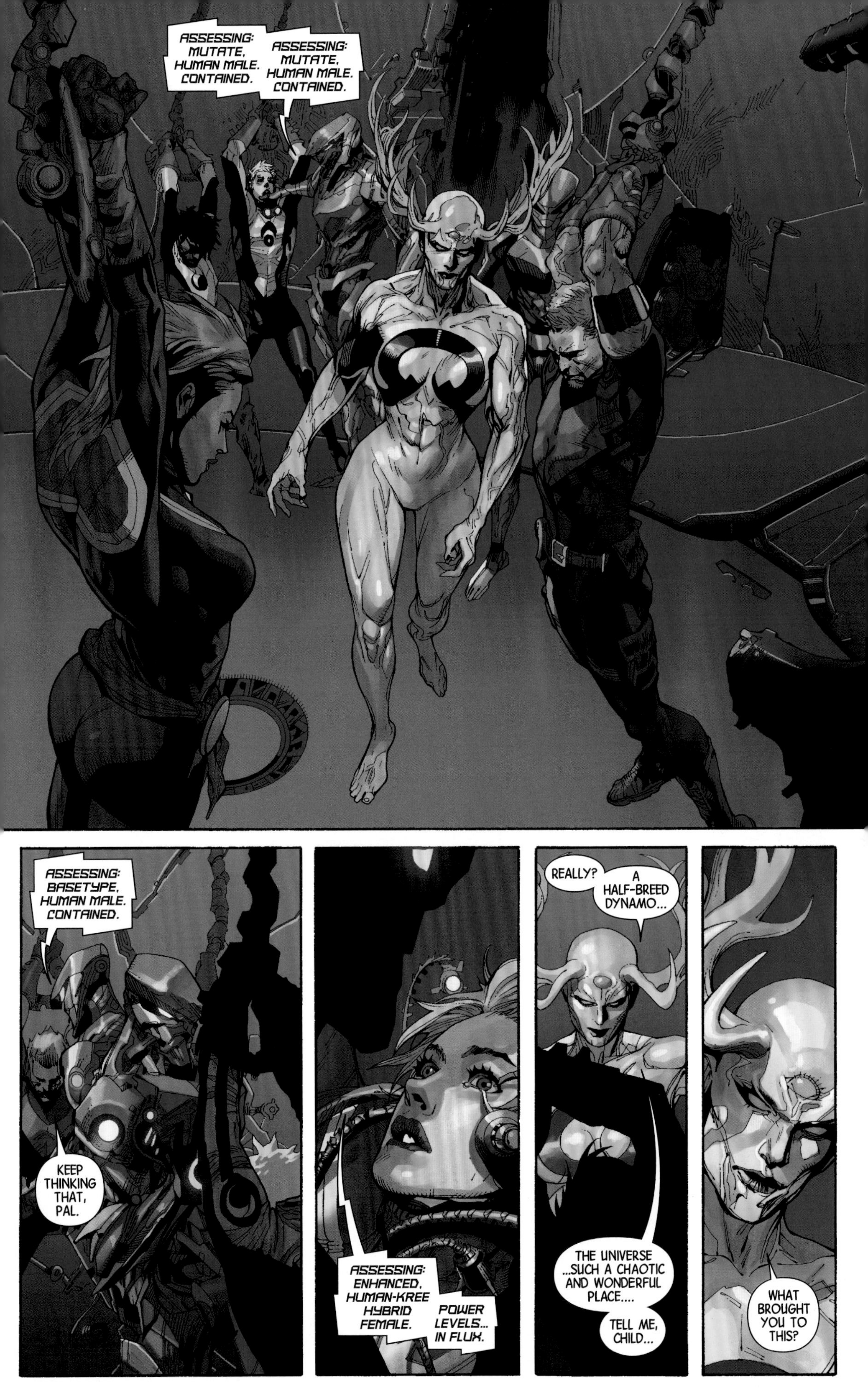
ASSESSING: MUTATE, HUMAN MALE. CONTAINED.
ASSESSING: MUTATE, HUMAN MALE. CONTAINED.
ASSESSING: BASETYPE, HUMAN MALE. CONTAINED.
KEEP THINKING THAT, PAL.
ASSESSING: ENHANCED, HUMAN-KREE HYBRID FEMALE.
POWER LEVELS... IN FLUX.
REALLY?
A HALF-BREED DYNAMO...
THE UNIVERSE ...SUCH A CHAOTIC AND WONDERFUL PLACE....
TELL ME, CHILD...
WHAT BROUGHT YOU TO THIS?

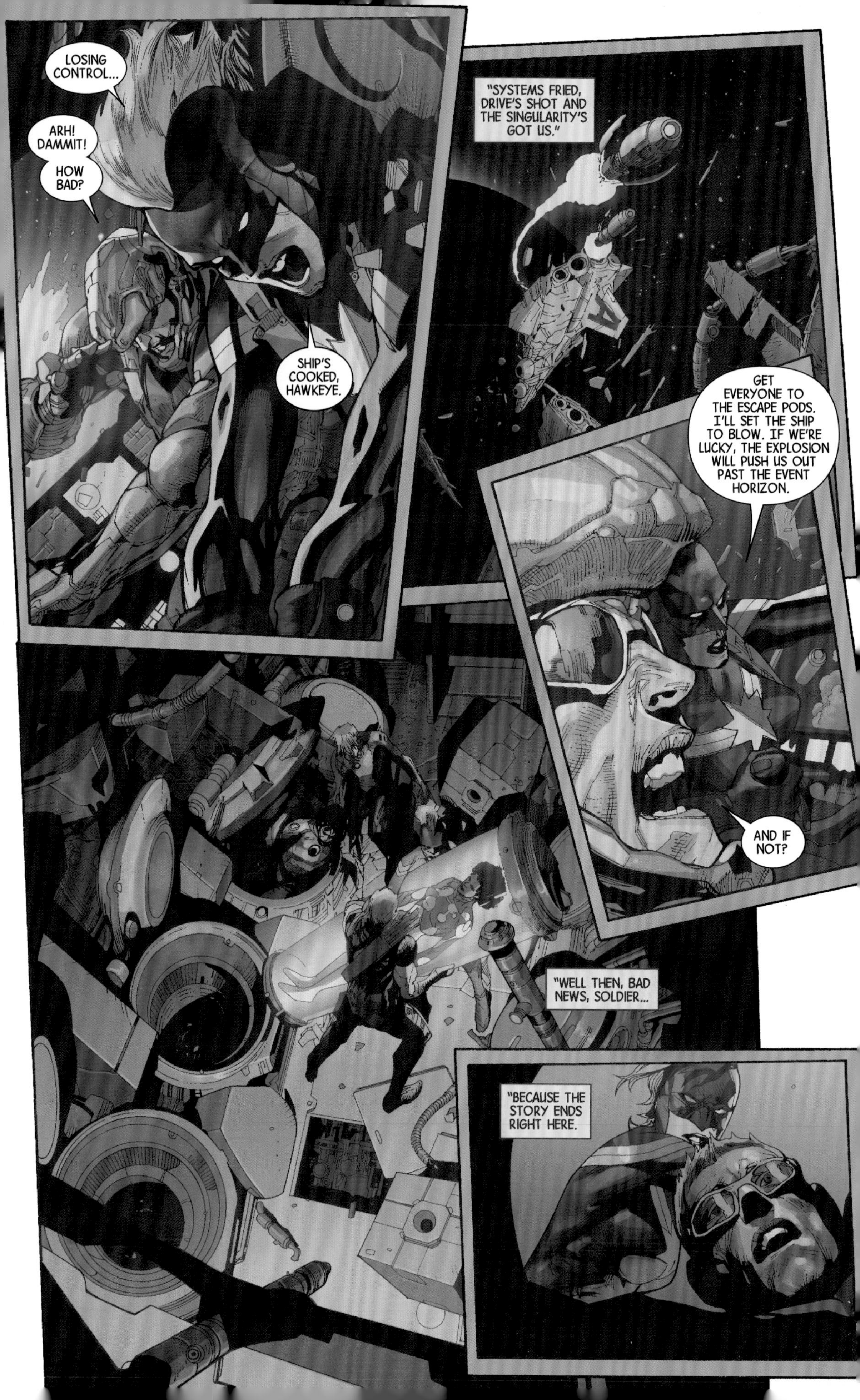
LOSING CONTROL...
ARH! DAMMIT!
HOW BAD?
SHIP'S COOKED, HAWKEYE.
"SYSTEMS FRIED, DRIVE'S SHOT AND THE SINGULARITY'S GOT US."
GET EVERYONE TO THE ESCAPE PODS. I'LL SET THE SHIP TO BLOW. IF WE'RE LUCKY, THE EXPLOSION WILL PUSH US OUT PAST THE EVENT HORIZON.
AND IF NOT?
"WELL THEN, BAD NEWS, SOLDIER...
"BECAUSE THE STORY ENDS RIGHT HERE.

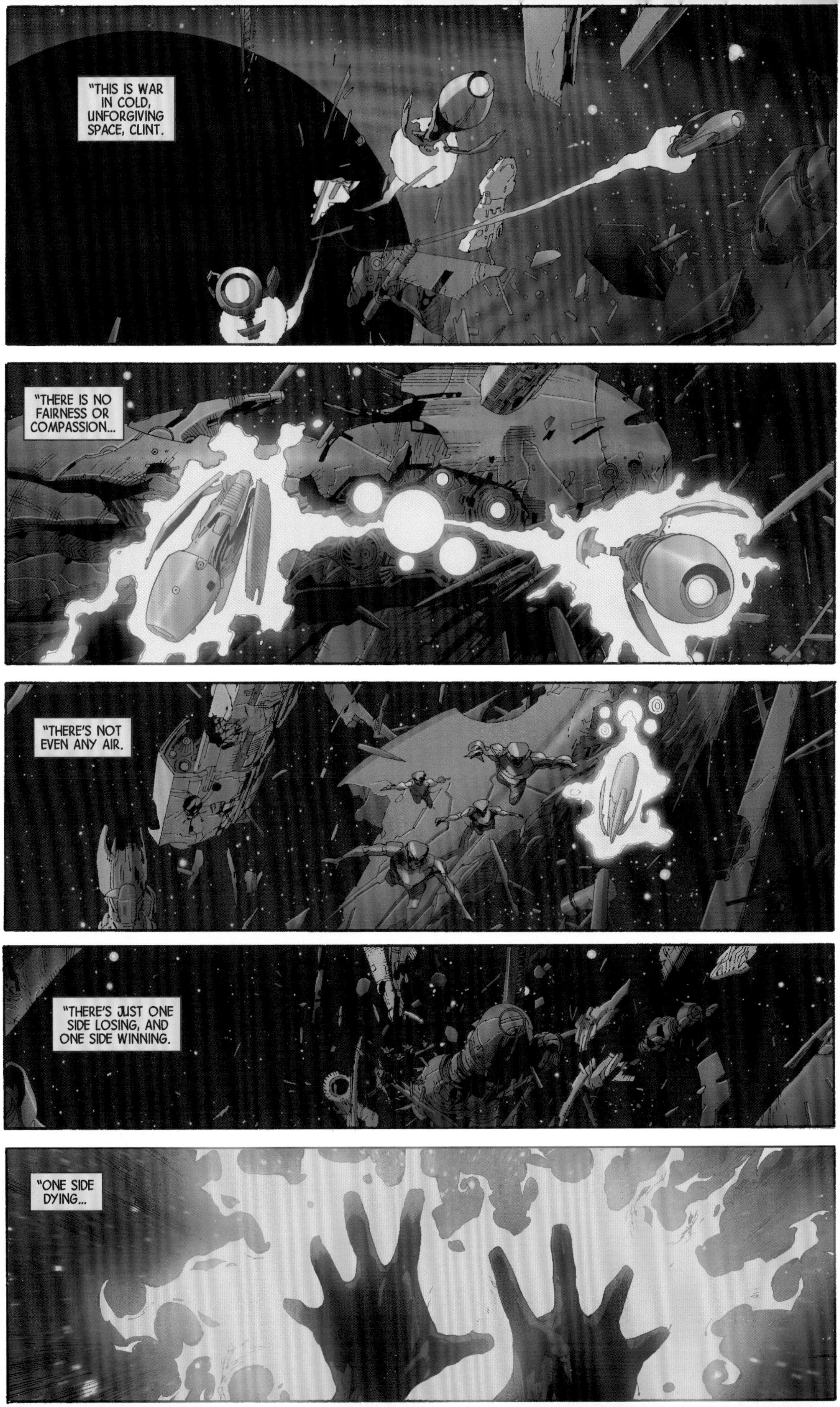
"THIS IS WAR IN COLD, UNFORGIVING SPACE, CLINT.
"THERE IS NO FAIRNESS OR COMPASSION...
"THERE'S NOT EVEN ANY AIR.
"THERE'S JUST ONE SIDE LOSING, AND ONE SIDE WINNING.
"ONE SIDE DYING...

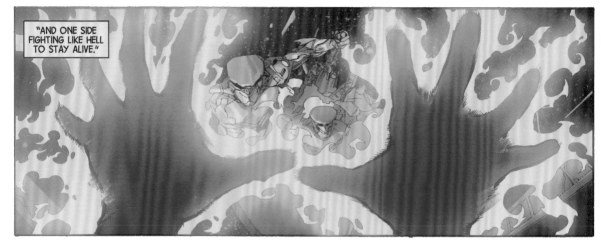

"AND ONE SIDE FIGHTING LIKE HELL TO STAY ALIVE."

"TELL ME, CHILD..."

AR

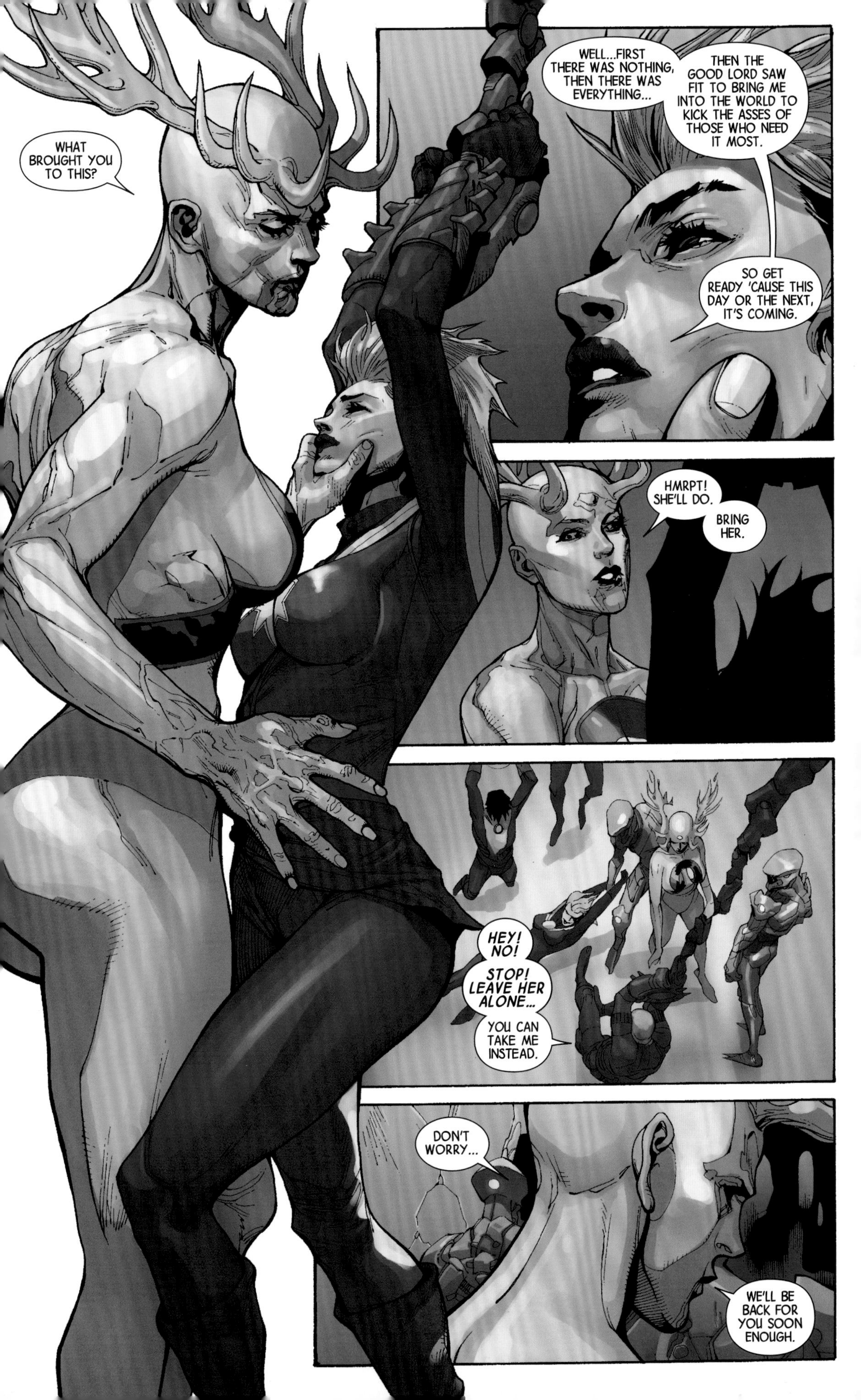
WHAT BROUGHT YOU TO THIS?
WELL...FIRST THERE WAS NOTHING, THEN THERE WAS EVERYTHING...
THEN THE GOOD LORD SAW FIT TO BRING ME INTO THE WORLD TO KICK THE ASSES OF THOSE WHO NEED IT MOST.
SO GET READY 'CAUSE THIS DAY OR THE NEXT, IT'S COMING.
HMRPT! SHE'LL DO.
BRING HER.
HEY! NO!
STOP! LEAVE HER ALONE...
YOU CAN TAKE ME INSTEAD.
DON'T WORRY...
WE'LL BE BACK FOR YOU SOON ENOUGH.

BEHEMOTH

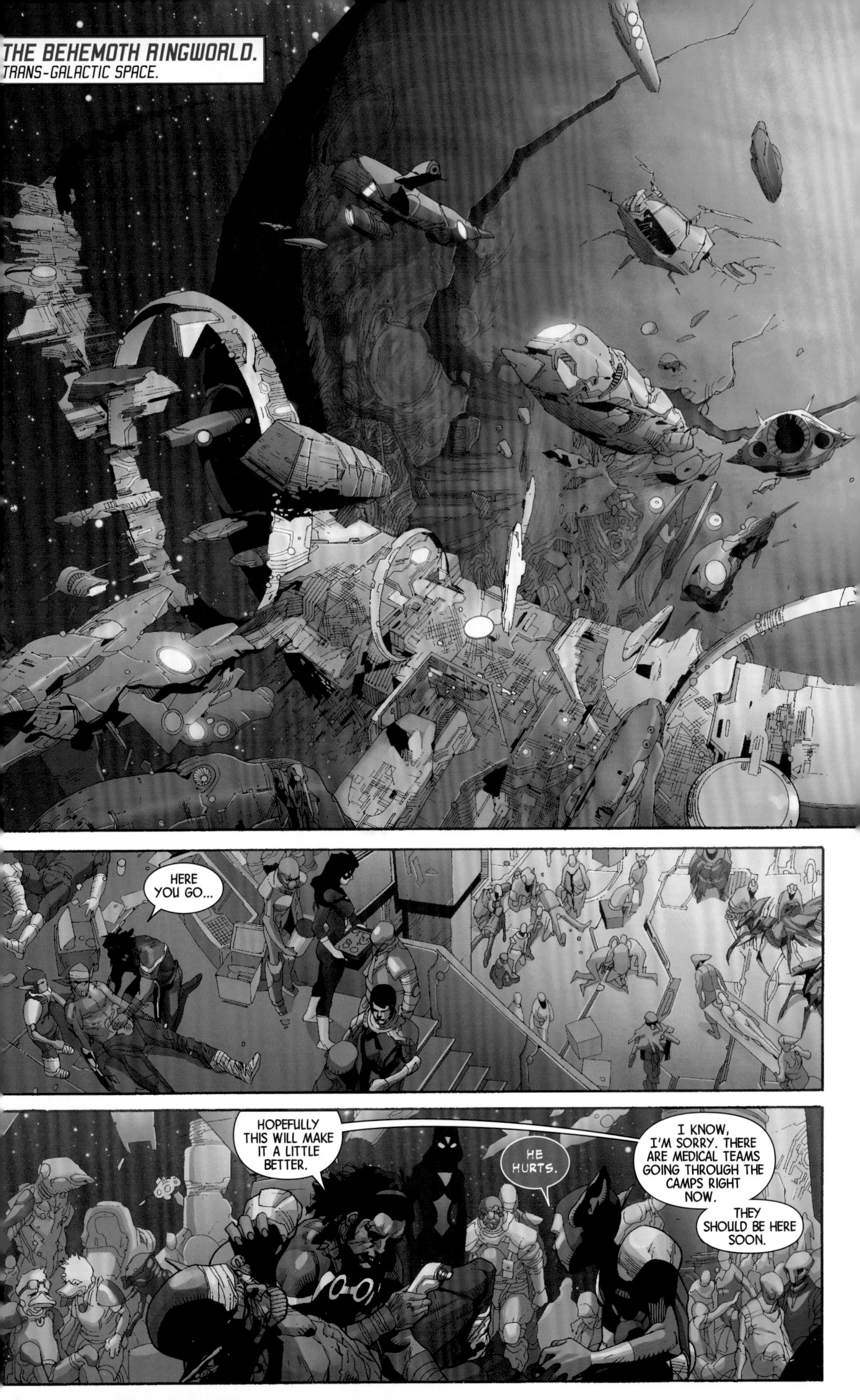
THE BEHEMOTH RINGWORLD.
TRANS-GALACTIC SPACE.
HERE YOU GO...
HOPEFULLY THIS WILL MAKE IT A LITTLE BETTER.
HE HURTS.
I KNOW, I'M SORRY. THERE ARE MEDICAL TEAMS GOING THROUGH THE CAMPS RIGHT NOW.
THEY SHOULD BE HERE SOON.

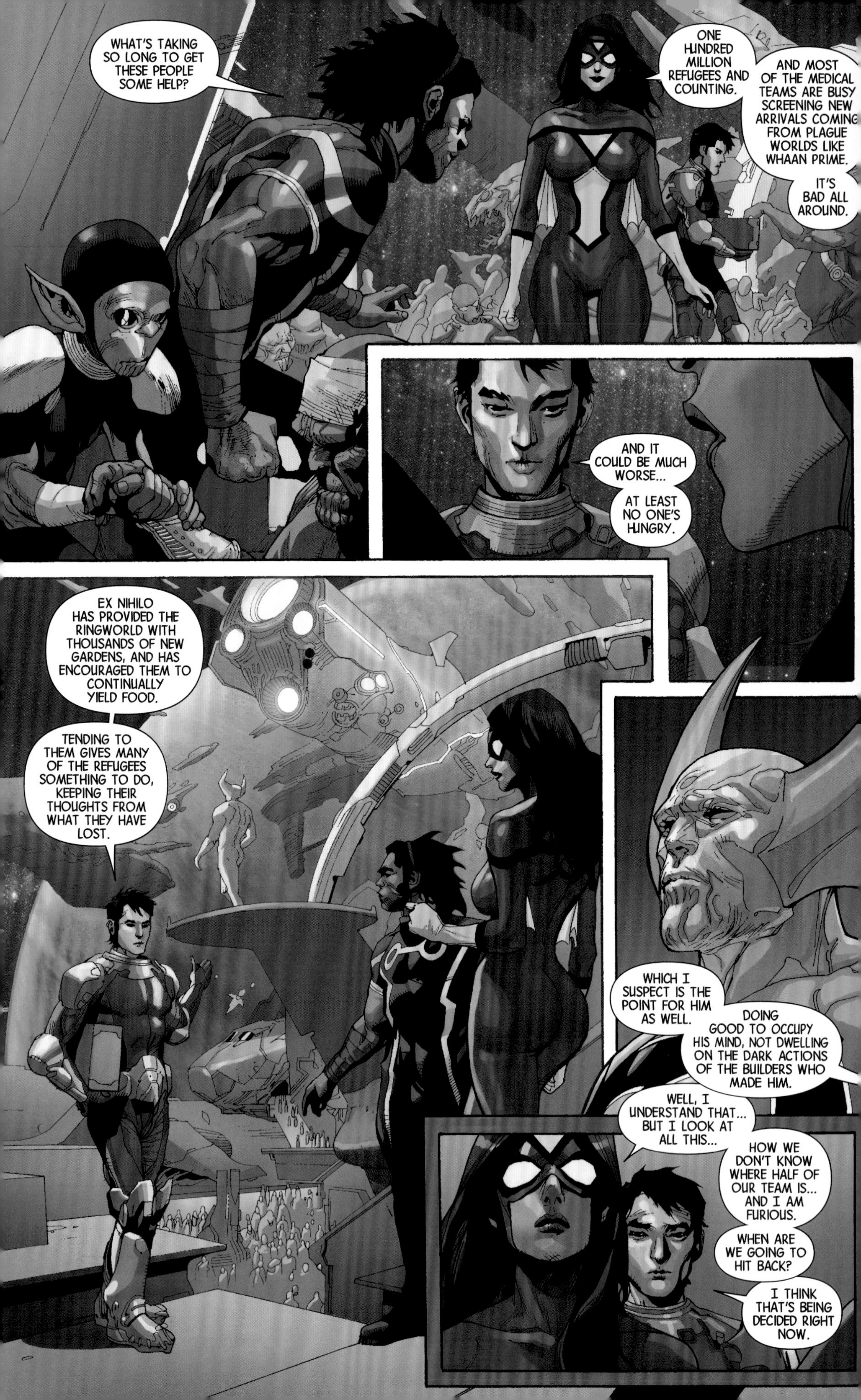
WHAT'S TAKING SO LONG TO GET THESE PEOPLE SOME HELP?
ONE HUNDRED MILLION REFUGEES AND COUNTING.
AND MOST OF THE MEDICAL TEAMS ARE BUSY SCREENING NEW ARRIVALS COMING FROM PLAGUE WORLDS LIKE WHAAN PRIME.
IT'S BAD ALL AROUND.
AND IT COULD BE MUCH WORSE...
AT LEAST NO ONE'S HUNGRY.
EX NIHILO HAS PROVIDED THE RINGWORLD WITH THOUSANDS OF NEW GARDENS, AND HAS ENCOURAGED THEM TO CONTINUALLY YIELD FOOD.
TENDING TO THEM GIVES MANY OF THE REFUGEES SOMETHING TO DO, KEEPING THEIR THOUGHTS FROM WHAT THEY HAVE LOST.
WHICH I SUSPECT IS THE POINT FOR HIM AS WELL.
DOING GOOD TO OCCUPY HIS MIND, NOT DWELLING ON THE DARK ACTIONS OF THE BUILDERS WHO MADE HIM.
WELL, I UNDERSTAND THAT... BUT I LOOK AT ALL THIS...
HOW WE DON'T KNOW WHERE HALF OF OUR TEAM IS... AND I AM FURIOUS.
WHEN ARE WE GOING TO HIT BACK?
I THINK THAT'S BEING DECIDED RIGHT NOW.

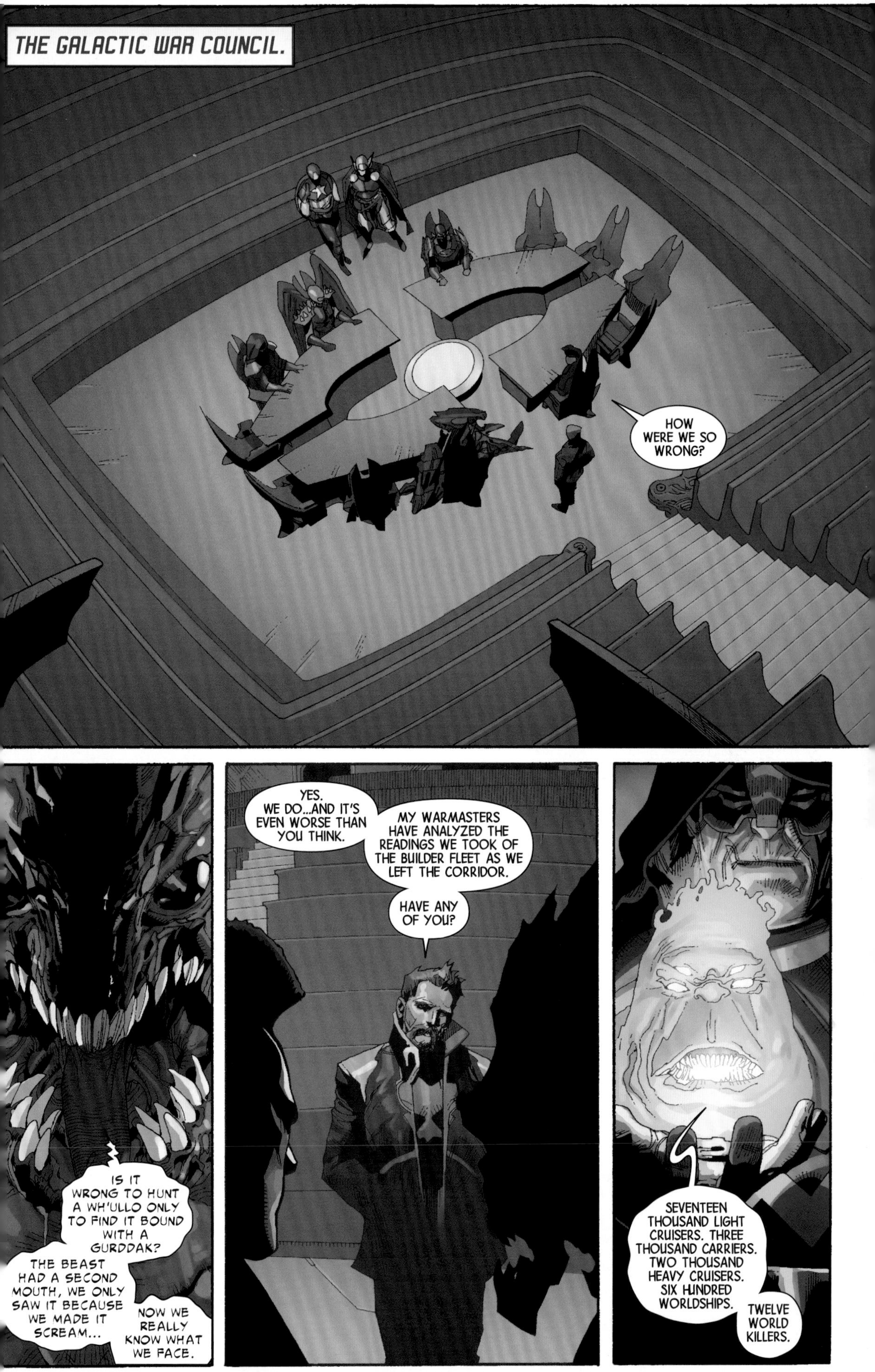
THE GALACTIC WAR COUNCIL.
HOW WERE WE SO WRONG?
IS IT WRONG TO HUNT A WH'ULLO ONLY TO FIND IT BOUND WITH A GURDDAK?
THE BEAST HAD A SECOND MOUTH, WE ONLY SAW IT BECAUSE WE MADE IT SCREAM...
NOW WE REALLY KNOW WHAT WE FACE.
YES. WE DO...AND IT'S EVEN WORSE THAN YOU THINK.
MY WARMASTERS HAVE ANALYZED THE READINGS WE TOOK OF THE BUILDER FLEET AS WE LEFT THE CORRIDOR.
HAVE ANY OF YOU?
SEVENTEEN THOUSAND LIGHT CRUISERS. THREE THOUSAND CARRIERS. TWO THOUSAND HEAVY CRUISERS. SIX HUNDRED WORLDSHIPS.
TWELVE WORLD KILLERS.

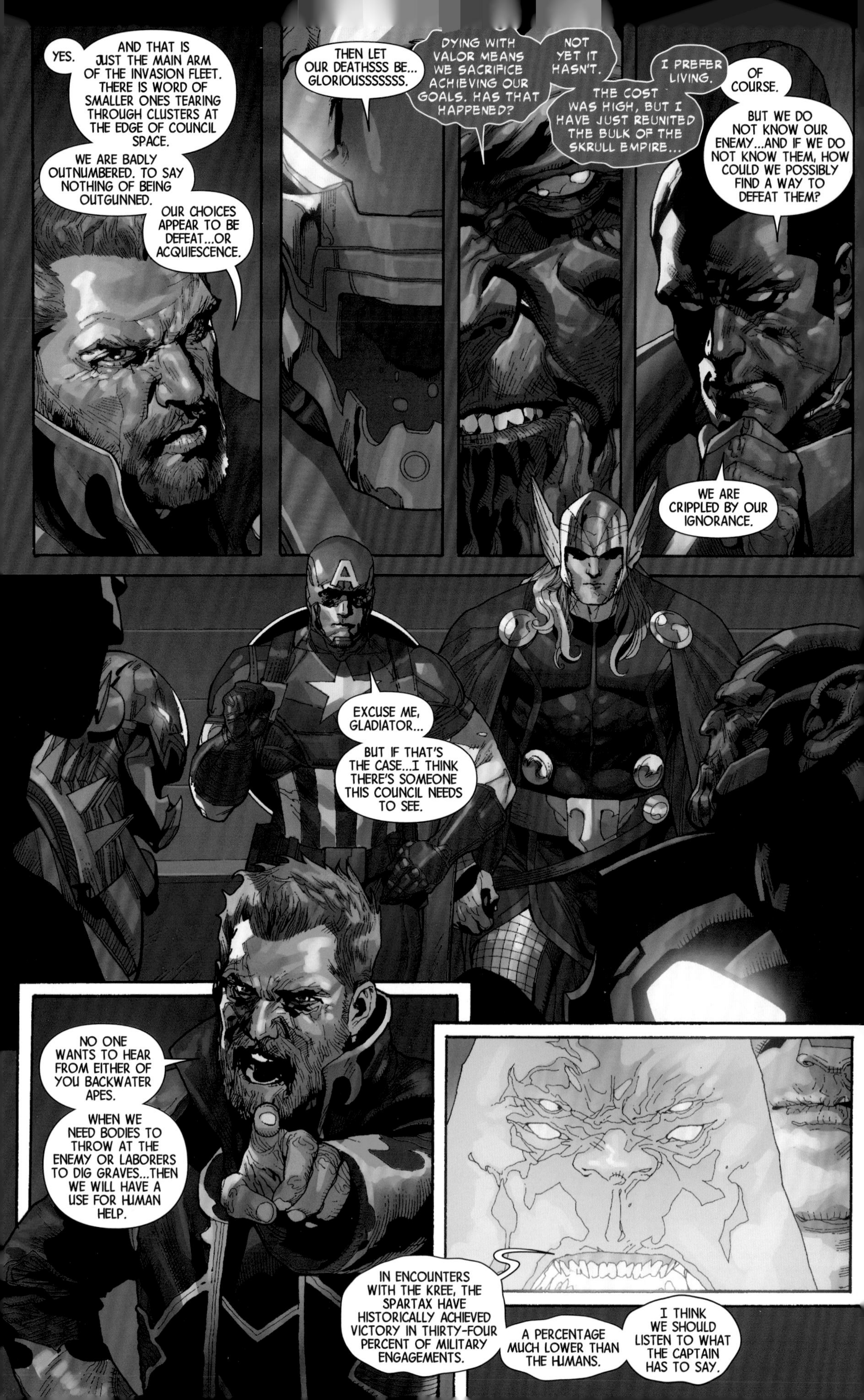

YES.
AND THAT IS JUST THE MAIN ARM OF THE INVASION FLEET. THERE IS WORD OF SMALLER ONES TEARING THROUGH CLUSTERS AT THE EDGE OF COUNCIL SPACE.
WE ARE BADLY OUTNUMBERED. TO SAY NOTHING OF BEING OUTGUNNED.
OUR CHOICES APPEAR TO BE DEFEAT...OR ACQUIESCENCE.
THEN LET OUR DEATHSSS BE... GLORIOUSSSSSSS.
DYING WITH VALOR MEANS WE SACRIFICE ACHIEVING OUR GOALS. HAS THAT HAPPENED?
NOT YET IT HASN'T.
THE COST WAS HIGH, BUT I HAVE JUST REUNITED THE BULK OF THE SKRULL EMPIRE...
I PREFER LIVING.
OF COURSE.
BUT WE DO NOT KNOW OUR ENEMY...AND IF WE DO NOT KNOW THEM, HOW COULD WE POSSIBLY FIND A WAY TO DEFEAT THEM?
WE ARE CRIPPLED BY OUR IGNORANCE.
EXCUSE ME, GLADIATOR...
BUT IF THAT'S THE CASE...I THINK THERE'S SOMEONE THIS COUNCIL NEEDS TO SEE.
NO ONE WANTS TO HEAR FROM EITHER OF YOU BACKWATER APES.
WHEN WE NEED BODIES TO THROW AT THE ENEMY OR LABORERS TO DIG GRAVES...THEN WE WILL HAVE A USE FOR HUMAN HELP.
IN ENCOUNTERS WITH THE KREE, THE SPARTAX HAVE HISTORICALLY ACHIEVED VICTORY IN THIRTY-FOUR PERCENT OF MILITARY ENGAGEMENTS.
A PERCENTAGE MUCH LOWER THAN THE HUMANS.
I THINK WE SHOULD LISTEN TO WHAT THE CAPTAIN HAS TO SAY.

ALL THESE THINGS
WE'VE MADE

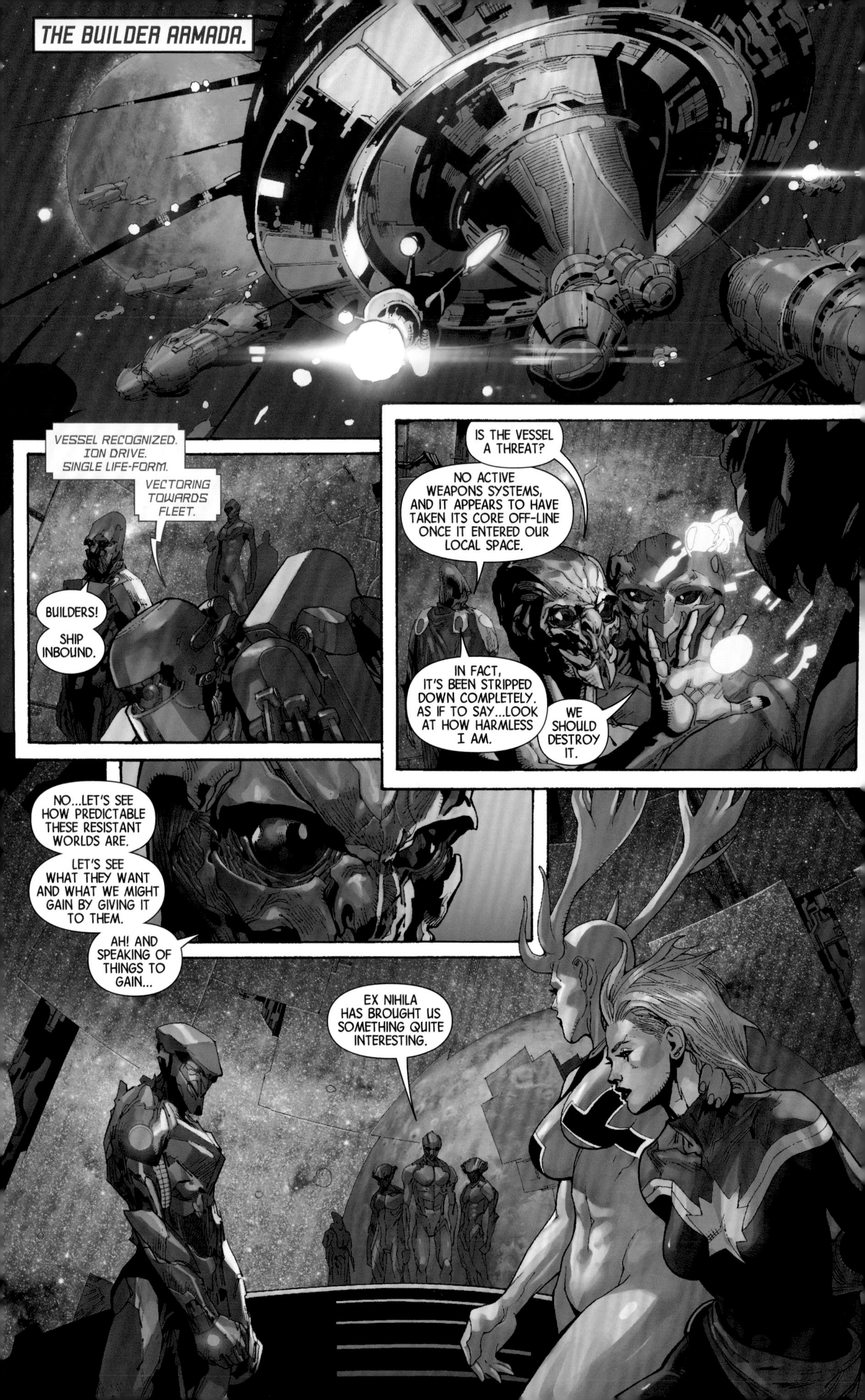
THE BUILDER ARMADA.
VESSEL RECOGNIZED. ION DRIVE. SINGLE LIFE-FORM.
VECTORING TOWARDS FLEET.
BUILDERS!
SHIP INBOUND.
IS THE VESSEL A THREAT?
NO ACTIVE WEAPONS SYSTEMS, AND IT APPEARS TO HAVE TAKEN ITS CORE OFF-LINE ONCE IT ENTERED OUR LOCAL SPACE.
IN FACT, IT'S BEEN STRIPPED DOWN COMPLETELY. AS IF TO SAY...LOOK AT HOW HARMLESS I AM.
WE SHOULD DESTROY IT.
NO...LET'S SEE HOW PREDICTABLE THESE RESISTANT WORLDS ARE.
LET'S SEE WHAT THEY WANT AND WHAT WE MIGHT GAIN BY GIVING IT TO THEM.
AH! AND SPEAKING OF THINGS TO GAIN...
EX NIHILA HAS BROUGHT US SOMETHING QUITE INTERESTING.

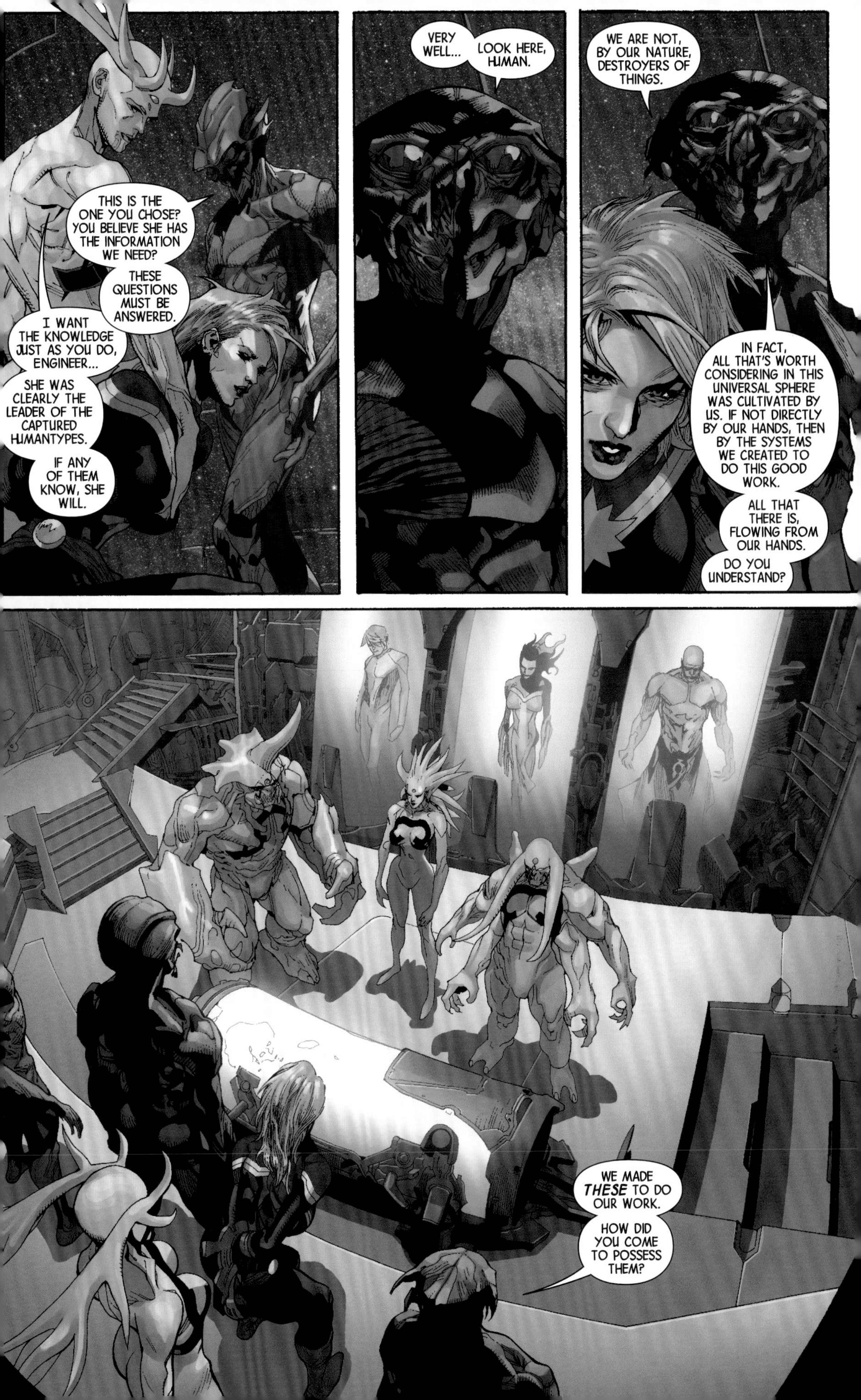
THIS IS THE ONE YOU CHOSE? YOU BELIEVE SHE HAS THE INFORMATION WE NEED?
THESE QUESTIONS MUST BE ANSWERED.
I WANT THE KNOWLEDGE JUST AS YOU DO, ENGINEER...
SHE WAS CLEARLY THE LEADER OF THE CAPTURED HUMANTYPES.
IF ANY OF THEM KNOW, SHE WILL.
VERY WELL...
LOOK HERE, HUMAN.
WE ARE NOT, BY OUR NATURE, DESTROYERS OF THINGS.
IN FACT, ALL THAT'S WORTH CONSIDERING IN THIS UNIVERSAL SPHERE WAS CULTIVATED BY US. IF NOT DIRECTLY BY OUR HANDS, THEN BY THE SYSTEMS WE CREATED TO DO THIS GOOD WORK.
ALL THAT THERE IS, FLOWING FROM OUR HANDS.
DO YOU UNDERSTAND?
WE MADE *THESE* TO DO OUR WORK.
HOW DID YOU COME TO POSSESS THEM?

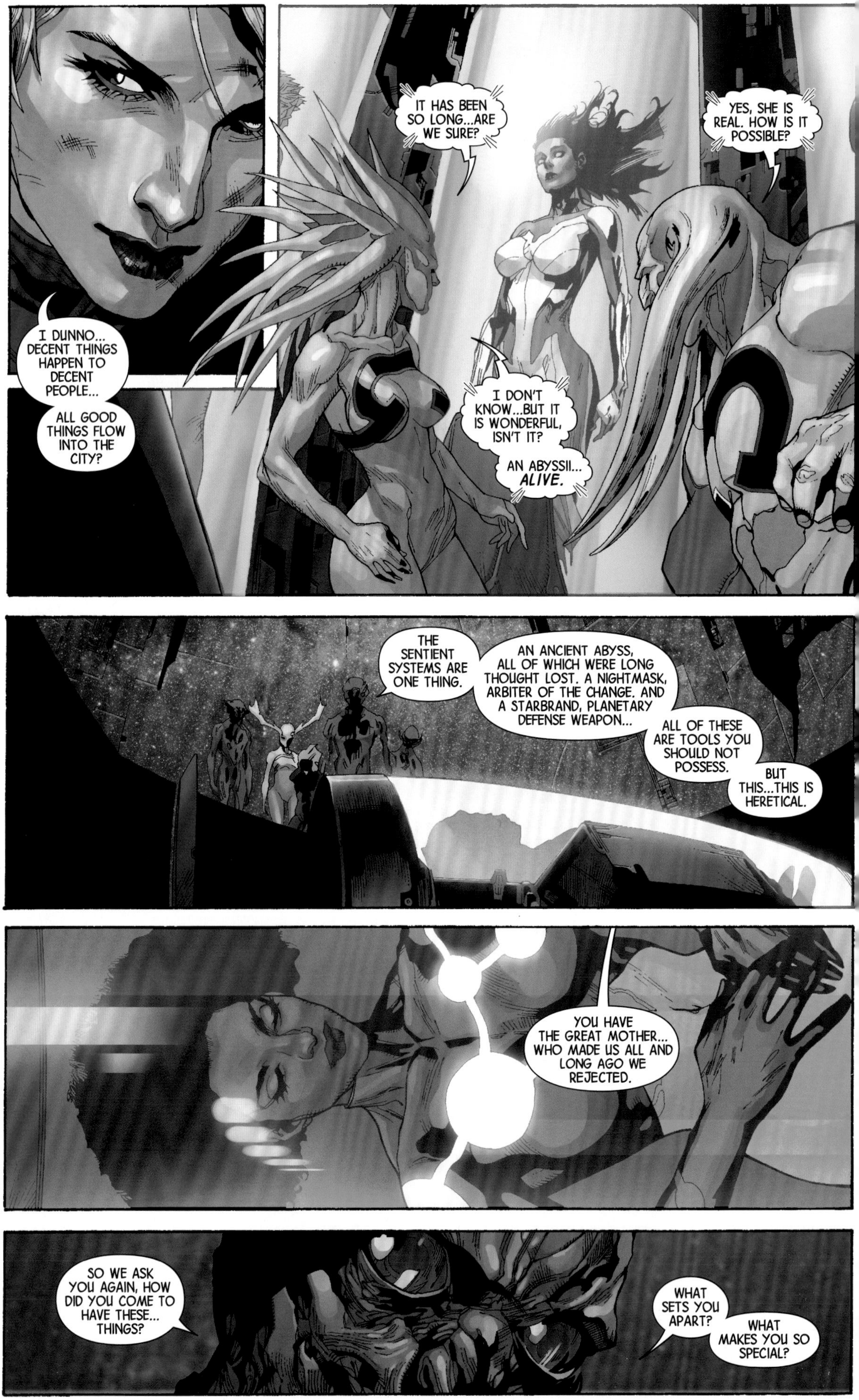
IT HAS BEEN SO LONG...ARE WE SURE?
YES, SHE IS REAL. HOW IS IT POSSIBLE?
I DUNNO... DECENT THINGS HAPPEN TO DECENT PEOPLE...
ALL GOOD THINGS FLOW INTO THE CITY?
I DON'T KNOW...BUT IT IS WONDERFUL, ISN'T IT?
AN ABYSSII... ALIVE.
THE SENTIENT SYSTEMS ARE ONE THING.
AN ANCIENT ABYSS, ALL OF WHICH WERE LONG THOUGHT LOST. A NIGHTMASK, ARBITER OF THE CHANGE. AND A STARBRAND, PLANETARY DEFENSE WEAPON...
ALL OF THESE ARE TOOLS YOU SHOULD NOT POSSESS.
BUT THIS...THIS IS HERETICAL.
YOU HAVE THE GREAT MOTHER... WHO MADE US ALL AND LONG AGO WE REJECTED.
SO WE ASK YOU AGAIN, HOW DID YOU COME TO HAVE THESE... THINGS?
WHAT SETS YOU APART?
WHAT MAKES YOU SO SPECIAL?

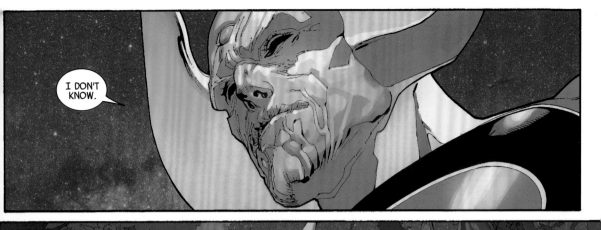

I DON'T KNOW.

MUCH OF WHAT I HAVE SEEN...CONFUSES ME.

I HAVE NEVER MET MY MAKERS, THESE BUILDERS. ALL I KNOW OF MY KIND ARE THE THINGS MY FATHER-ALEPH TAUGHT ME.

AND THE FIRST LESSON HE TAUGHT ME? BEFORE ALL OTHER THINGS, I AM TO BE LIFE-CREATING.

SO WATCHING THAT...OTHER ME... KILL HIMSELF AND POISON THAT WORLD...

SOMETHING HAS GONE VERY, VERY WRONG...

AND IT MUST BE STOPPED.

SO WHATEVER YOU MIGHT NEED FROM ME, YOU WILL HAVE IT.

WHY?

WHAT DO YOU MEAN?

I MEAN, WHY?

WHY ARE THEY DOING THIS? WHAT DO THEY WANT?

WHAT IS THE DAMNED POINT?

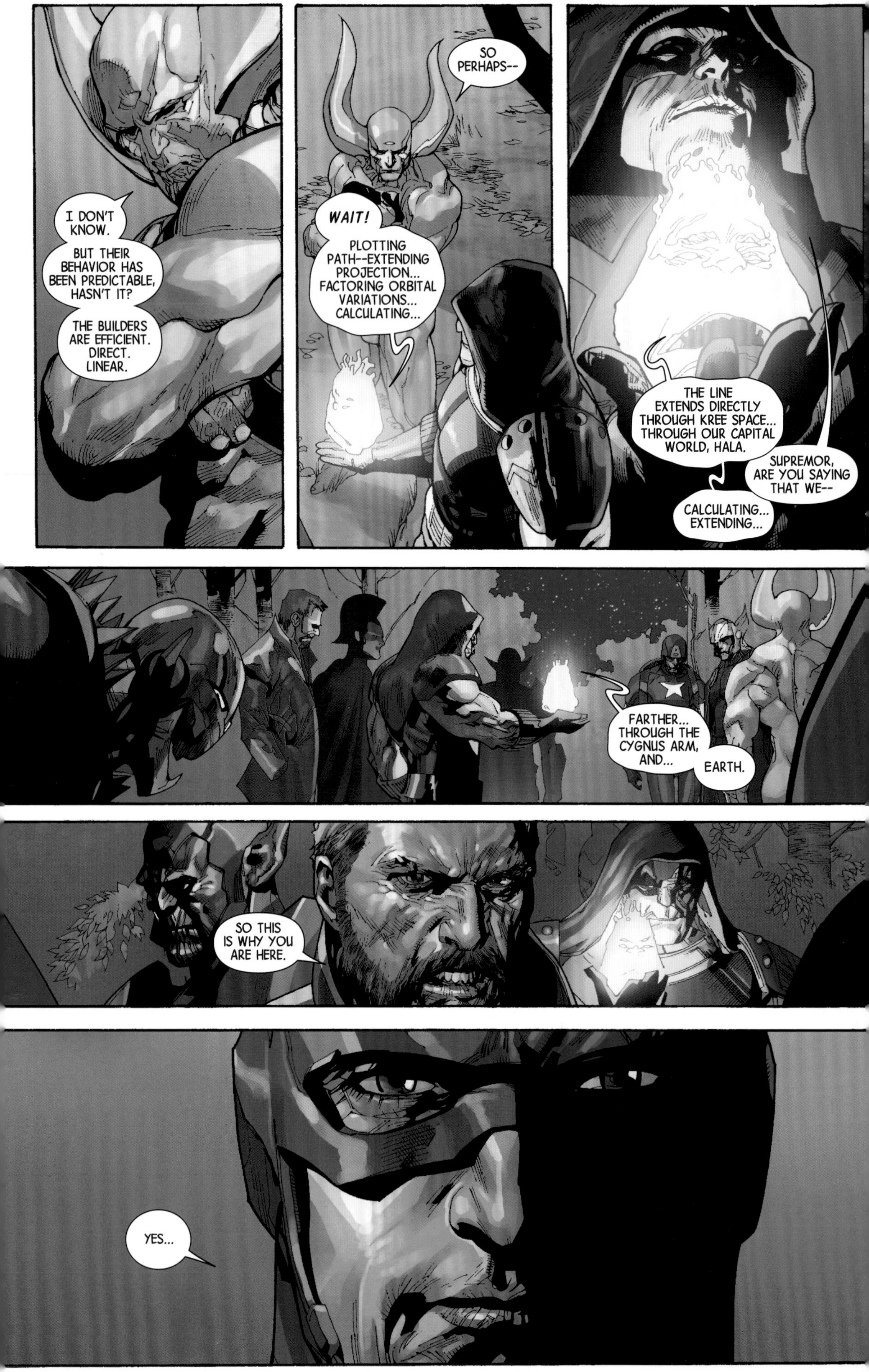
I DON'T KNOW.
BUT THEIR BEHAVIOR HAS BEEN PREDICTABLE, HASN'T IT?
THE BUILDERS ARE EFFICIENT. DIRECT. LINEAR.
SO PERHAPS--
WAIT!
PLOTTING PATH--EXTENDING PROJECTION... FACTORING ORBITAL VARIATIONS... CALCULATING...
THE LINE EXTENDS DIRECTLY THROUGH KREE SPACE... THROUGH OUR CAPITAL WORLD, HALA.
SUPREMOR, ARE YOU SAYING THAT WE--
CALCULATING... EXTENDING...
FARTHER... THROUGH THE CYGNUS ARM, AND...
EARTH.
SO THIS IS WHY YOU ARE HERE.
YES...

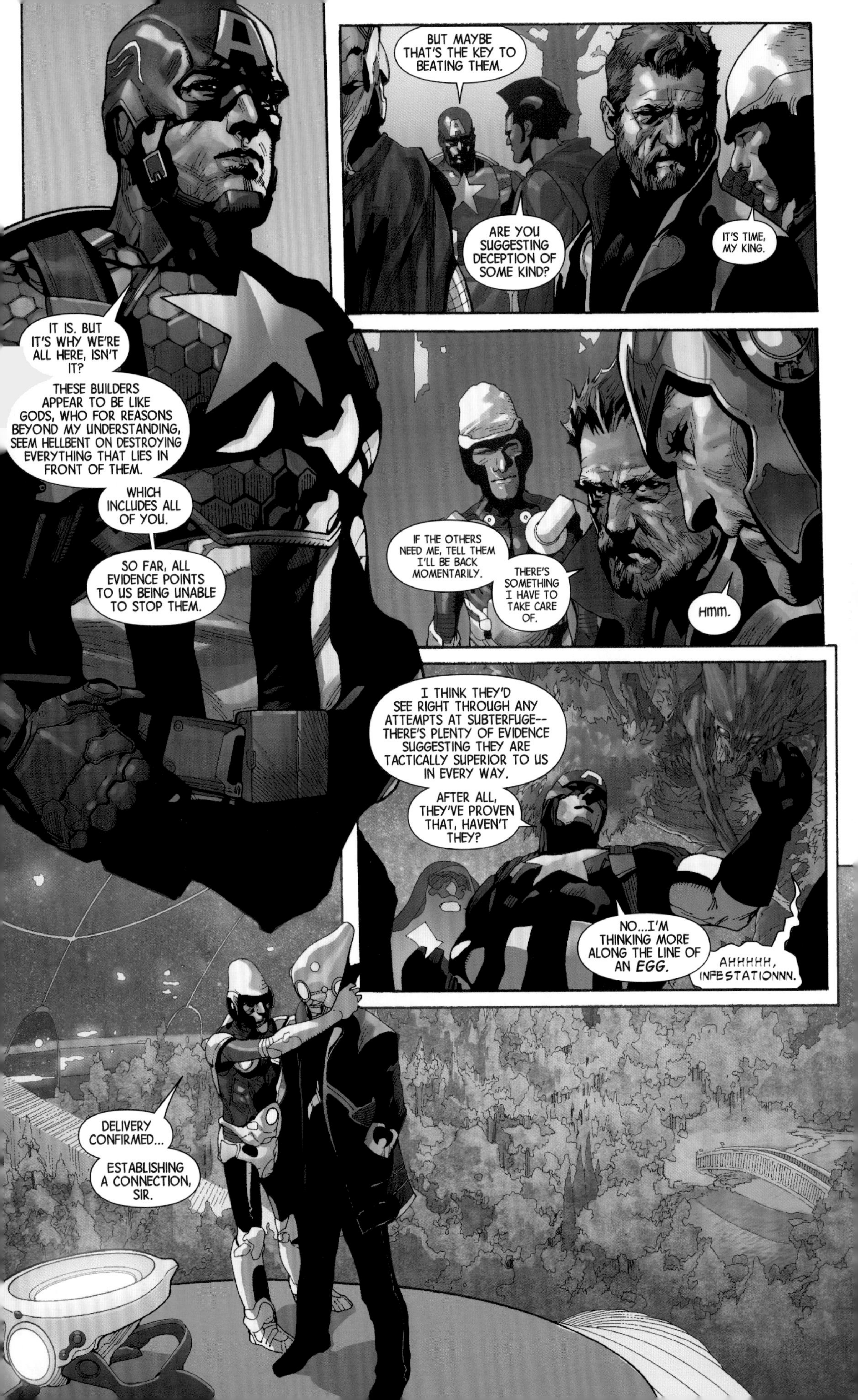

IT IS. BUT IT'S WHY WE'RE ALL HERE, ISN'T IT?
THESE BUILDERS APPEAR TO BE LIKE GODS, WHO FOR REASONS BEYOND MY UNDERSTANDING, SEEM HELLBENT ON DESTROYING EVERYTHING THAT LIES IN FRONT OF THEM.
WHICH INCLUDES ALL OF YOU.
SO FAR, ALL EVIDENCE POINTS TO US BEING UNABLE TO STOP THEM.
BUT MAYBE THAT'S THE KEY TO BEATING THEM.
ARE YOU SUGGESTING DECEPTION OF SOME KIND?
IT'S TIME, MY KING.
IF THE OTHERS NEED ME, TELL THEM I'LL BE BACK MOMENTARILY.
THERE'S SOMETHING I HAVE TO TAKE CARE OF.
HMM.
I THINK THEY'D SEE RIGHT THROUGH ANY ATTEMPTS AT SUBTERFUGE-- THERE'S PLENTY OF EVIDENCE SUGGESTING THEY ARE TACTICALLY SUPERIOR TO US IN EVERY WAY.
AFTER ALL, THEY'VE PROVEN THAT, HAVEN'T THEY?
NO...I'M THINKING MORE ALONG THE LINE OF AN EGG.
AHHHHH, INFESTATIONNN.
DELIVERY CONFIRMED...
ESTABLISHING A CONNECTION, SIR.

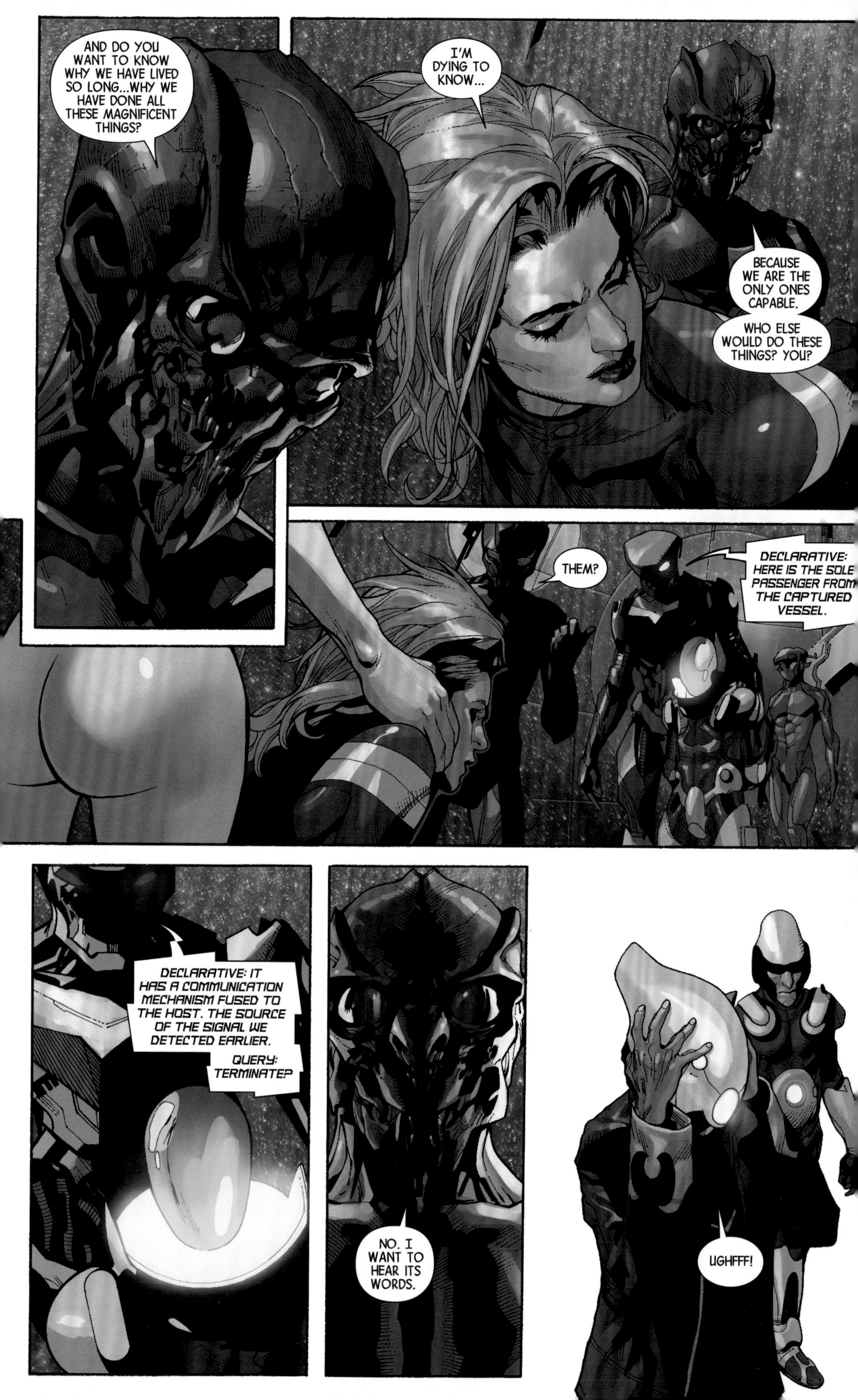
AND DO YOU WANT TO KNOW WHY WE HAVE LIVED SO LONG...WHY WE HAVE DONE ALL THESE MAGNIFICENT THINGS?
I'M DYING TO KNOW...
BECAUSE WE ARE THE ONLY ONES CAPABLE.
WHO ELSE WOULD DO THESE THINGS? YOU?
THEM?
DECLARATIVE: HERE IS THE SOLE PASSENGER FROM THE CAPTURED VESSEL.
DECLARATIVE: IT HAS A COMMUNICATION MECHANISM FUSED TO THE HOST. THE SOURCE OF THE SIGNAL WE DETECTED EARLIER.
QUERY: TERMINATE?
NO. I WANT TO HEAR ITS WORDS.
UGHFFF!

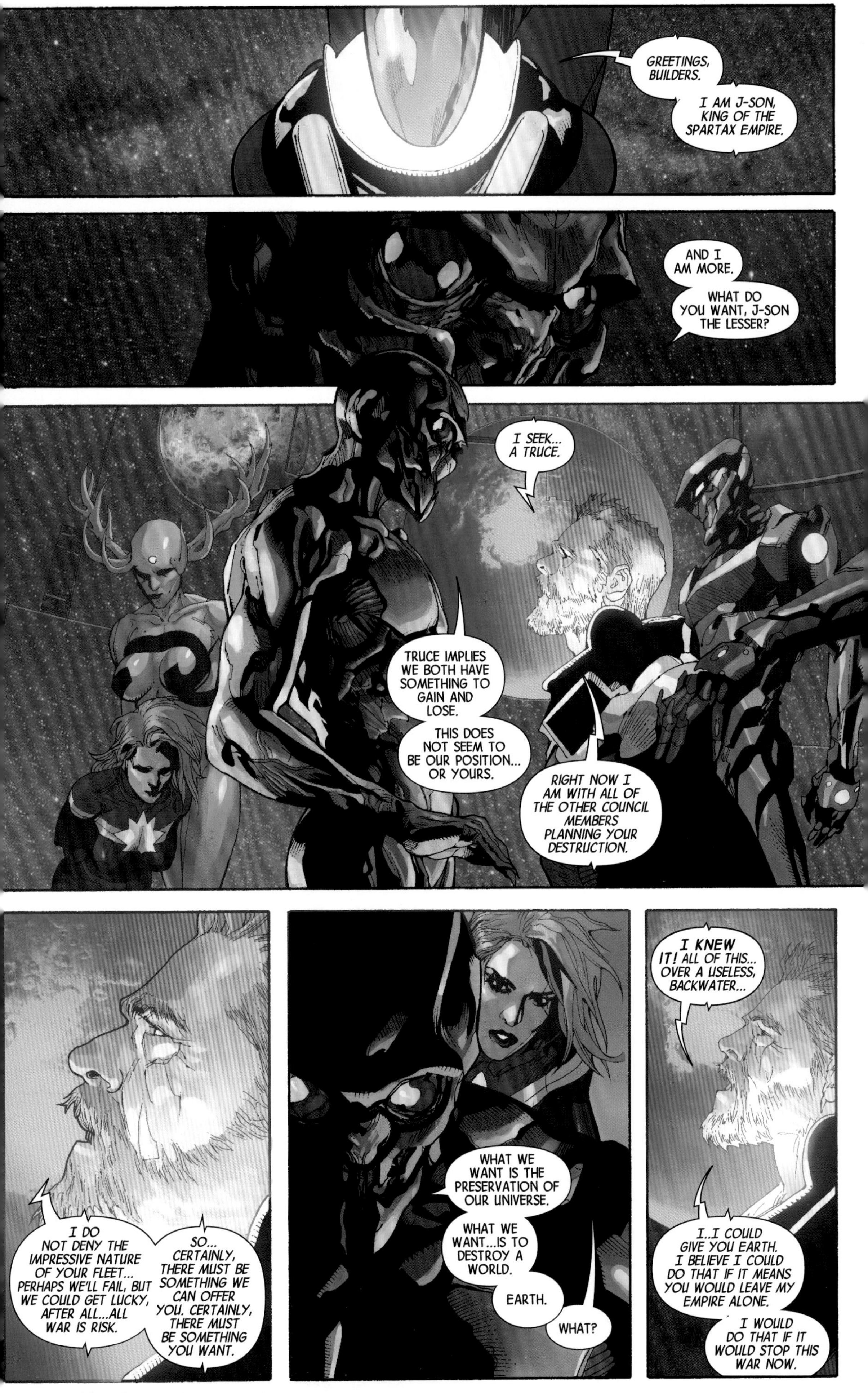
GREETINGS, BUILDERS.
I AM J-SON, KING OF THE SPARTAX EMPIRE.
AND I AM MORE.
WHAT DO YOU WANT, J-SON THE LESSER?
I SEEK... A TRUCE.
TRUCE IMPLIES WE BOTH HAVE SOMETHING TO GAIN AND LOSE.
THIS DOES NOT SEEM TO BE OUR POSITION... OR YOURS.
RIGHT NOW I AM WITH ALL OF THE OTHER COUNCIL MEMBERS PLANNING YOUR DESTRUCTION.
I DO NOT DENY THE IMPRESSIVE NATURE OF YOUR FLEET... PERHAPS WE'LL FAIL, BUT WE COULD GET LUCKY, AFTER ALL...ALL WAR IS RISK.
SO... CERTAINLY, THERE MUST BE SOMETHING WE CAN OFFER YOU. CERTAINLY, THERE MUST BE SOMETHING YOU WANT.
WHAT WE WANT IS THE PRESERVATION OF OUR UNIVERSE.
WHAT WE WANT...IS TO DESTROY A WORLD.
EARTH.
WHAT?
I KNEW IT! ALL OF THIS... OVER A USELESS, BACKWATER...
I..I COULD GIVE YOU EARTH. I BELIEVE I COULD DO THAT IF IT MEANS YOU WOULD LEAVE MY EMPIRE ALONE.
I WOULD DO THAT IF IT WOULD STOP THIS WAR NOW.

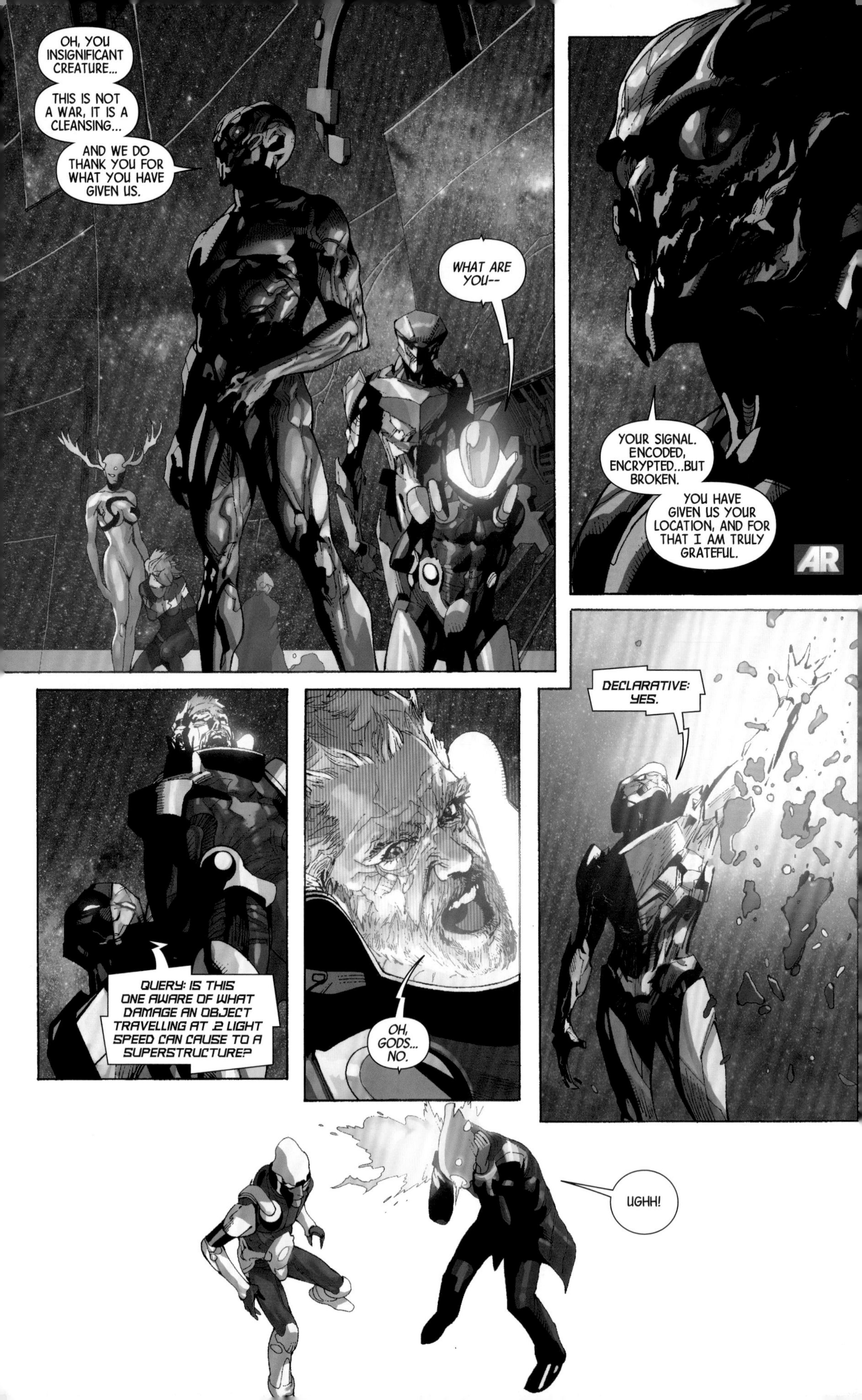

OH, YOU INSIGNIFICANT CREATURE...
THIS IS NOT A WAR, IT IS A CLEANSING...
AND WE DO THANK YOU FOR WHAT YOU HAVE GIVEN US.
WHAT ARE YOU--
YOUR SIGNAL. ENCODED, ENCRYPTED...BUT BROKEN.
YOU HAVE GIVEN US YOUR LOCATION, AND FOR THAT I AM TRULY GRATEFUL.
AR
QUERY: IS THIS ONE AWARE OF WHAT DAMAGE AN OBJECT TRAVELLING AT .2 LIGHT SPEED CAN CAUSE TO A SUPERSTRUCTURE?
OH, GODS... NO.
DECLARATIVE: YES.
UGHH!

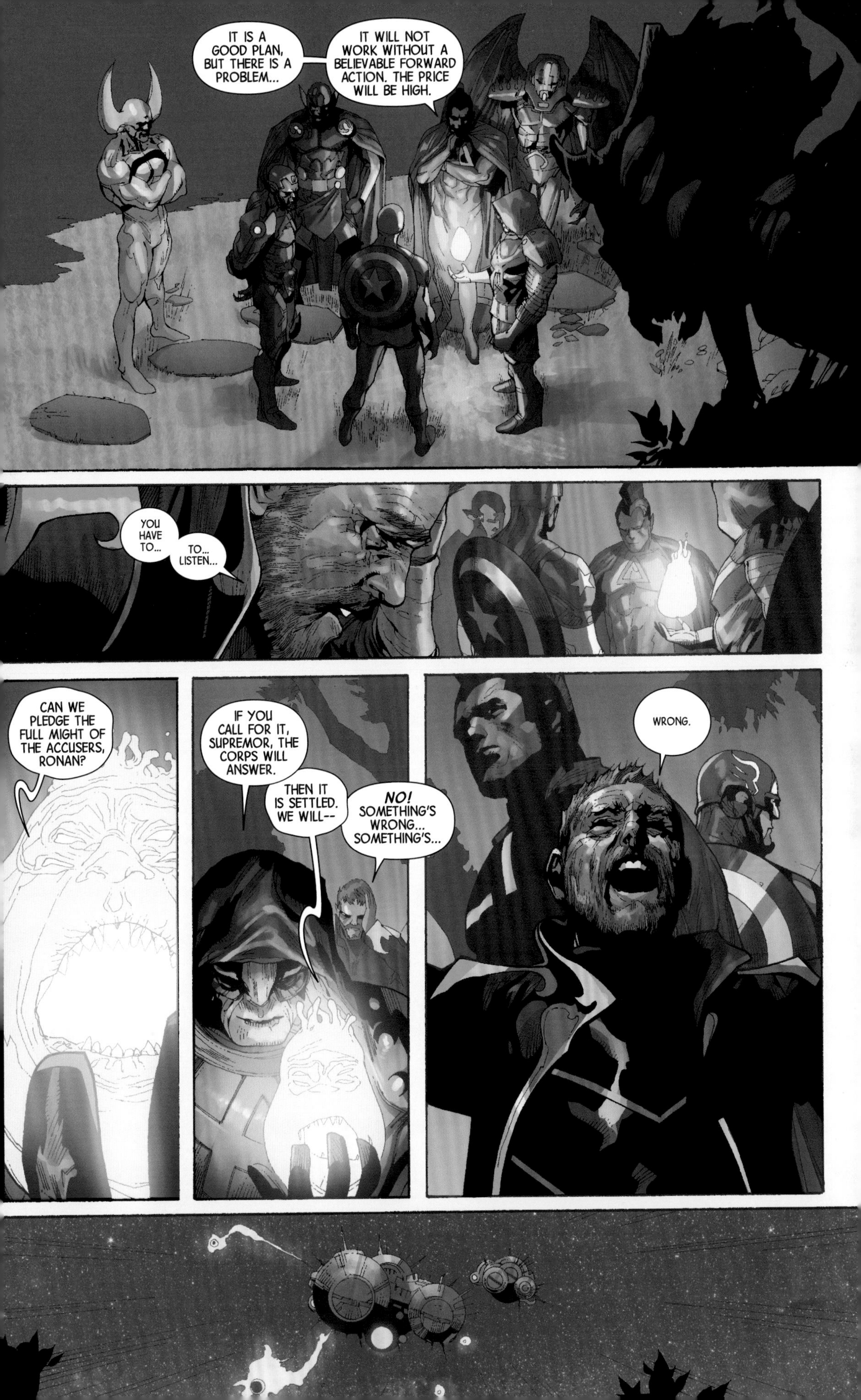
IT IS A GOOD PLAN, BUT THERE IS A PROBLEM...
IT WILL NOT WORK WITHOUT A BELIEVABLE FORWARD ACTION. THE PRICE WILL BE HIGH.
YOU HAVE TO...
TO... LISTEN...
CAN WE PLEDGE THE FULL MIGHT OF THE ACCUSERS, RONAN?
IF YOU CALL FOR IT, SUPREMOR, THE CORPS WILL ANSWER.
THEN IT IS SETTLED. WE WILL--
NO! SOMETHING'S WRONG... SOMETHING'S...
WRONG.

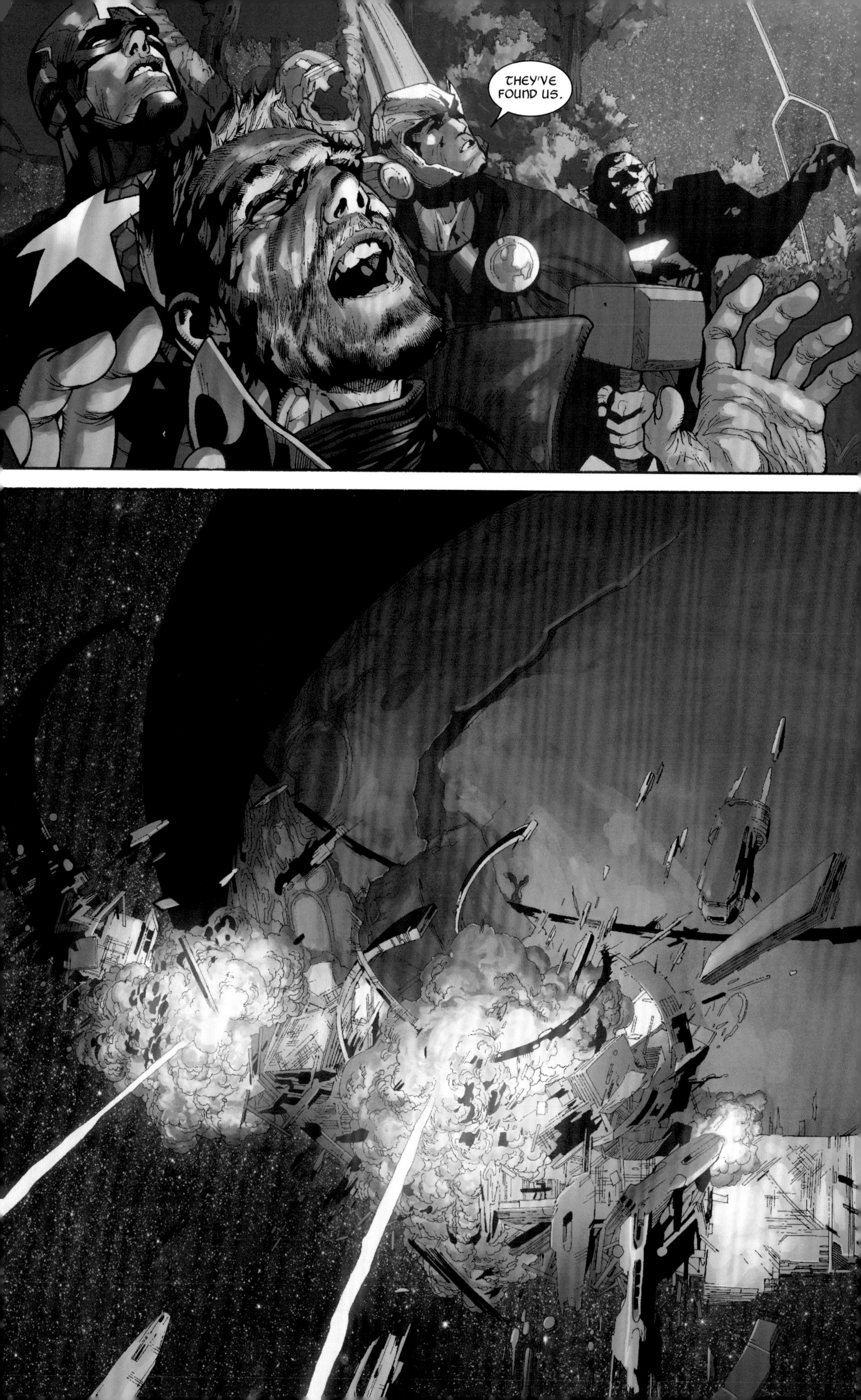
THEY'VE FOUND US.

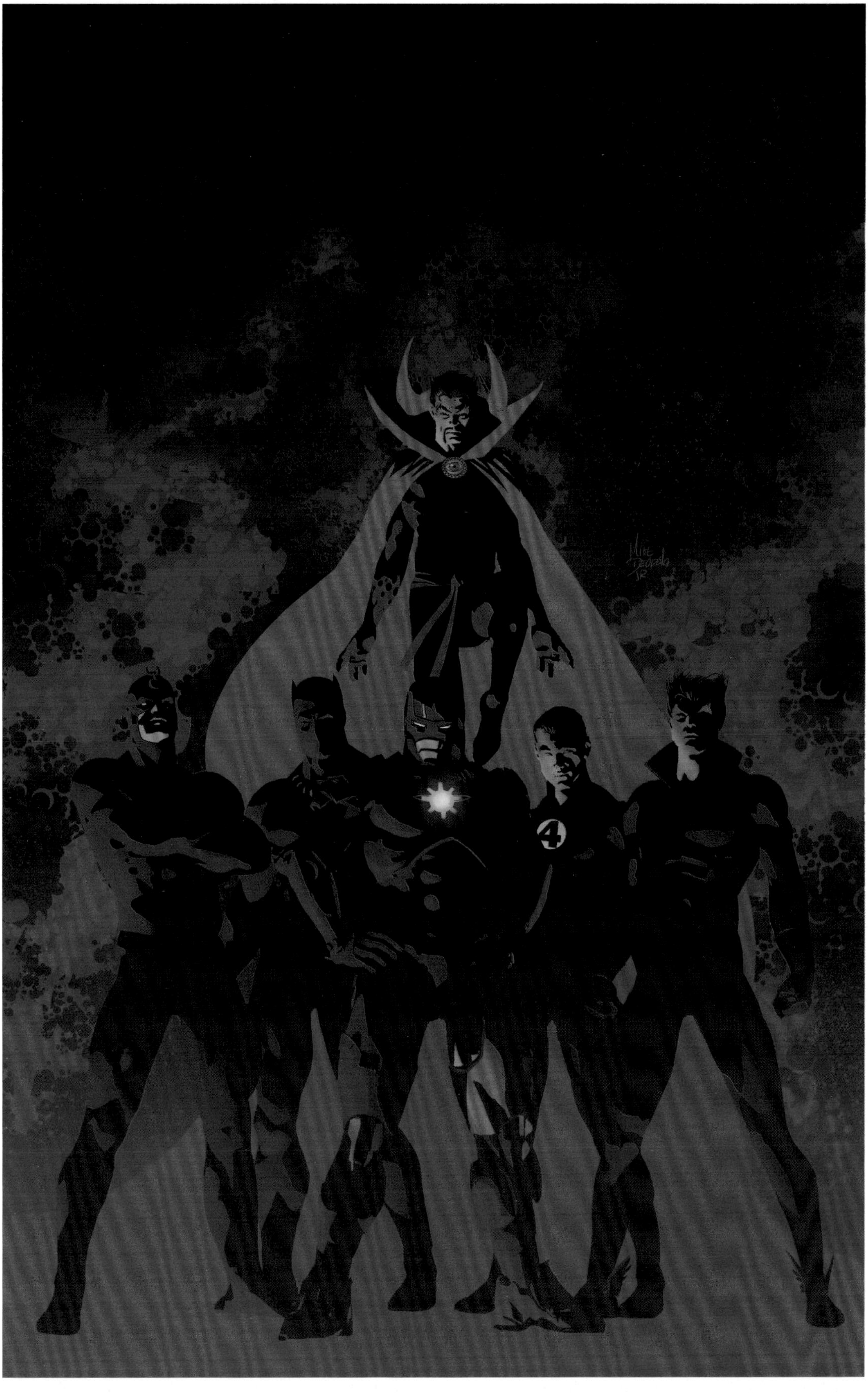

THE THANOS SEED

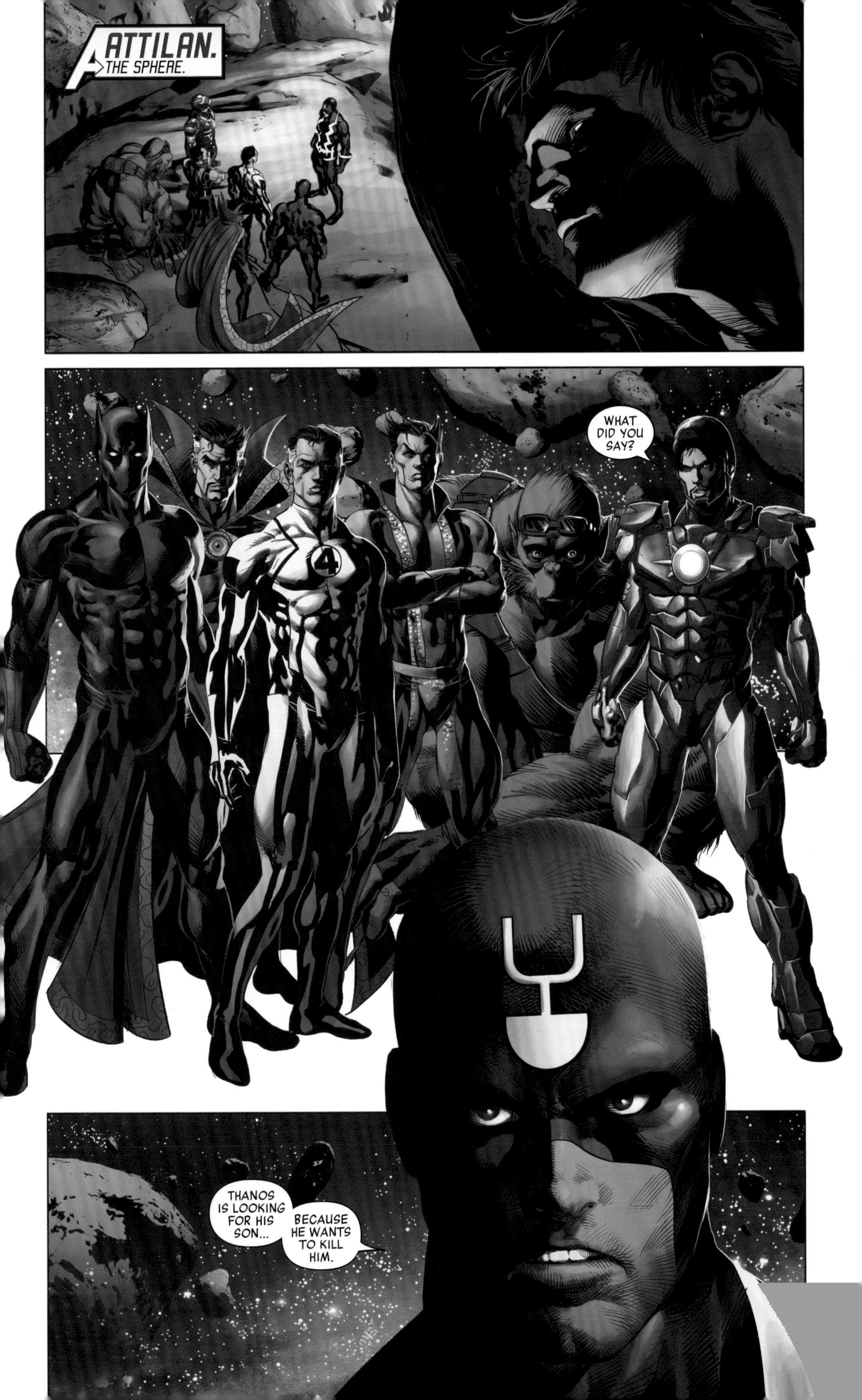
ATTILAN.
THE SPHERE.
WHAT DID YOU SAY?
THANOS IS LOOKING FOR HIS SON...
BECAUSE HE WANTS TO KILL HIM.

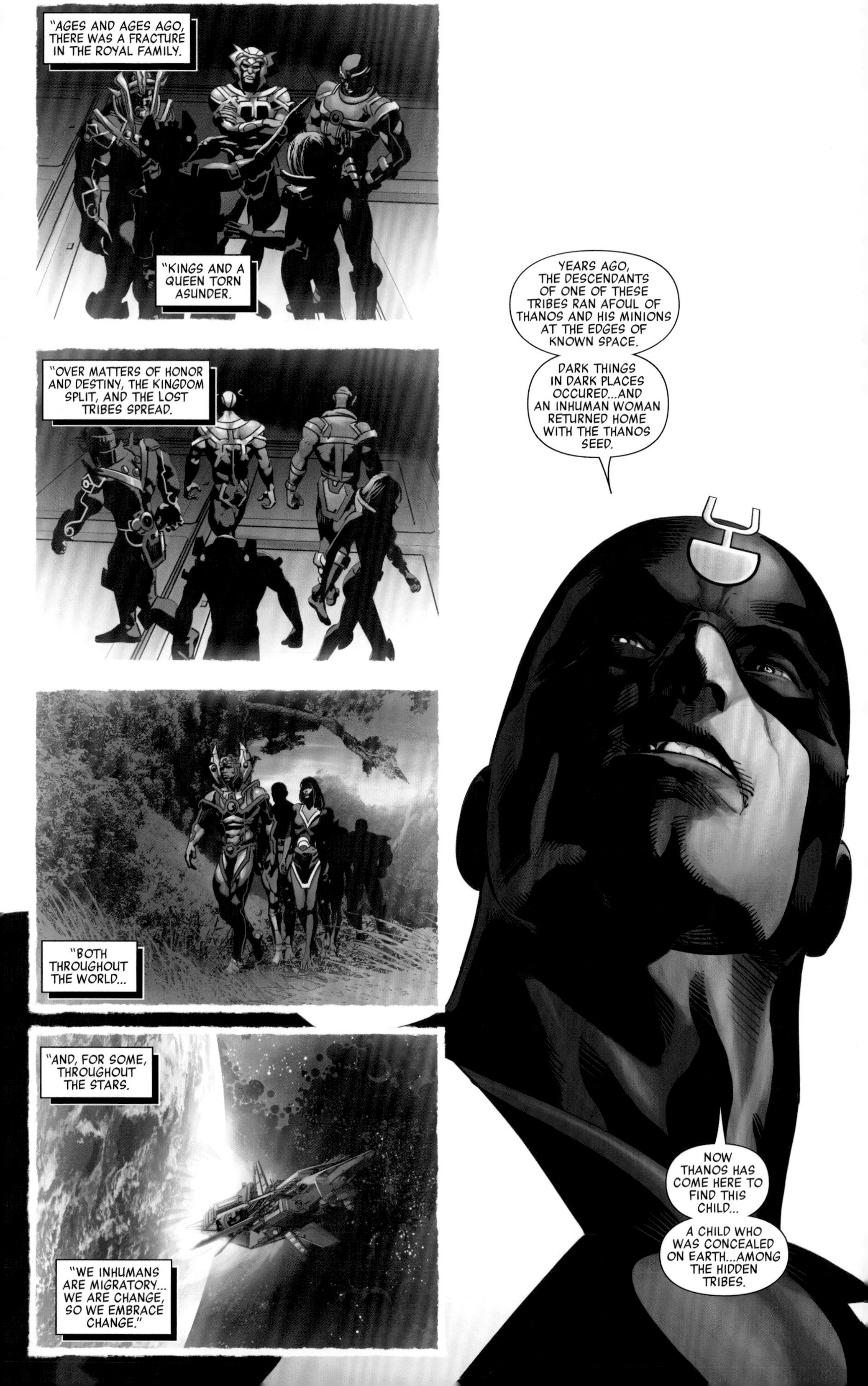
"AGES AND AGES AGO, THERE WAS A FRACTURE IN THE ROYAL FAMILY.
"KINGS AND A QUEEN TORN ASUNDER.
"OVER MATTERS OF HONOR AND DESTINY, THE KINGDOM SPLIT, AND THE LOST TRIBES SPREAD.
"BOTH THROUGHOUT THE WORLD...
"AND, FOR SOME, THROUGHOUT THE STARS.
"WE INHUMANS ARE MIGRATORY... WE ARE CHANGE, SO WE EMBRACE CHANGE."
YEARS AGO, THE DESCENDANTS OF ONE OF THESE TRIBES RAN AFOUL OF THANOS AND HIS MINIONS AT THE EDGES OF KNOWN SPACE.
DARK THINGS IN DARK PLACES OCCURED...AND AN INHUMAN WOMAN RETURNED HOME WITH THE THANOS SEED.
NOW THANOS HAS COME HERE TO FIND THIS CHILD...
A CHILD WHO WAS CONCEALED ON EARTH...AMONG THE HIDDEN TRIBES.

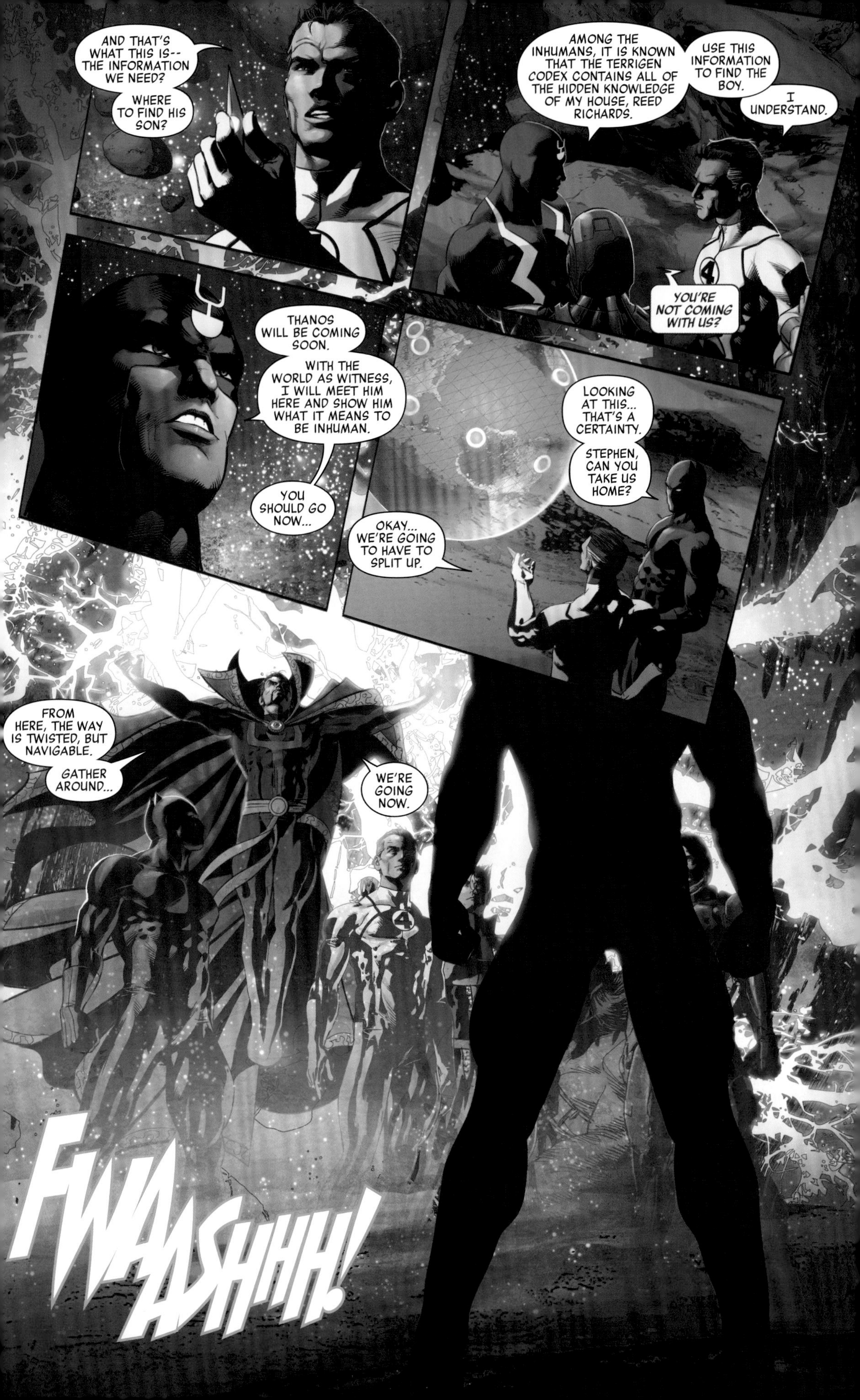
AND THAT'S WHAT THIS IS-- THE INFORMATION WE NEED?
WHERE TO FIND HIS SON?
AMONG THE INHUMANS, IT IS KNOWN THAT THE TERRIGEN CODEX CONTAINS ALL OF THE HIDDEN KNOWLEDGE OF MY HOUSE, REED RICHARDS.
USE THIS INFORMATION TO FIND THE BOY.
I UNDERSTAND.
YOU'RE NOT COMING WITH US?
THANOS WILL BE COMING SOON.
WITH THE WORLD AS WITNESS, I WILL MEET HIM HERE AND SHOW HIM WHAT IT MEANS TO BE INHUMAN.
YOU SHOULD GO NOW...
LOOKING AT THIS... THAT'S A CERTAINTY.
STEPHEN, CAN YOU TAKE US HOME?
OKAY... WE'RE GOING TO HAVE TO SPLIT UP.
FROM HERE, THE WAY IS TWISTED, BUT NAVIGABLE.
GATHER AROUND...
WE'RE GOING NOW.
FWAASHHH!

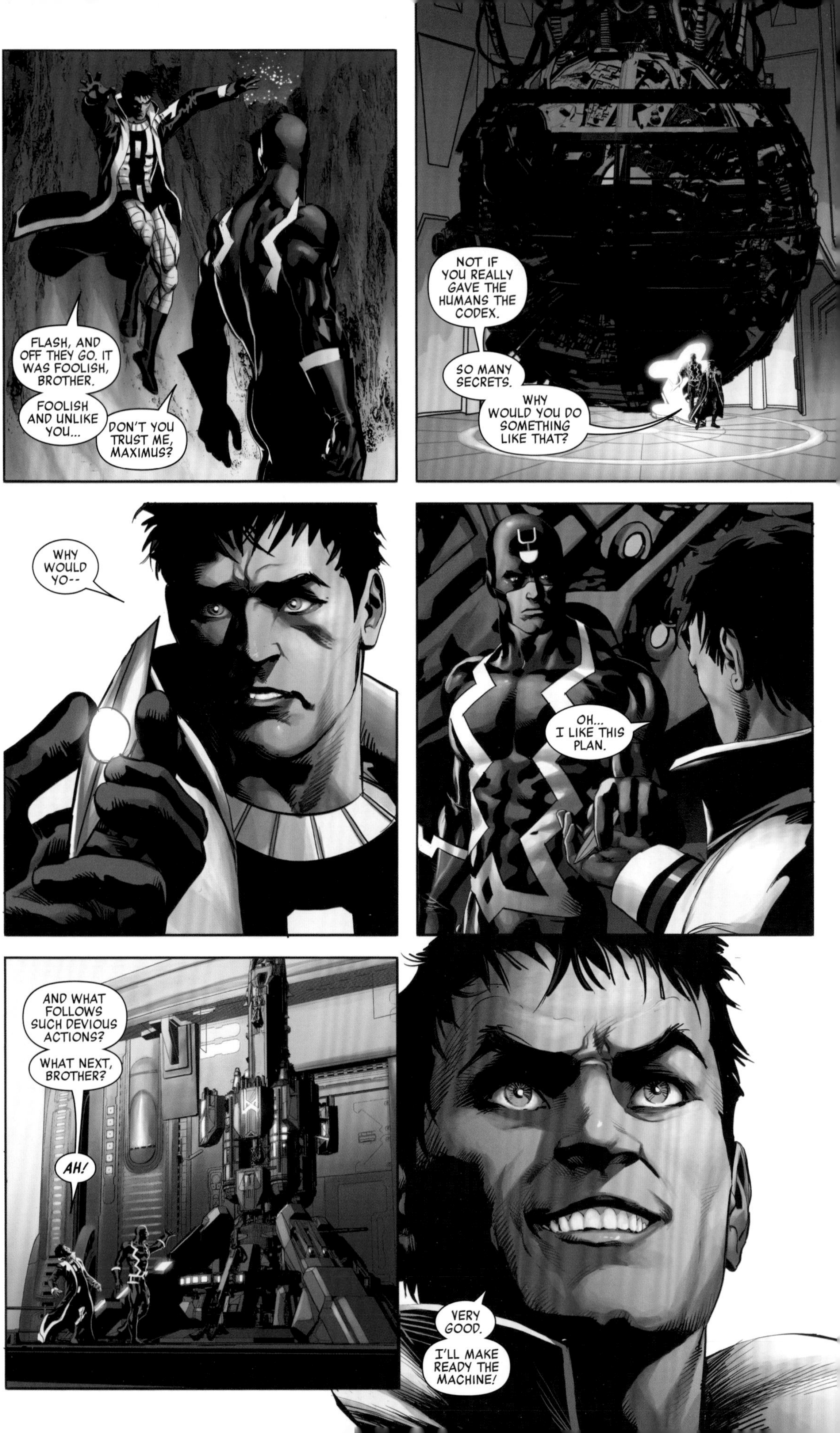

FLASH, AND OFF THEY GO. IT WAS FOOLISH, BROTHER.
FOOLISH AND UNLIKE YOU...
DON'T YOU TRUST ME, MAXIMUS?
NOT IF YOU REALLY GAVE THE HUMANS THE CODEX.
SO MANY SECRETS.
WHY WOULD YOU DO SOMETHING LIKE THAT?
WHY WOULD YO--
OH... I LIKE THIS PLAN.
AND WHAT FOLLOWS SUCH DEVIOUS ACTIONS?
WHAT NEXT, BROTHER?
AH!
VERY GOOD.
I'LL MAKE READY THE MACHINE!

FAVOR AND DISFAVOR

◆

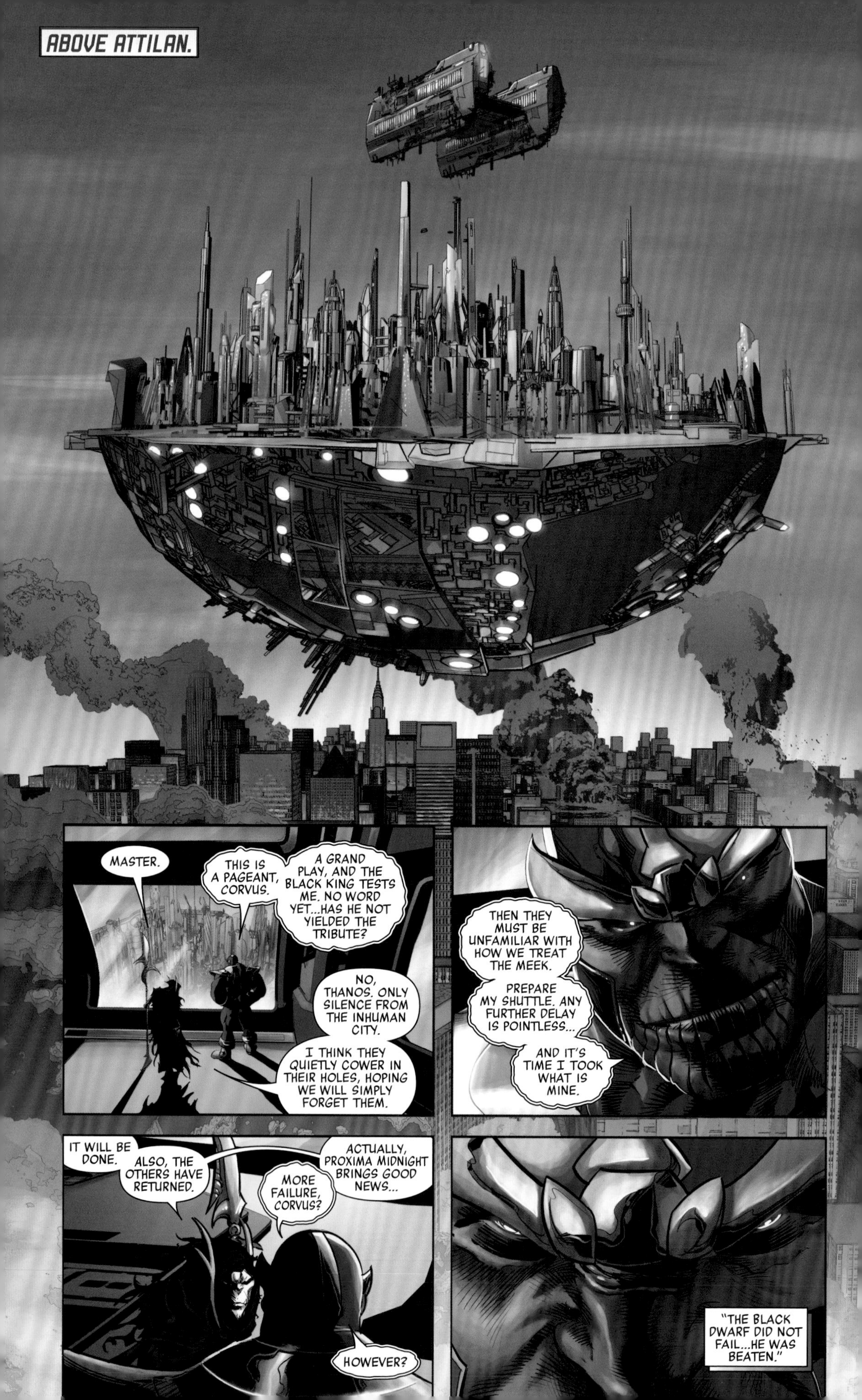
ABOVE ATTILAN.
MASTER.
THIS IS A PAGEANT, CORVUS.
A GRAND PLAY, AND THE BLACK KING TESTS ME. NO WORD YET...HAS HE NOT YIELDED THE TRIBUTE?
NO, THANOS. ONLY SILENCE FROM THE INHUMAN CITY.
I THINK THEY QUIETLY COWER IN THEIR HOLES, HOPING WE WILL SIMPLY FORGET THEM.
THEN THEY MUST BE UNFAMILIAR WITH HOW WE TREAT THE MEEK.
PREPARE MY SHUTTLE. ANY FURTHER DELAY IS POINTLESS...
AND IT'S TIME I TOOK WHAT IS MINE.
IT WILL BE DONE.
ALSO, THE OTHERS HAVE RETURNED.
MORE FAILURE, CORVUS?
ACTUALLY, PROXIMA MIDNIGHT BRINGS GOOD NEWS...
HOWEVER?
"THE BLACK DWARF DID NOT FAIL...HE WAS BEATEN."

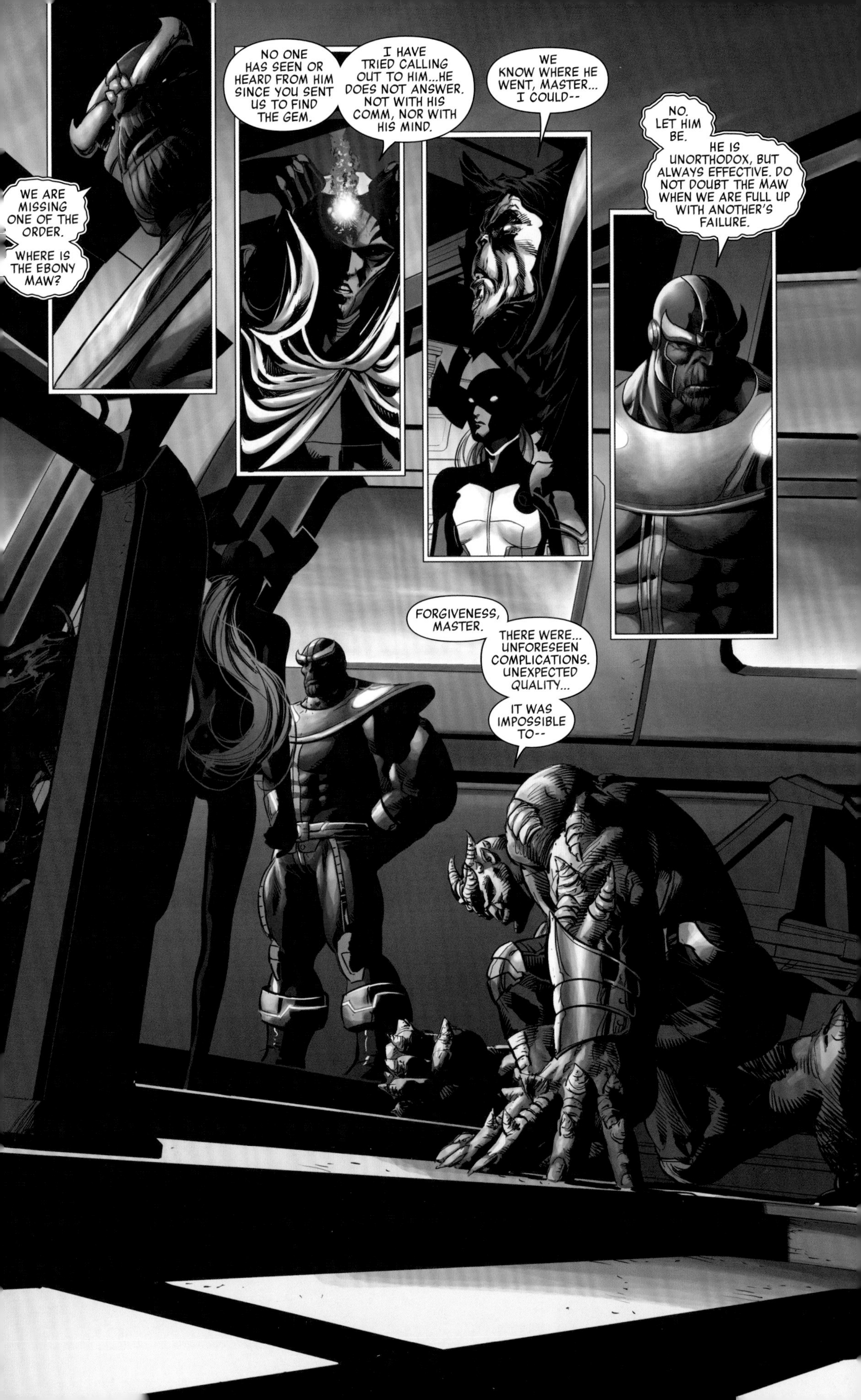
WE ARE MISSING ONE OF THE ORDER.
WHERE IS THE EBONY MAW?
NO ONE HAS SEEN OR HEARD FROM HIM SINCE YOU SENT US TO FIND THE GEM.
I HAVE TRIED CALLING OUT TO HIM...HE DOES NOT ANSWER. NOT WITH HIS COMM, NOR WITH HIS MIND.
WE KNOW WHERE HE WENT, MASTER... I COULD--
NO. LET HIM BE.
HE IS UNORTHODOX, BUT ALWAYS EFFECTIVE. DO NOT DOUBT THE MAW WHEN WE ARE FULL UP WITH ANOTHER'S FAILURE.
FORGIVENESS, MASTER.
THERE WERE... UNFORESEEN COMPLICATIONS. UNEXPECTED QUALITY...
IT WAS IMPOSSIBLE TO--

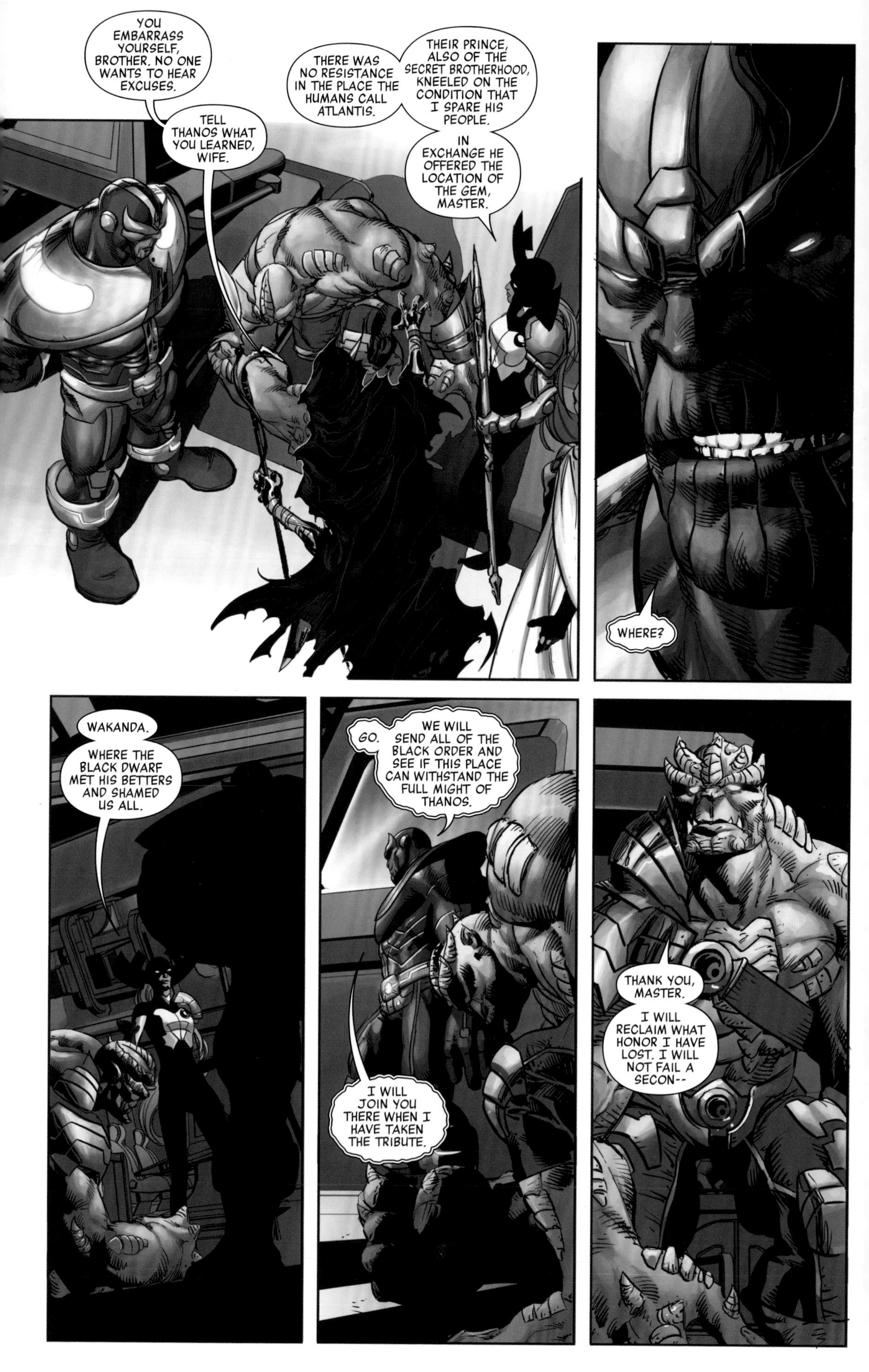
YOU EMBARRASS YOURSELF, BROTHER. NO ONE WANTS TO HEAR EXCUSES.
TELL THANOS WHAT YOU LEARNED, WIFE.
THERE WAS NO RESISTANCE IN THE PLACE THE HUMANS CALL ATLANTIS.
THEIR PRINCE, ALSO OF THE SECRET BROTHERHOOD, KNEELED ON THE CONDITION THAT I SPARE HIS PEOPLE.
IN EXCHANGE HE OFFERED THE LOCATION OF THE GEM, MASTER.
WHERE?
WAKANDA.
WHERE THE BLACK DWARF MET HIS BETTERS AND SHAMED US ALL.
GO.
WE WILL SEND ALL OF THE BLACK ORDER AND SEE IF THIS PLACE CAN WITHSTAND THE FULL MIGHT OF THANOS.
I WILL JOIN YOU THERE WHEN I HAVE TAKEN THE TRIBUTE.
THANK YOU, MASTER.
I WILL RECLAIM WHAT HONOR I HAVE LOST. I WILL NOT FAIL A SECON--

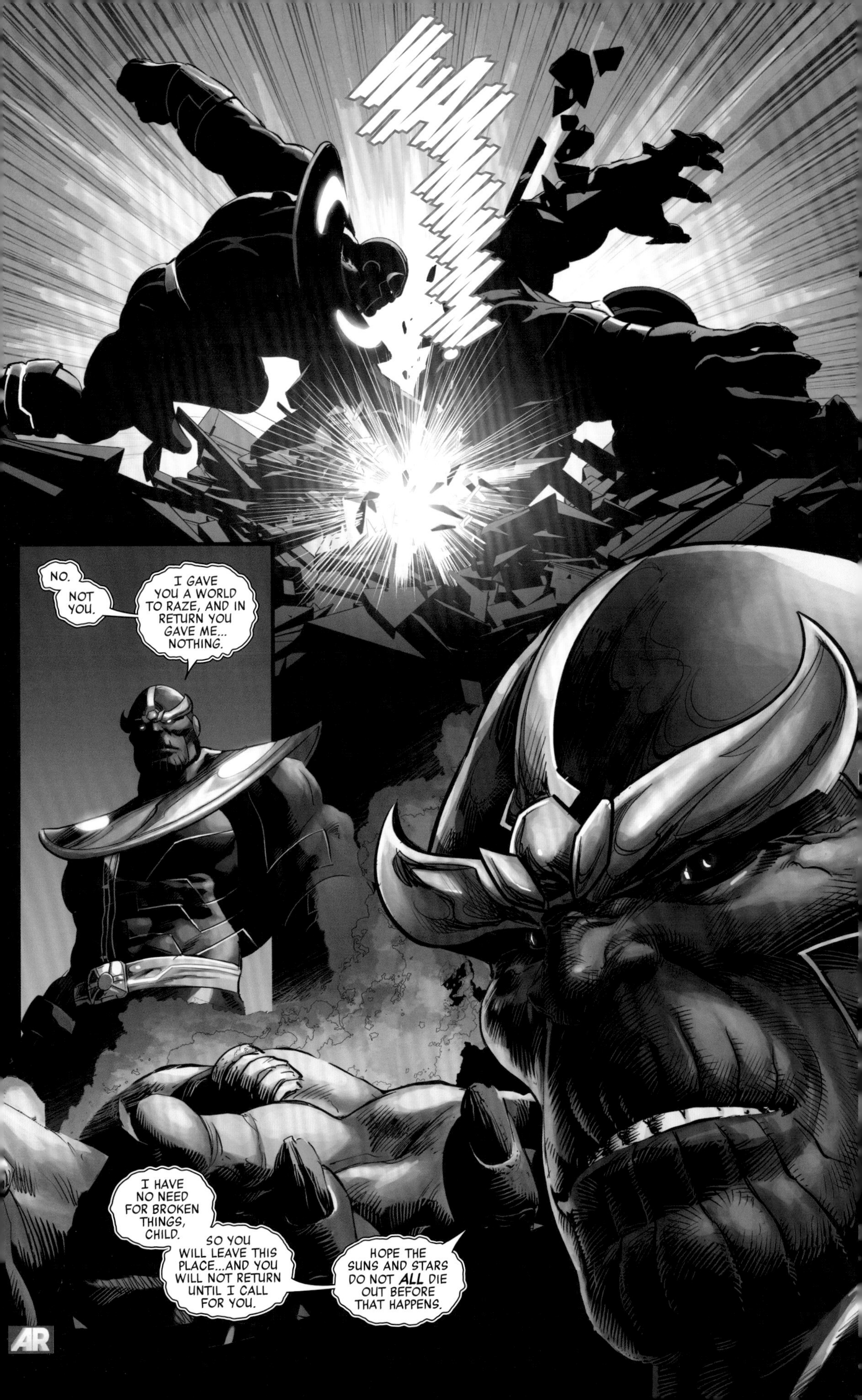

NO.
NOT YOU.
I GAVE YOU A WORLD TO RAZE, AND IN RETURN YOU GAVE ME... NOTHING.
I HAVE NO NEED FOR BROKEN THINGS, CHILD.
SO YOU WILL LEAVE THIS PLACE...AND YOU WILL NOT RETURN UNTIL I CALL FOR YOU.
HOPE THE SUNS AND STARS DO NOT *ALL* DIE OUT BEFORE THAT HAPPENS.

THE HUNT

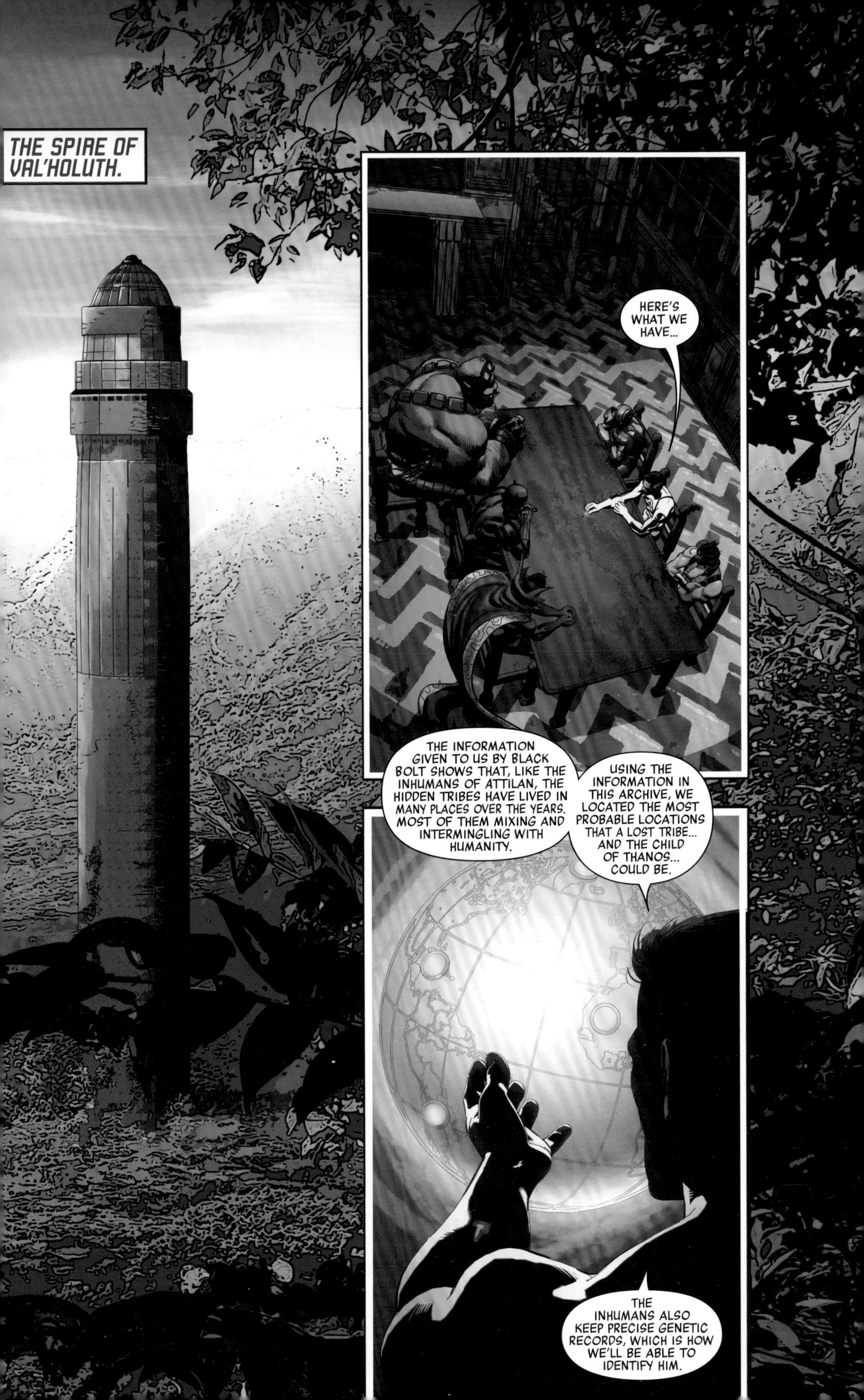
THE SPIRE OF VAL'HOLUTH.
HERE'S WHAT WE HAVE...
THE INFORMATION GIVEN TO US BY BLACK BOLT SHOWS THAT, LIKE THE INHUMANS OF ATTILAN, THE HIDDEN TRIBES HAVE LIVED IN MANY PLACES OVER THE YEARS. MOST OF THEM MIXING AND INTERMINGLING WITH HUMANITY.
USING THE INFORMATION IN THIS ARCHIVE, WE LOCATED THE MOST PROBABLE LOCATIONS THAT A LOST TRIBE... AND THE CHILD OF THANOS... COULD BE.
THE INHUMANS ALSO KEEP PRECISE GENETIC RECORDS, WHICH IS HOW WE'LL BE ABLE TO IDENTIFY HIM.

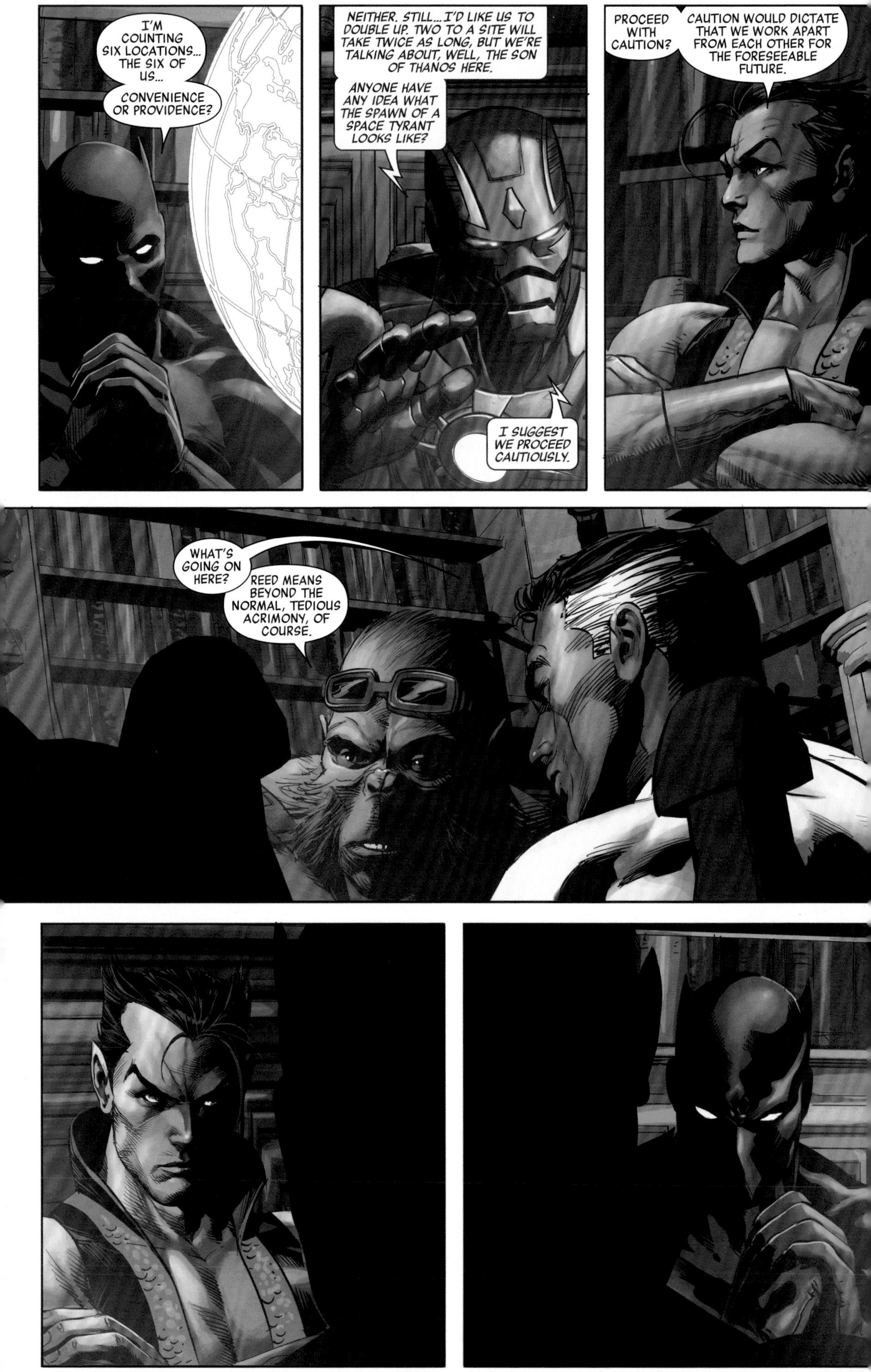
I'M COUNTING SIX LOCATIONS... THE SIX OF US...
CONVENIENCE OR PROVIDENCE?
NEITHER. STILL... I'D LIKE US TO DOUBLE UP. TWO TO A SITE WILL TAKE TWICE AS LONG, BUT WE'RE TALKING ABOUT, WELL, THE SON OF THANOS HERE.
ANYONE HAVE ANY IDEA WHAT THE SPAWN OF A SPACE TYRANT LOOKS LIKE?
I SUGGEST WE PROCEED CAUTIOUSLY.
PROCEED WITH CAUTION?
CAUTION WOULD DICTATE THAT WE WORK APART FROM EACH OTHER FOR THE FORESEEABLE FUTURE.
WHAT'S GOING ON HERE?
REED MEANS BEYOND THE NORMAL, TEDIOUS ACRIMONY, OF COURSE.

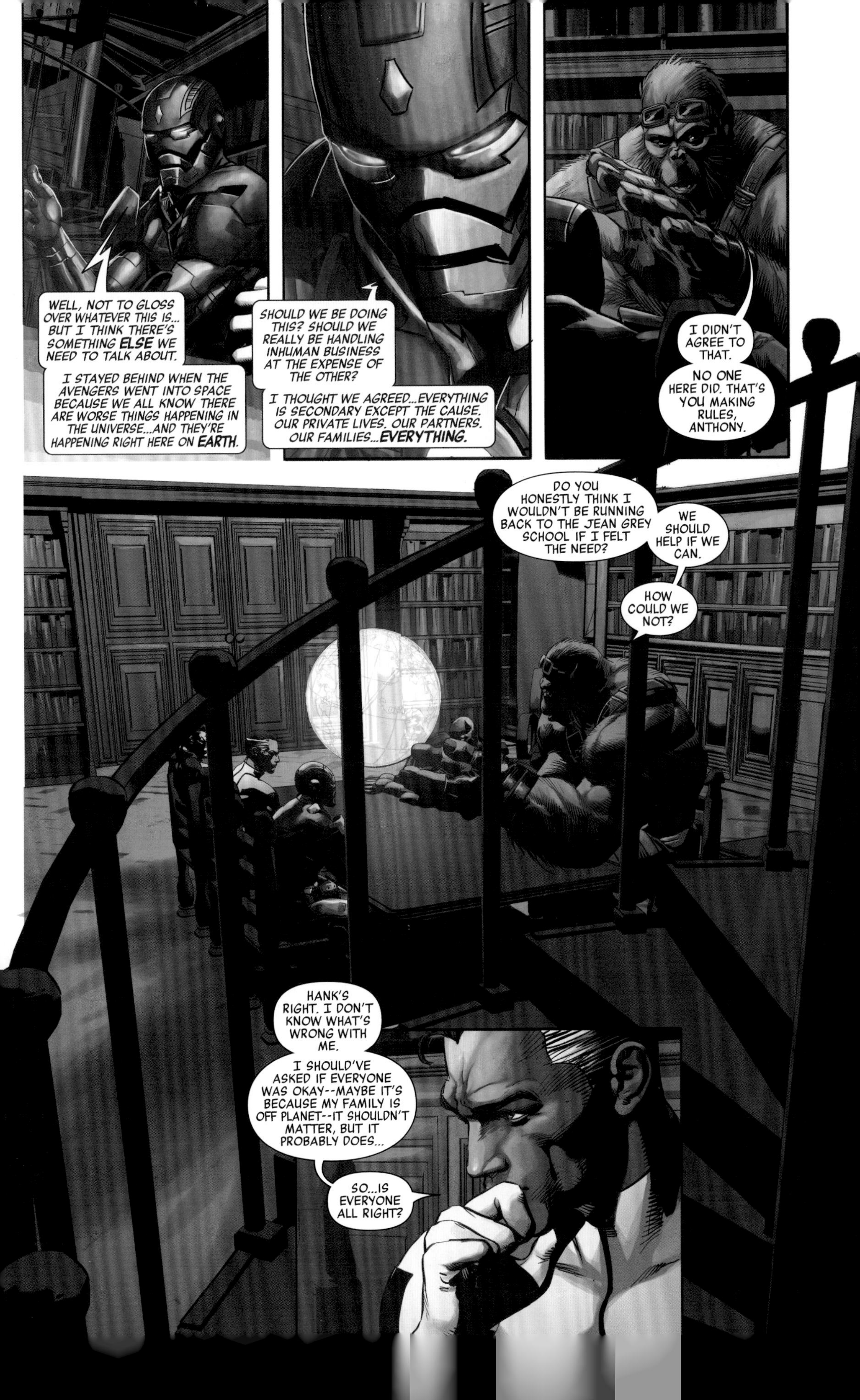
WELL, NOT TO GLOSS OVER WHATEVER THIS IS... BUT I THINK THERE'S SOMETHING ELSE WE NEED TO TALK ABOUT.
I STAYED BEHIND WHEN THE AVENGERS WENT INTO SPACE BECAUSE WE ALL KNOW THERE ARE WORSE THINGS HAPPENING IN THE UNIVERSE...AND THEY'RE HAPPENING RIGHT HERE ON EARTH.
SHOULD WE BE DOING THIS? SHOULD WE REALLY BE HANDLING INHUMAN BUSINESS AT THE EXPENSE OF THE OTHER?
I THOUGHT WE AGREED...EVERYTHING IS SECONDARY EXCEPT THE CAUSE. OUR PRIVATE LIVES. OUR PARTNERS. OUR FAMILIES...EVERYTHING.
I DIDN'T AGREE TO THAT.
NO ONE HERE DID. THAT'S YOU MAKING RULES, ANTHONY.
DO YOU HONESTLY THINK I WOULDN'T BE RUNNING BACK TO THE JEAN GREY SCHOOL IF I FELT THE NEED?
WE SHOULD HELP IF WE CAN.
HOW COULD WE NOT?
HANK'S RIGHT. I DON'T KNOW WHAT'S WRONG WITH ME.
I SHOULD'VE ASKED IF EVERYONE WAS OKAY--MAYBE IT'S BECAUSE MY FAMILY IS OFF PLANET--IT SHOULDN'T MATTER, BUT IT PROBABLY DOES...
SO...IS EVERYONE ALL RIGHT?

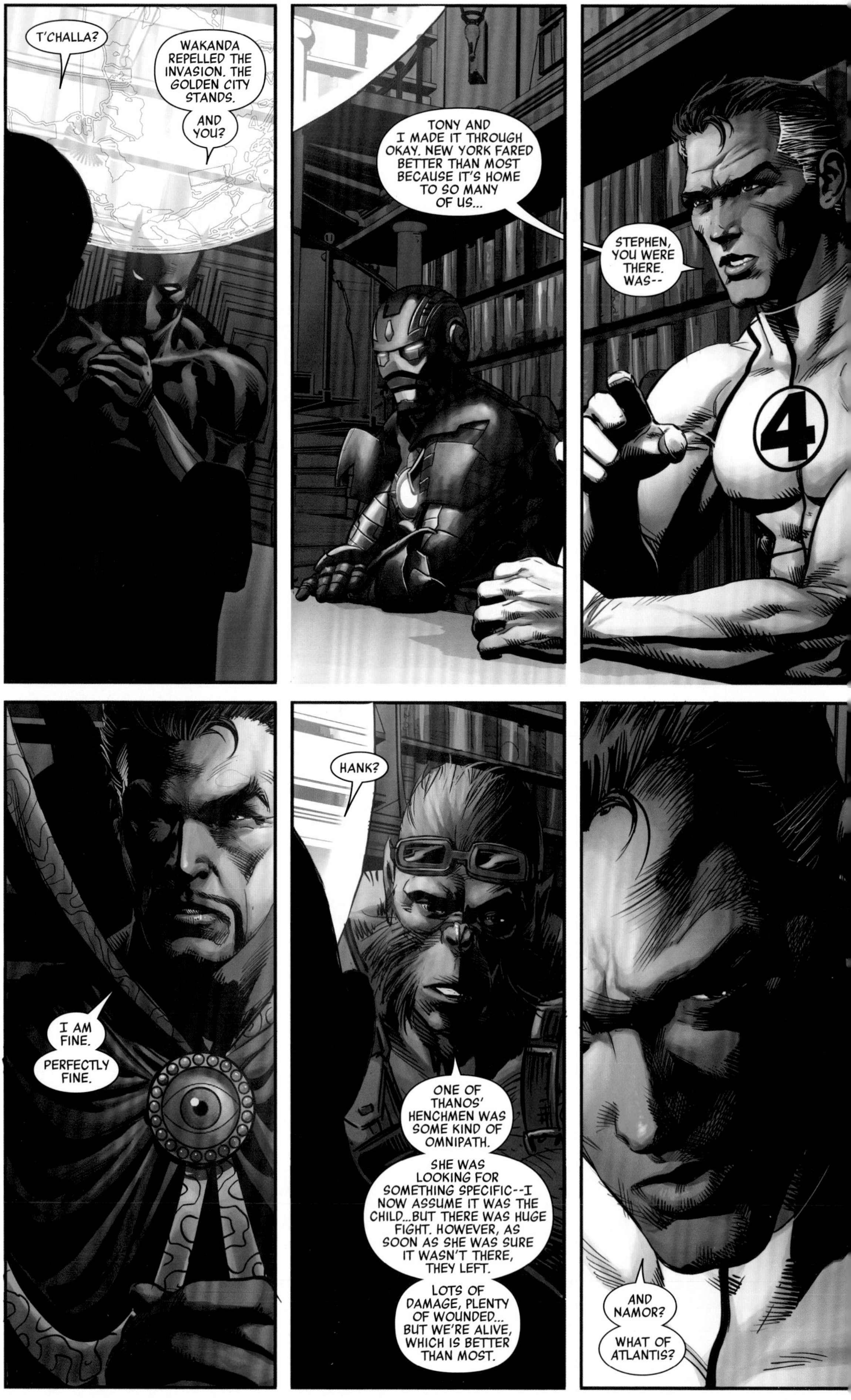
T'CHALLA?
WAKANDA REPELLED THE INVASION. THE GOLDEN CITY STANDS.
AND YOU?
TONY AND I MADE IT THROUGH OKAY. NEW YORK FARED BETTER THAN MOST BECAUSE IT'S HOME TO SO MANY OF US...
STEPHEN, YOU WERE THERE. WAS--
I AM FINE.
PERFECTLY FINE.
HANK?
ONE OF THANOS' HENCHMEN WAS SOME KIND OF OMNIPATH.
SHE WAS LOOKING FOR SOMETHING SPECIFIC--I NOW ASSUME IT WAS THE CHILD...BUT THERE WAS HUGE FIGHT. HOWEVER, AS SOON AS SHE WAS SURE IT WASN'T THERE, THEY LEFT.
LOTS OF DAMAGE, PLENTY OF WOUNDED... BUT WE'RE ALIVE, WHICH IS BETTER THAN MOST.
AND NAMOR?
WHAT OF ATLANTIS?

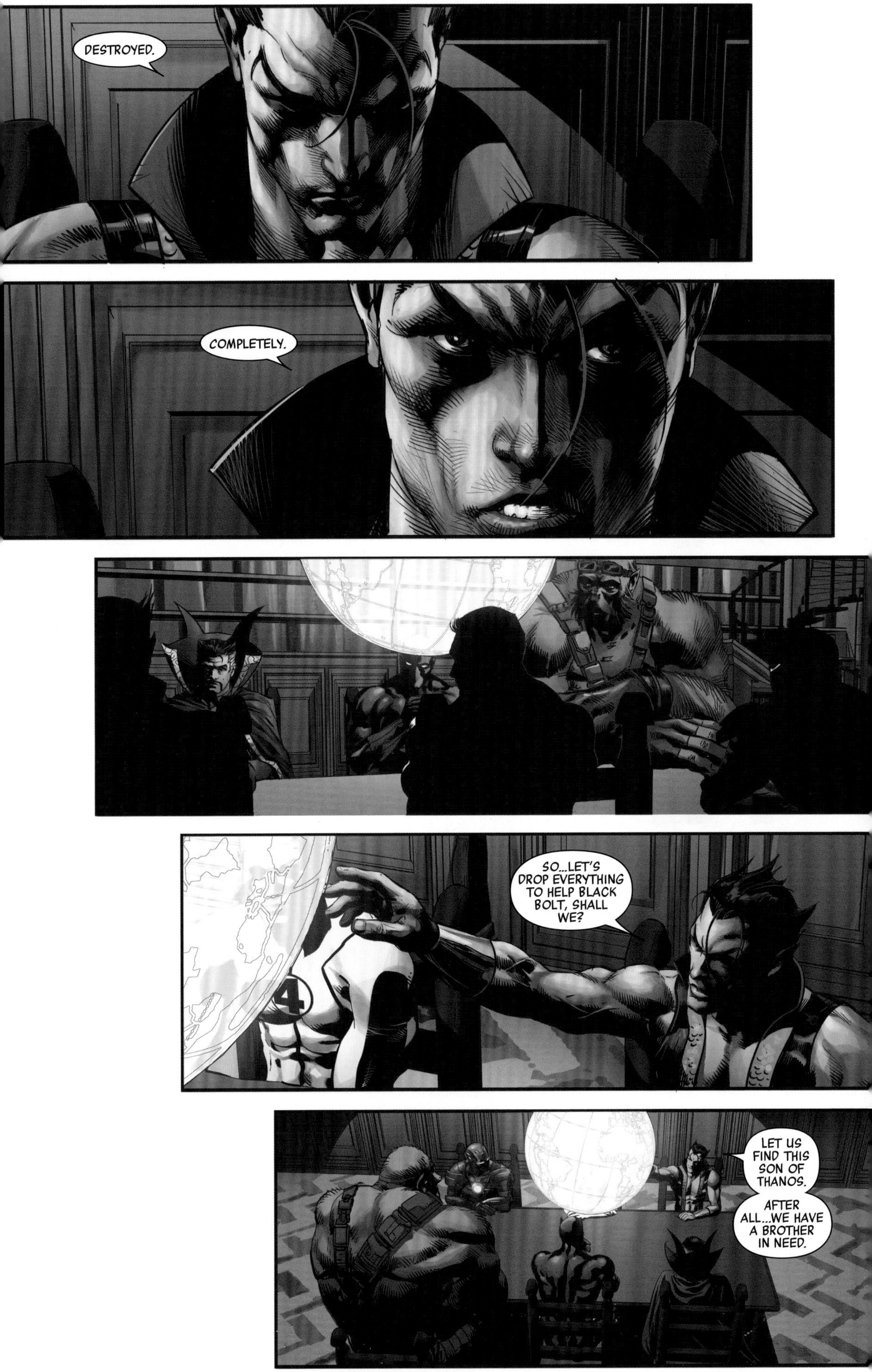
DESTROYED.
COMPLETELY.
SO...LET'S DROP EVERYTHING TO HELP BLACK BOLT, SHALL WE?
LET US FIND THIS SON OF THANOS.
AFTER ALL...WE HAVE A BROTHER IN NEED.

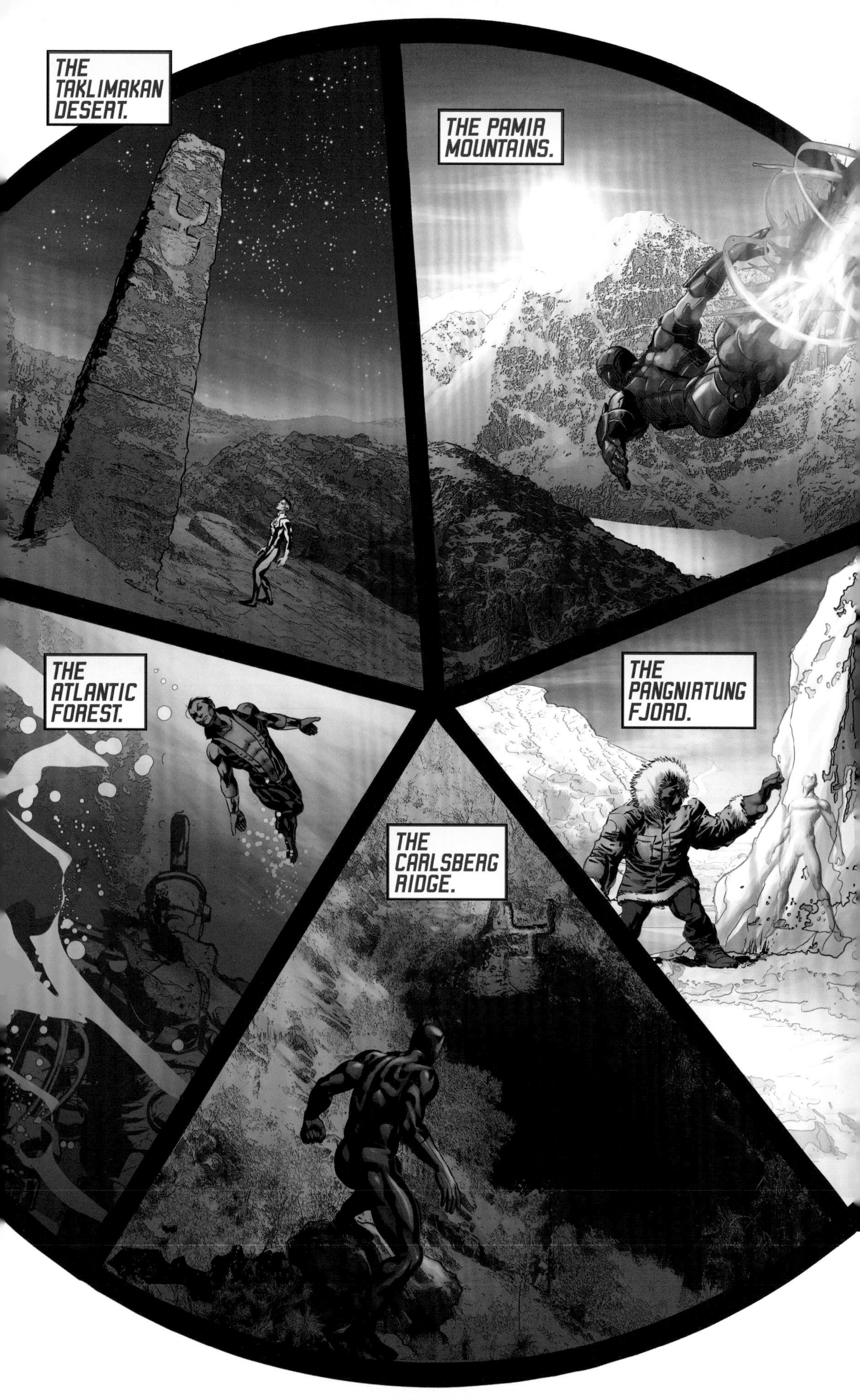

THE TAKLIMAKAN DESERT.
THE PAMIR MOUNTAINS.
THE ATLANTIC FOREST.
THE CARLSBERG RIDGE.
THE PANGNIRTUNG FJORD.

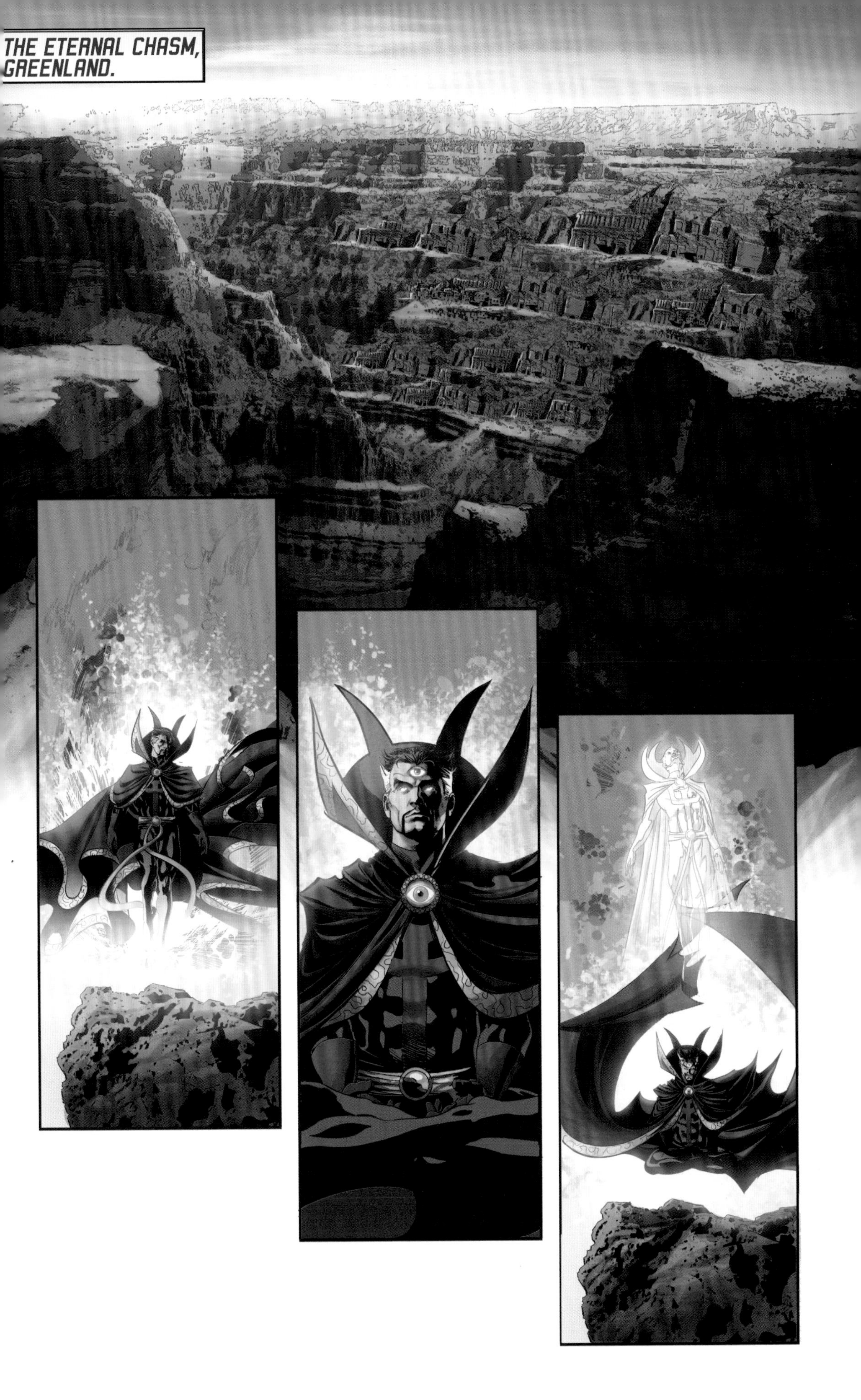
THE ETERNAL CHASM, GREENLAND.

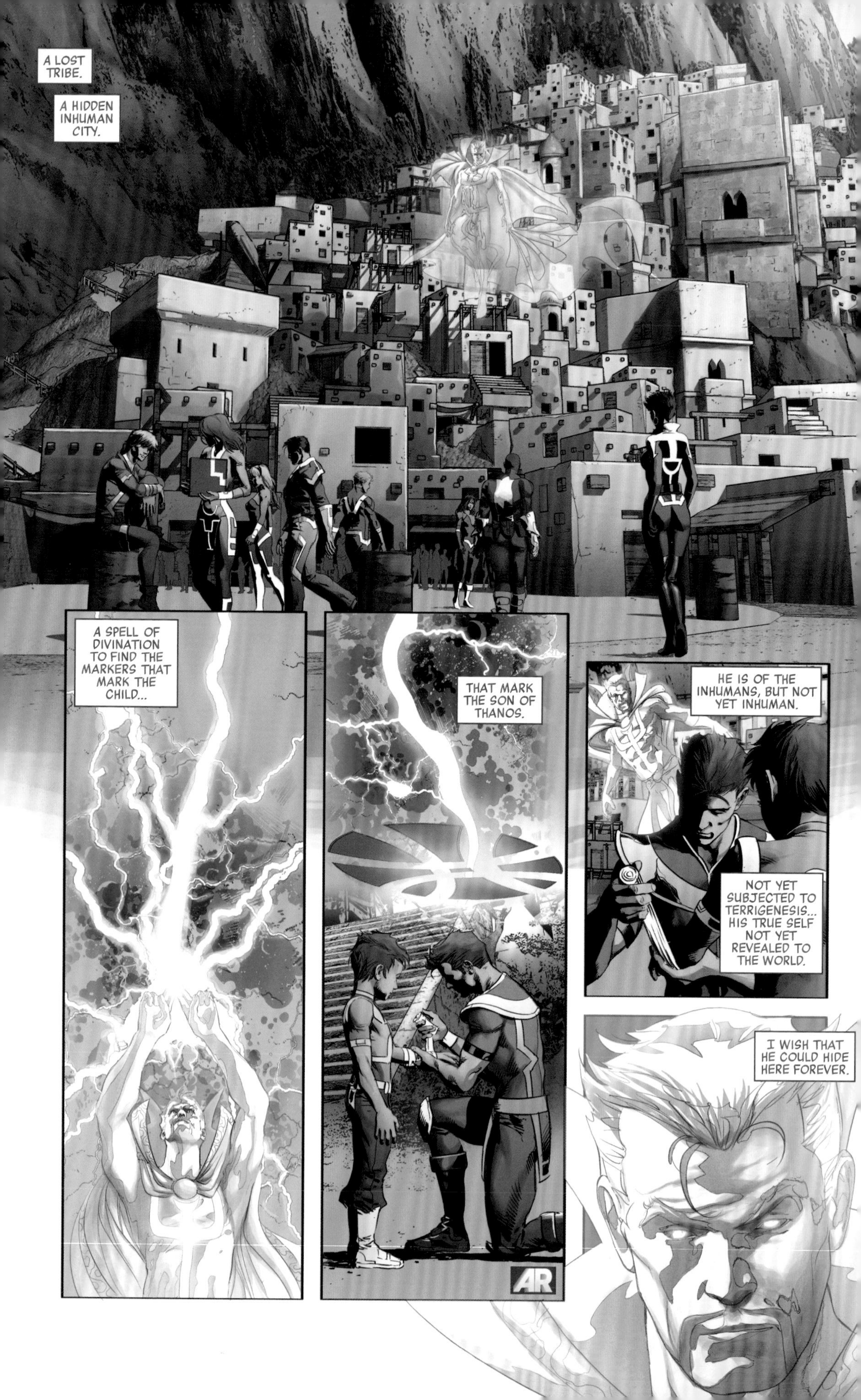
A LOST TRIBE.
A HIDDEN INHUMAN CITY.
A SPELL OF DIVINATION TO FIND THE MARKERS THAT MARK THE CHILD...
THAT MARK THE SON OF THANOS.
HE IS OF THE INHUMANS, BUT NOT YET INHUMAN.
NOT YET SUBJECTED TO TERRIGENESIS... HIS TRUE SELF NOT YET REVEALED TO THE WORLD.
I WISH THAT HE COULD HIDE HERE FOREVER.
AR

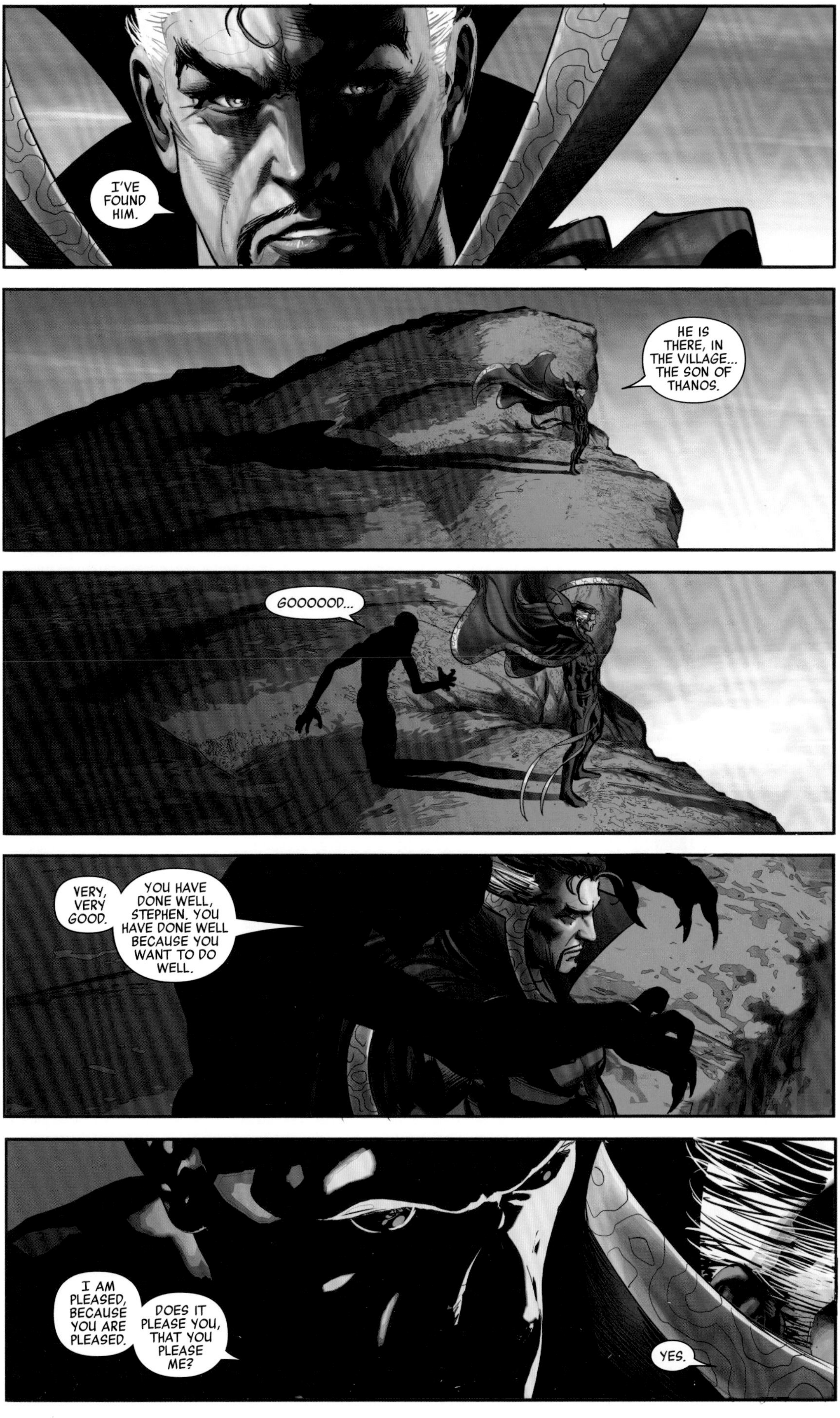

I'VE FOUND HIM.
HE IS THERE, IN THE VILLAGE... THE SON OF THANOS.
GOOOOOD...
VERY, VERY GOOD.
YOU HAVE DONE WELL, STEPHEN. YOU HAVE DONE WELL BECAUSE YOU WANT TO DO WELL.
I AM PLEASED, BECAUSE YOU ARE PLEASED.
DOES IT PLEASE YOU, THAT YOU PLEASE ME?
YES.

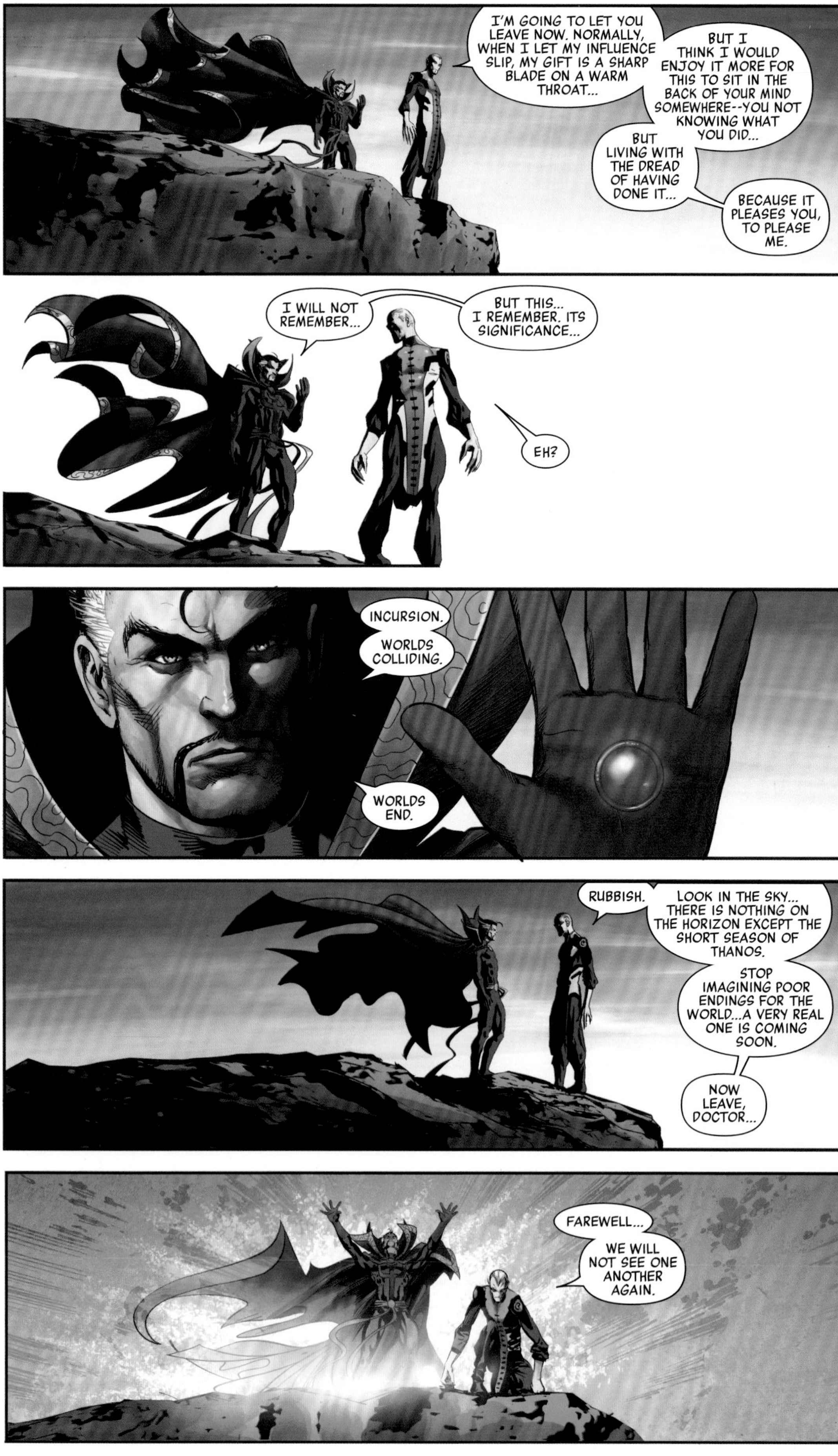
I'M GOING TO LET YOU LEAVE NOW. NORMALLY, WHEN I LET MY INFLUENCE SLIP, MY GIFT IS A SHARP BLADE ON A WARM THROAT...
BUT I THINK I WOULD ENJOY IT MORE FOR THIS TO SIT IN THE BACK OF YOUR MIND SOMEWHERE--YOU NOT KNOWING WHAT YOU DID...
BUT LIVING WITH THE DREAD OF HAVING DONE IT...
BECAUSE IT PLEASES YOU, TO PLEASE ME.
I WILL NOT REMEMBER...
BUT THIS... I REMEMBER. ITS SIGNIFICANCE...
EH?
INCURSION.
WORLDS COLLIDING.
WORLDS END.
RUBBISH.
LOOK IN THE SKY... THERE IS NOTHING ON THE HORIZON EXCEPT THE SHORT SEASON OF THANOS.
STOP IMAGINING POOR ENDINGS FOR THE WORLD...A VERY REAL ONE IS COMING SOON.
NOW LEAVE, DOCTOR...
FAREWELL...
WE WILL NOT SEE ONE ANOTHER AGAIN.

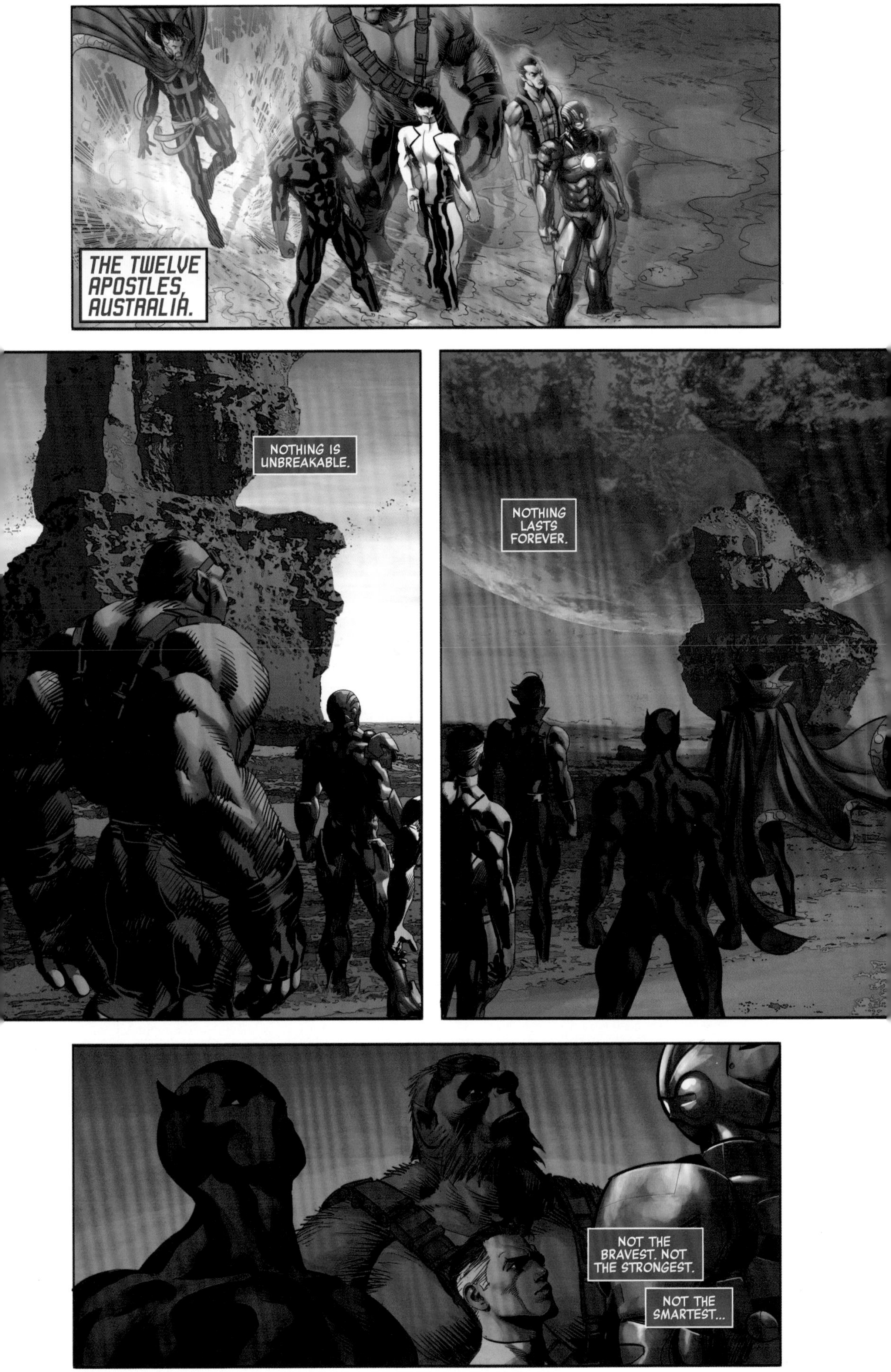
THE TWELVE APOSTLES, AUSTRALIA.
NOTHING IS UNBREAKABLE.
NOTHING LASTS FOREVER.
NOT THE BRAVEST. NOT THE STRONGEST.
NOT THE SMARTEST...

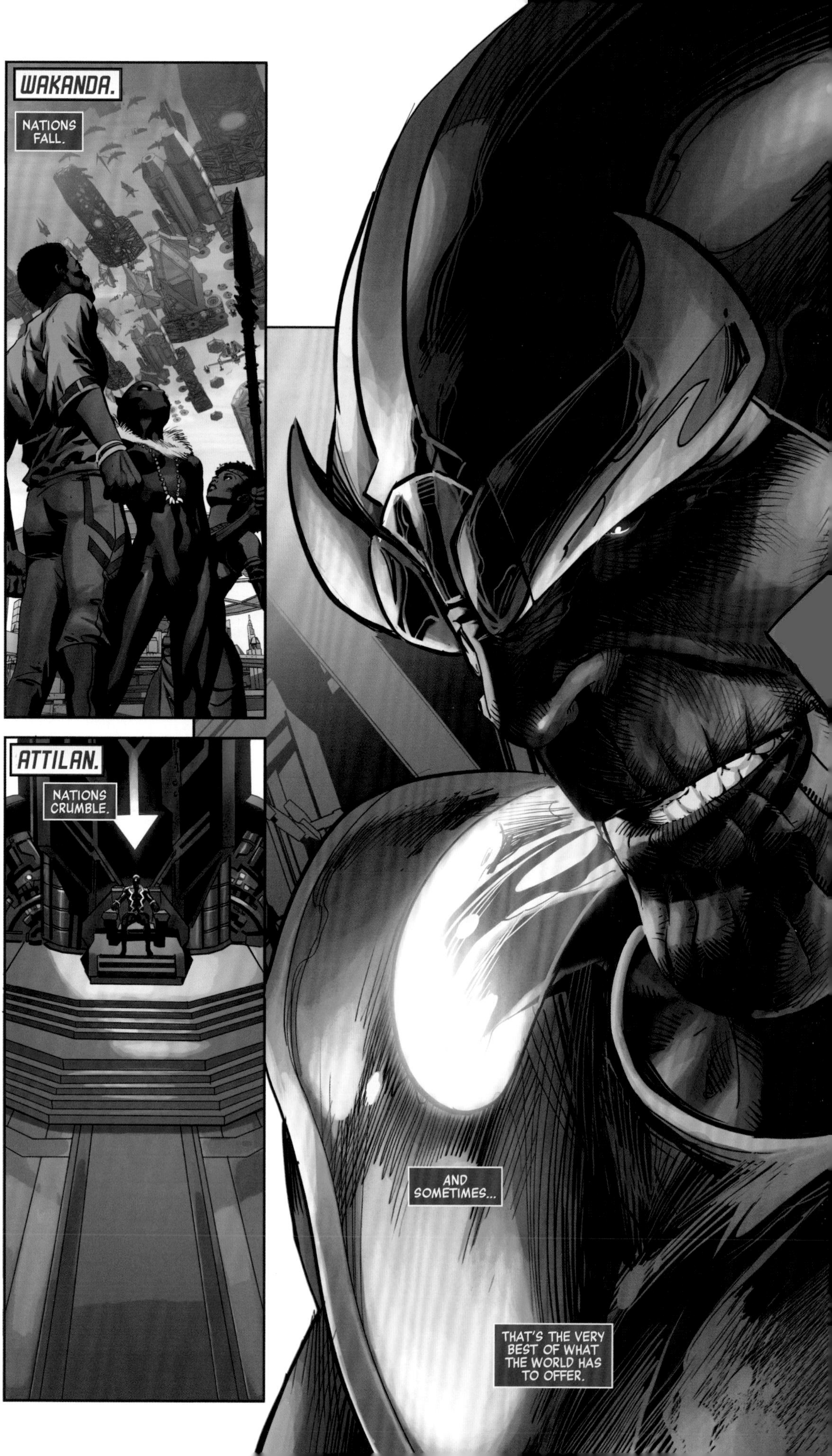
WAKANDA.
NATIONS FALL.
ATTILAN.
NATIONS CRUMBLE.
AND SOMETIMES...
THAT'S THE VERY BEST OF WHAT THE WORLD HAS TO OFFER.

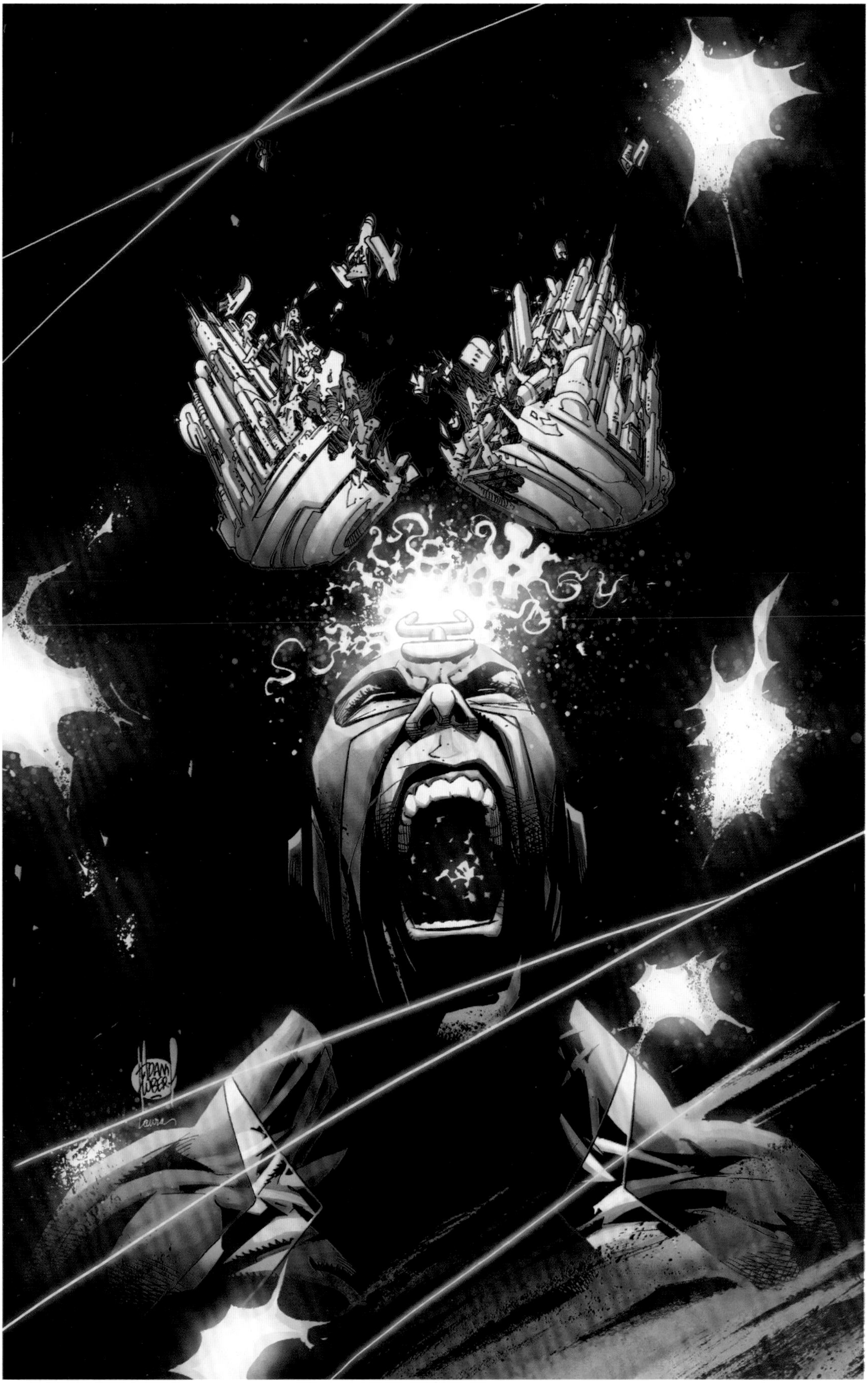

SUBMIT OR
PERISH

◆

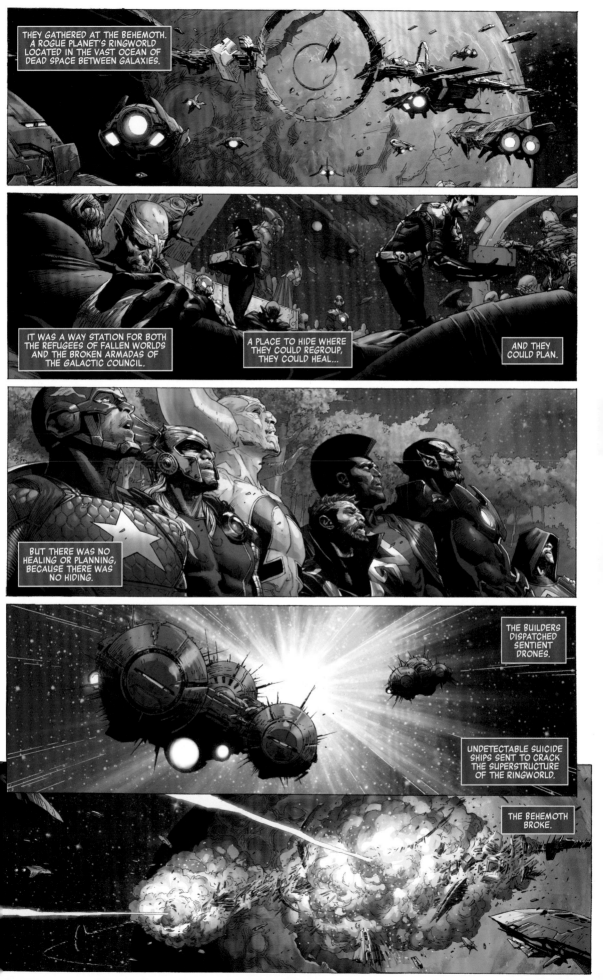

THEY GATHERED AT THE BEHEMOTH. A ROGUE PLANET'S RINGWORLD LOCATED IN THE VAST OCEAN OF DEAD SPACE BETWEEN GALAXIES.

IT WAS A WAY STATION FOR BOTH THE REFUGEES OF FALLEN WORLDS AND THE BROKEN ARMADAS OF THE GALACTIC COUNCIL.

A PLACE TO HIDE WHERE THEY COULD REGROUP, THEY COULD HEAL...

AND THEY COULD PLAN.

BUT THERE WAS NO HEALING OR PLANNING, BECAUSE THERE WAS NO HIDING.

THE BUILDERS DISPATCHED SENTIENT DRONES.

UNDETECTABLE SUICIDE SHIPS SENT TO CRACK THE SUPERSTRUCTURE OF THE RINGWORLD.

THE BEHEMOTH BROKE.

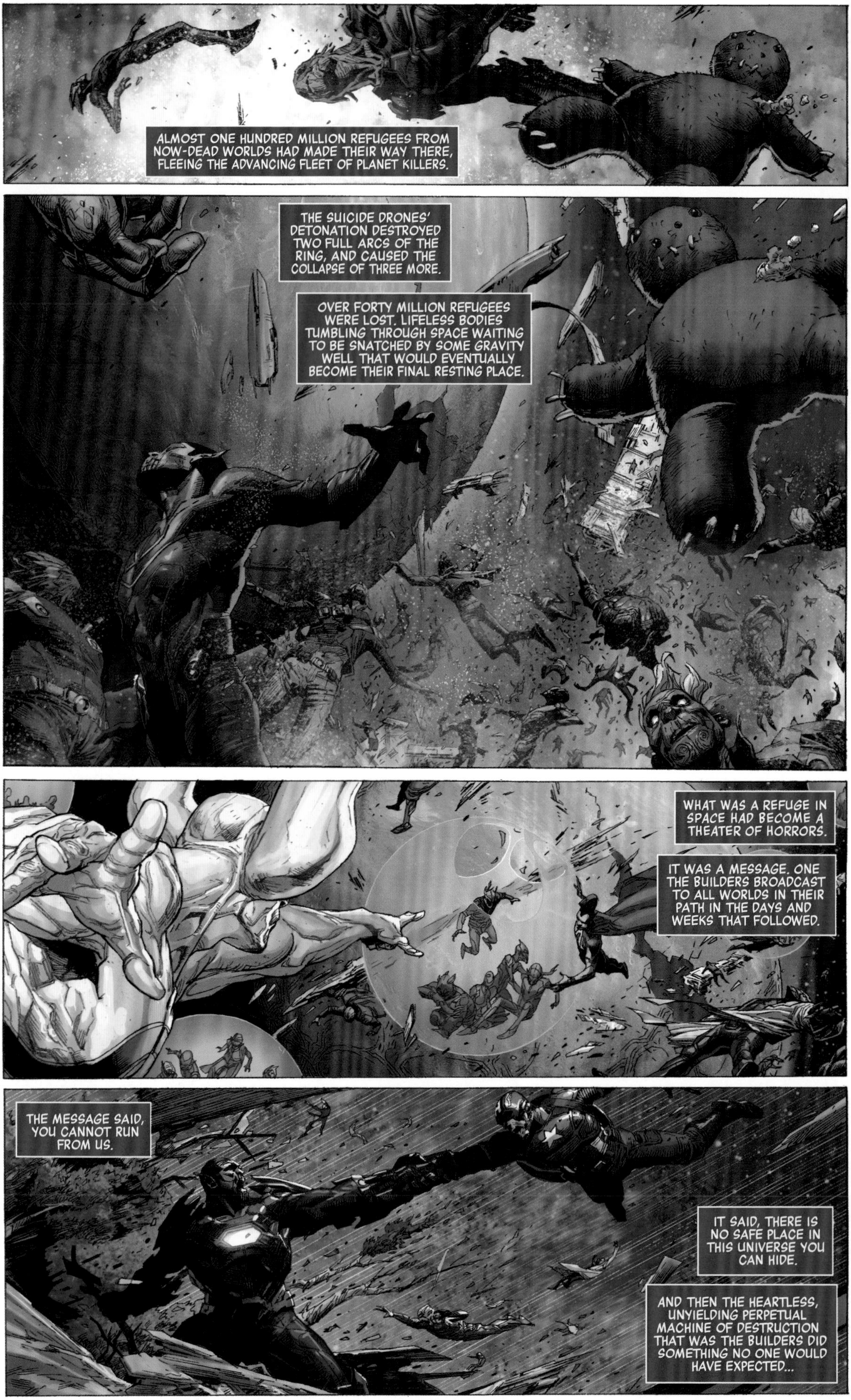
ALMOST ONE HUNDRED MILLION REFUGEES FROM NOW-DEAD WORLDS HAD MADE THEIR WAY THERE, FLEEING THE ADVANCING FLEET OF PLANET KILLERS.
THE SUICIDE DRONES' DETONATION DESTROYED TWO FULL ARCS OF THE RING, AND CAUSED THE COLLAPSE OF THREE MORE.
OVER FORTY MILLION REFUGEES WERE LOST. LIFELESS BODIES TUMBLING THROUGH SPACE WAITING TO BE SNATCHED BY SOME GRAVITY WELL THAT WOULD EVENTUALLY BECOME THEIR FINAL RESTING PLACE.
WHAT WAS A REFUGE IN SPACE HAD BECOME A THEATER OF HORRORS.
IT WAS A MESSAGE. ONE THE BUILDERS BROADCAST TO ALL WORLDS IN THEIR PATH IN THE DAYS AND WEEKS THAT FOLLOWED.
THE MESSAGE SAID, YOU CANNOT RUN FROM US.
IT SAID, THERE IS NO SAFE PLACE IN THIS UNIVERSE YOU CAN HIDE.
AND THEN THE HEARTLESS, UNYIELDING PERPETUAL MACHINE OF DESTRUCTION THAT WAS THE BUILDERS DID SOMETHING NO ONE WOULD HAVE EXPECTED...

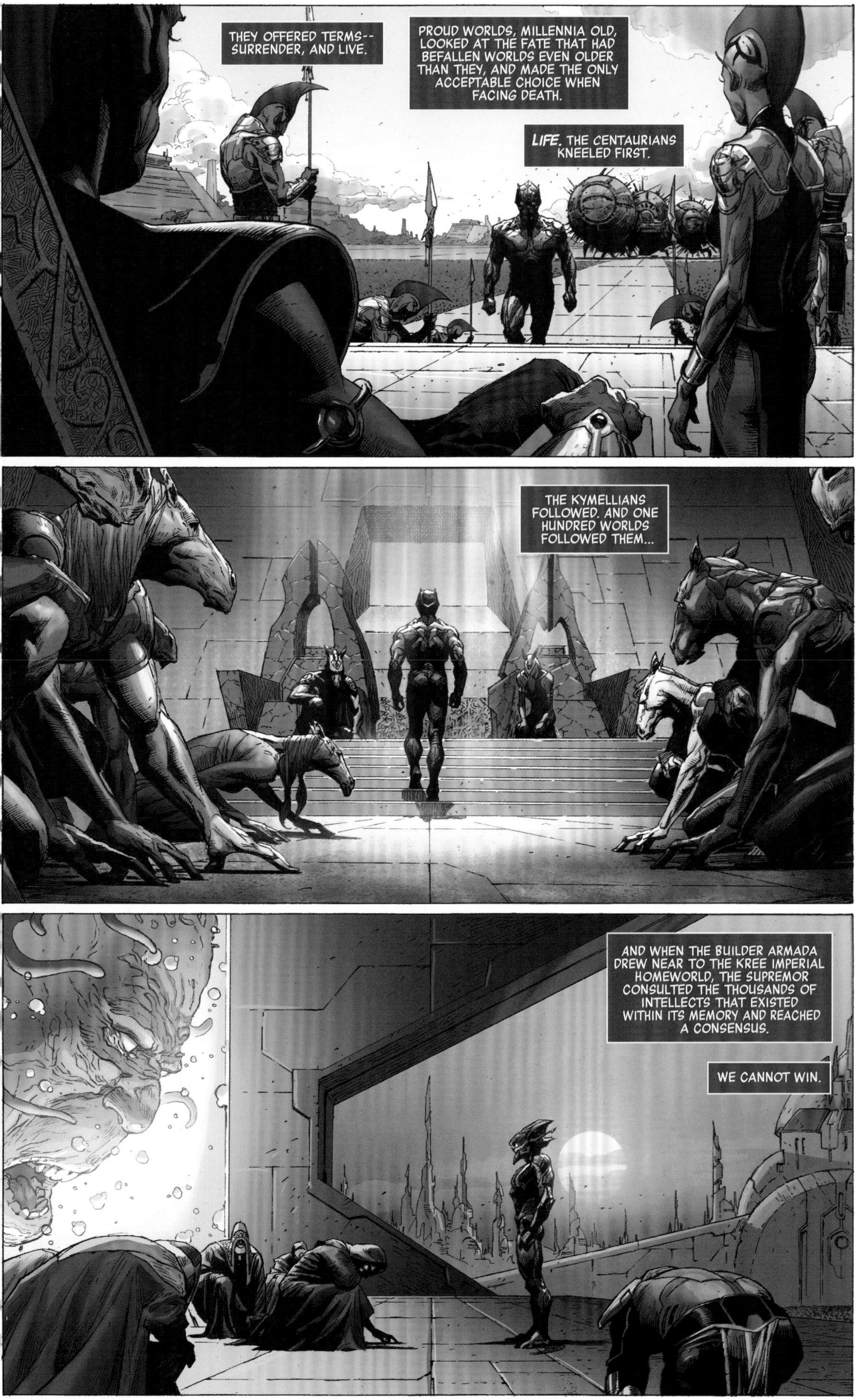

THEY OFFERED TERMS--SURRENDER, AND LIVE.
PROUD WORLDS, MILLENNIA OLD, LOOKED AT THE FATE THAT HAD BEFALLEN WORLDS EVEN OLDER THAN THEY, AND MADE THE ONLY ACCEPTABLE CHOICE WHEN FACING DEATH.
LIFE. THE CENTAURIANS KNEELED FIRST.
THE KYMELLIANS FOLLOWED. AND ONE HUNDRED WORLDS FOLLOWED THEM...
AND WHEN THE BUILDER ARMADA DREW NEAR TO THE KREE IMPERIAL HOMEWORLD, THE SUPREMOR CONSULTED THE THOUSANDS OF INTELLECTS THAT EXISTED WITHIN ITS MEMORY AND REACHED A CONSENSUS.
WE CANNOT WIN.

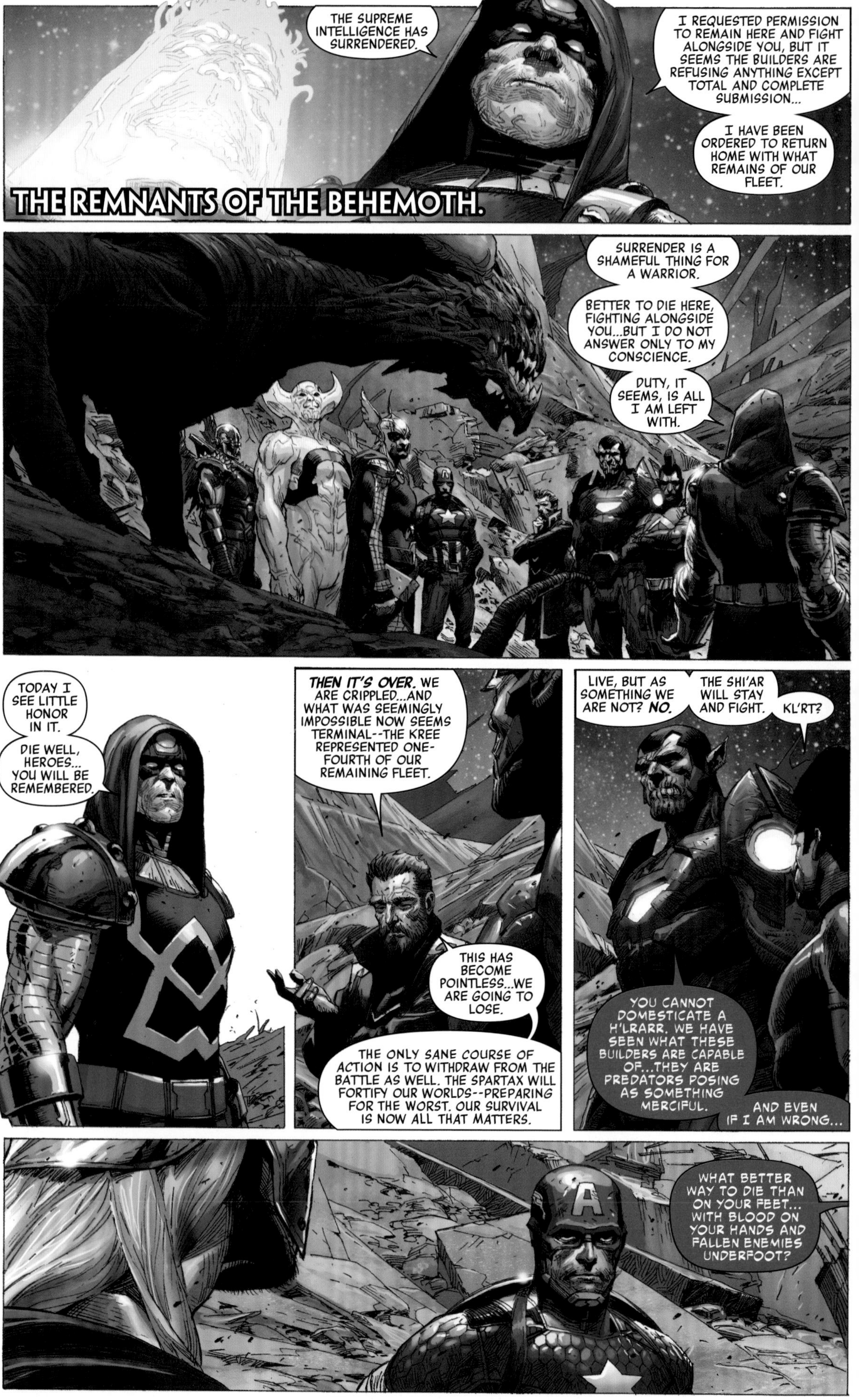
THE SUPREME INTELLIGENCE HAS SURRENDERED.
I REQUESTED PERMISSION TO REMAIN HERE AND FIGHT ALONGSIDE YOU, BUT IT SEEMS THE BUILDERS ARE REFUSING ANYTHING EXCEPT TOTAL AND COMPLETE SUBMISSION...
I HAVE BEEN ORDERED TO RETURN HOME WITH WHAT REMAINS OF OUR FLEET.
THE REMNANTS OF THE BEHEMOTH.
SURRENDER IS A SHAMEFUL THING FOR A WARRIOR.
BETTER TO DIE HERE, FIGHTING ALONGSIDE YOU...BUT I DO NOT ANSWER ONLY TO MY CONSCIENCE.
DUTY, IT SEEMS, IS ALL I AM LEFT WITH.
TODAY I SEE LITTLE HONOR IN IT.
DIE WELL, HEROES... YOU WILL BE REMEMBERED.
THEN IT'S OVER. WE ARE CRIPPLED...AND WHAT WAS SEEMINGLY IMPOSSIBLE NOW SEEMS TERMINAL--THE KREE REPRESENTED ONE-FOURTH OF OUR REMAINING FLEET.
THIS HAS BECOME POINTLESS...WE ARE GOING TO LOSE.
THE ONLY SANE COURSE OF ACTION IS TO WITHDRAW FROM THE BATTLE AS WELL. THE SPARTAX WILL FORTIFY OUR WORLDS--PREPARING FOR THE WORST. OUR SURVIVAL IS NOW ALL THAT MATTERS.
LIVE, BUT AS SOMETHING WE ARE NOT? NO.
THE SHI'AR WILL STAY AND FIGHT.
KL'RT?
YOU CANNOT DOMESTICATE A H'LRARR. WE HAVE SEEN WHAT THESE BUILDERS ARE CAPABLE OF...THEY ARE PREDATORS POSING AS SOMETHING MERCIFUL.
AND EVEN IF I AM WRONG...
WHAT BETTER WAY TO DIE THAN ON YOUR FEET... WITH BLOOD ON YOUR HANDS AND FALLEN ENEMIES UNDERFOOT?

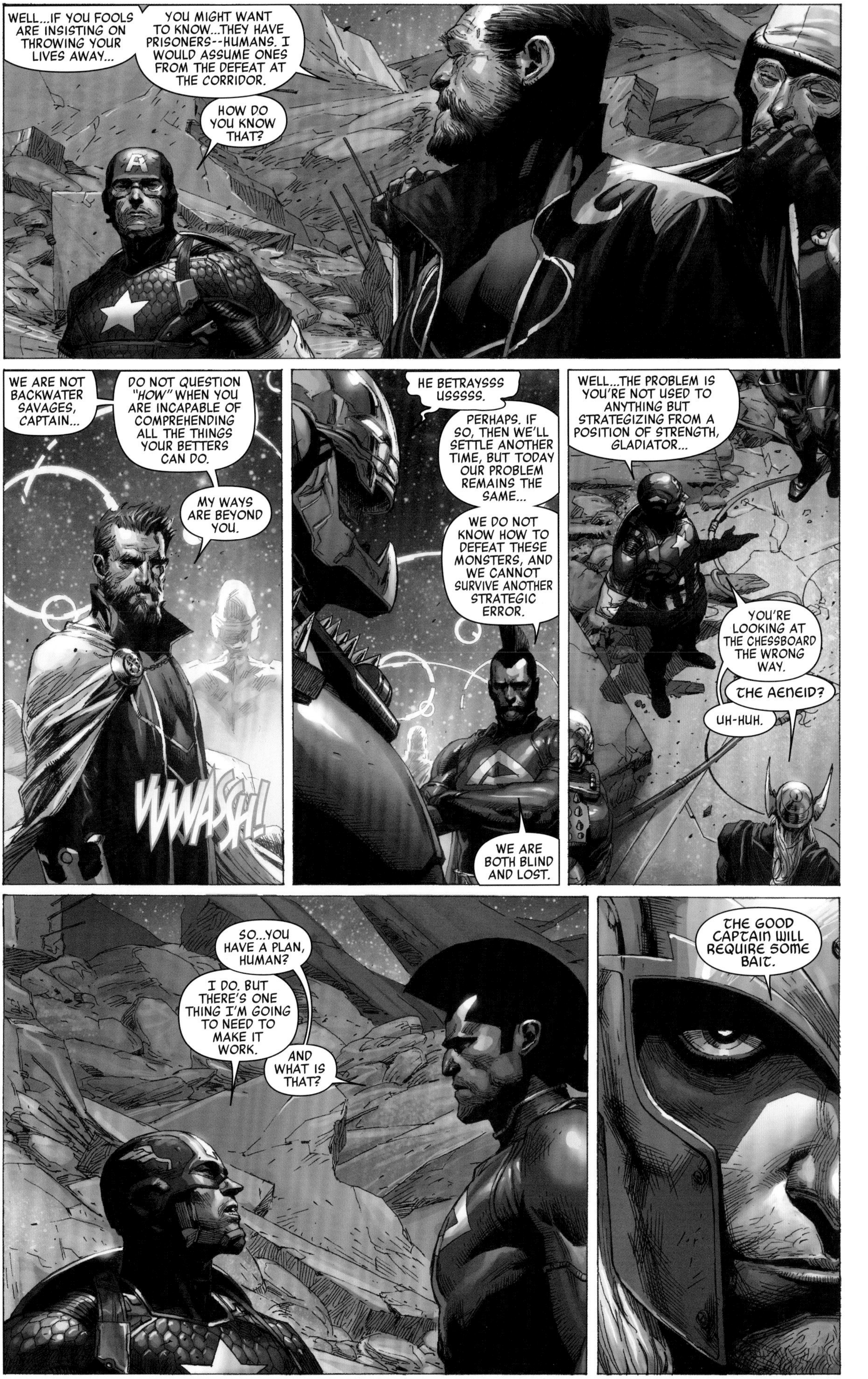
WELL...IF YOU FOOLS ARE INSISTING ON THROWING YOUR LIVES AWAY...
YOU MIGHT WANT TO KNOW...THEY HAVE PRISONERS--HUMANS. I WOULD ASSUME ONES FROM THE DEFEAT AT THE CORRIDOR.
HOW DO YOU KNOW THAT?
WE ARE NOT BACKWATER SAVAGES, CAPTAIN...
DO NOT QUESTION "HOW" WHEN YOU ARE INCAPABLE OF COMPREHENDING ALL THE THINGS YOUR BETTERS CAN DO.
MY WAYS ARE BEYOND YOU.
VVWASH!
HE BETRAYSSS USSSSS.
PERHAPS. IF SO, THEN WE'LL SETTLE ANOTHER TIME, BUT TODAY OUR PROBLEM REMAINS THE SAME...
WE DO NOT KNOW HOW TO DEFEAT THESE MONSTERS, AND WE CANNOT SURVIVE ANOTHER STRATEGIC ERROR.
WE ARE BOTH BLIND AND LOST.
WELL...THE PROBLEM IS YOU'RE NOT USED TO ANYTHING BUT STRATEGIZING FROM A POSITION OF STRENGTH, GLADIATOR...
YOU'RE LOOKING AT THE CHESSBOARD THE WRONG WAY.
THE AENEID?
UH-HUH.
SO...YOU HAVE A PLAN, HUMAN?
I DO. BUT THERE'S ONE THING I'M GOING TO NEED TO MAKE IT WORK.
AND WHAT IS THAT?
THE GOOD CAPTAIN WILL REQUIRE SOME BAIT.

WORLD KILLERS

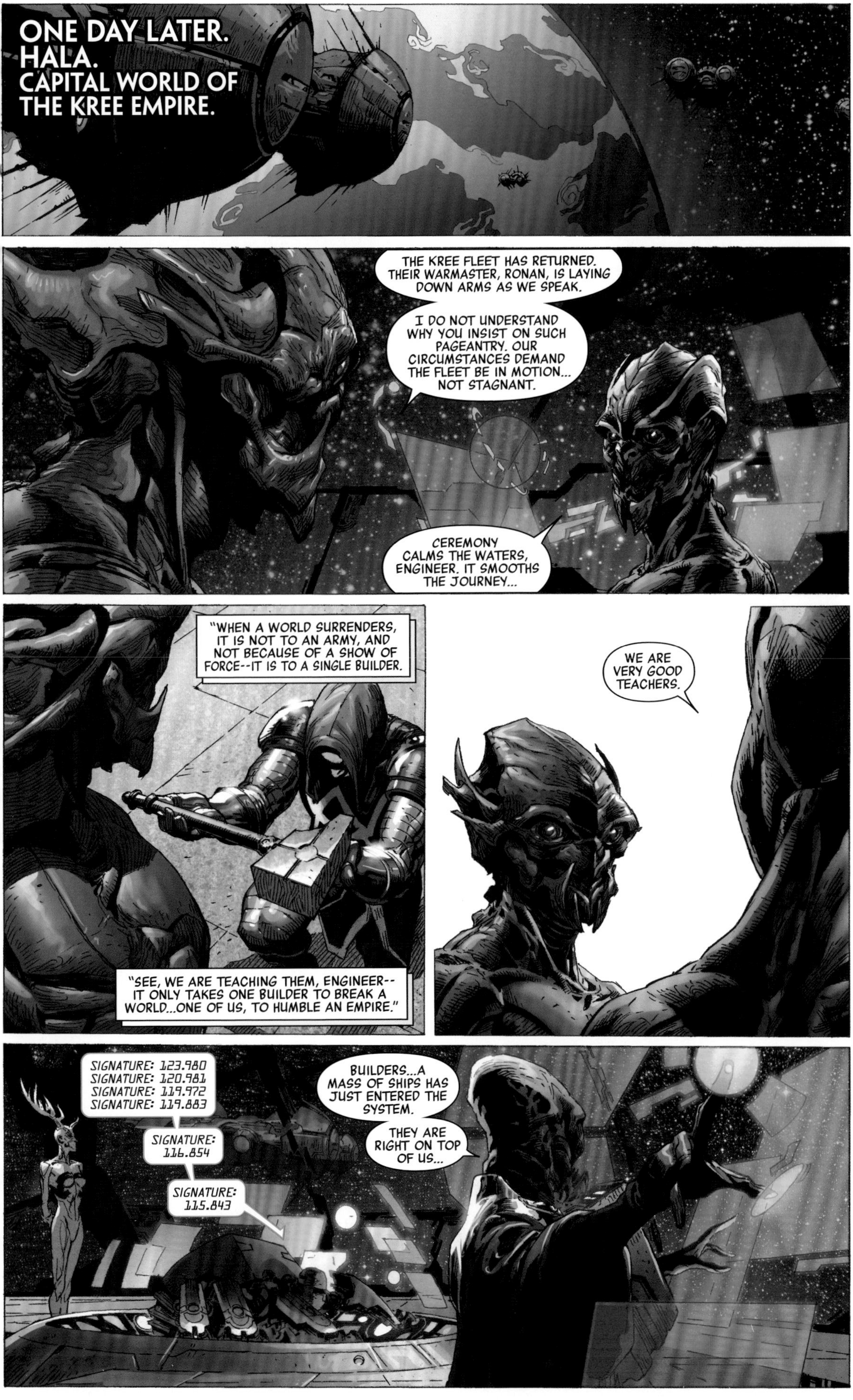
ONE DAY LATER. HALA. CAPITAL WORLD OF THE KREE EMPIRE.
THE KREE FLEET HAS RETURNED. THEIR WARMASTER, RONAN, IS LAYING DOWN ARMS AS WE SPEAK.
I DO NOT UNDERSTAND WHY YOU INSIST ON SUCH PAGEANTRY. OUR CIRCUMSTANCES DEMAND THE FLEET BE IN MOTION... NOT STAGNANT.
CEREMONY CALMS THE WATERS, ENGINEER. IT SMOOTHS THE JOURNEY...
"WHEN A WORLD SURRENDERS, IT IS NOT TO AN ARMY, AND NOT BECAUSE OF A SHOW OF FORCE--IT IS TO A SINGLE BUILDER.
"SEE, WE ARE TEACHING THEM, ENGINEER-- IT ONLY TAKES ONE BUILDER TO BREAK A WORLD...ONE OF US, TO HUMBLE AN EMPIRE."
WE ARE VERY GOOD TEACHERS.
SIGNATURE: 123.980 SIGNATURE: 120.981 SIGNATURE: 119.972 SIGNATURE: 119.883
SIGNATURE: 116.854
SIGNATURE: 115.843
BUILDERS...A MASS OF SHIPS HAS JUST ENTERED THE SYSTEM.
THEY ARE RIGHT ON TOP OF US...

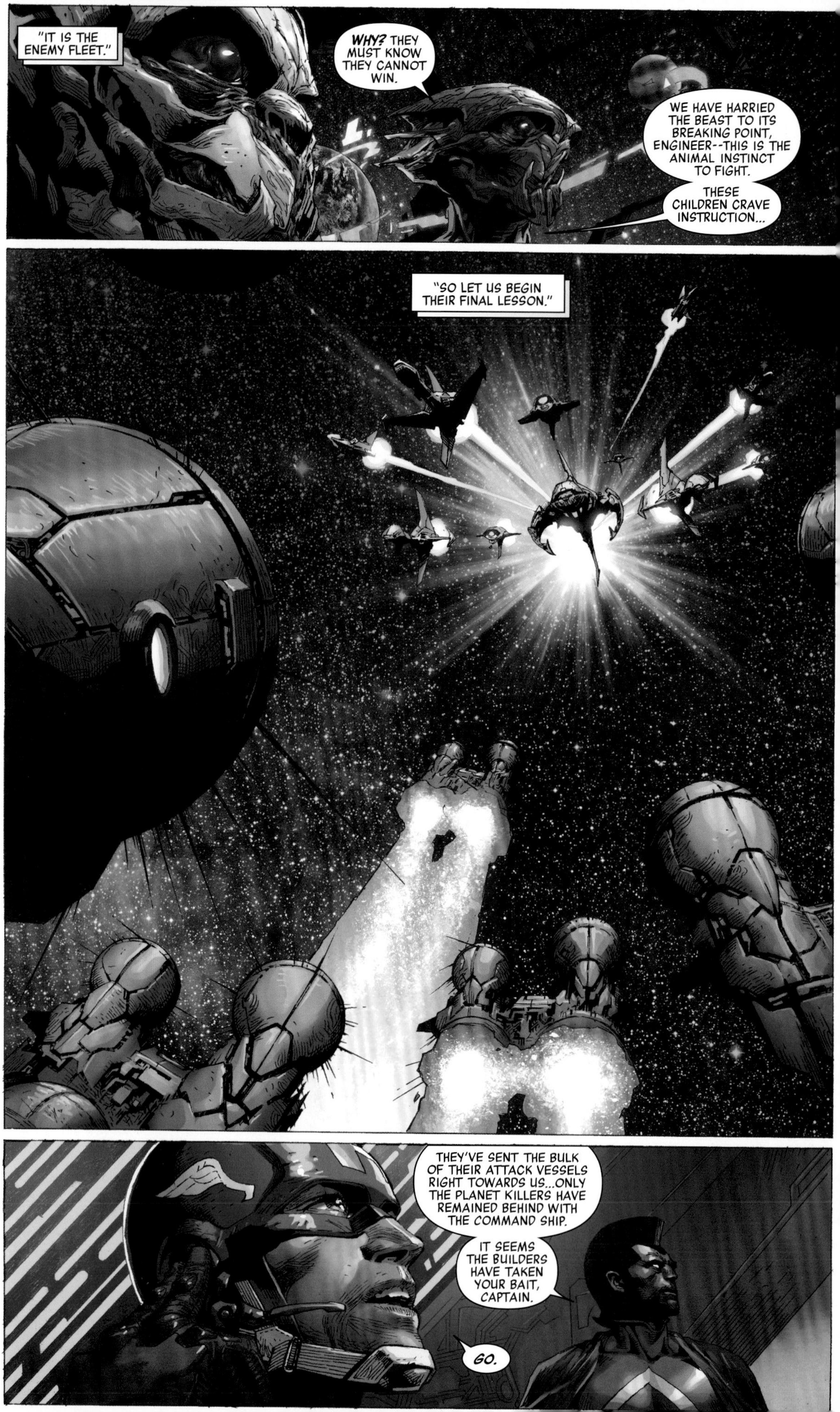
"IT IS THE ENEMY FLEET."
WHY? THEY MUST KNOW THEY CANNOT WIN.
WE HAVE HARRIED THE BEAST TO ITS BREAKING POINT, ENGINEER--THIS IS THE ANIMAL INSTINCT TO FIGHT.
THESE CHILDREN CRAVE INSTRUCTION...
"SO LET US BEGIN THEIR FINAL LESSON."
THEY'VE SENT THE BULK OF THEIR ATTACK VESSELS RIGHT TOWARDS US...ONLY THE PLANET KILLERS HAVE REMAINED BEHIND WITH THE COMMAND SHIP.
IT SEEMS THE BUILDERS HAVE TAKEN YOUR BAIT, CAPTAIN.
GO.

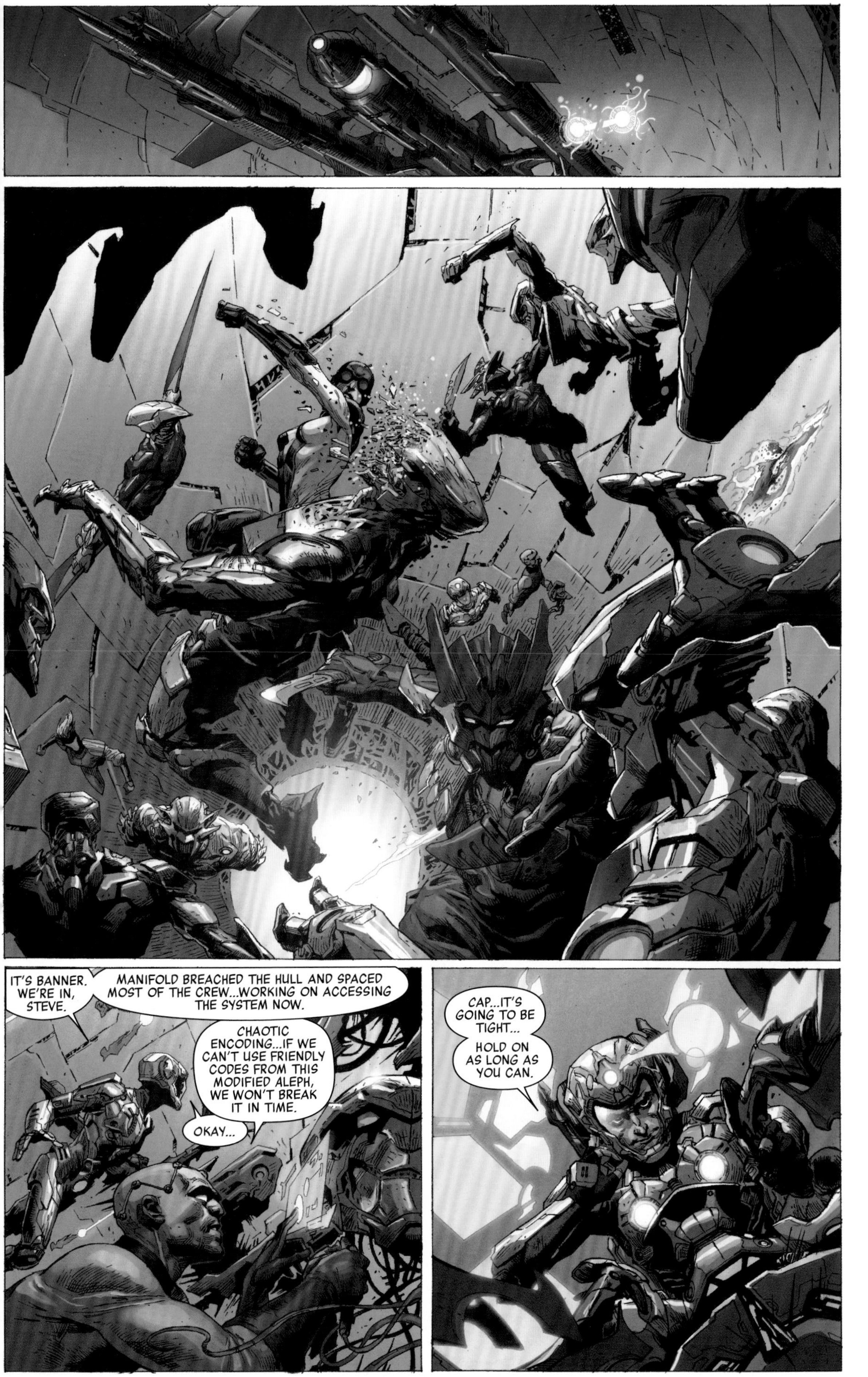
IT'S BANNER. WE'RE IN, STEVE.
MANIFOLD BREACHED THE HULL AND SPACED MOST OF THE CREW...WORKING ON ACCESSING THE SYSTEM NOW.
CHAOTIC ENCODING...IF WE CAN'T USE FRIENDLY CODES FROM THIS MODIFIED ALEPH, WE WON'T BREAK IT IN TIME.
OKAY...
CAP...IT'S GOING TO BE TIGHT...
HOLD ON AS LONG AS YOU CAN.

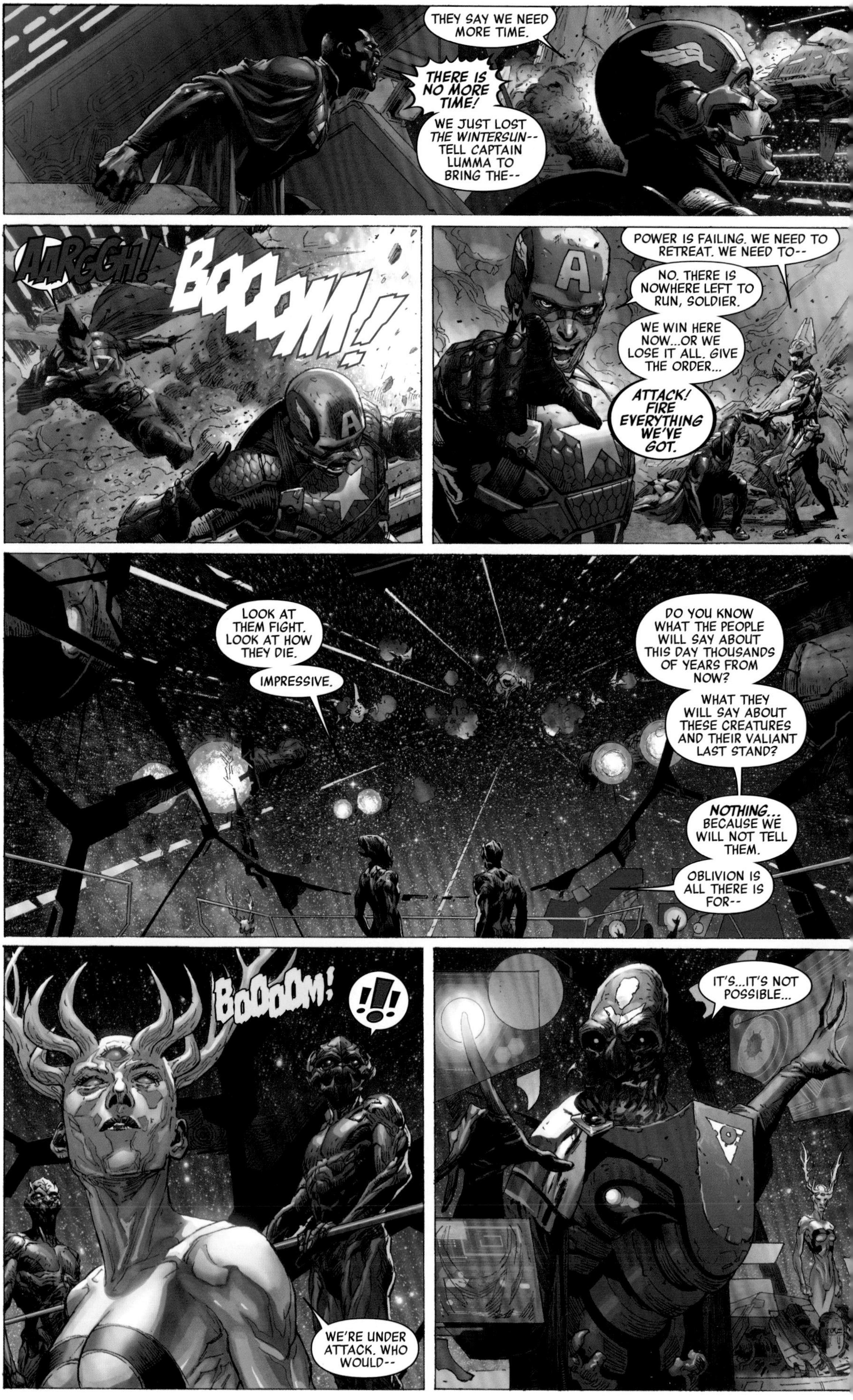
THEY SAY WE NEED MORE TIME.
THERE IS NO MORE TIME!
WE JUST LOST THE WINTERSUN-- TELL CAPTAIN LUMMA TO BRING THE--
AARGGH!
BOOOOM!!
POWER IS FAILING. WE NEED TO RETREAT. WE NEED TO--
NO. THERE IS NOWHERE LEFT TO RUN, SOLDIER.
WE WIN HERE NOW...OR WE LOSE IT ALL. GIVE THE ORDER...
ATTACK! FIRE EVERYTHING WE'VE GOT.
LOOK AT THEM FIGHT. LOOK AT HOW THEY DIE.
IMPRESSIVE.
DO YOU KNOW WHAT THE PEOPLE WILL SAY ABOUT THIS DAY THOUSANDS OF YEARS FROM NOW?
WHAT THEY WILL SAY ABOUT THESE CREATURES AND THEIR VALIANT LAST STAND?
NOTHING... BECAUSE WE WILL NOT TELL THEM.
OBLIVION IS ALL THERE IS FOR--
BOOOOM!
!!
WE'RE UNDER ATTACK. WHO WOULD--
IT'S...IT'S NOT POSSIBLE...

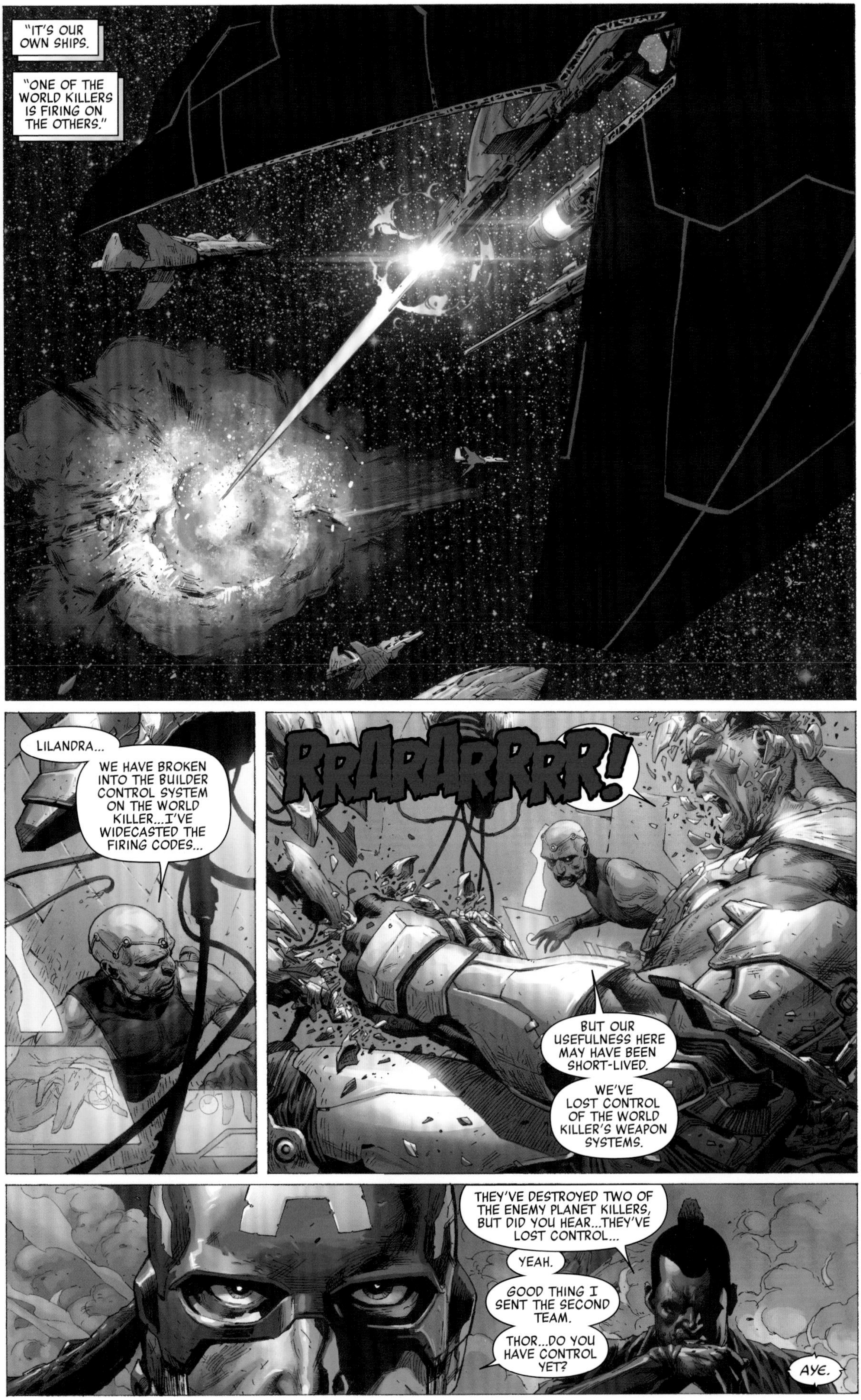
"IT'S OUR OWN SHIPS.
"ONE OF THE WORLD KILLERS IS FIRING ON THE OTHERS."
LILANDRA...
WE HAVE BROKEN INTO THE BUILDER CONTROL SYSTEM ON THE WORLD KILLER...I'VE WIDECASTED THE FIRING CODES...
RRARARRRR!
BUT OUR USEFULNESS HERE MAY HAVE BEEN SHORT-LIVED.
WE'VE LOST CONTROL OF THE WORLD KILLER'S WEAPON SYSTEMS.
THEY'VE DESTROYED TWO OF THE ENEMY PLANET KILLERS, BUT DID YOU HEAR...THEY'VE LOST CONTROL...
YEAH.
GOOD THING I SENT THE SECOND TEAM.
THOR...DO YOU HAVE CONTROL YET?
AYE.

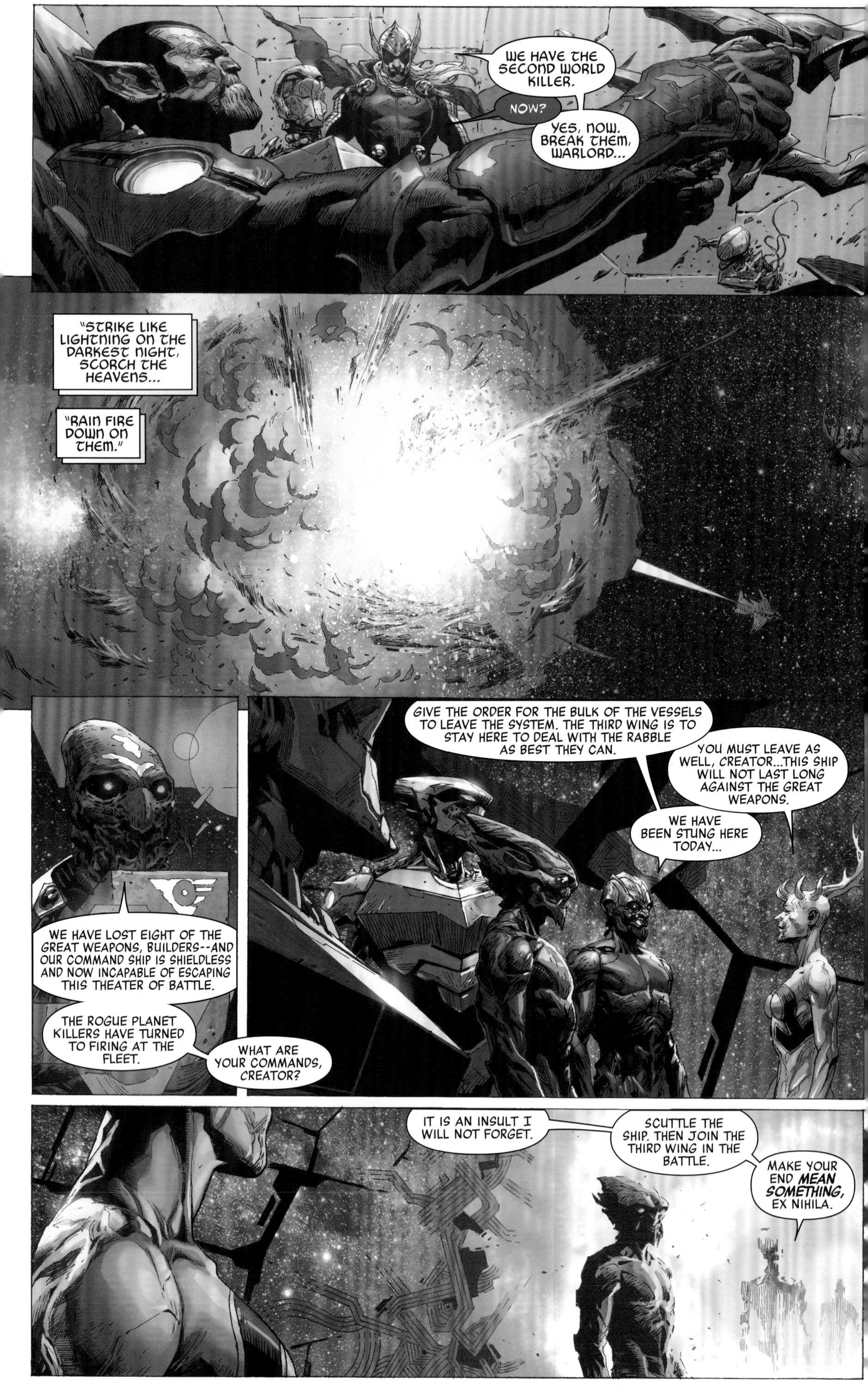
WE HAVE THE SECOND WORLD KILLER.
NOW?
YES, NOW. BREAK THEM, WARLORD...
"STRIKE LIKE LIGHTNING ON THE DARKEST NIGHT, SCORCH THE HEAVENS...
"RAIN FIRE DOWN ON THEM."
WE HAVE LOST EIGHT OF THE GREAT WEAPONS, BUILDERS--AND OUR COMMAND SHIP IS SHIELDLESS AND NOW INCAPABLE OF ESCAPING THIS THEATER OF BATTLE.
THE ROGUE PLANET KILLERS HAVE TURNED TO FIRING AT THE FLEET.
WHAT ARE YOUR COMMANDS, CREATOR?
GIVE THE ORDER FOR THE BULK OF THE VESSELS TO LEAVE THE SYSTEM. THE THIRD WING IS TO STAY HERE TO DEAL WITH THE RABBLE AS BEST THEY CAN.
WE HAVE BEEN STUNG HERE TODAY...
YOU MUST LEAVE AS WELL, CREATOR...THIS SHIP WILL NOT LAST LONG AGAINST THE GREAT WEAPONS.
IT IS AN INSULT I WILL NOT FORGET.
SCUTTLE THE SHIP. THEN JOIN THE THIRD WING IN THE BATTLE.
MAKE YOUR END **MEAN SOMETHING,** EX NIHILA.

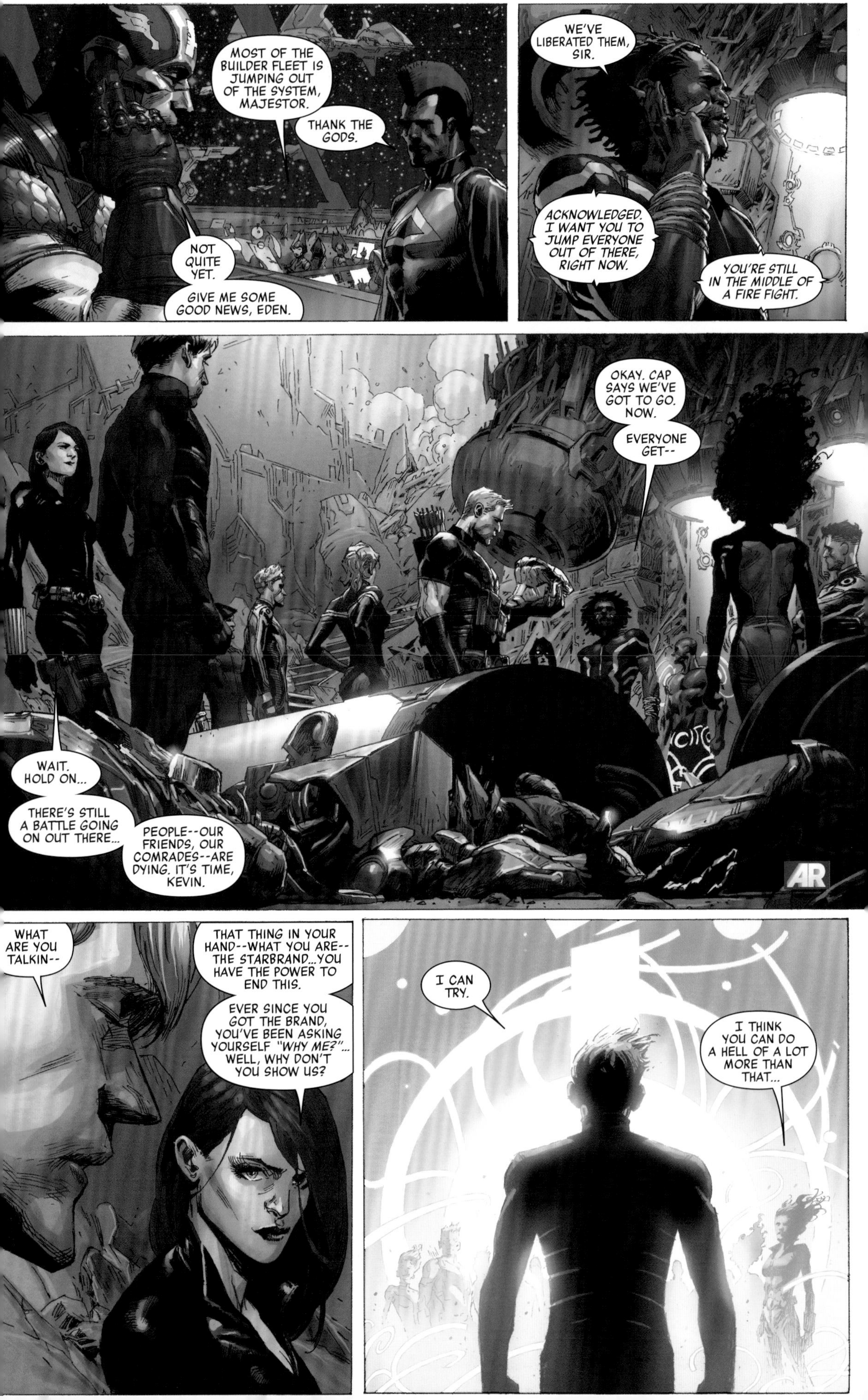

MOST OF THE BUILDER FLEET IS JUMPING OUT OF THE SYSTEM, MAJESTOR.
THANK THE GODS.
NOT QUITE YET.
GIVE ME SOME GOOD NEWS, EDEN.
WE'VE LIBERATED THEM, SIR.
ACKNOWLEDGED. I WANT YOU TO JUMP EVERYONE OUT OF THERE, RIGHT NOW.
YOU'RE STILL IN THE MIDDLE OF A FIRE FIGHT.
OKAY. CAP SAYS WE'VE GOT TO GO. NOW.
EVERYONE GET--
WAIT. HOLD ON...
THERE'S STILL A BATTLE GOING ON OUT THERE...
PEOPLE--OUR FRIENDS, OUR COMRADES--ARE DYING. IT'S TIME, KEVIN.
WHAT ARE YOU TALKIN--
THAT THING IN YOUR HAND--WHAT YOU ARE--THE STARBRAND...YOU HAVE THE POWER TO END THIS.
EVER SINCE YOU GOT THE BRAND, YOU'VE BEEN ASKING YOURSELF "WHY ME?"... WELL, WHY DON'T YOU SHOW US?
I CAN TRY.
I THINK YOU CAN DO A HELL OF A LOT MORE THAN THAT...

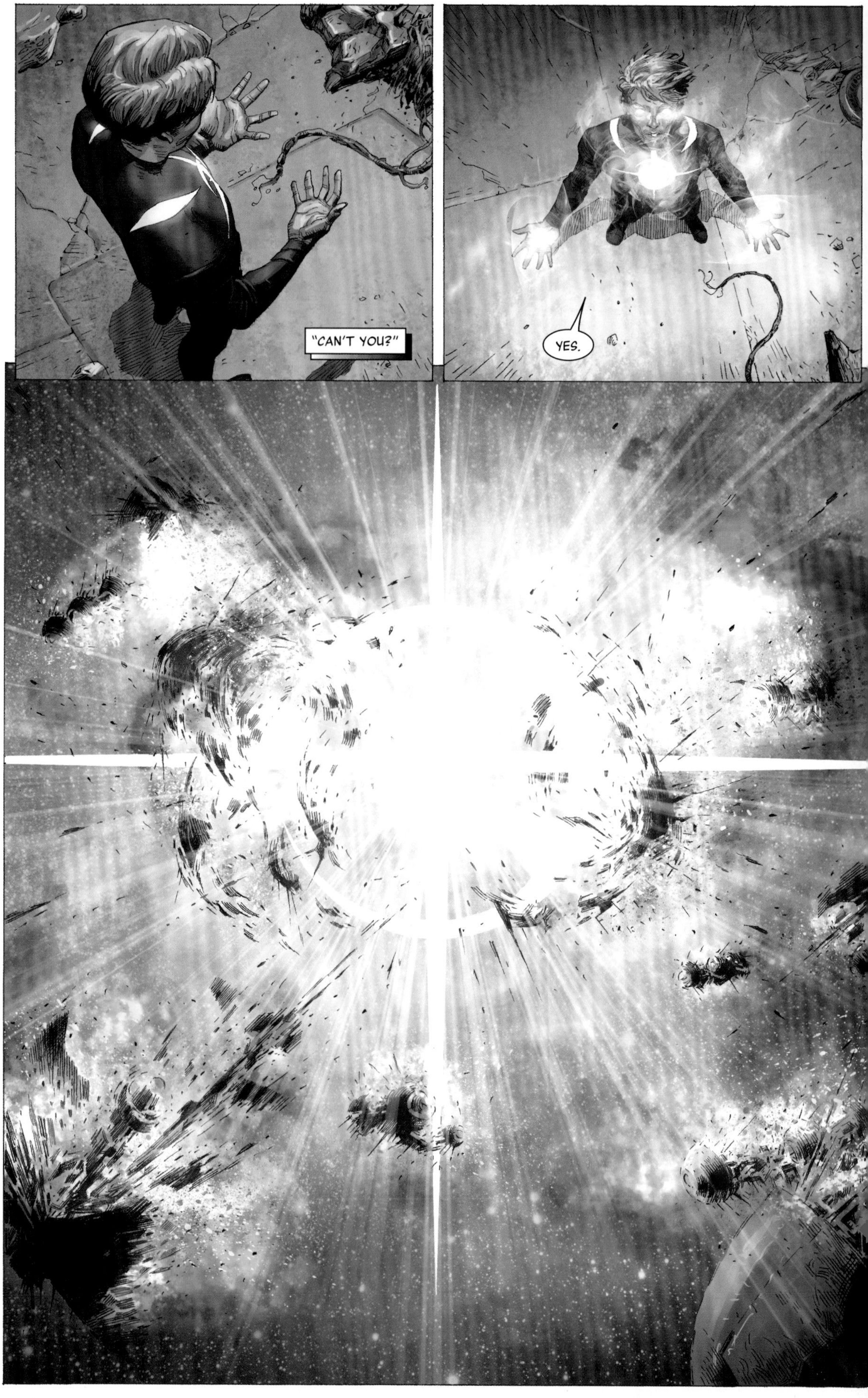
"CAN'T YOU?"
YES.

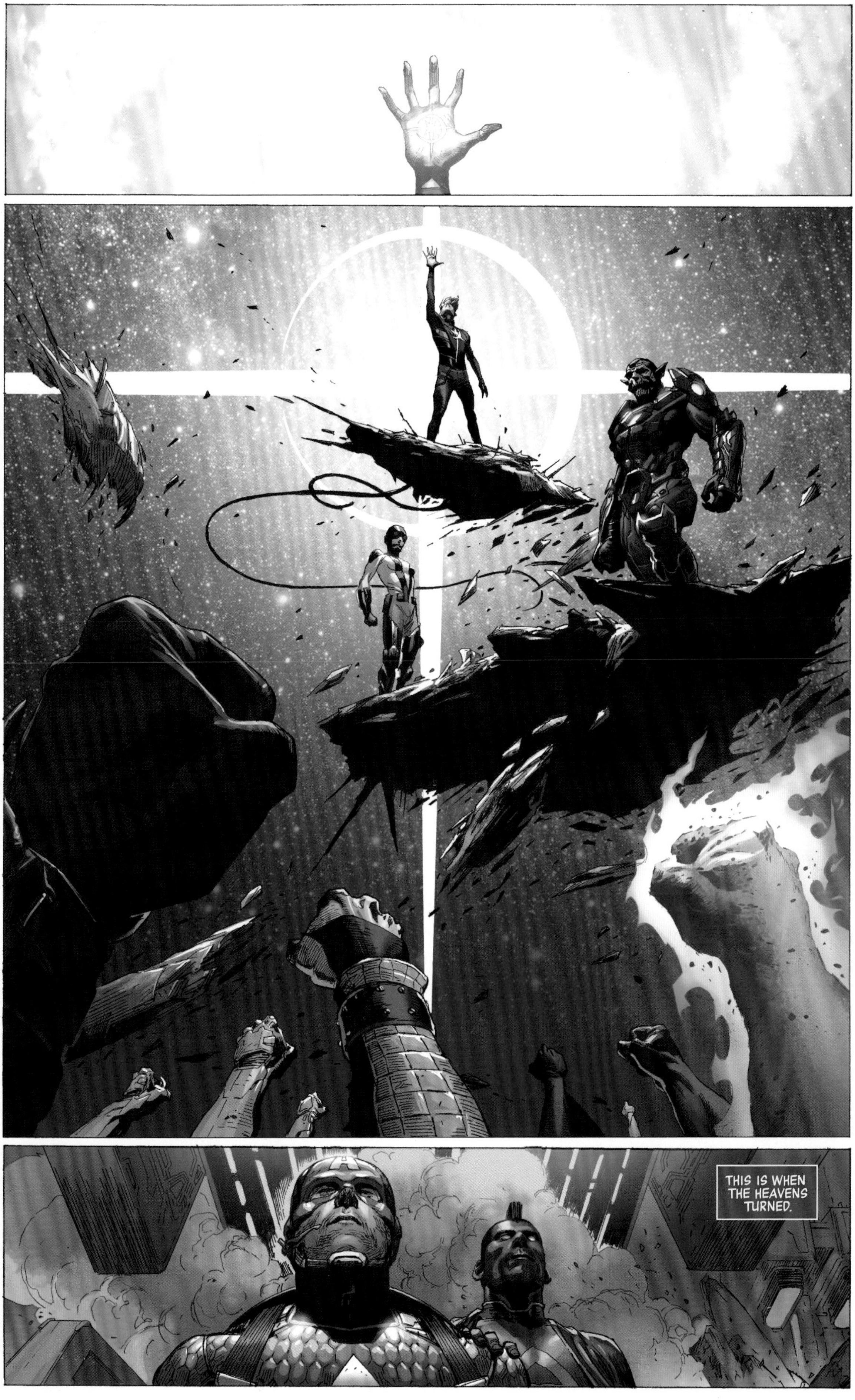
THIS IS WHEN THE HEAVENS TURNED.

WHAT MAXIMUS
BUILT

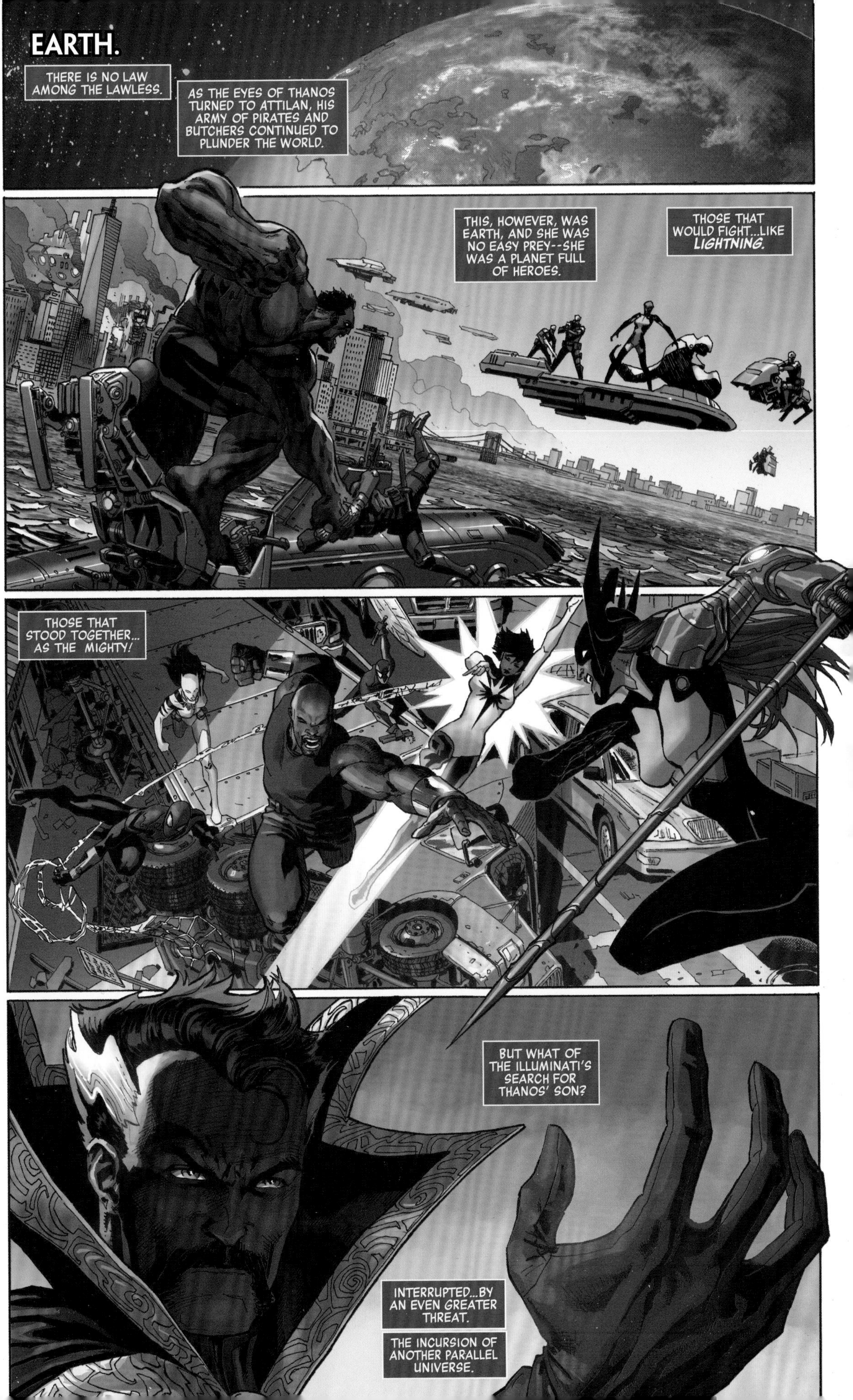
EARTH.
THERE IS NO LAW AMONG THE LAWLESS.
AS THE EYES OF THANOS TURNED TO ATTILAN, HIS ARMY OF PIRATES AND BUTCHERS CONTINUED TO PLUNDER THE WORLD.
THIS, HOWEVER, WAS EARTH, AND SHE WAS NO EASY PREY--SHE WAS A PLANET FULL OF HEROES.
THOSE THAT WOULD FIGHT...LIKE LIGHTNING.
THOSE THAT STOOD TOGETHER... AS THE MIGHTY!
BUT WHAT OF THE ILLUMINATI'S SEARCH FOR THANOS' SON?
INTERRUPTED...BY AN EVEN GREATER THREAT.
THE INCURSION OF ANOTHER PARALLEL UNIVERSE.

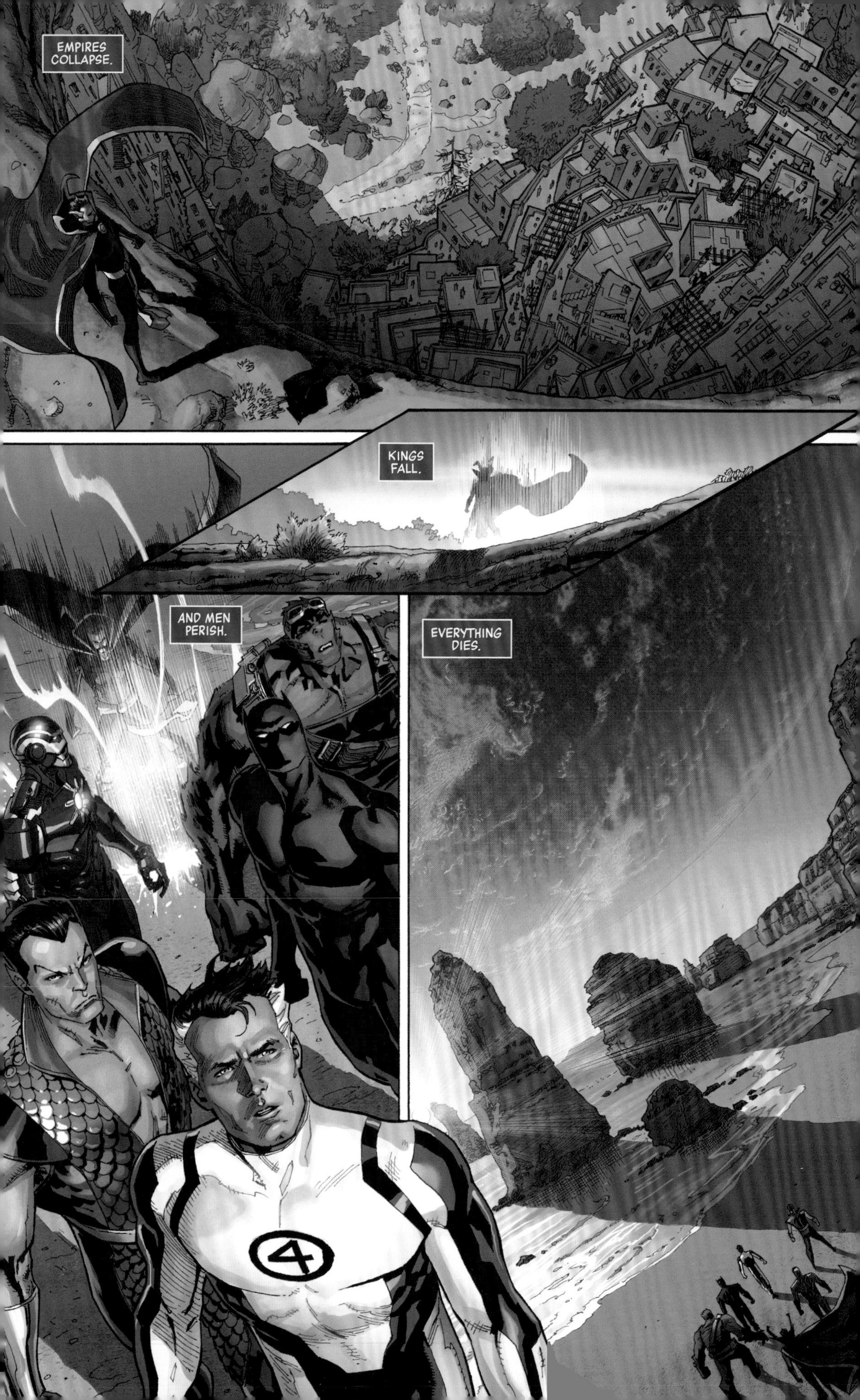
EMPIRES COLLAPSE.
KINGS FALL.
AND MEN PERISH.
EVERYTHING DIES.

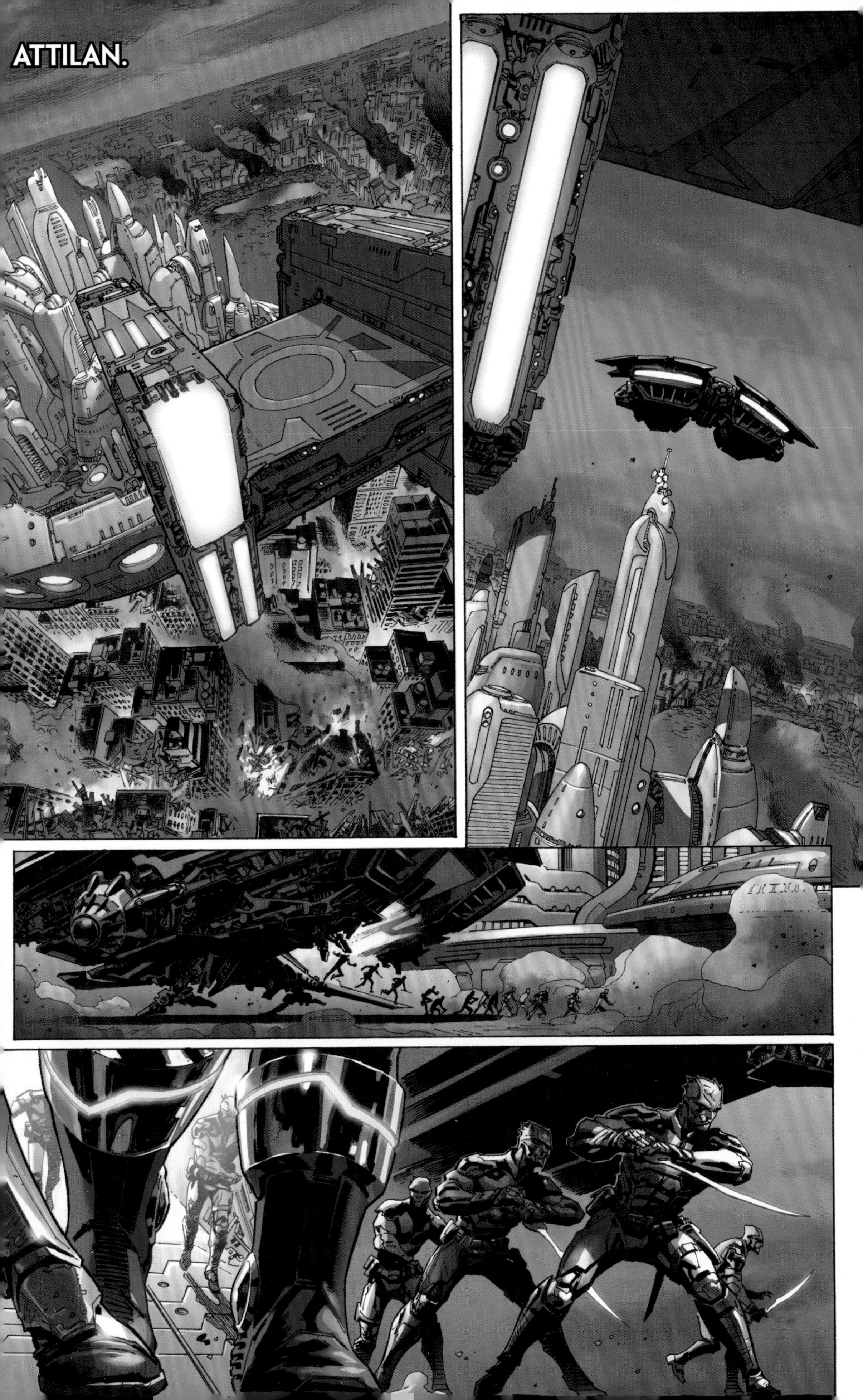
ATTILAN.

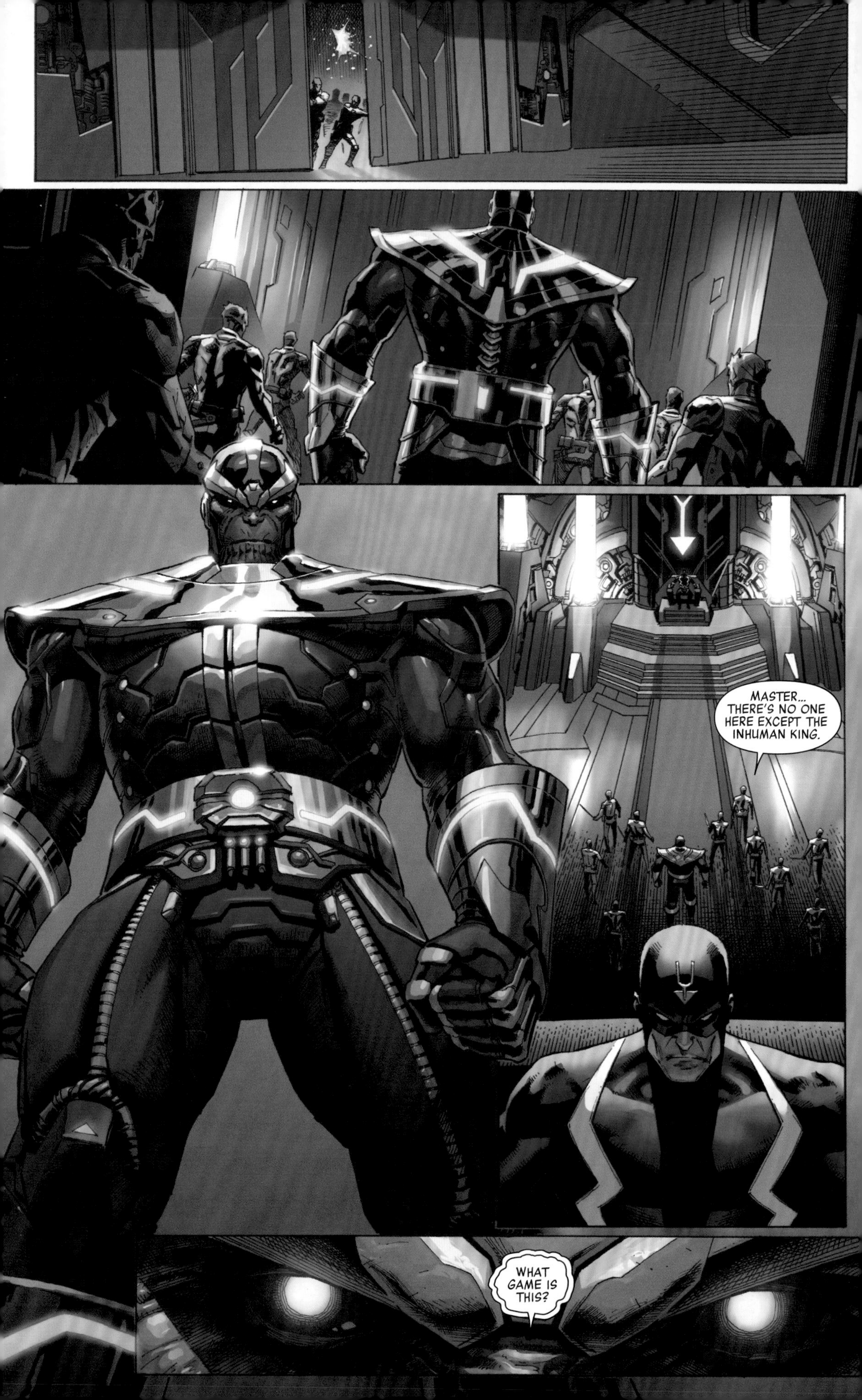
MASTER... THERE'S NO ONE HERE EXCEPT THE INHUMAN KING.
WHAT GAME IS THIS?

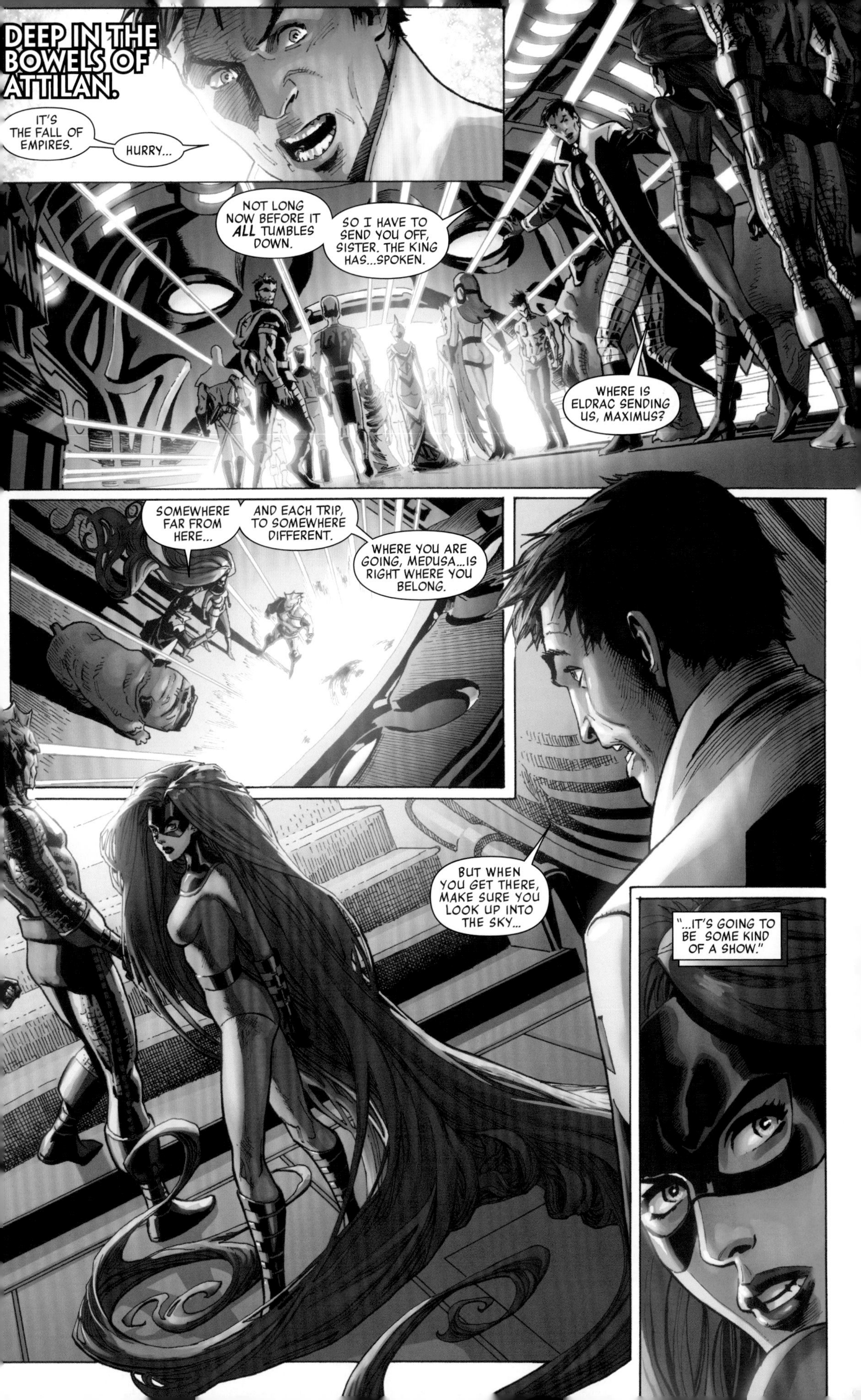

DEEP IN THE BOWELS OF ATTILAN.
IT'S THE FALL OF EMPIRES.
HURRY...
NOT LONG NOW BEFORE IT ALL TUMBLES DOWN.
SO I HAVE TO SEND YOU OFF, SISTER. THE KING HAS...SPOKEN.
WHERE IS ELDRAC SENDING US, MAXIMUS?
SOMEWHERE FAR FROM HERE...
AND EACH TRIP, TO SOMEWHERE DIFFERENT.
WHERE YOU ARE GOING, MEDUSA...IS RIGHT WHERE YOU BELONG.
BUT WHEN YOU GET THERE, MAKE SURE YOU LOOK UP INTO THE SKY...
"...IT'S GOING TO BE SOME KIND OF A SHOW."

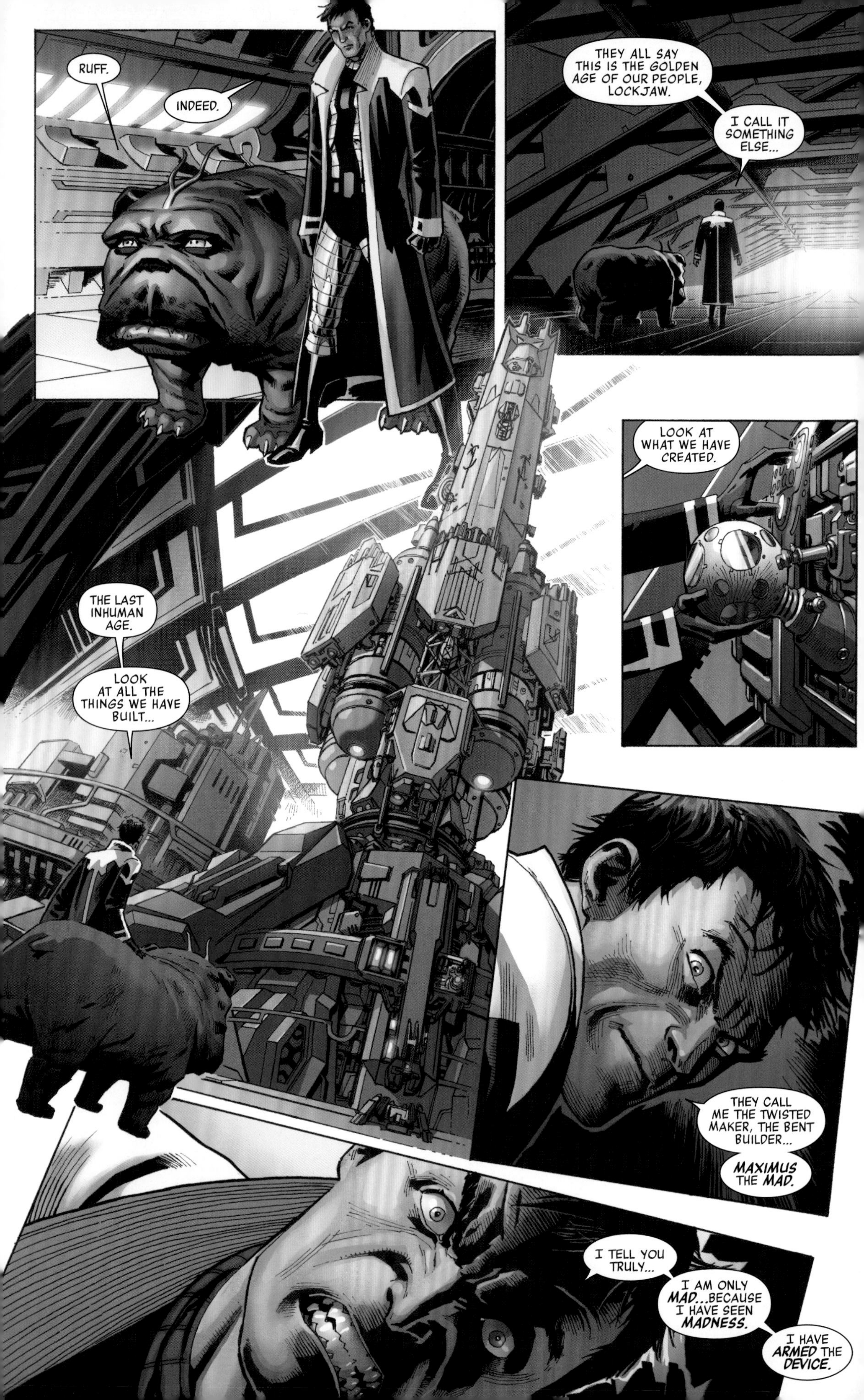
RUFF.
INDEED.
THEY ALL SAY THIS IS THE GOLDEN AGE OF OUR PEOPLE, LOCKJAW.
I CALL IT SOMETHING ELSE...
THE LAST INHUMAN AGE.
LOOK AT ALL THE THINGS WE HAVE BUILT...
LOOK AT WHAT WE HAVE CREATED.
THEY CALL ME THE TWISTED MAKER, THE BENT BUILDER...
MAXIMUS THE MAD.
I TELL YOU TRULY...
I AM ONLY MAD...BECAUSE I HAVE SEEN MADNESS.
I HAVE ARMED THE DEVICE.

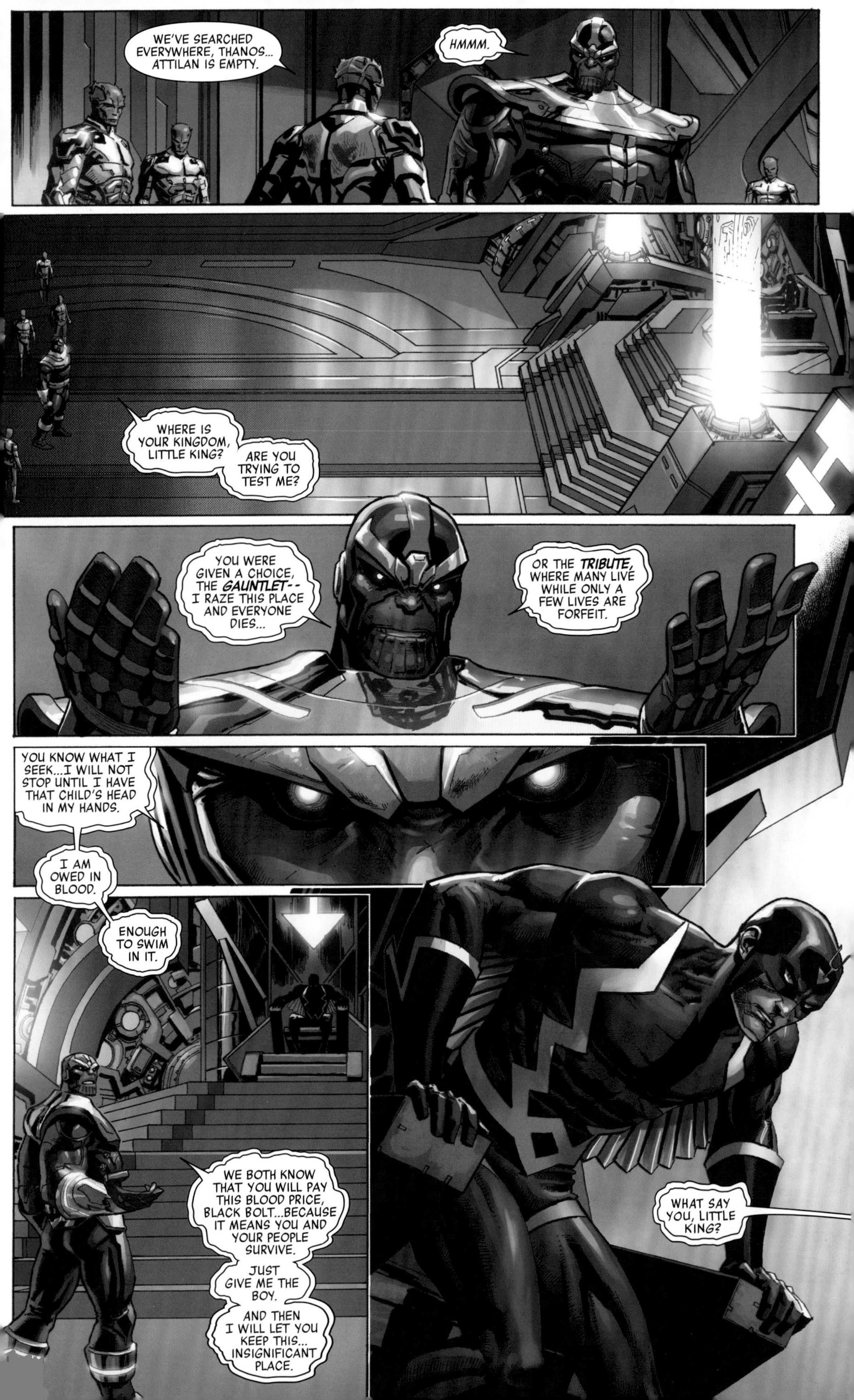
WE'VE SEARCHED EVERYWHERE, THANOS... ATTILAN IS EMPTY.
HMMM.
WHERE IS YOUR KINGDOM, LITTLE KING?
ARE YOU TRYING TO TEST ME?
YOU WERE GIVEN A CHOICE, THE GAUNTLET-- I RAZE THIS PLACE AND EVERYONE DIES...
OR THE TRIBUTE, WHERE MANY LIVE WHILE ONLY A FEW LIVES ARE FORFEIT.
YOU KNOW WHAT I SEEK...I WILL NOT STOP UNTIL I HAVE THAT CHILD'S HEAD IN MY HANDS.
I AM OWED IN BLOOD.
ENOUGH TO SWIM IN IT.
WE BOTH KNOW THAT YOU WILL PAY THIS BLOOD PRICE, BLACK BOLT...BECAUSE IT MEANS YOU AND YOUR PEOPLE SURVIVE.
JUST GIVE ME THE BOY.
AND THEN I WILL LET YOU KEEP THIS... INSIGNIFICANT PLACE.
WHAT SAY YOU, LITTLE KING?

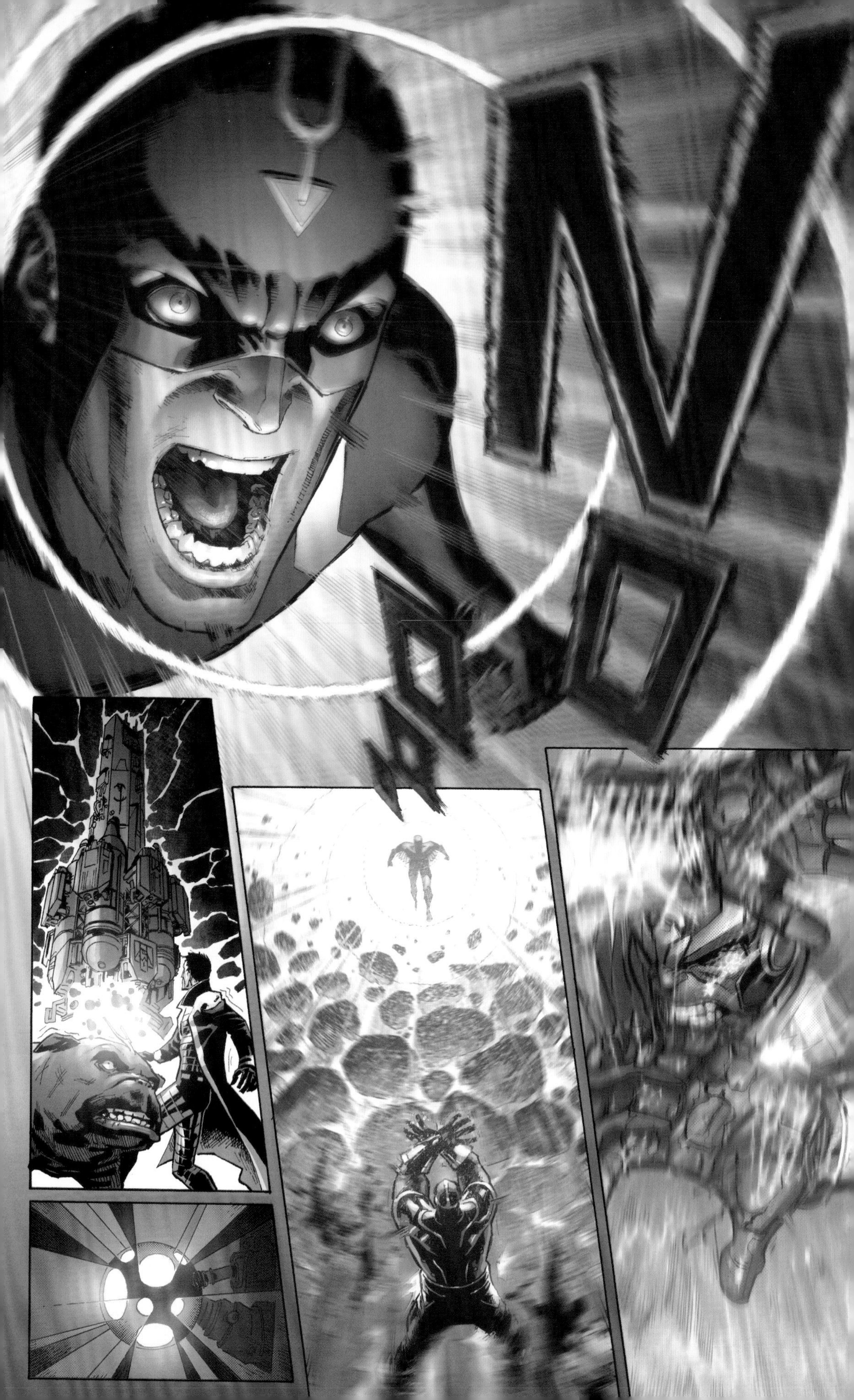
NO

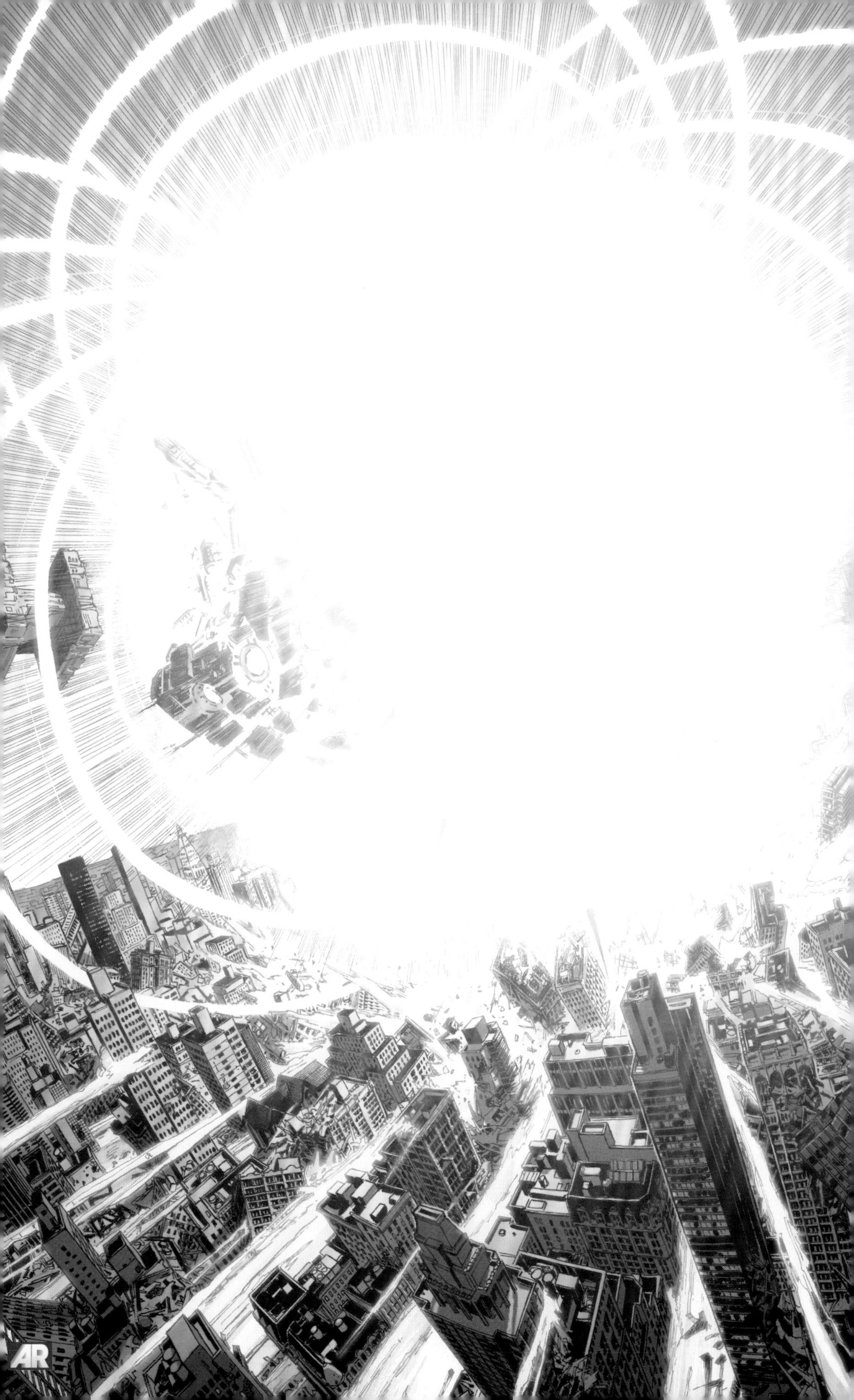

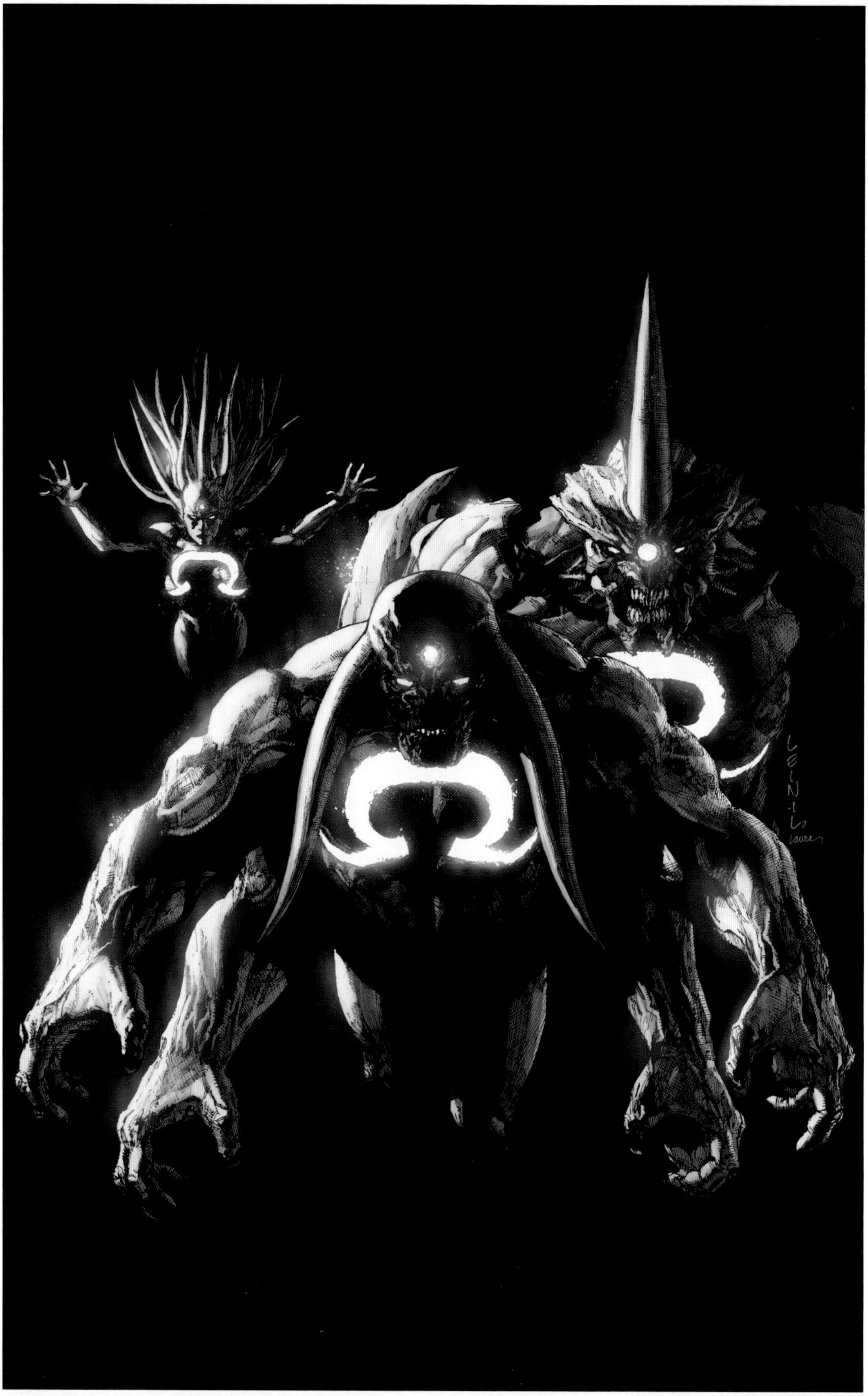

THE WORDS OF A
GARDENER

◆

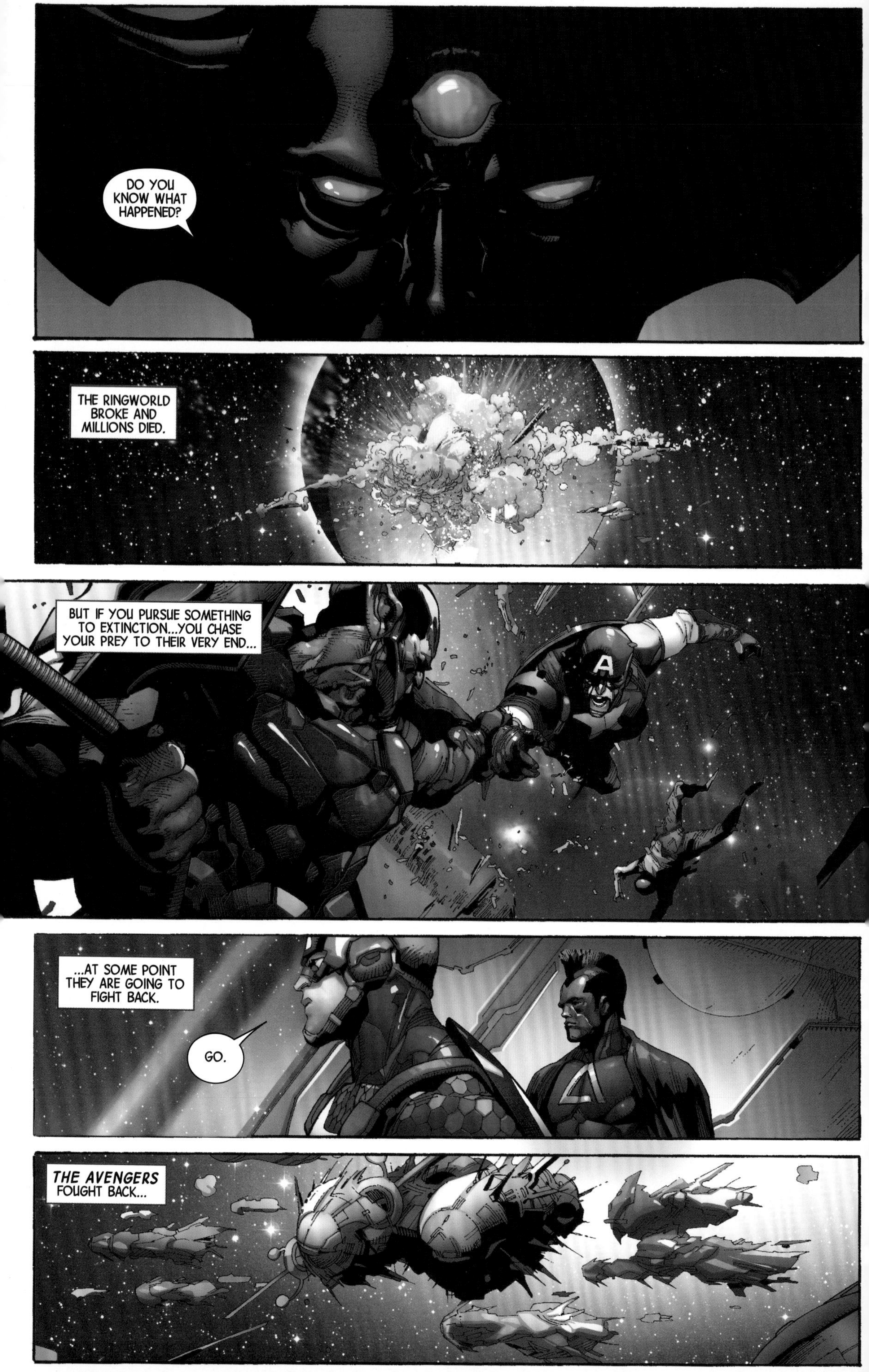
DO YOU KNOW WHAT HAPPENED?
THE RINGWORLD BROKE AND MILLIONS DIED.
BUT IF YOU PURSUE SOMETHING TO EXTINCTION...YOU CHASE YOUR PREY TO THEIR VERY END...
...AT SOME POINT THEY ARE GOING TO FIGHT BACK.
GO.
THE AVENGERS FOUGHT BACK...

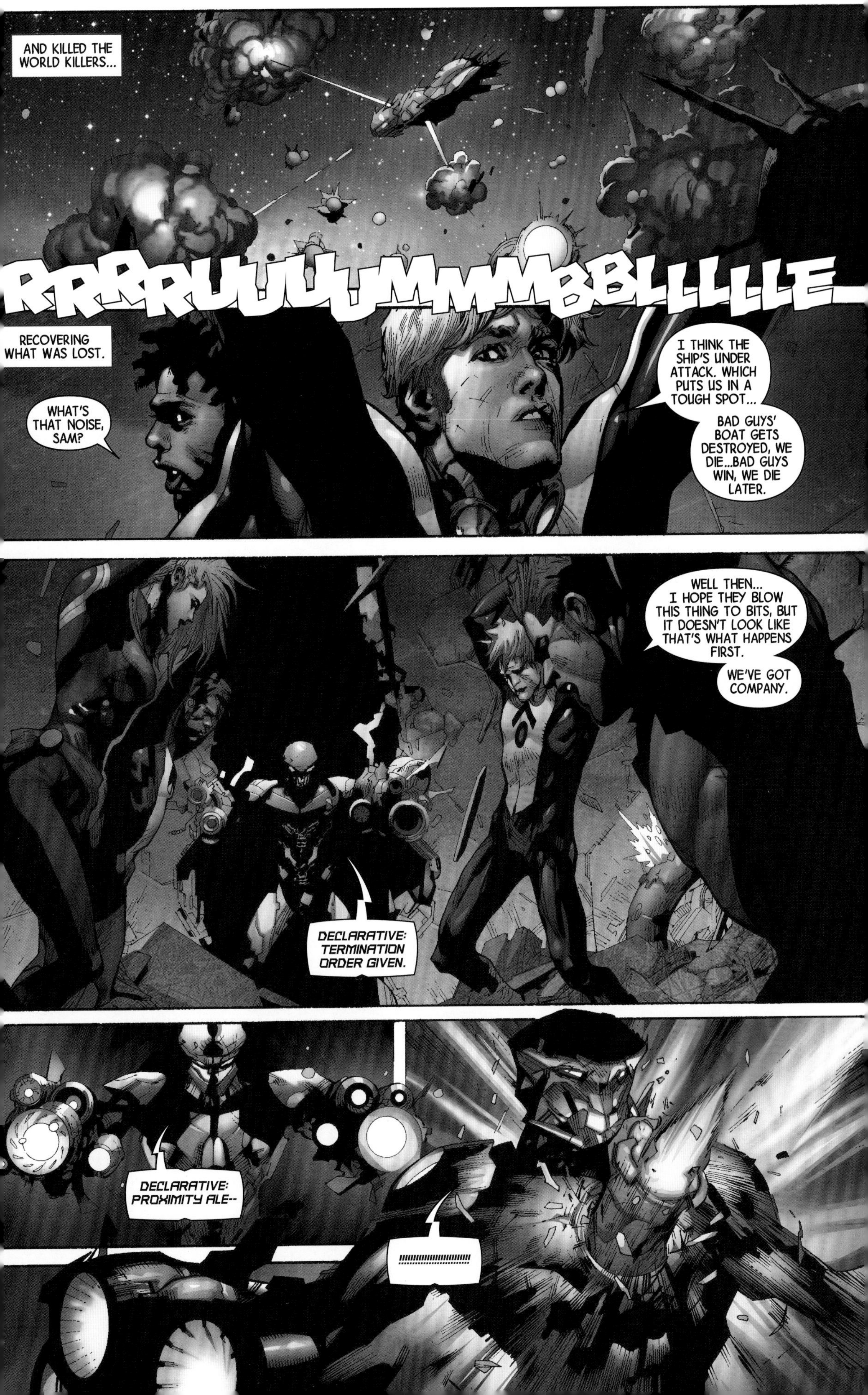
AND KILLED THE WORLD KILLERS...
RRRRUUUUMMMMBBLLLLLE
RECOVERING WHAT WAS LOST.
WHAT'S THAT NOISE, SAM?
I THINK THE SHIP'S UNDER ATTACK. WHICH PUTS US IN A TOUGH SPOT...
BAD GUYS' BOAT GETS DESTROYED, WE DIE...BAD GUYS WIN, WE DIE LATER.
WELL THEN... I HOPE THEY BLOW THIS THING TO BITS, BUT IT DOESN'T LOOK LIKE THAT'S WHAT HAPPENS FIRST.
WE'VE GOT COMPANY.
DECLARATIVE: TERMINATION ORDER GIVEN.
DECLARATIVE: PROXIMITY ALE--

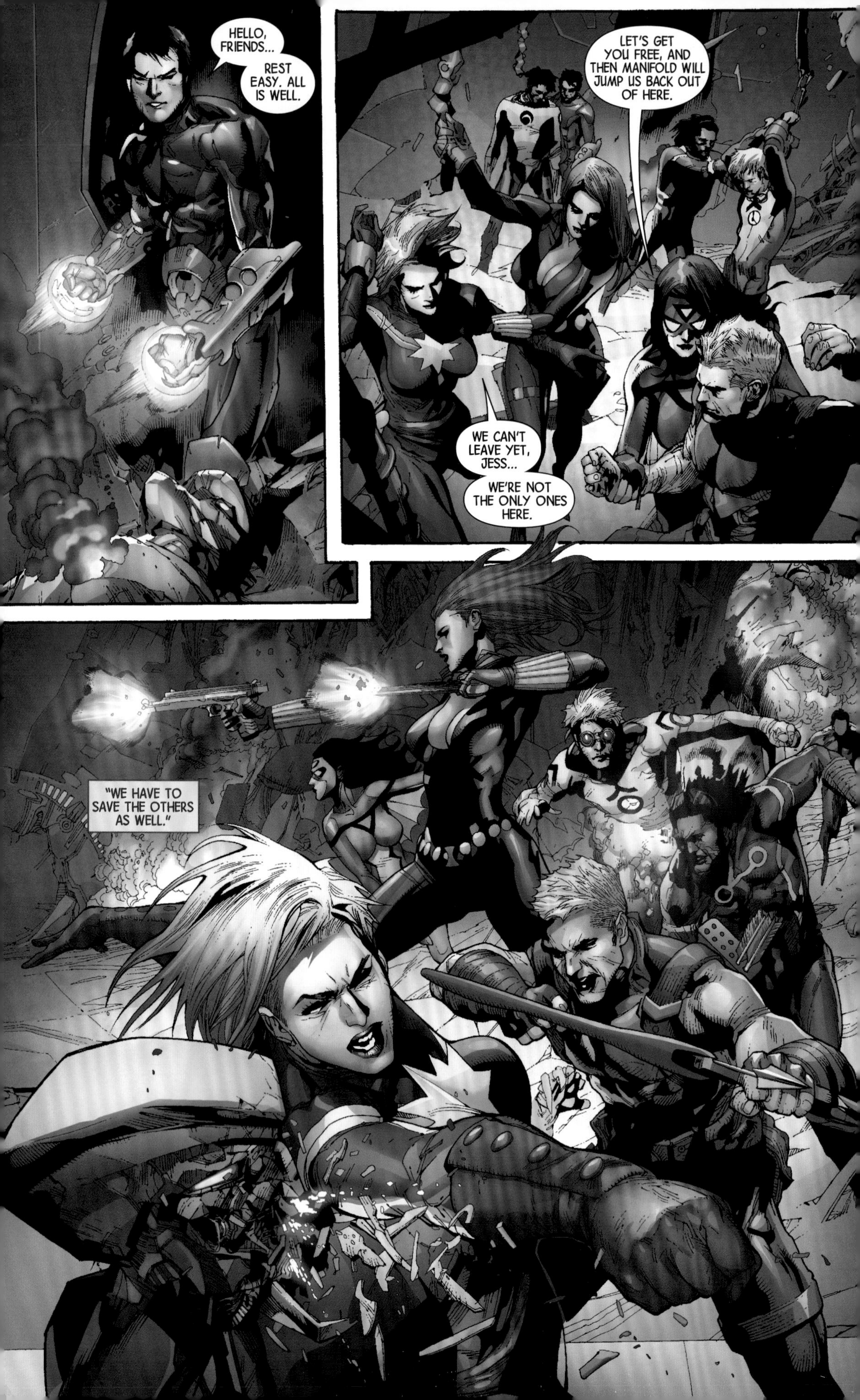
HELLO, FRIENDS...
REST EASY. ALL IS WELL.
LET'S GET YOU FREE, AND THEN MANIFOLD WILL JUMP US BACK OUT OF HERE.
WE CAN'T LEAVE YET, JESS...
WE'RE NOT THE ONLY ONES HERE.
"WE HAVE TO SAVE THE OTHERS AS WELL."

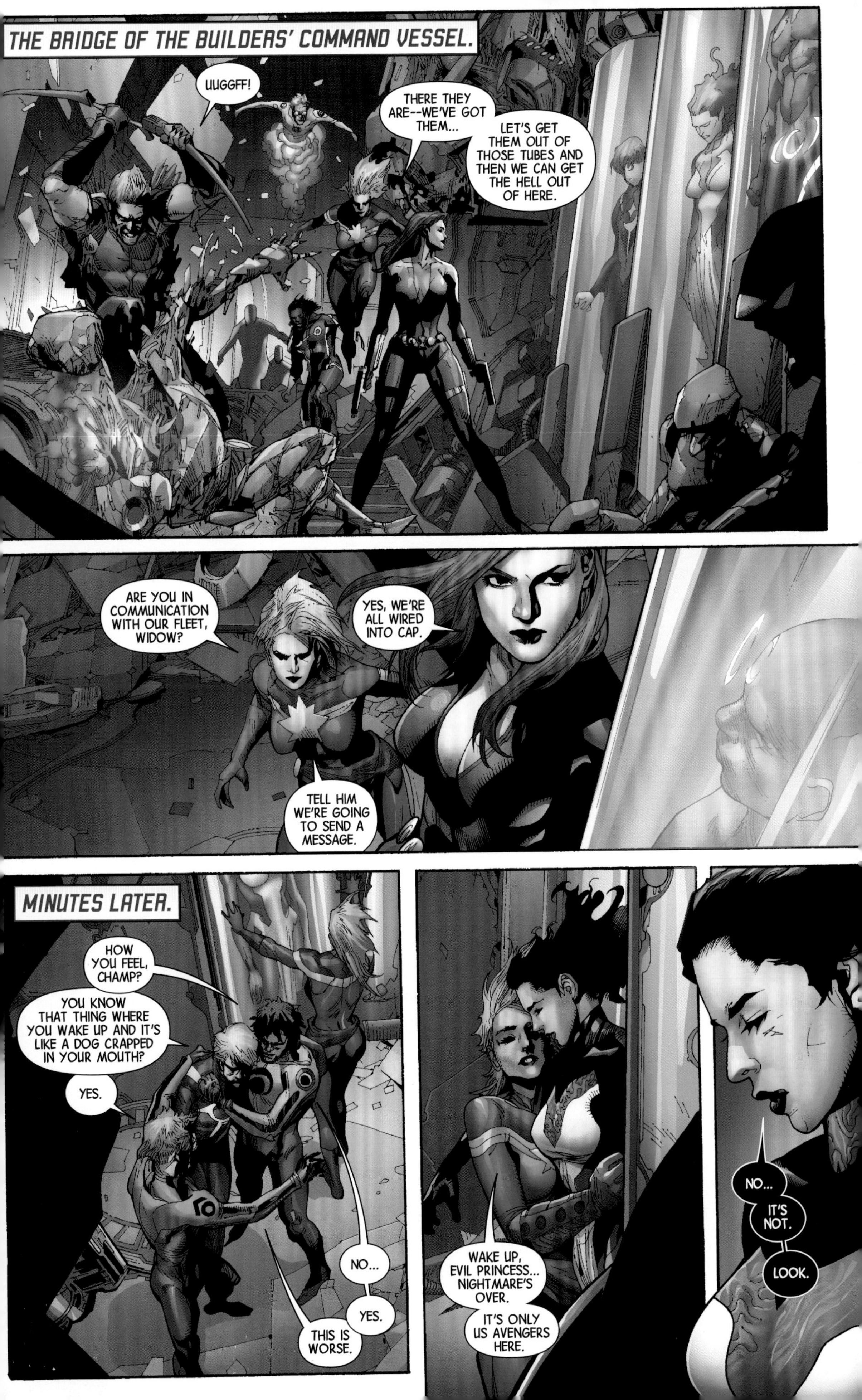
THE BRIDGE OF THE BUILDERS' COMMAND VESSEL.
UUGGFF!
THERE THEY ARE--WE'VE GOT THEM...
LET'S GET THEM OUT OF THOSE TUBES AND THEN WE CAN GET THE HELL OUT OF HERE.
ARE YOU IN COMMUNICATION WITH OUR FLEET, WIDOW?
YES, WE'RE ALL WIRED INTO CAP.
TELL HIM WE'RE GOING TO SEND A MESSAGE.
MINUTES LATER.
HOW YOU FEEL, CHAMP?
YOU KNOW THAT THING WHERE YOU WAKE UP AND IT'S LIKE A DOG CRAPPED IN YOUR MOUTH?
YES.
NO...
YES.
THIS IS WORSE.
WAKE UP, EVIL PRINCESS... NIGHTMARE'S OVER.
IT'S ONLY US AVENGERS HERE.
NO...
IT'S NOT.
LOOK.

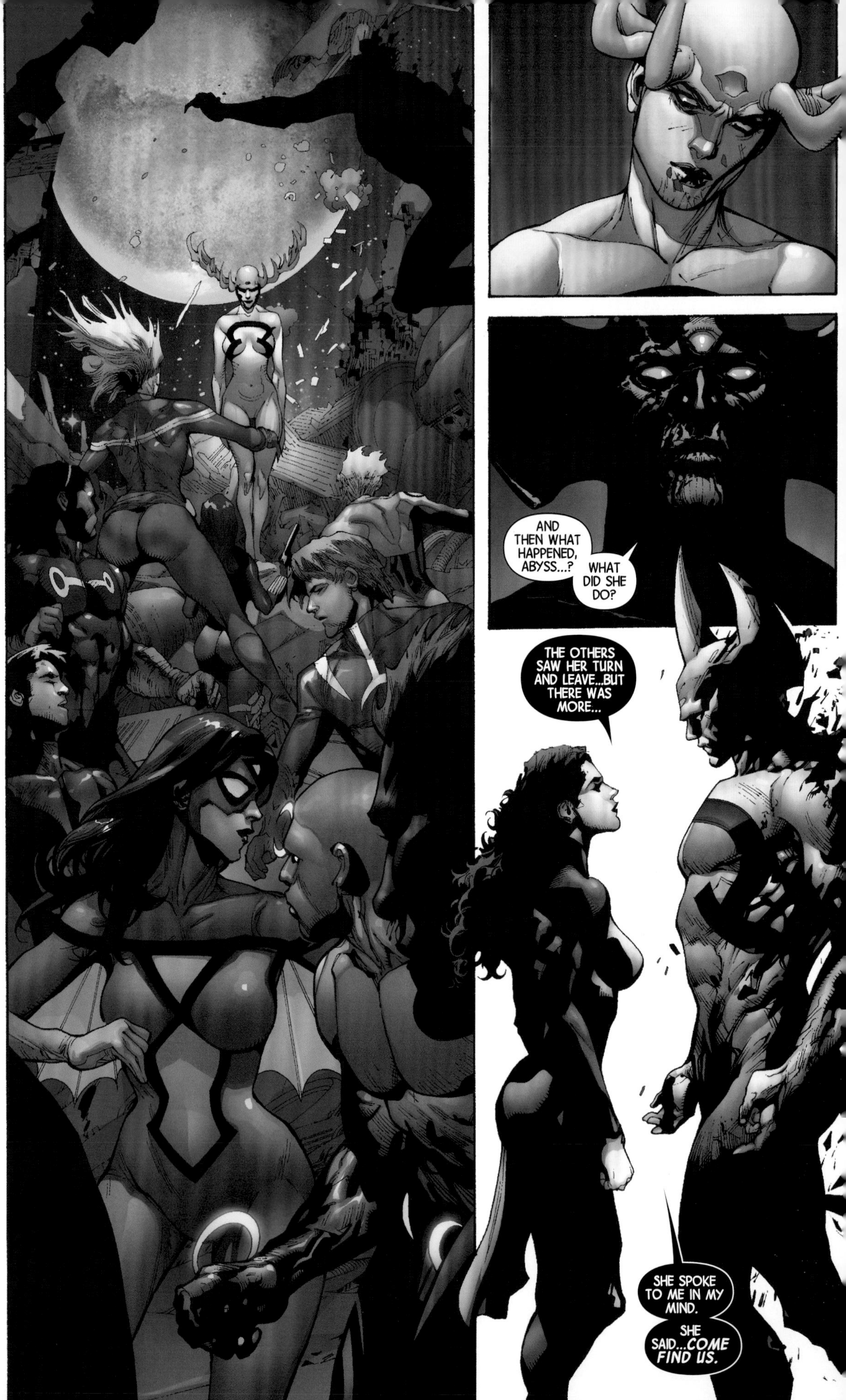
AND THEN WHAT HAPPENED, ABYSS...?
WHAT DID SHE DO?
THE OTHERS SAW HER TURN AND LEAVE...BUT THERE WAS MORE...
SHE SPOKE TO ME IN MY MIND.
SHE SAID...COME FIND US.

THE EDGE OF
ANNIHILATION

◆

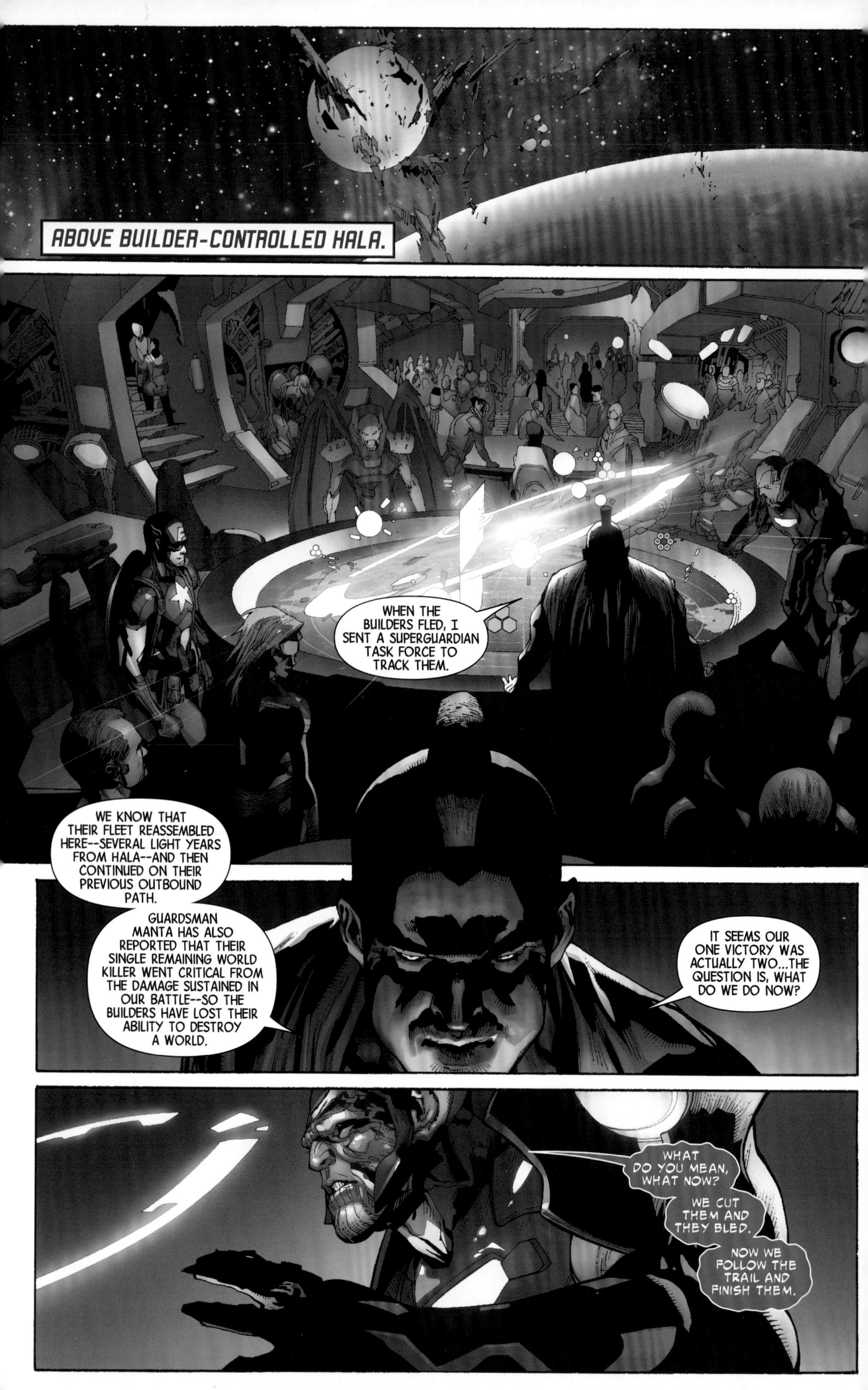
ABOVE BUILDER-CONTROLLED HALA.
WHEN THE BUILDERS FLED, I SENT A SUPERGUARDIAN TASK FORCE TO TRACK THEM.
WE KNOW THAT THEIR FLEET REASSEMBLED HERE--SEVERAL LIGHT YEARS FROM HALA--AND THEN CONTINUED ON THEIR PREVIOUS OUTBOUND PATH.
GUARDSMAN MANTA HAS ALSO REPORTED THAT THEIR SINGLE REMAINING WORLD KILLER WENT CRITICAL FROM THE DAMAGE SUSTAINED IN OUR BATTLE--SO THE BUILDERS HAVE LOST THEIR ABILITY TO DESTROY A WORLD.
IT SEEMS OUR ONE VICTORY WAS ACTUALLY TWO...THE QUESTION IS, WHAT DO WE DO NOW?
WHAT DO YOU MEAN, WHAT NOW?
WE CUT THEM AND THEY BLED.
NOW WE FOLLOW THE TRAIL AND FINISH THEM.

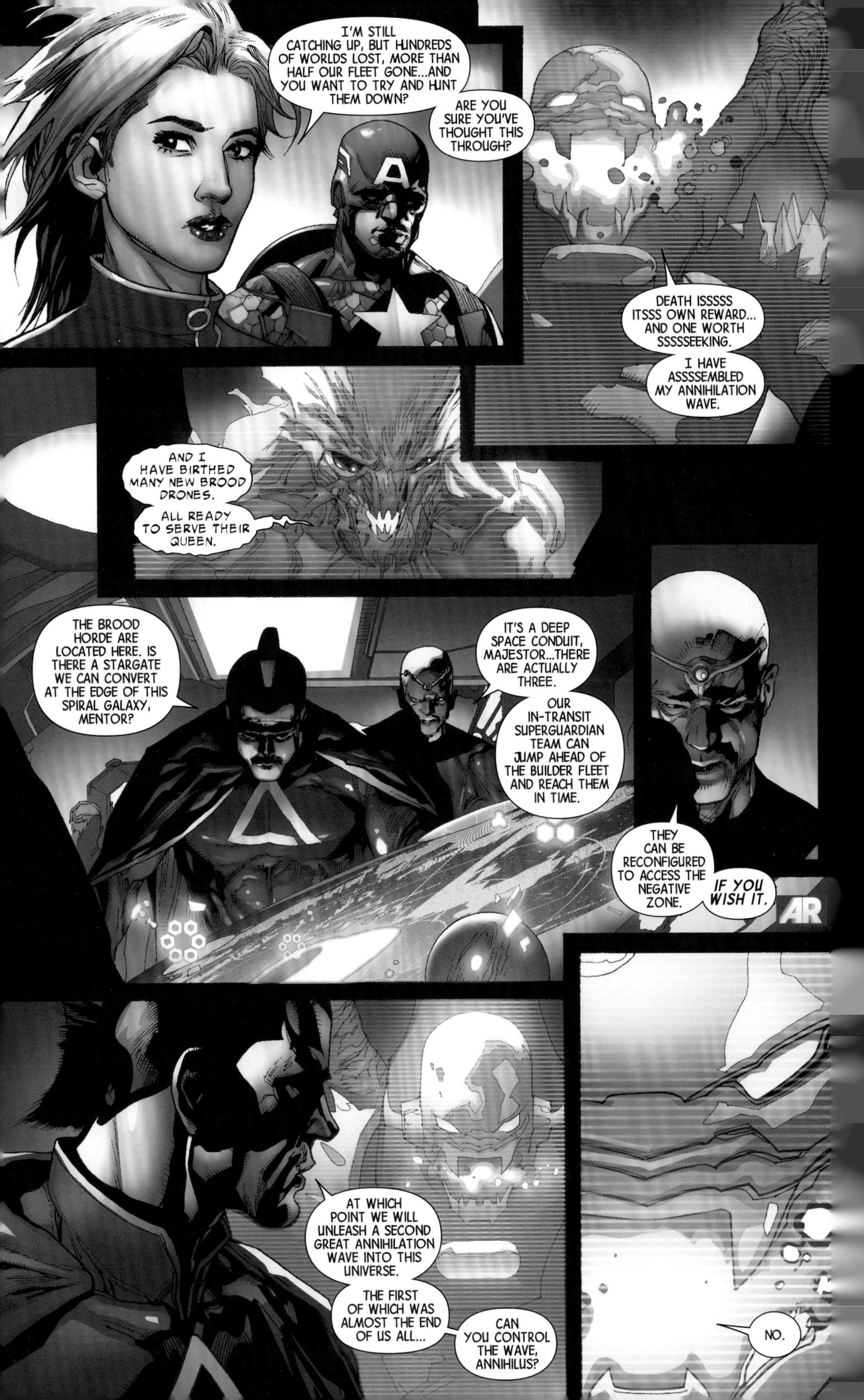
I'M STILL CATCHING UP, BUT HUNDREDS OF WORLDS LOST, MORE THAN HALF OUR FLEET GONE...AND YOU WANT TO TRY AND HUNT THEM DOWN?
ARE YOU SURE YOU'VE THOUGHT THIS THROUGH?
DEATH ISSSSS ITSSS OWN REWARD... AND ONE WORTH SSSSSEEKING.
I HAVE ASSSSEMBLED MY ANNIHILATION WAVE.
AND I HAVE BIRTHED MANY NEW BROOD DRONES.
ALL READY TO SERVE THEIR QUEEN.
THE BROOD HORDE ARE LOCATED HERE. IS THERE A STARGATE WE CAN CONVERT AT THE EDGE OF THIS SPIRAL GALAXY, MENTOR?
IT'S A DEEP SPACE CONDUIT, MAJESTOR...THERE ARE ACTUALLY THREE.
OUR IN-TRANSIT SUPERGUARDIAN TEAM CAN JUMP AHEAD OF THE BUILDER FLEET AND REACH THEM IN TIME.
THEY CAN BE RECONFIGURED TO ACCESS THE NEGATIVE ZONE.
IF YOU WISH IT.
AT WHICH POINT WE WILL UNLEASH A SECOND GREAT ANNIHILATION WAVE INTO THIS UNIVERSE.
THE FIRST OF WHICH WAS ALMOST THE END OF US ALL...
CAN YOU CONTROL THE WAVE, ANNIHILUS?
NO.

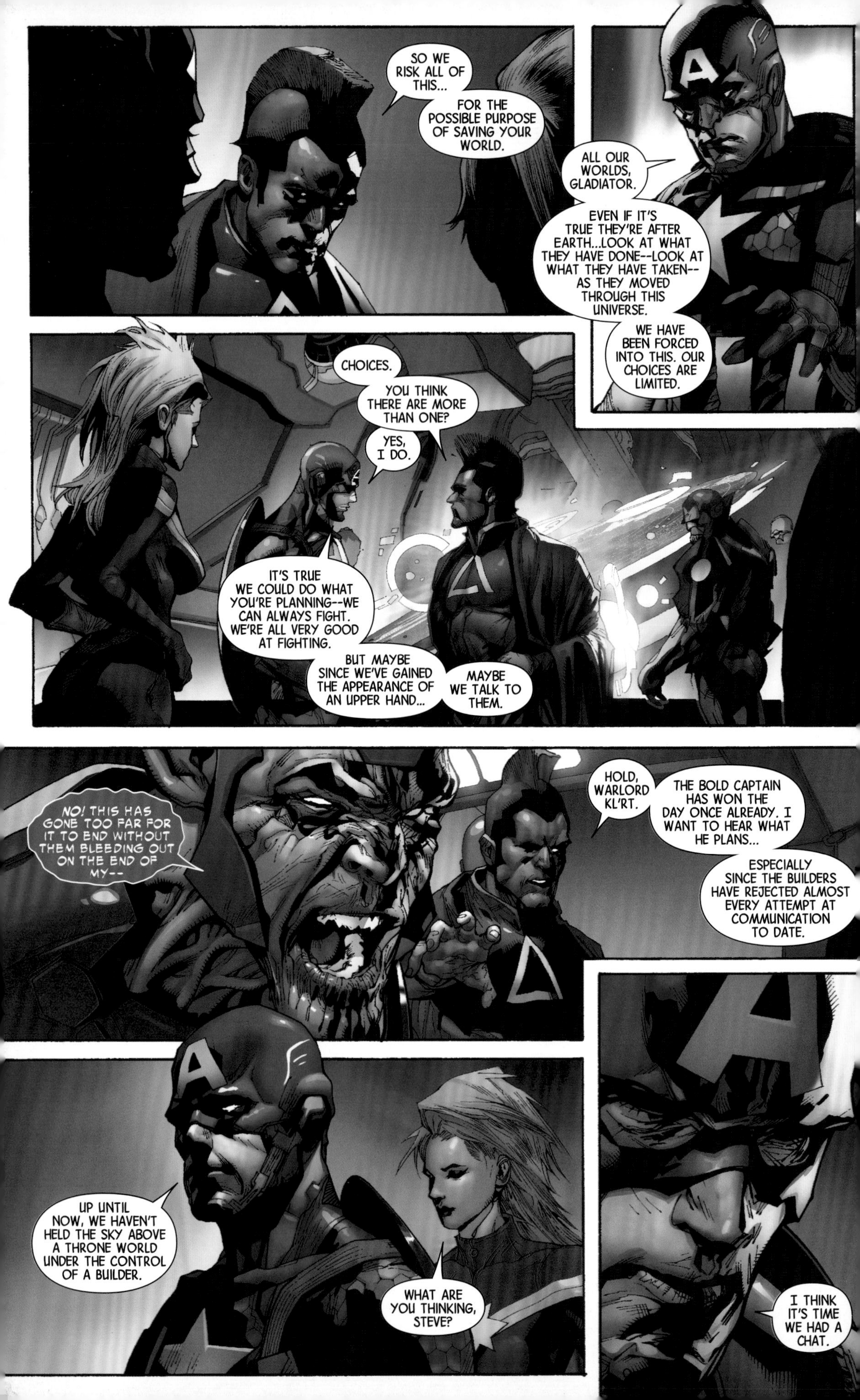

SO WE RISK ALL OF THIS...
FOR THE POSSIBLE PURPOSE OF SAVING YOUR WORLD.
ALL OUR WORLDS, GLADIATOR.
EVEN IF IT'S TRUE THEY'RE AFTER EARTH...LOOK AT WHAT THEY HAVE DONE--LOOK AT WHAT THEY HAVE TAKEN--AS THEY MOVED THROUGH THIS UNIVERSE.
WE HAVE BEEN FORCED INTO THIS. OUR CHOICES ARE LIMITED.
CHOICES.
YOU THINK THERE ARE MORE THAN ONE?
YES, I DO.
IT'S TRUE WE COULD DO WHAT YOU'RE PLANNING--WE CAN ALWAYS FIGHT. WE'RE ALL VERY GOOD AT FIGHTING.
BUT MAYBE SINCE WE'VE GAINED THE APPEARANCE OF AN UPPER HAND...
MAYBE WE TALK TO THEM.
NO! THIS HAS GONE TOO FAR FOR IT TO END WITHOUT THEM BLEEDING OUT ON THE END OF MY--
HOLD, WARLORD KL'RT.
THE BOLD CAPTAIN HAS WON THE DAY ONCE ALREADY. I WANT TO HEAR WHAT HE PLANS...
ESPECIALLY SINCE THE BUILDERS HAVE REJECTED ALMOST EVERY ATTEMPT AT COMMUNICATION TO DATE.
UP UNTIL NOW, WE HAVEN'T HELD THE SKY ABOVE A THRONE WORLD UNDER THE CONTROL OF A BUILDER.
WHAT ARE YOU THINKING, STEVE?
I THINK IT'S TIME WE HAD A CHAT.

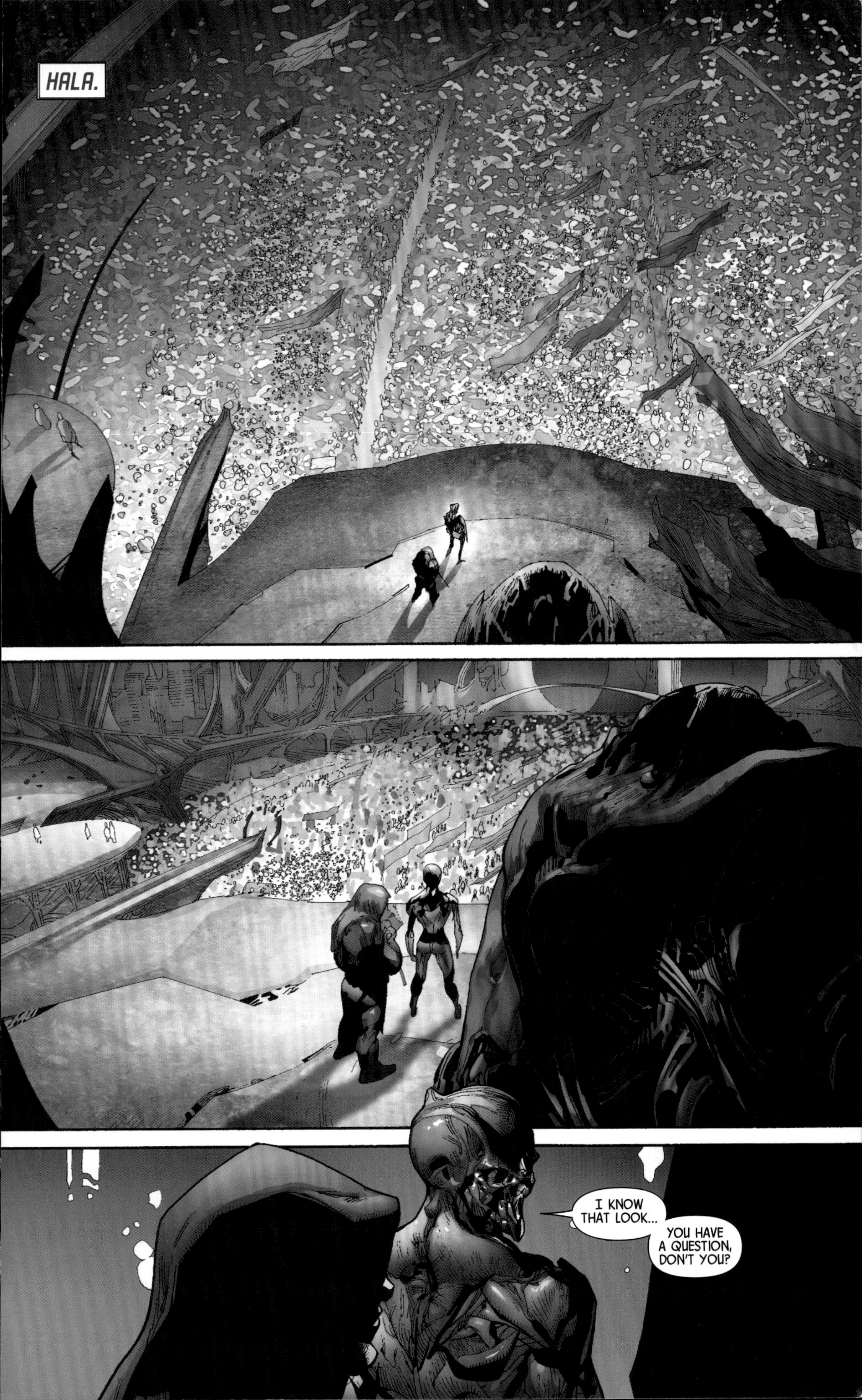
HALA.
I KNOW THAT LOOK...
YOU HAVE A QUESTION, DON'T YOU?

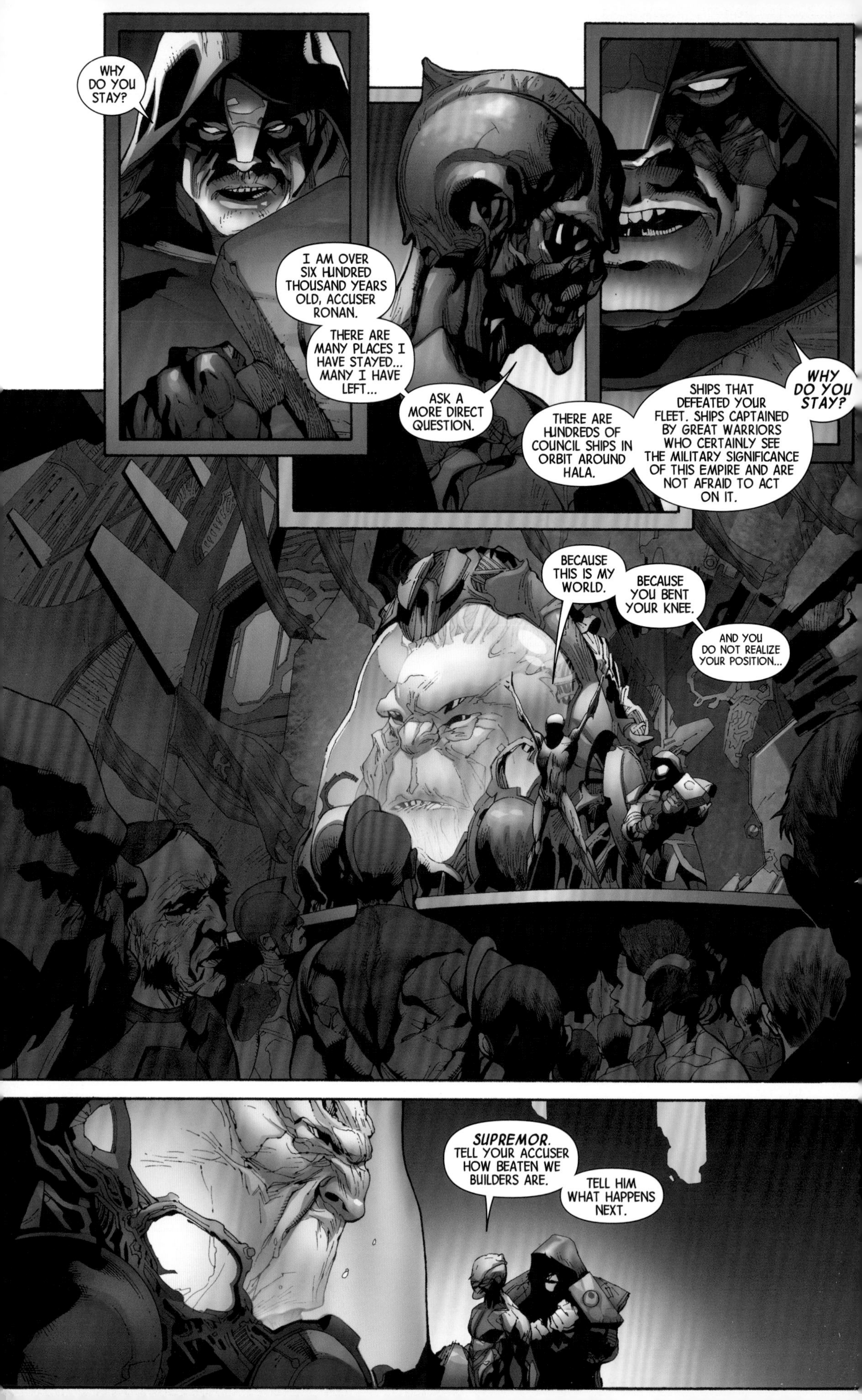
WHY DO YOU STAY?
I AM OVER SIX HUNDRED THOUSAND YEARS OLD, ACCUSER RONAN.
THERE ARE MANY PLACES I HAVE STAYED... MANY I HAVE LEFT...
ASK A MORE DIRECT QUESTION.
THERE ARE HUNDREDS OF COUNCIL SHIPS IN ORBIT AROUND HALA.
SHIPS THAT DEFEATED YOUR FLEET. SHIPS CAPTAINED BY GREAT WARRIORS WHO CERTAINLY SEE THE MILITARY SIGNIFICANCE OF THIS EMPIRE AND ARE NOT AFRAID TO ACT ON IT.
WHY DO YOU STAY?
BECAUSE THIS IS MY WORLD.
BECAUSE YOU BENT YOUR KNEE.
AND YOU DO NOT REALIZE YOUR POSITION...
SUPREMOR. TELL YOUR ACCUSER HOW BEATEN WE BUILDERS ARE.
TELL HIM WHAT HAPPENS NEXT.

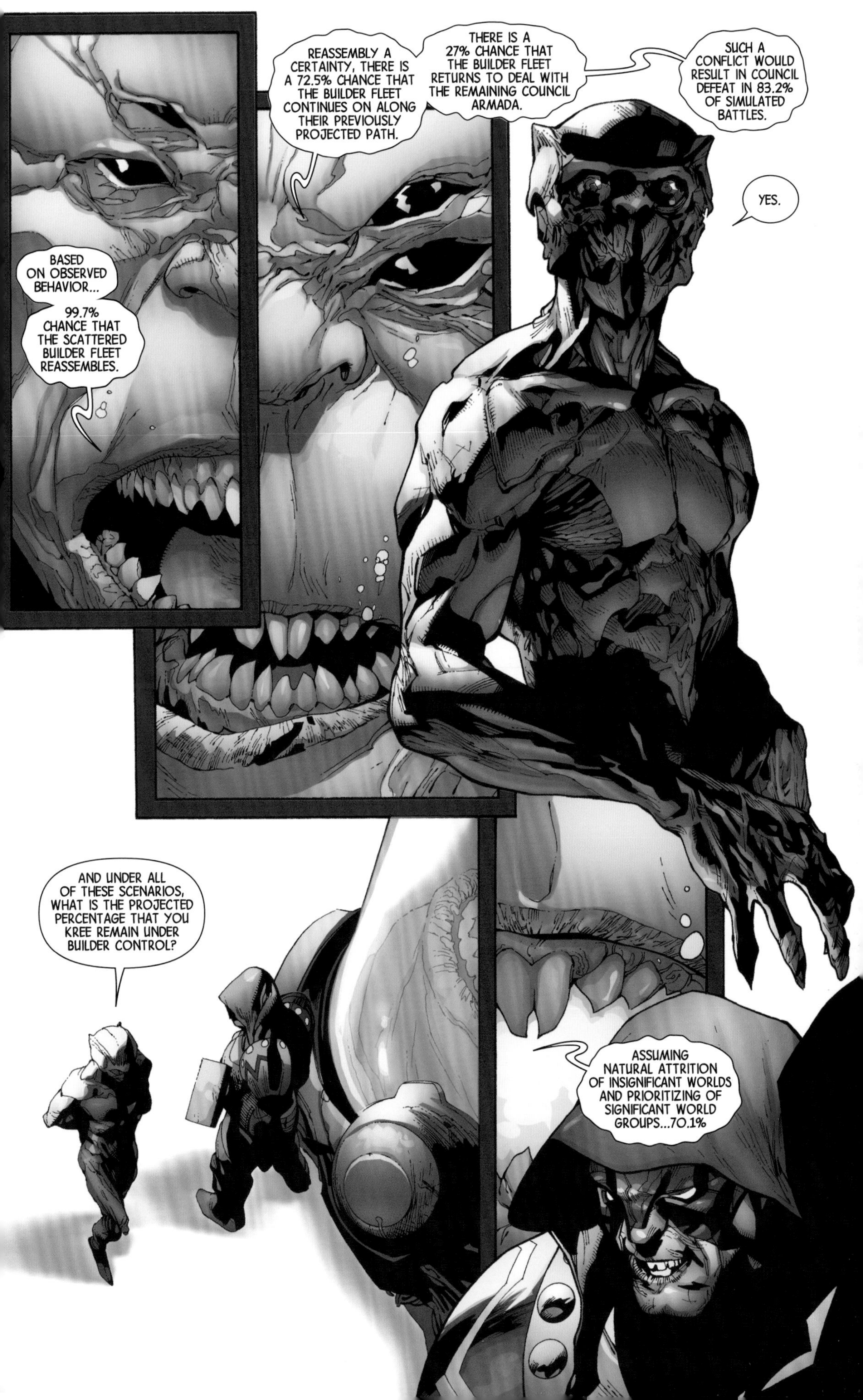
BASED ON OBSERVED BEHAVIOR...
99.7% CHANCE THAT THE SCATTERED BUILDER FLEET REASSEMBLES.
REASSEMBLY A CERTAINTY, THERE IS A 72.5% CHANCE THAT THE BUILDER FLEET CONTINUES ON ALONG THEIR PREVIOUSLY PROJECTED PATH.
THERE IS A 27% CHANCE THAT THE BUILDER FLEET RETURNS TO DEAL WITH THE REMAINING COUNCIL ARMADA.
SUCH A CONFLICT WOULD RESULT IN COUNCIL DEFEAT IN 83.2% OF SIMULATED BATTLES.
YES.
AND UNDER ALL OF THESE SCENARIOS, WHAT IS THE PROJECTED PERCENTAGE THAT YOU KREE REMAIN UNDER BUILDER CONTROL?
ASSUMING NATURAL ATTRITION OF INSIGNIFICANT WORLDS AND PRIORITIZING OF SIGNIFICANT WORLD GROUPS...70.1%

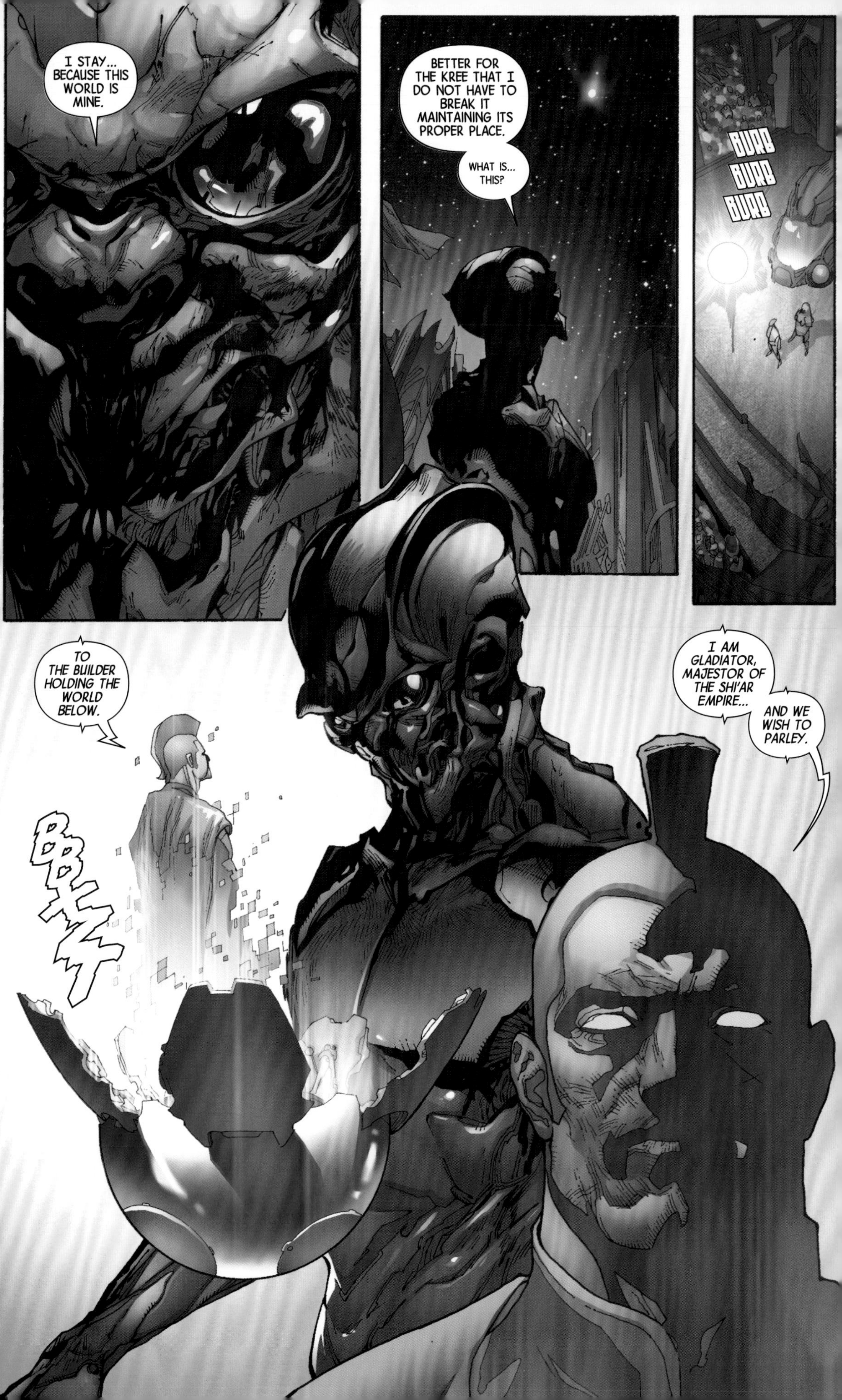
I STAY... BECAUSE THIS WORLD IS MINE.
BETTER FOR THE KREE THAT I DO NOT HAVE TO BREAK IT MAINTAINING ITS PROPER PLACE.
WHAT IS... THIS?
BURB BURB BURB
TO THE BUILDER HOLDING THE WORLD BELOW.
BBZZT
I AM GLADIATOR, MAJESTOR OF THE SHI'AR EMPIRE...
AND WE WISH TO PARLEY.

WITHOUT JUDGES
WE ARE LOST

◆

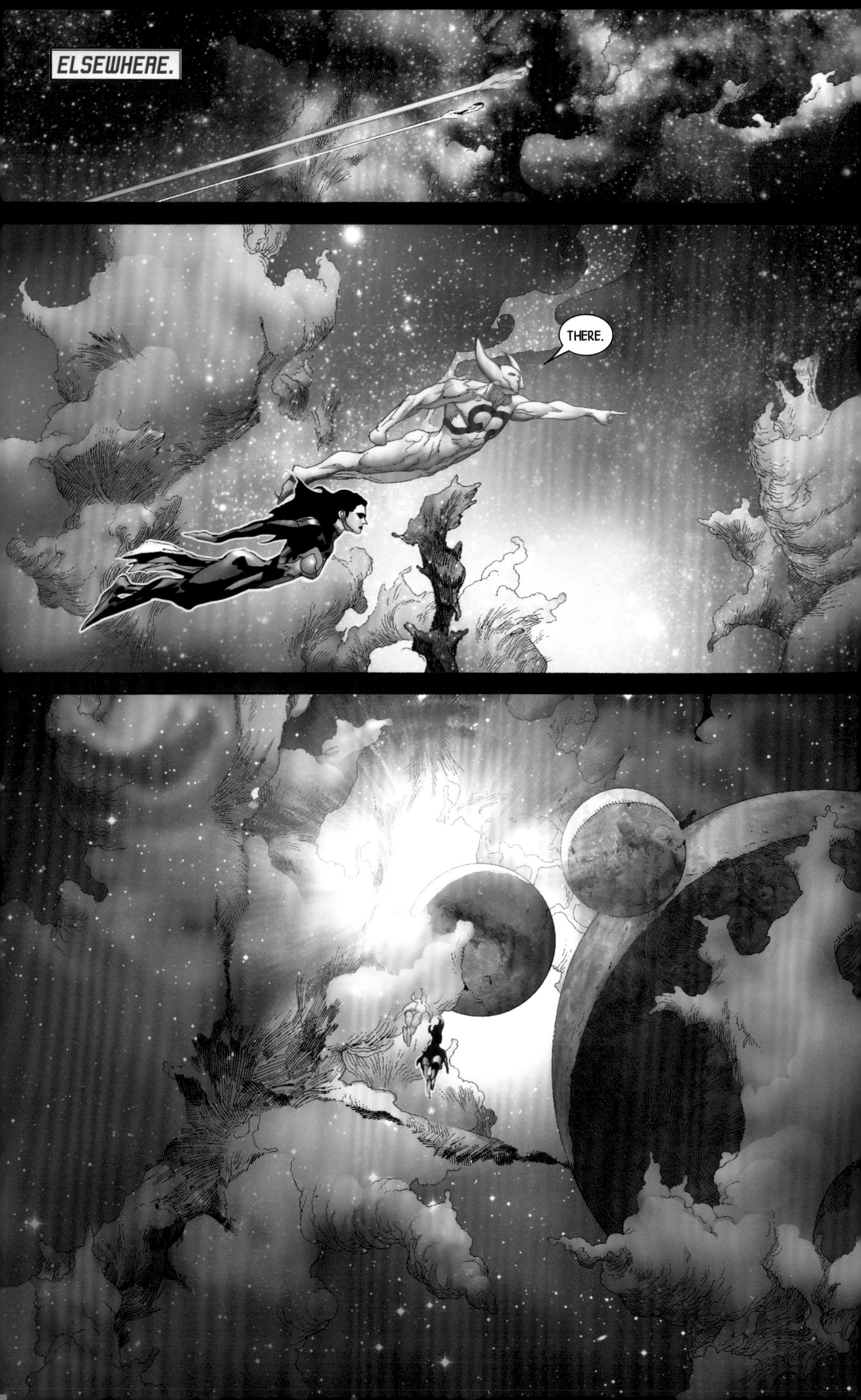
ELSEWHERE.
THERE.

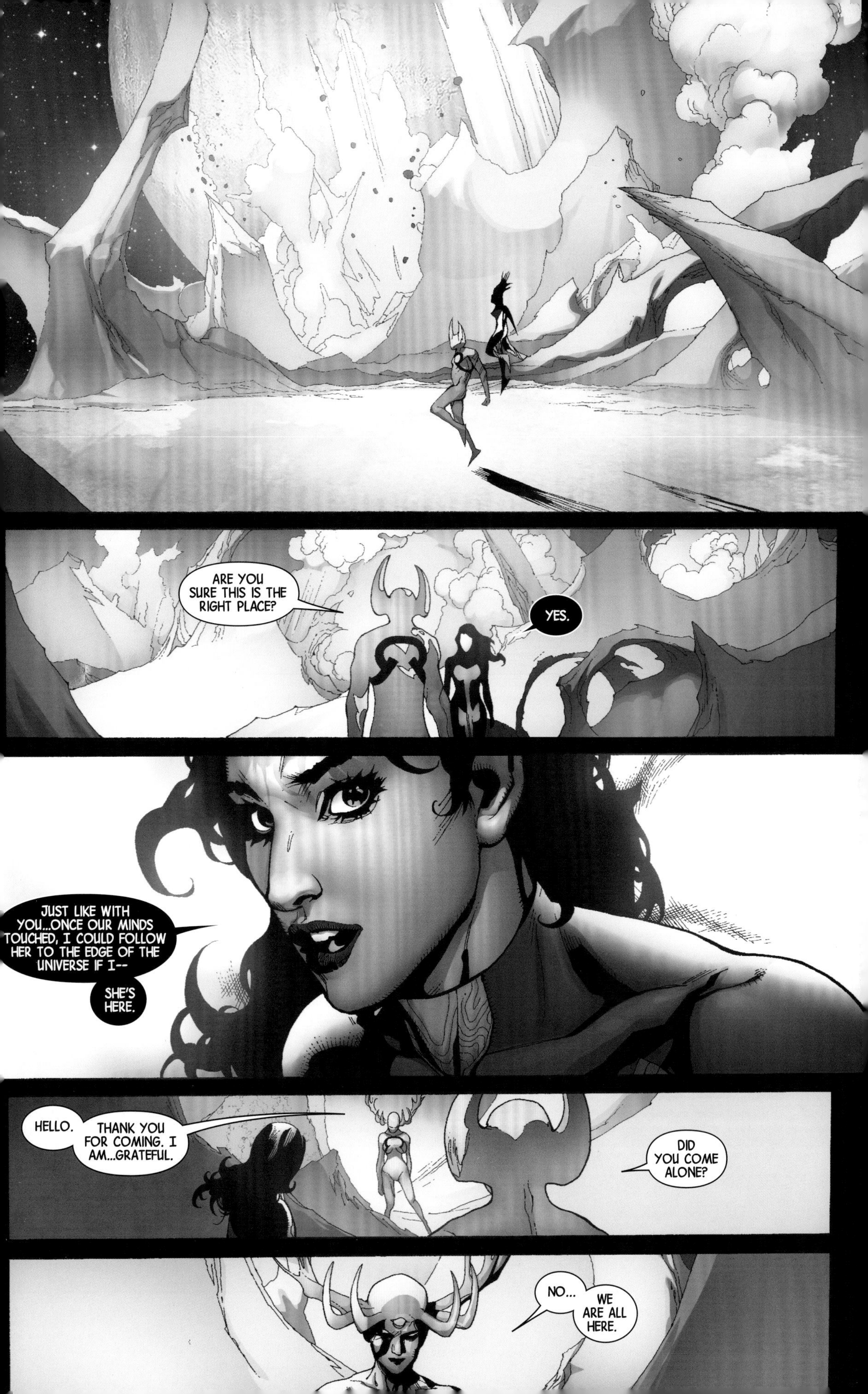
ARE YOU SURE THIS IS THE RIGHT PLACE?
YES.
JUST LIKE WITH YOU...ONCE OUR MINDS TOUCHED, I COULD FOLLOW HER TO THE EDGE OF THE UNIVERSE IF I--
SHE'S HERE.
HELLO.
THANK YOU FOR COMING. I AM...GRATEFUL.
DID YOU COME ALONE?
NO...
WE ARE ALL HERE.

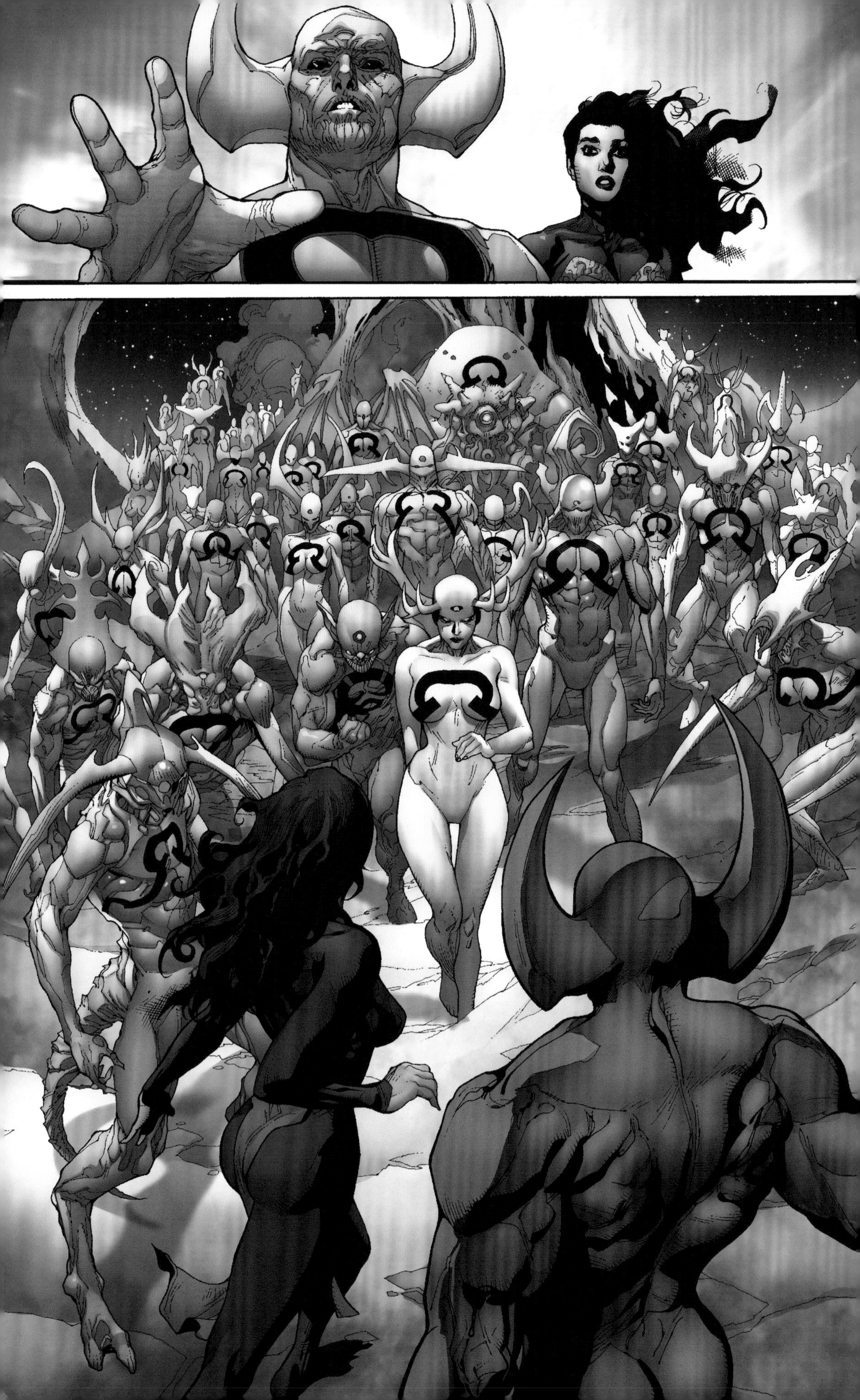

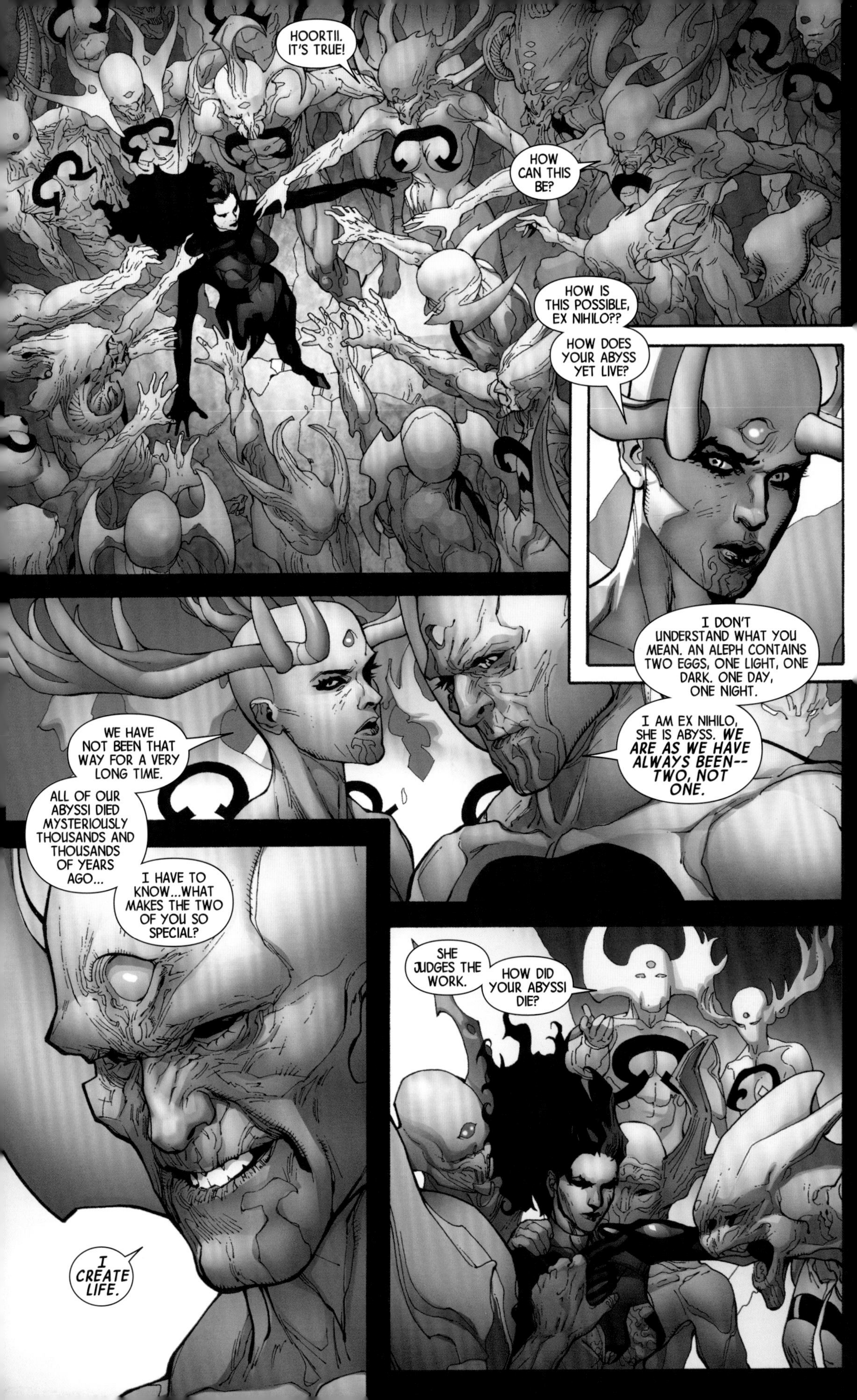
HOORTII. IT'S TRUE!
HOW CAN THIS BE?
HOW IS THIS POSSIBLE, EX NIHILO??
HOW DOES YOUR ABYSS YET LIVE?
I DON'T UNDERSTAND WHAT YOU MEAN. AN ALEPH CONTAINS TWO EGGS, ONE LIGHT, ONE DARK. ONE DAY, ONE NIGHT.
I AM EX NIHILO, SHE IS ABYSS. WE ARE AS WE HAVE ALWAYS BEEN-- TWO, NOT ONE.
WE HAVE NOT BEEN THAT WAY FOR A VERY LONG TIME.
ALL OF OUR ABYSSI DIED MYSTERIOUSLY THOUSANDS AND THOUSANDS OF YEARS AGO...
I HAVE TO KNOW...WHAT MAKES THE TWO OF YOU SO SPECIAL?
I CREATE LIFE.
SHE JUDGES THE WORK.
HOW DID YOUR ABYSSI DIE?

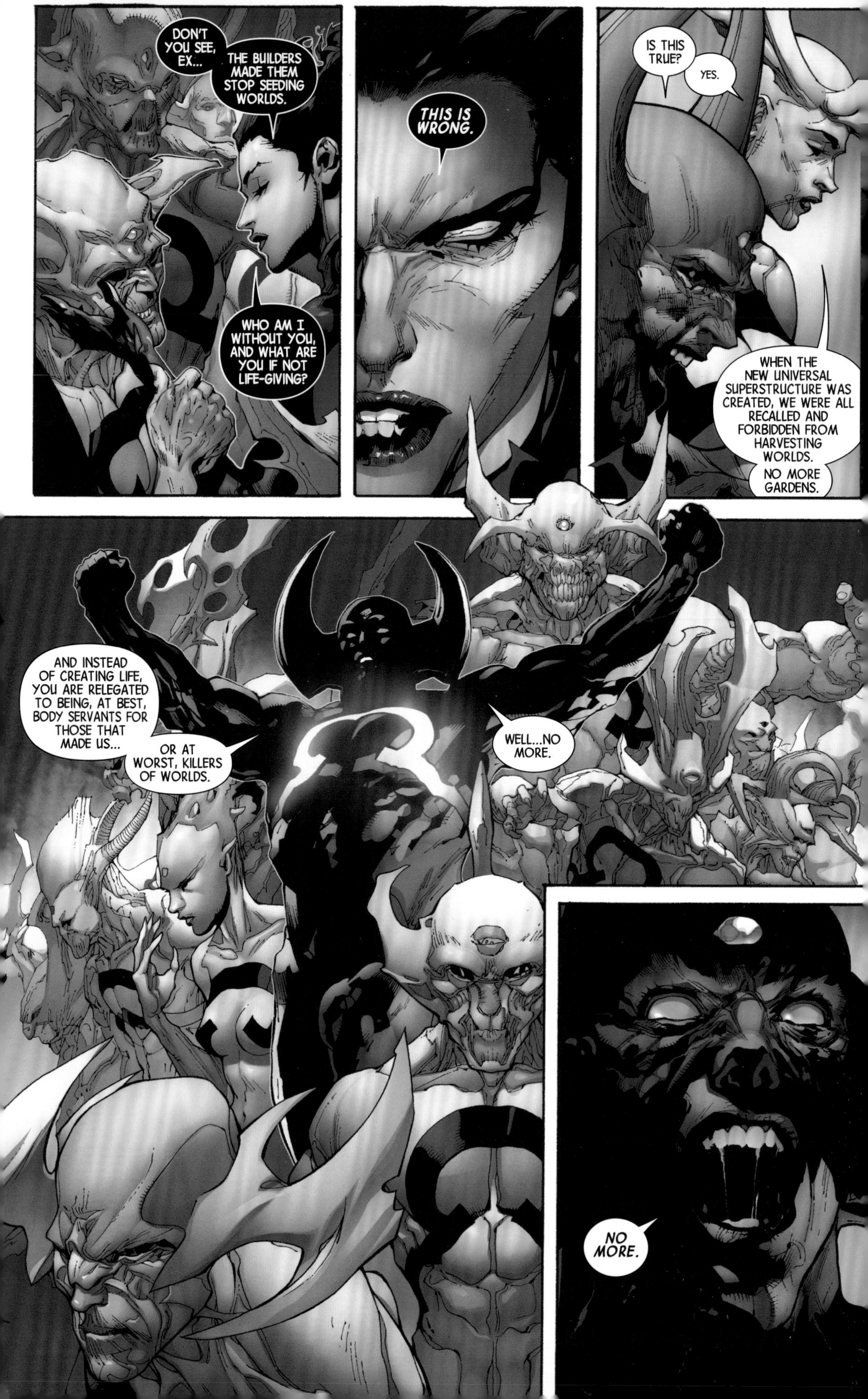
DON'T YOU SEE, EX...
THE BUILDERS MADE THEM STOP SEEDING WORLDS.
WHO AM I WITHOUT YOU, AND WHAT ARE YOU IF NOT LIFE-GIVING?
THIS IS WRONG.
IS THIS TRUE?
YES.
WHEN THE NEW UNIVERSAL SUPERSTRUCTURE WAS CREATED, WE WERE ALL RECALLED AND FORBIDDEN FROM HARVESTING WORLDS.
NO MORE GARDENS.
AND INSTEAD OF CREATING LIFE, YOU ARE RELEGATED TO BEING, AT BEST, BODY SERVANTS FOR THOSE THAT MADE US...
OR AT WORST, KILLERS OF WORLDS.
WELL...NO MORE.
NO MORE.

ONE MAN KNEELS

◆

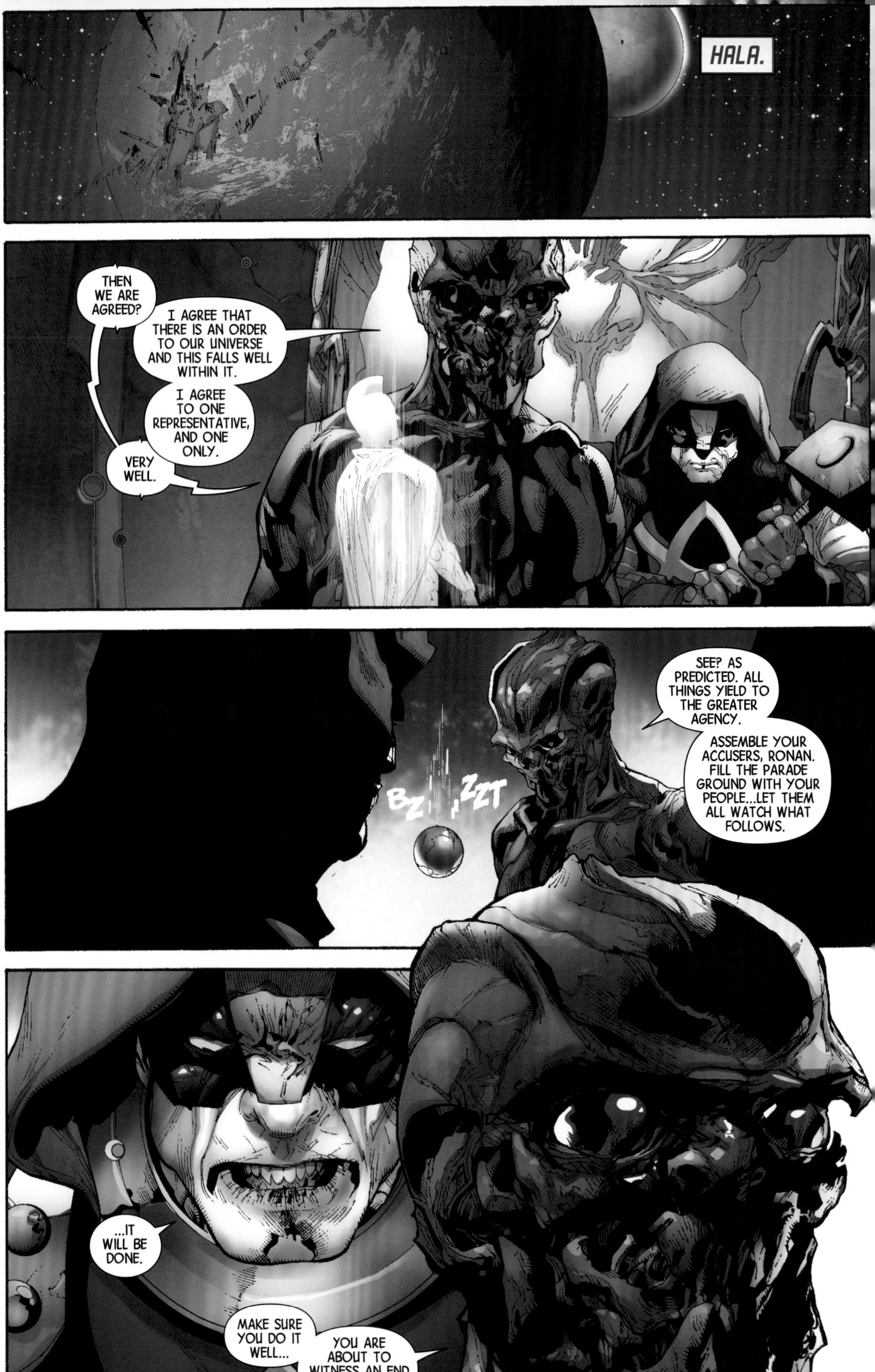
HALA.
THEN WE ARE AGREED?
I AGREE THAT THERE IS AN ORDER TO OUR UNIVERSE AND THIS FALLS WELL WITHIN IT.
I AGREE TO ONE REPRESENTATIVE, AND ONE ONLY.
VERY WELL.
SEE? AS PREDICTED. ALL THINGS YIELD TO THE GREATER AGENCY.
ASSEMBLE YOUR ACCUSERS, RONAN. FILL THE PARADE GROUND WITH YOUR PEOPLE...LET THEM ALL WATCH WHAT FOLLOWS.
BZ ZZT
...IT WILL BE DONE.
MAKE SURE YOU DO IT WELL...
YOU ARE ABOUT TO WITNESS AN END TO OUR LITTLE WAR.
AR

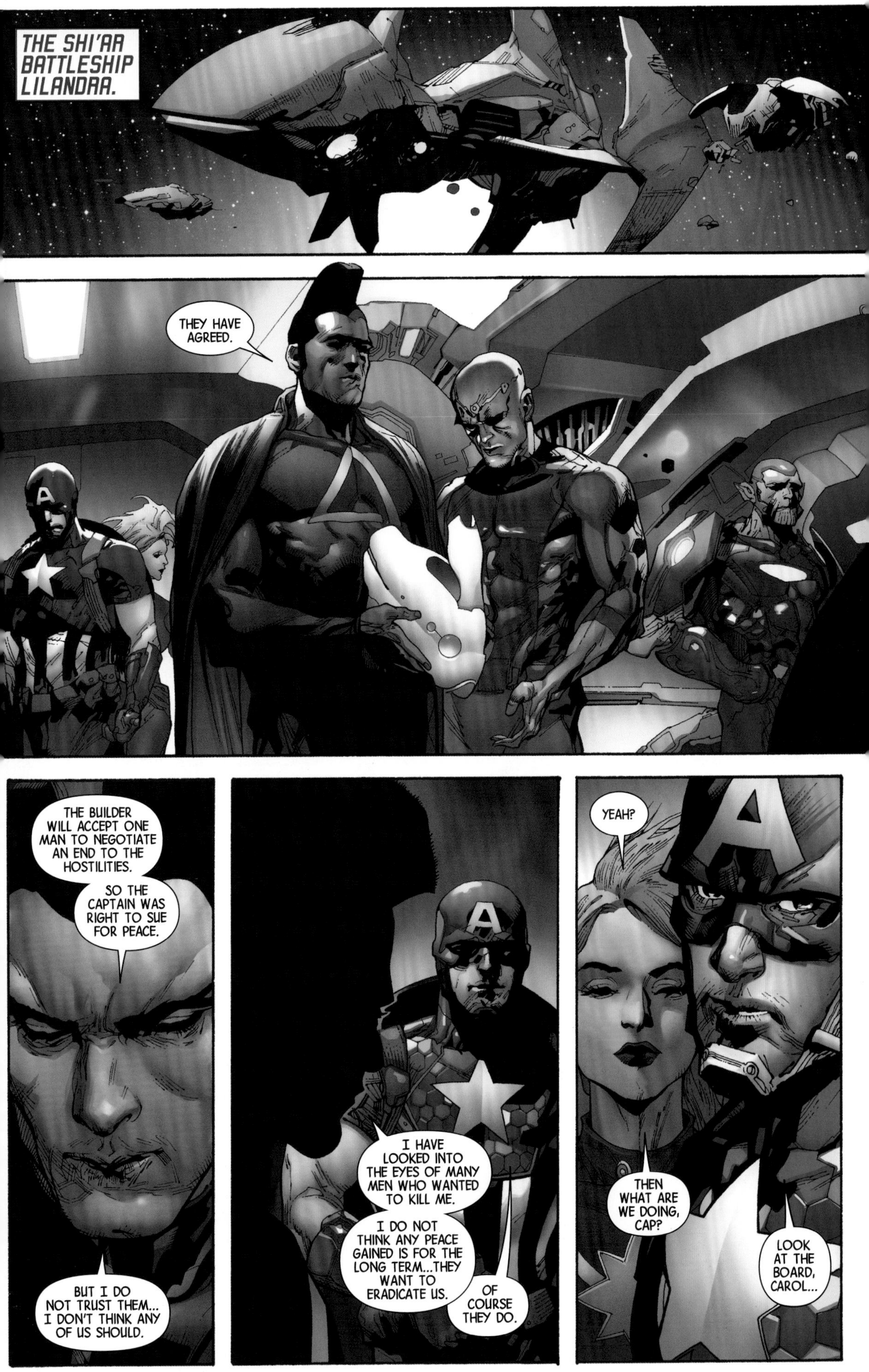
THE SHI'AR BATTLESHIP LILANDRA.
THEY HAVE AGREED.
THE BUILDER WILL ACCEPT ONE MAN TO NEGOTIATE AN END TO THE HOSTILITIES.
SO THE CAPTAIN WAS RIGHT TO SUE FOR PEACE.
BUT I DO NOT TRUST THEM... I DON'T THINK ANY OF US SHOULD.
I HAVE LOOKED INTO THE EYES OF MANY MEN WHO WANTED TO KILL ME.
I DO NOT THINK ANY PEACE GAINED IS FOR THE LONG TERM...THEY WANT TO ERADICATE US.
OF COURSE THEY DO.
YEAH?
THEN WHAT ARE WE DOING, CAP?
LOOK AT THE BOARD, CAROL...

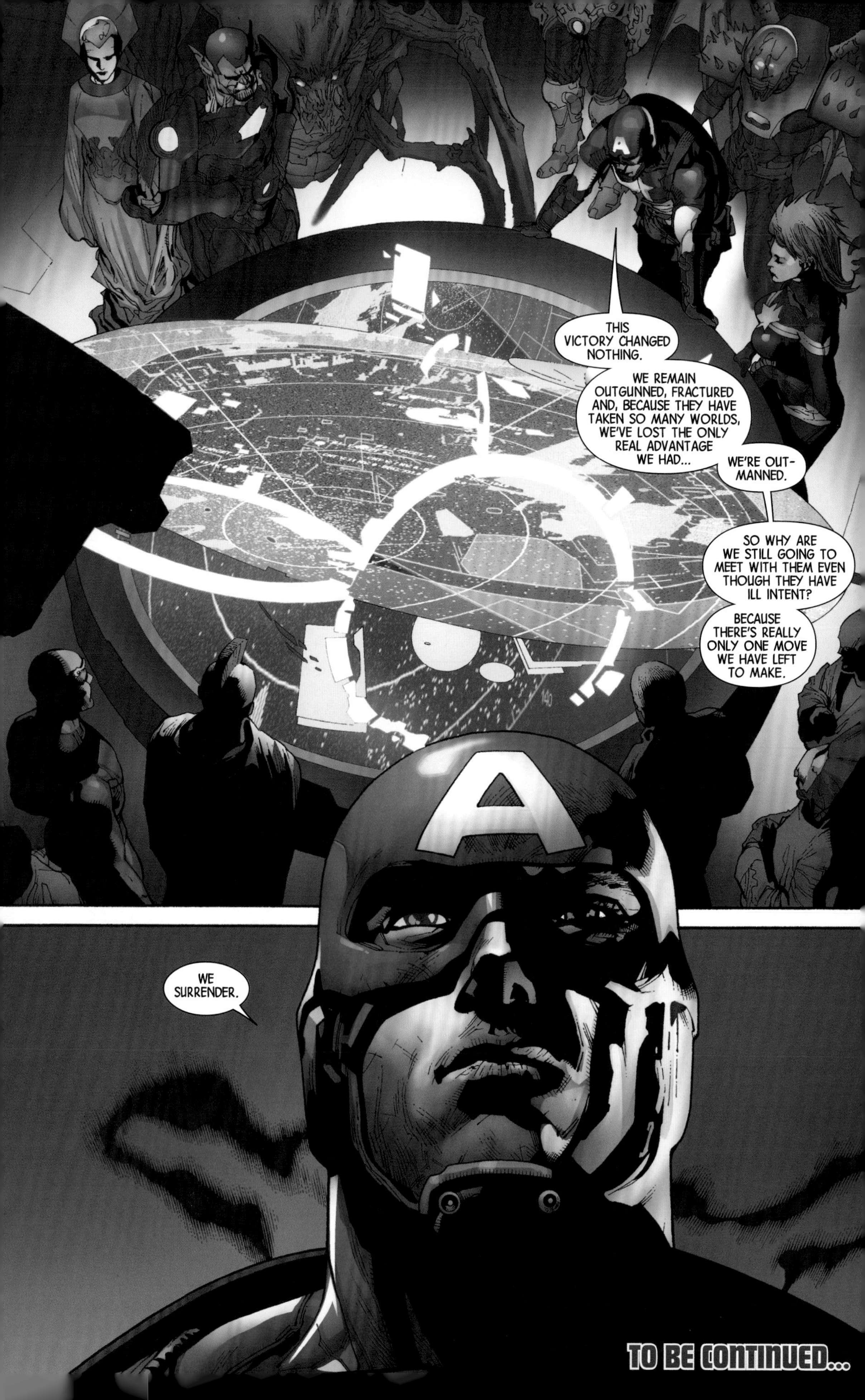
THIS VICTORY CHANGED NOTHING.
WE REMAIN OUTGUNNED, FRACTURED AND, BECAUSE THEY HAVE TAKEN SO MANY WORLDS, WE'VE LOST THE ONLY REAL ADVANTAGE WE HAD...
WE'RE OUT-MANNED.
SO WHY ARE WE STILL GOING TO MEET WITH THEM EVEN THOUGH THEY HAVE ILL INTENT?
BECAUSE THERE'S REALLY ONLY ONE MOVE WE HAVE LEFT TO MAKE.
WE SURRENDER.
TO BE CONTINUED...

INFINITY™

Variant Cover Gallery

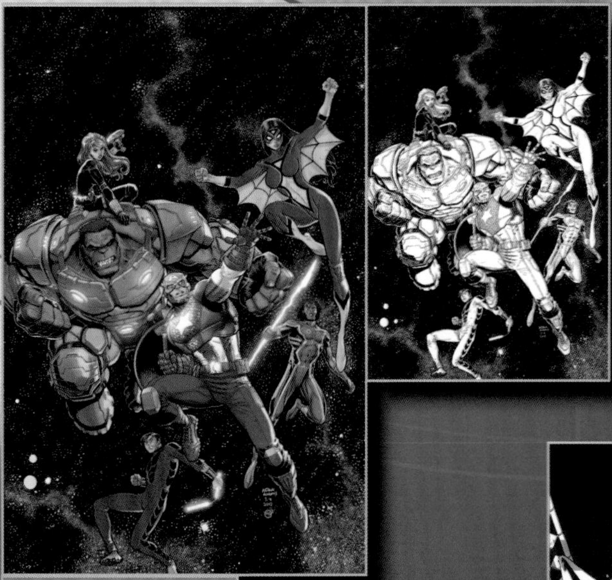

Infinity #1 by Art Adams

Infinity #1 by Mark Brooks

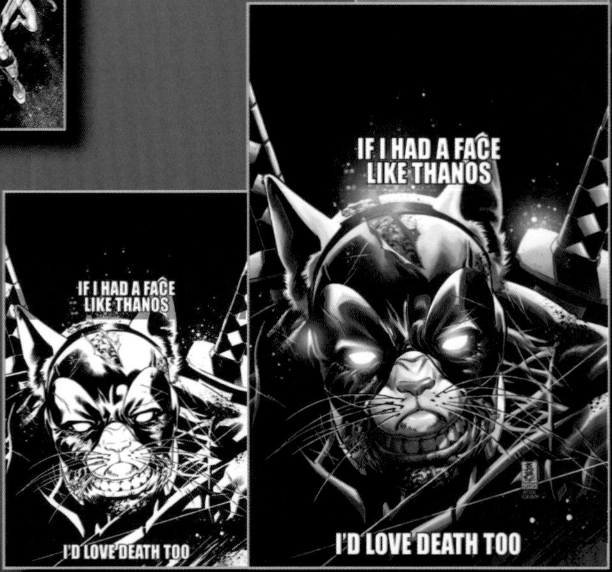
IF I HAD A FACE LIKE THANOS
I'D LOVE DEATH TOO
IF I HAD A FACE LIKE THANOS
I'D LOVE DEATH TOO

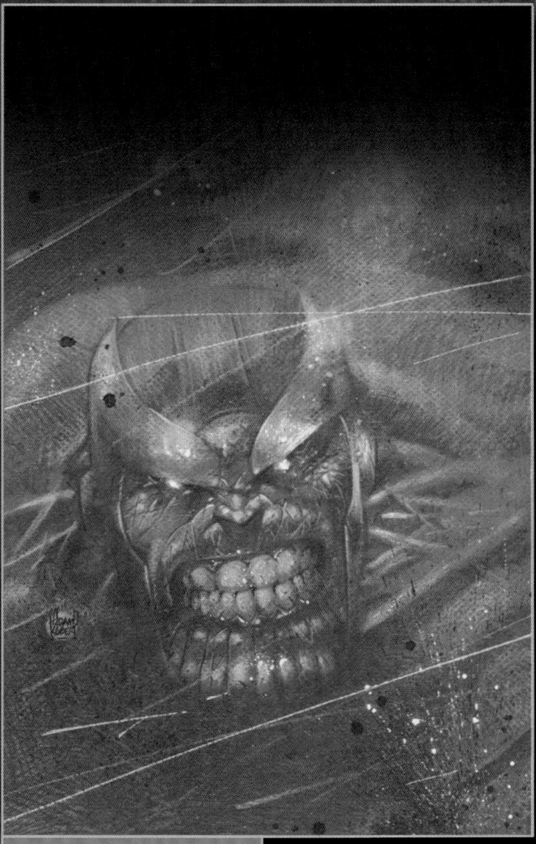

Infinity #1 by Adam Kubert

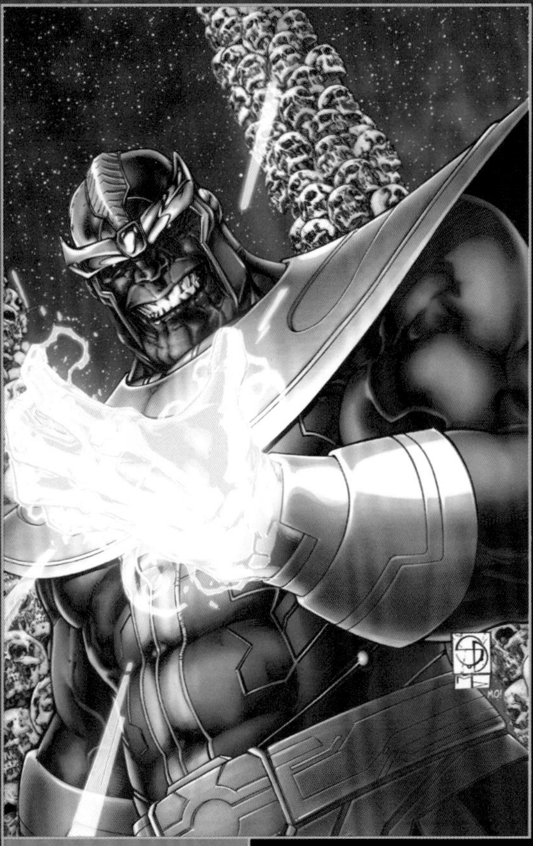

Infinity #1 by Shane Davis

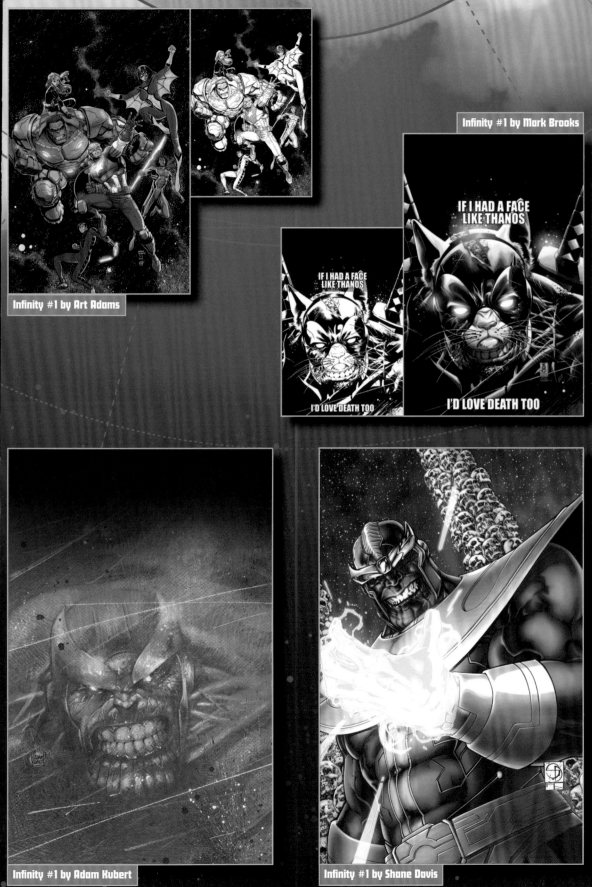

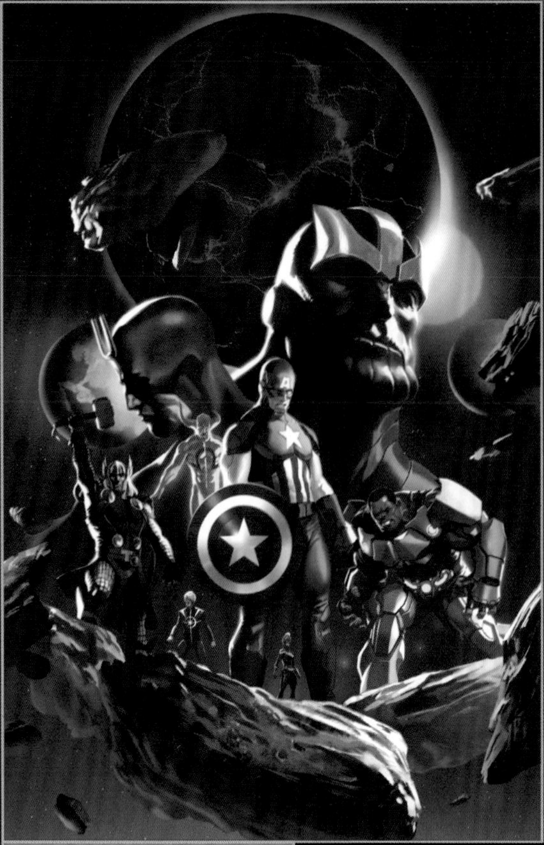

Infinity #1 by Marko Djurdjevic

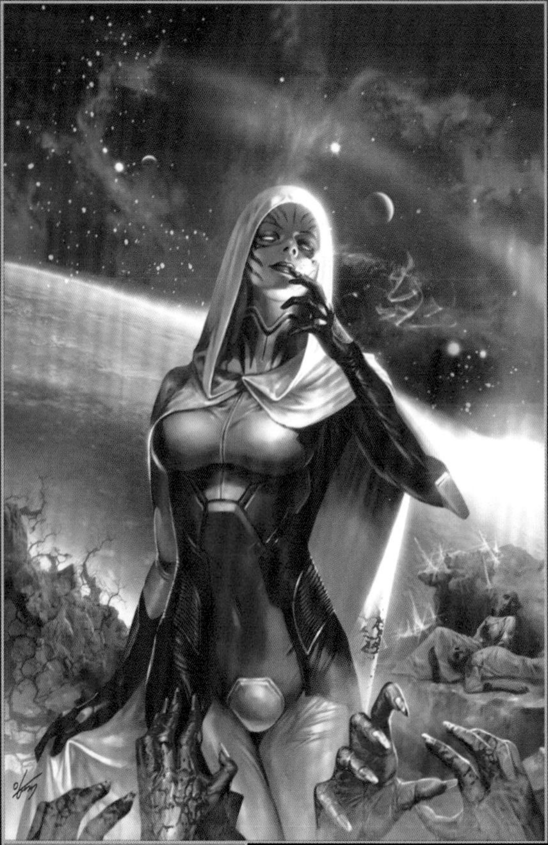

Infinity #1 by In-Hyuk Lee

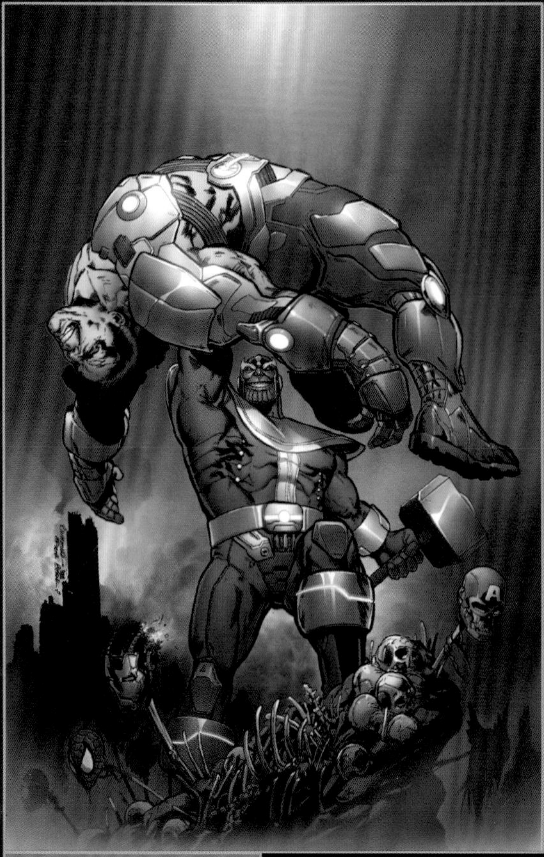

Infinity #1 by Phil Jimenez

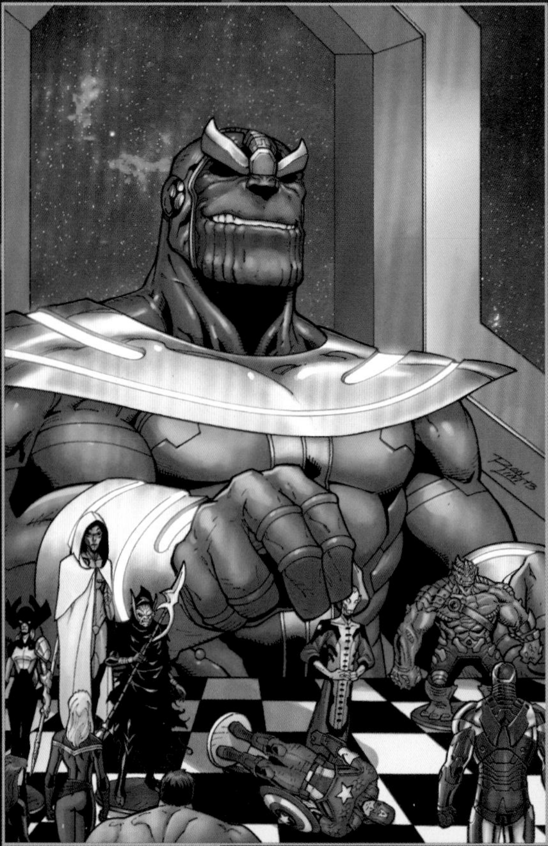

Infinity #1 by Ron Lim

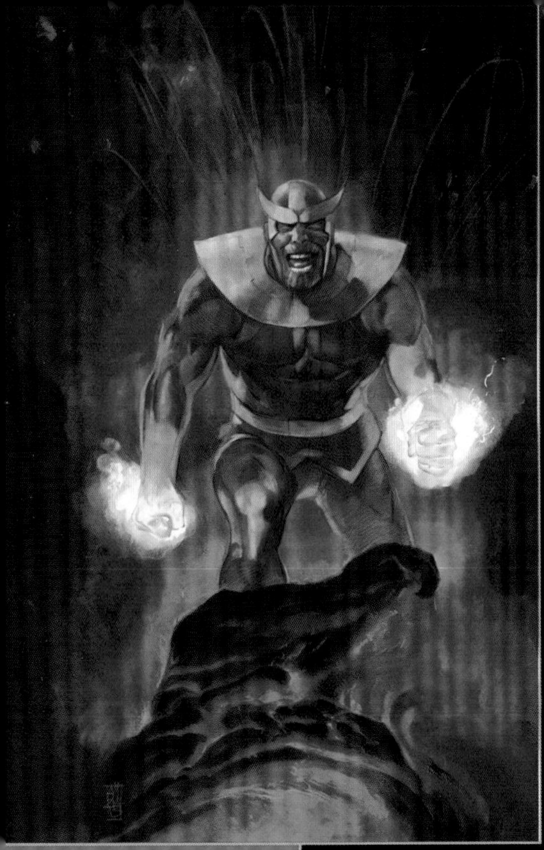

Infinity #1 by Alexander Maleev

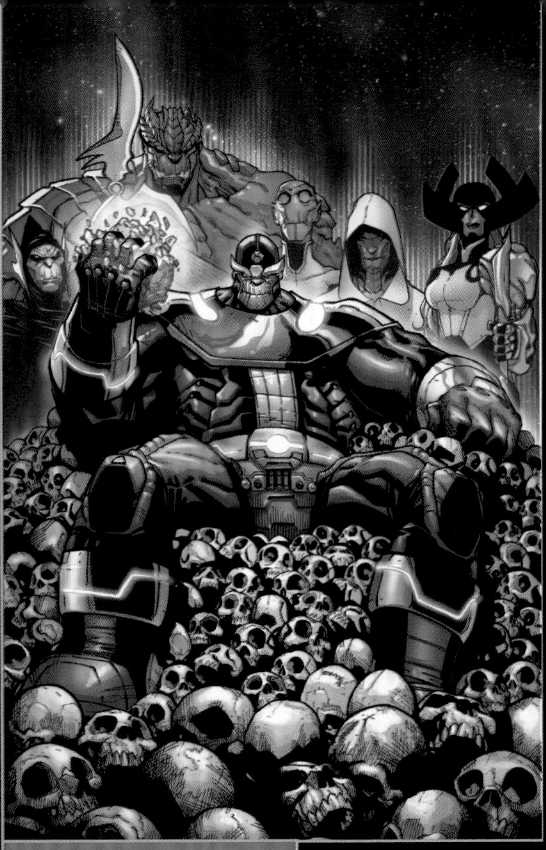

Infinity #1 by Humberto Ramos

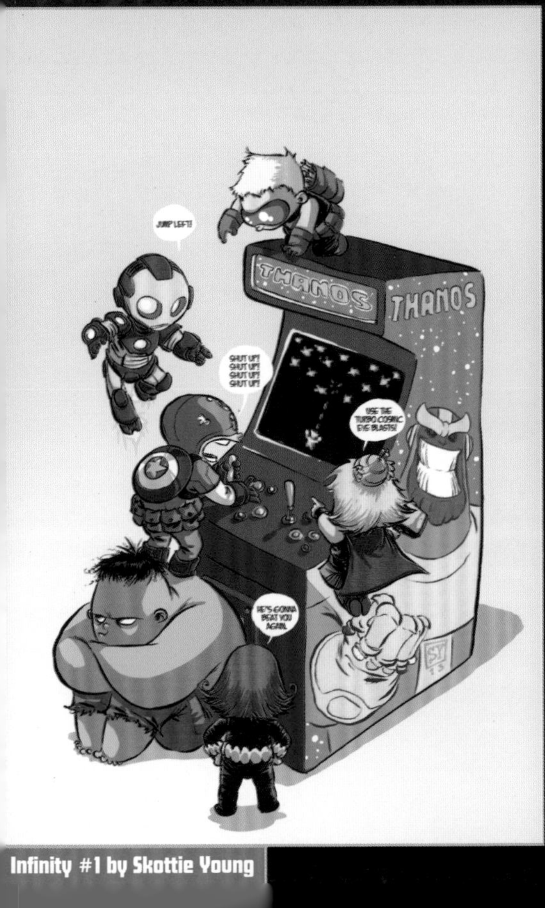
JUMP LEFT!
THANOS
THANOS
SHUT UP!
SHUT UP!
SHUT UP!
SHUT UP!
USE THE TURBO COSMIC EYE BLASTS!
HE'S GONNA BEAT YOU AGAIN.

Infinity #1 by Skottie Young

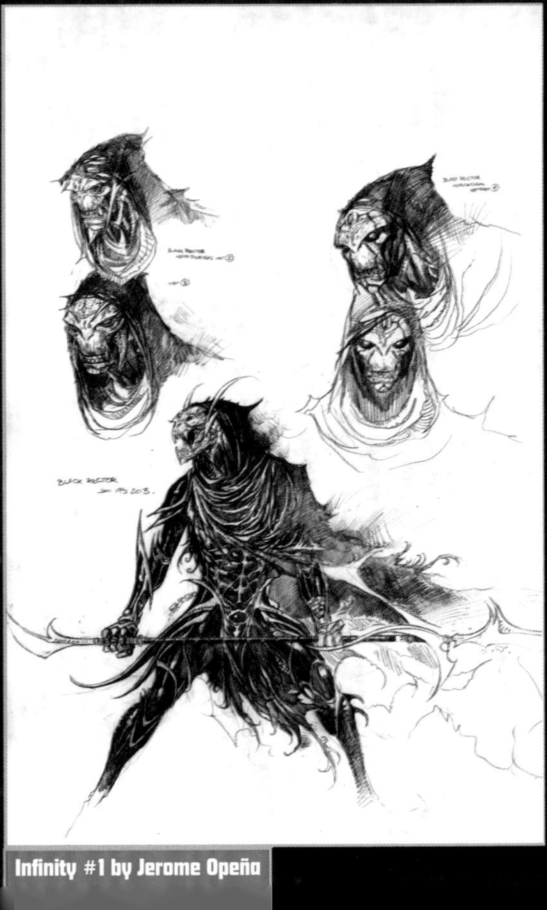

Infinity #1 by Jerome Opeña

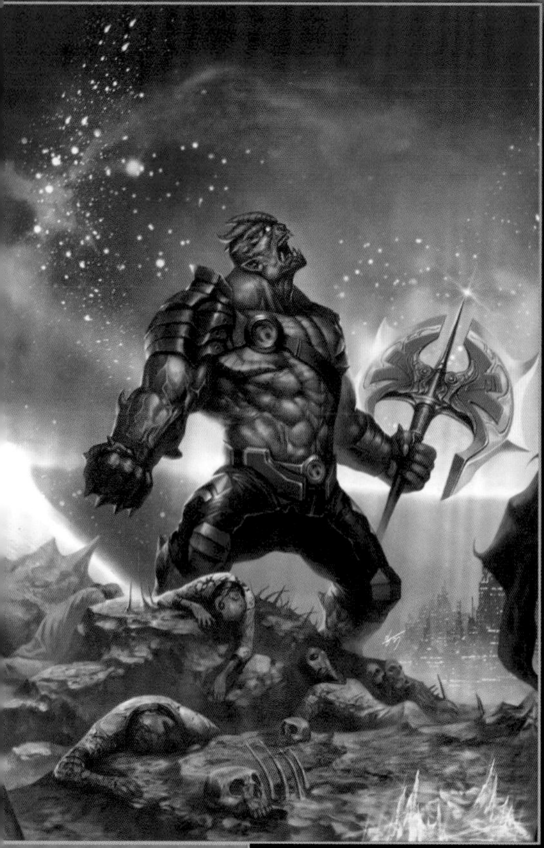

Infinity #2 by In-Hyuk Lee

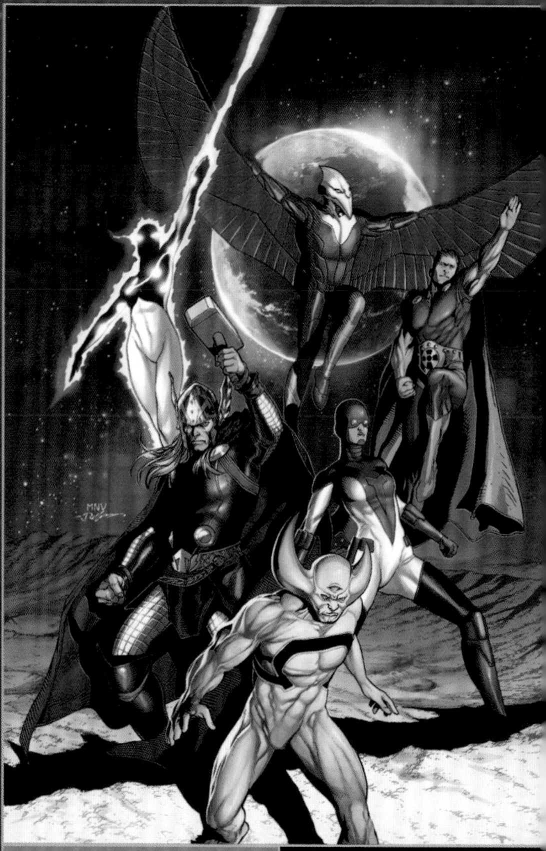

Infinity #2 by Steve McNiven

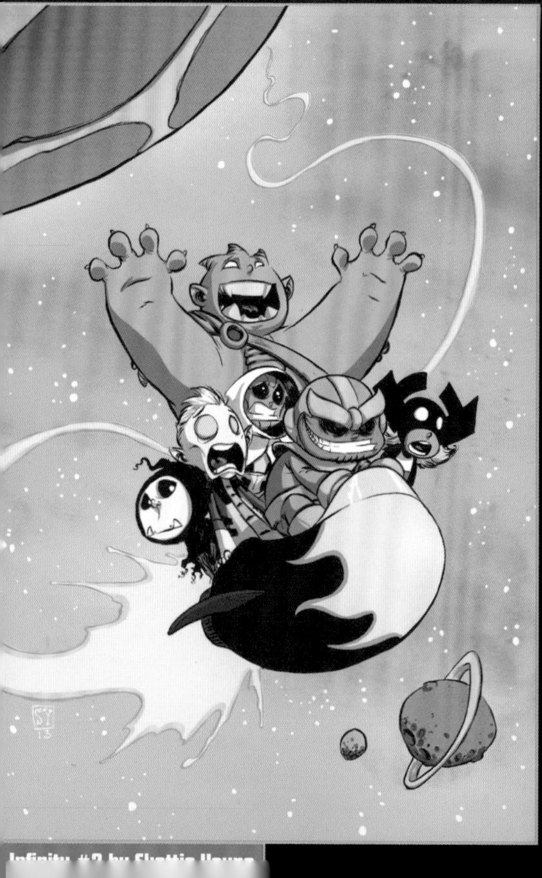

Infinity #2 by Skottie Young

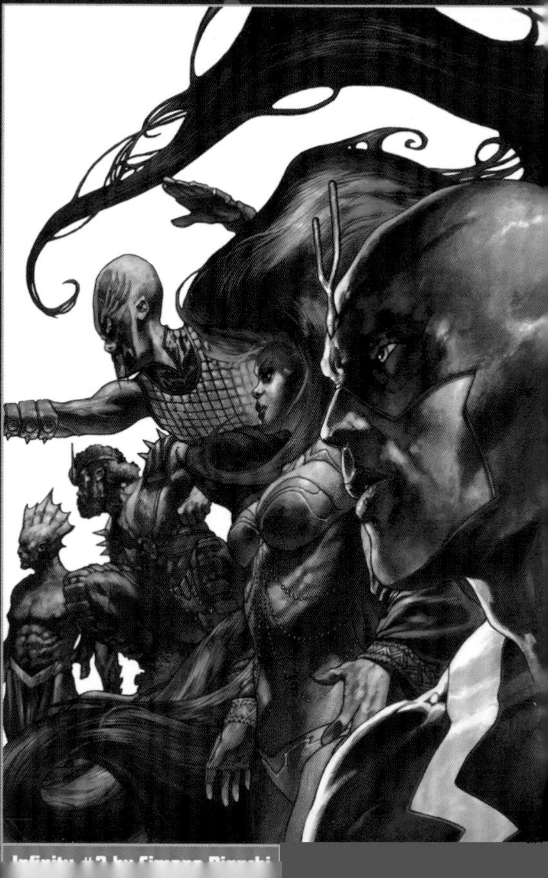

Infinity #2 by Simone Bianchi

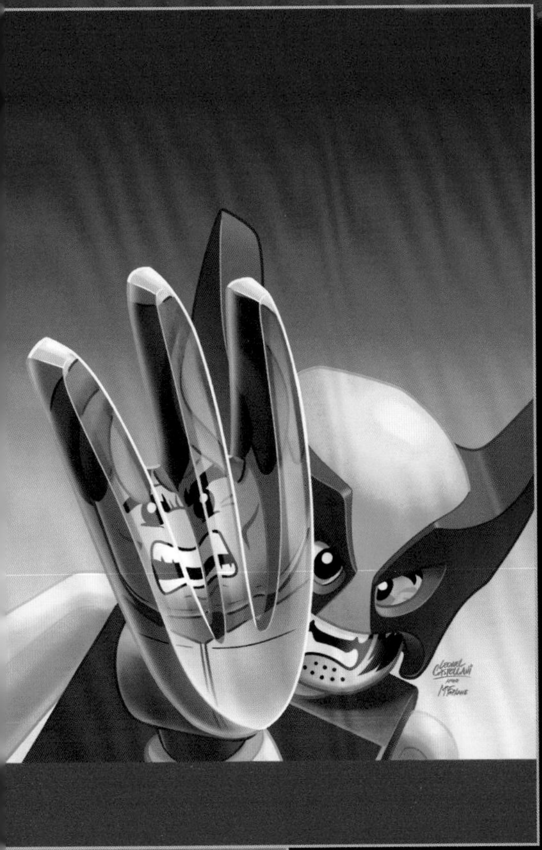

Infinity #3 by Leonel Castellani

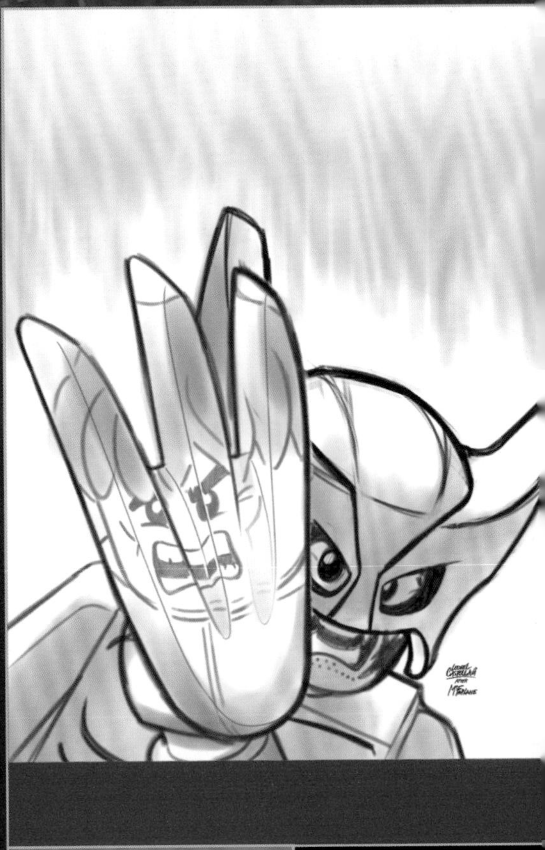

Infinity #3 by Leonel Castellani

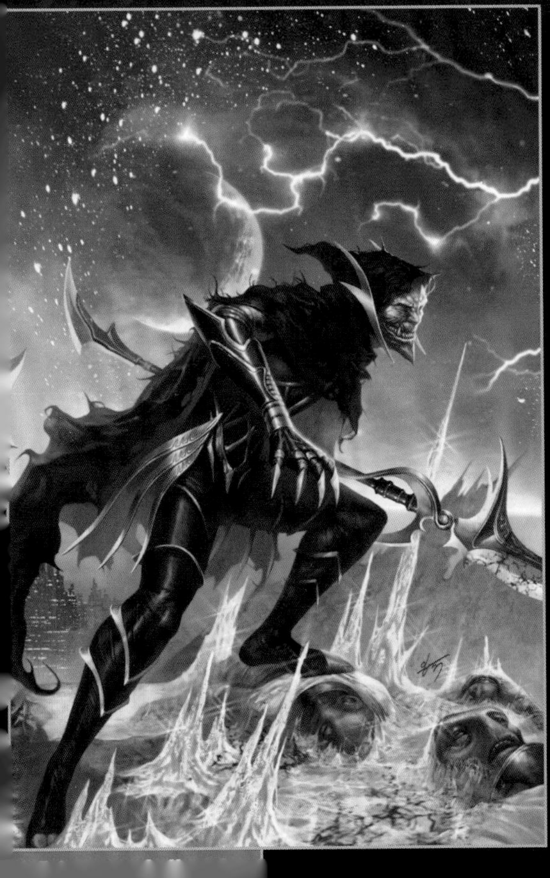

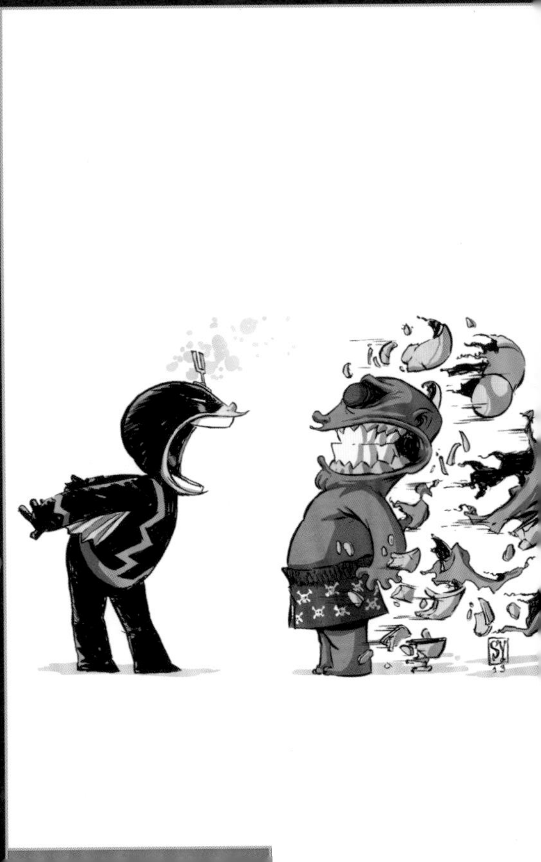

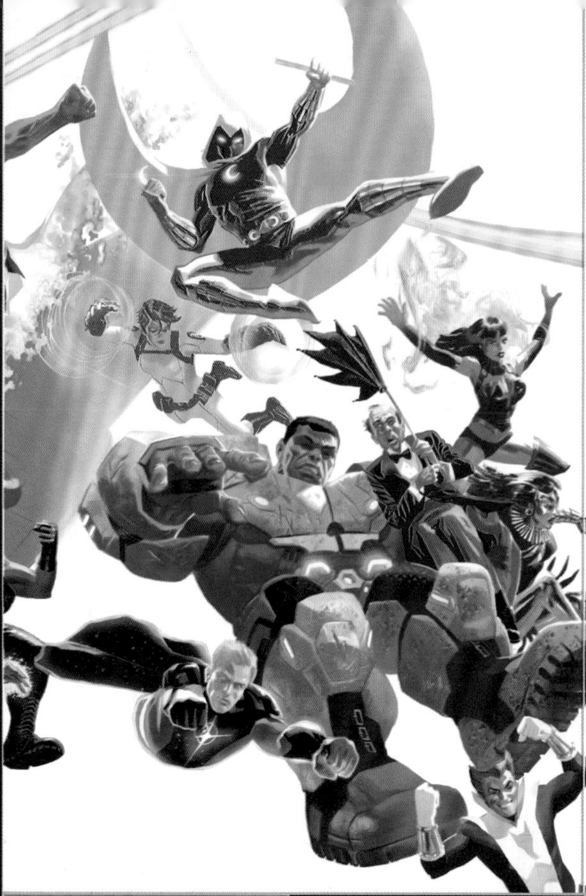

Avengers #18 by Daniel Acuña

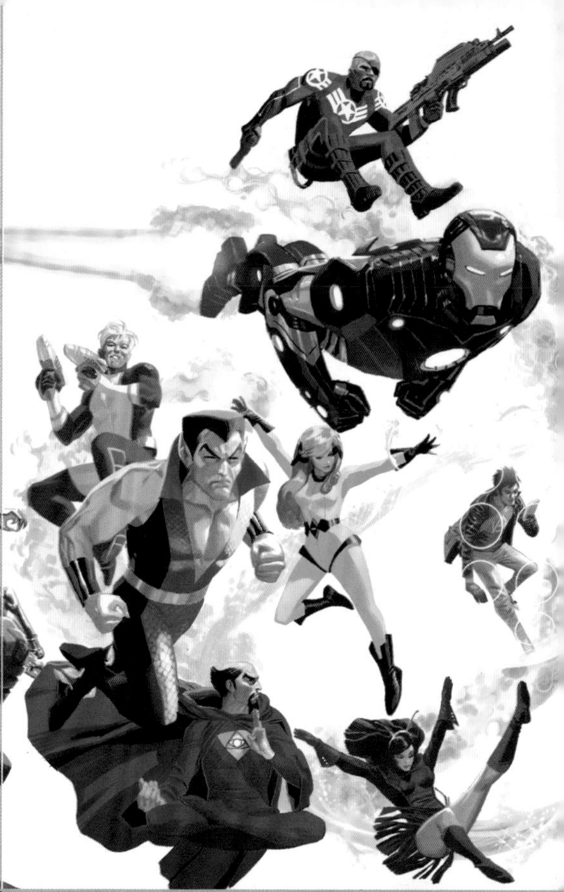

Avengers #20 by Daniel Acuña

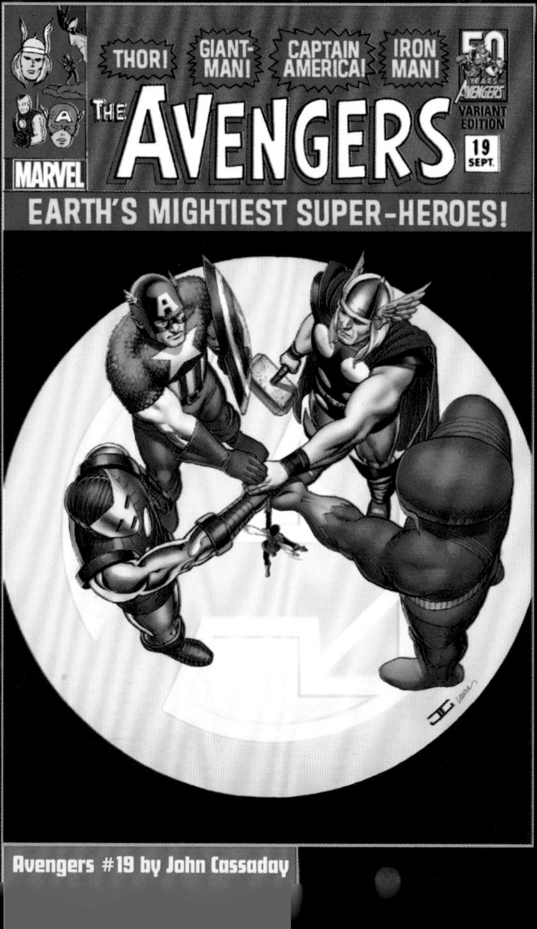
THOR!
GIANT-MAN!
CAPTAIN AMERICA!
IRON MAN!
50 YEARS AVENGERS
THE AVENGERS
VARIANT EDITION
19 SEPT.
MARVEL
EARTH'S MIGHTIEST SUPER-HEROES!

Avengers #19 by John Cassaday

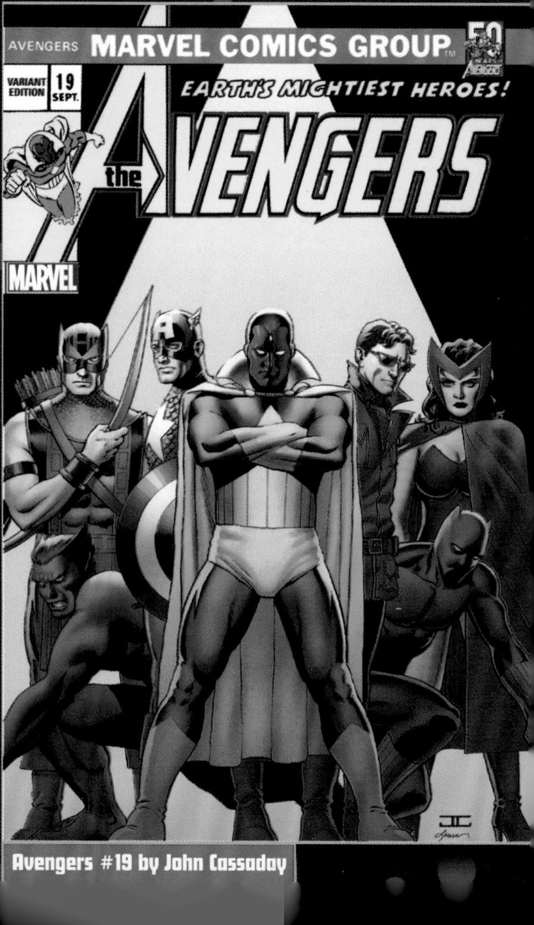
AVENGERS
MARVEL COMICS GROUP
50 YEARS AVENGERS
VARIANT EDITION
19 SEPT.
EARTH'S MIGHTIEST HEROES!
the AVENGERS
MARVEL

Avengers #19 by John Cassaday